Volume 1

By

Becky Cloonan

TOKYOPOP®

HAMBURG // LONDON // LOS ANGELES // TOKYO

East Coast Rising Volume 1
Created by Becky Cloonan

Tones - Vasilis Lolos
Lettering - Fawn Lau
Cover Design - Kyle Plummer

Editor - Tim Beedle
Digital Imaging Manager - Chris Buford
Production Manager - Jennifer Miller
Managing Editor - Lindsey Johnston
Editorial Director - Jeremy Ross
VP of Production - Ron Klamert
Publisher and E.I.C. - Mike Kiley
President and C.O.O. - John Parker
C.E.O. and Chief Creative Officer - Stuart Levy

A  Manga

TOKYOPOP Inc.
5900 Wilshire Blvd. Suite 2000
Los Angeles, CA 90036

E-mail: info@TOKYOPOP.com
Come visit us online at www.TOKYOPOP.com

ISBN: 1-59816-468-6

First TOKYOPOP printing: April 2006
10 9 8 7 6 5 4 3 2 1
Printed in the USA

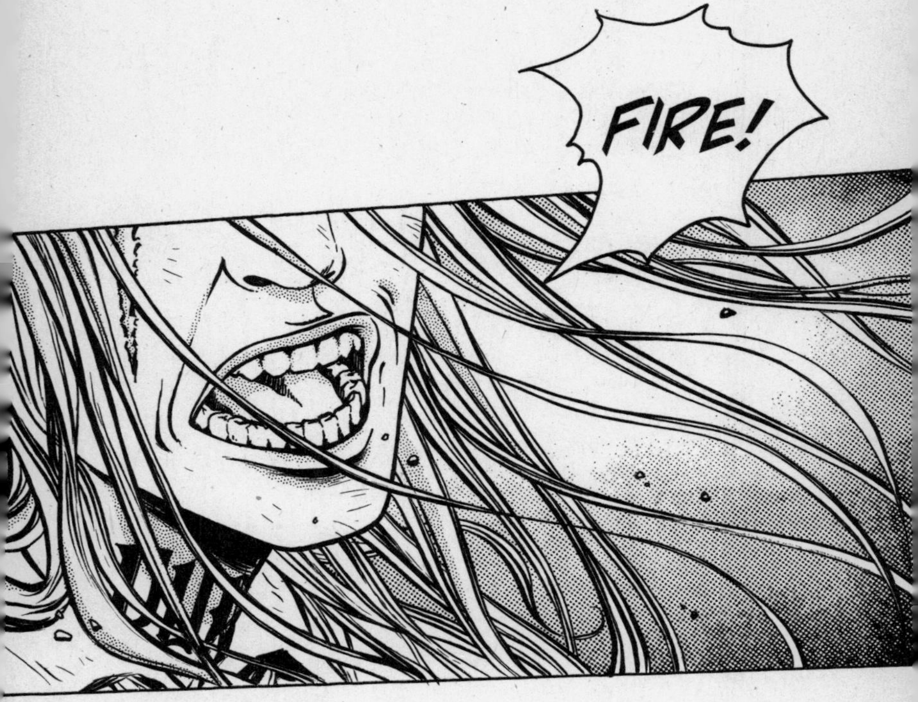
FIRE!

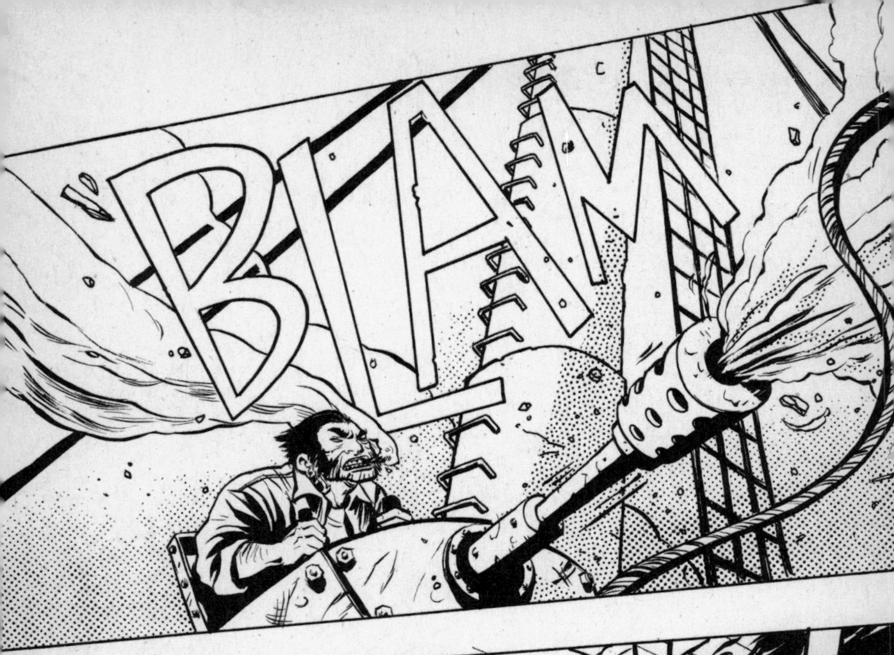
BLAM
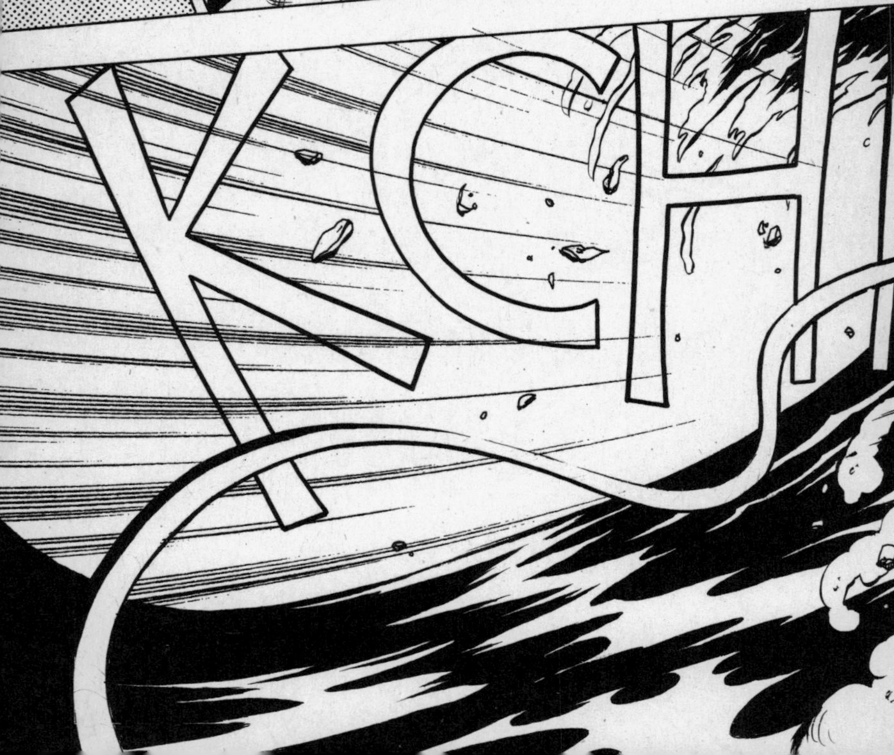
KCH

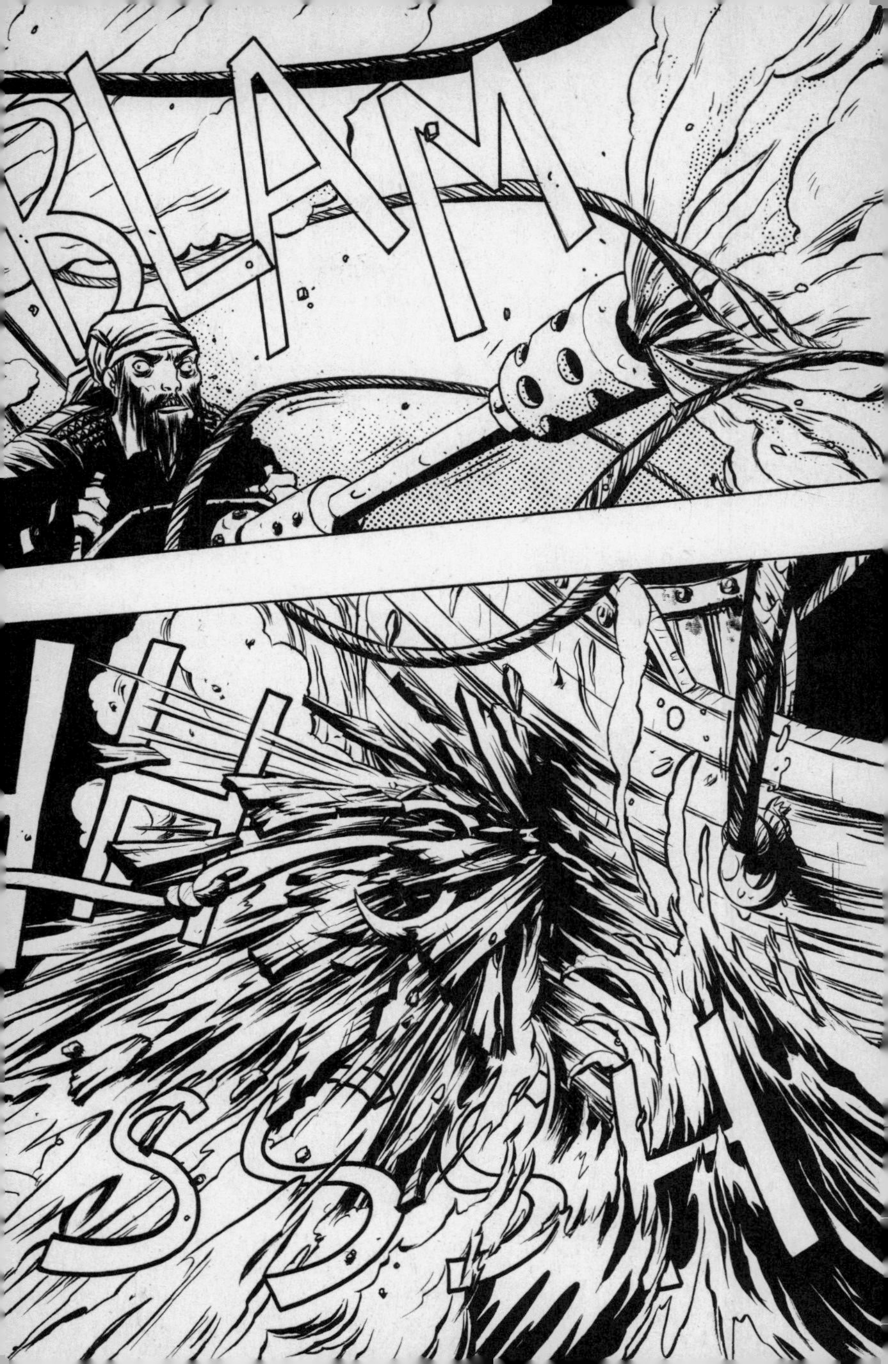
BLAM

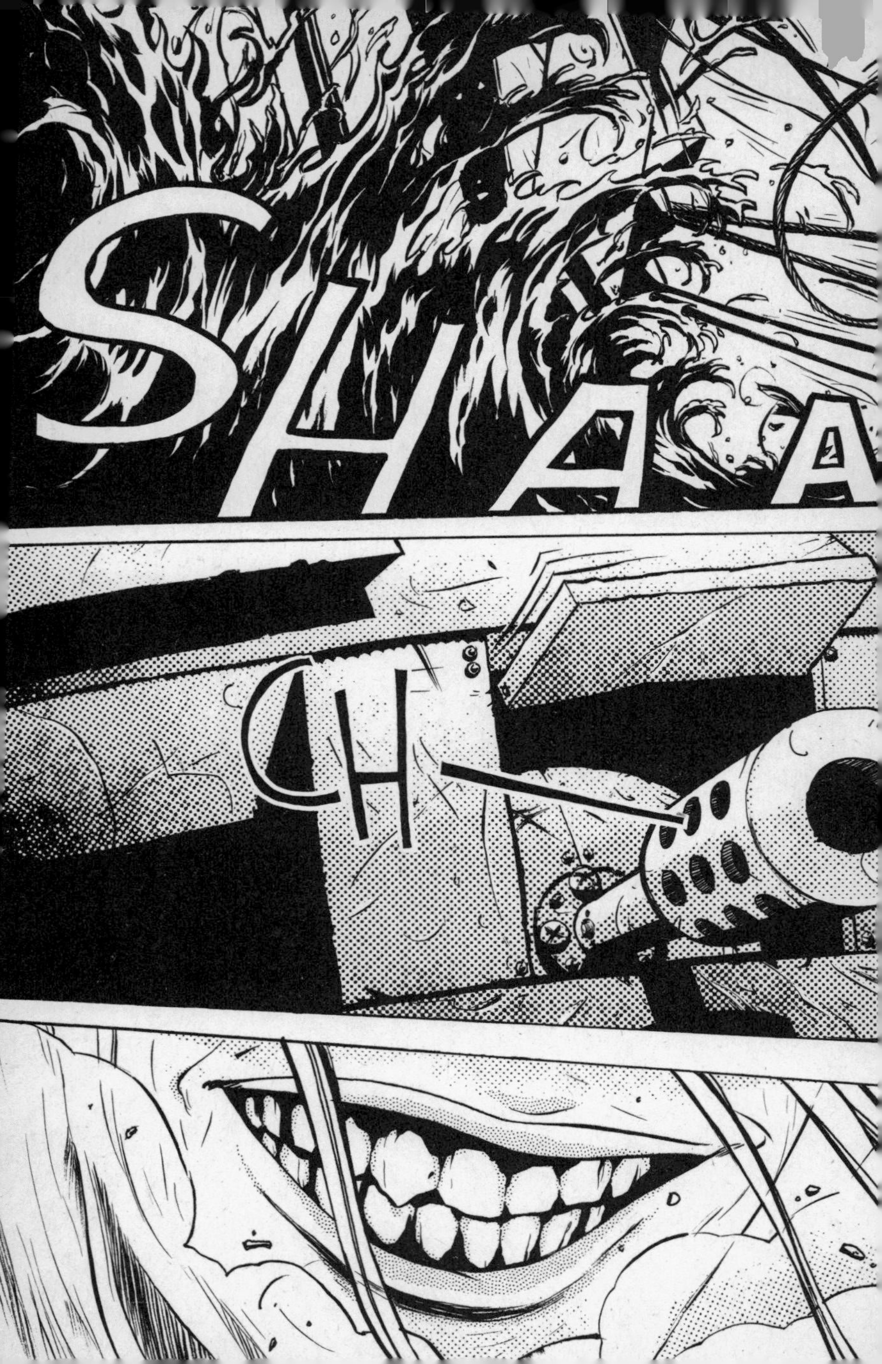
SHAA
CH

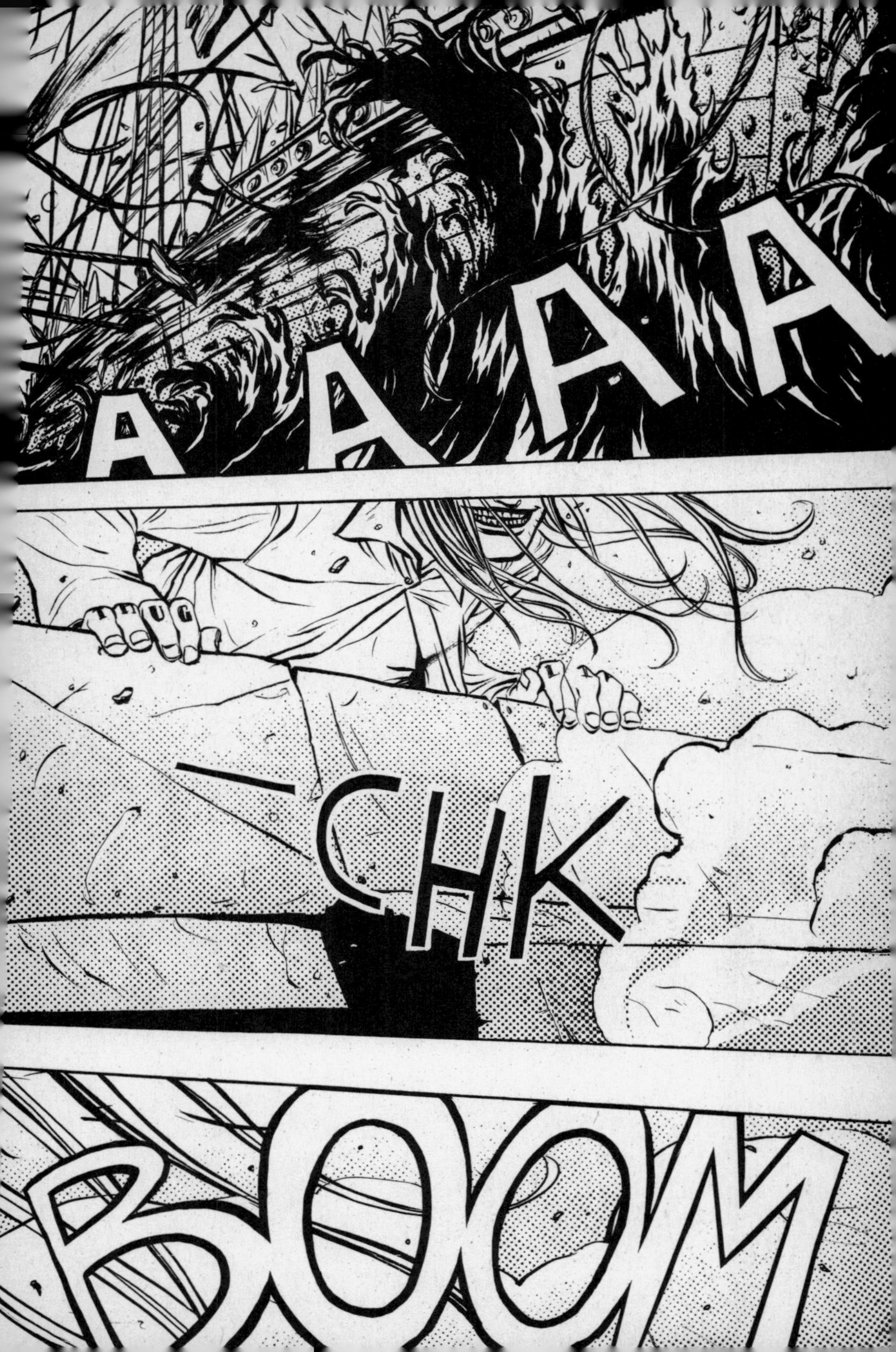
AAAAA
THUG
CHK
BOOM

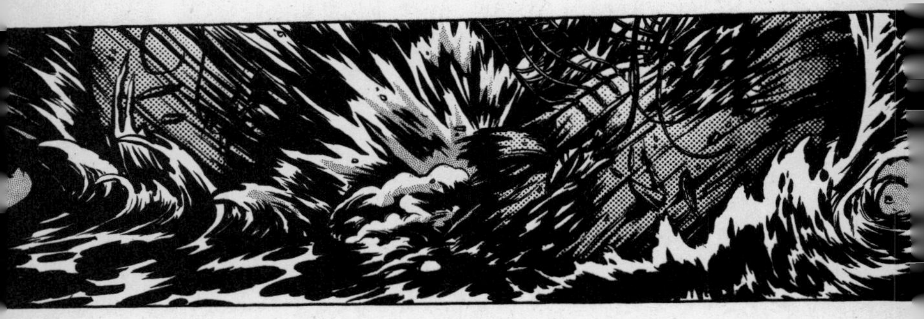
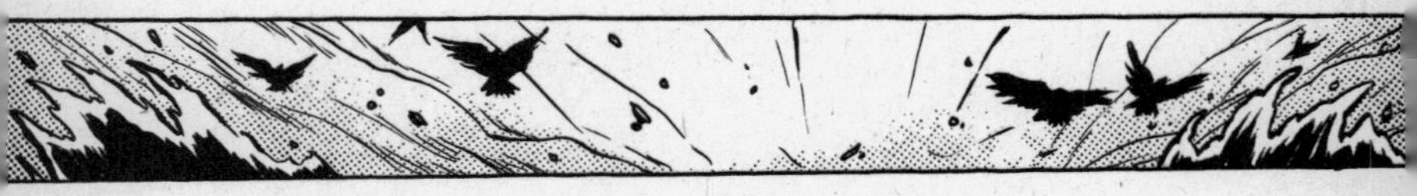
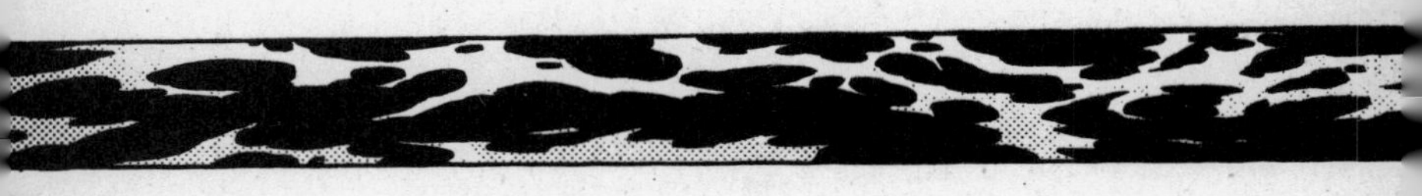

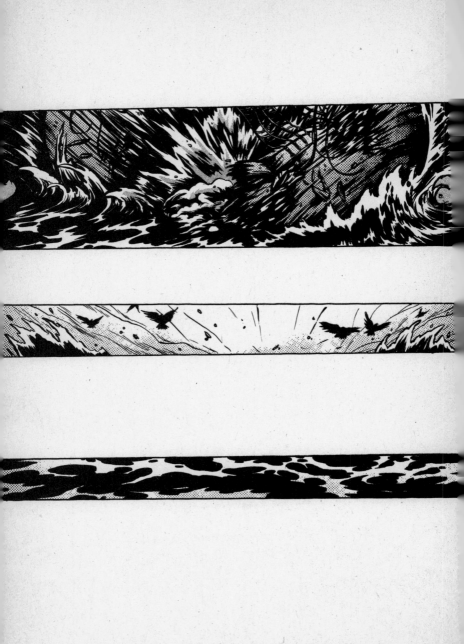

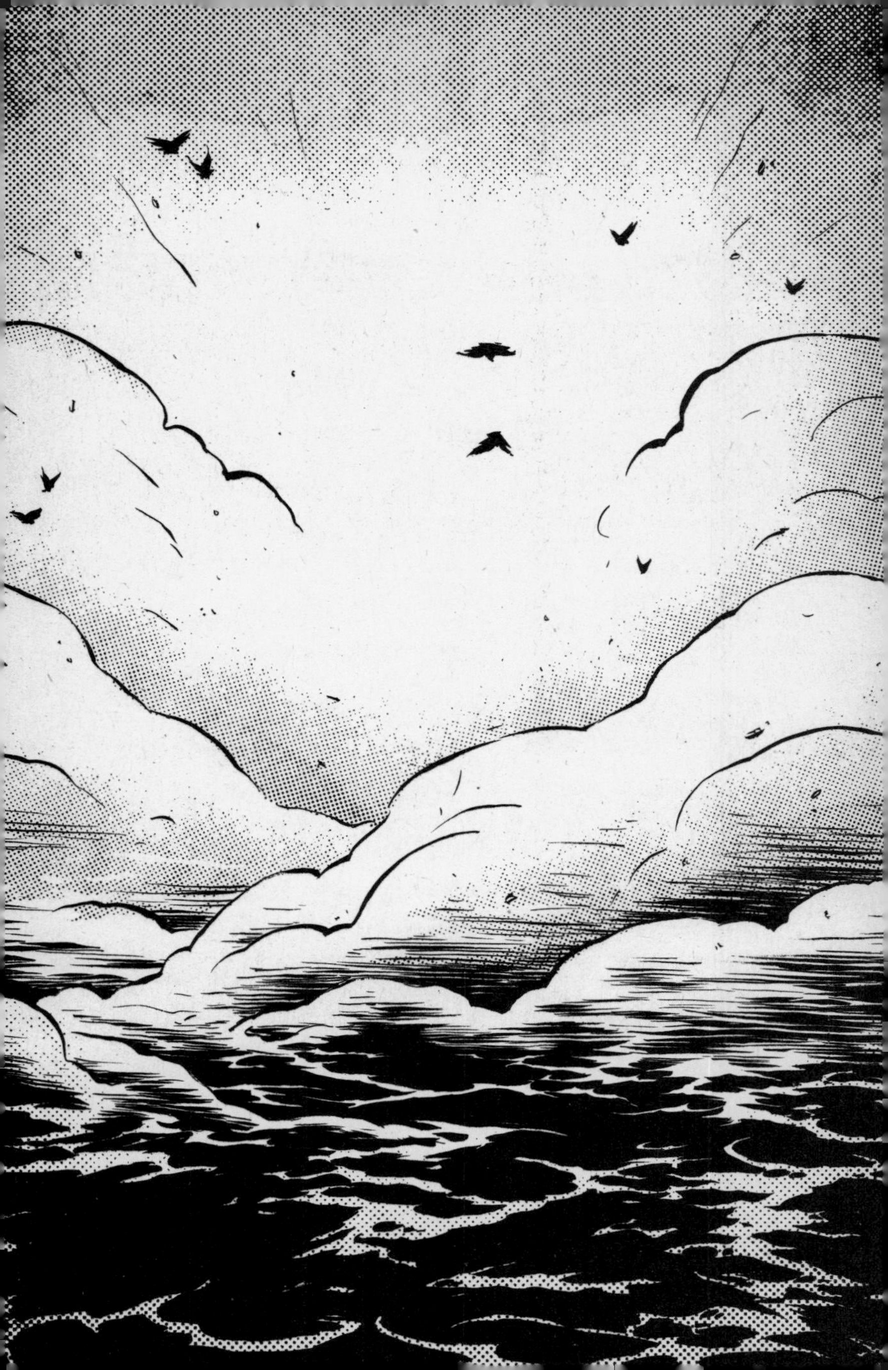

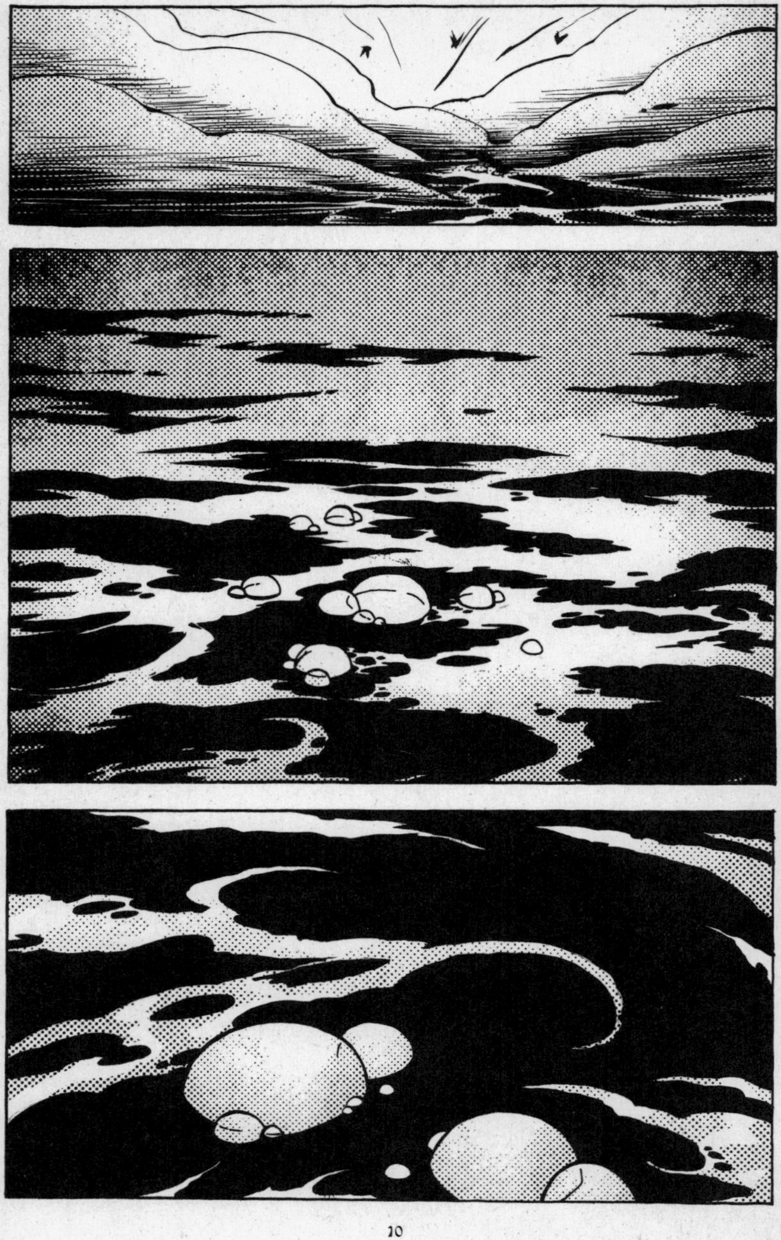

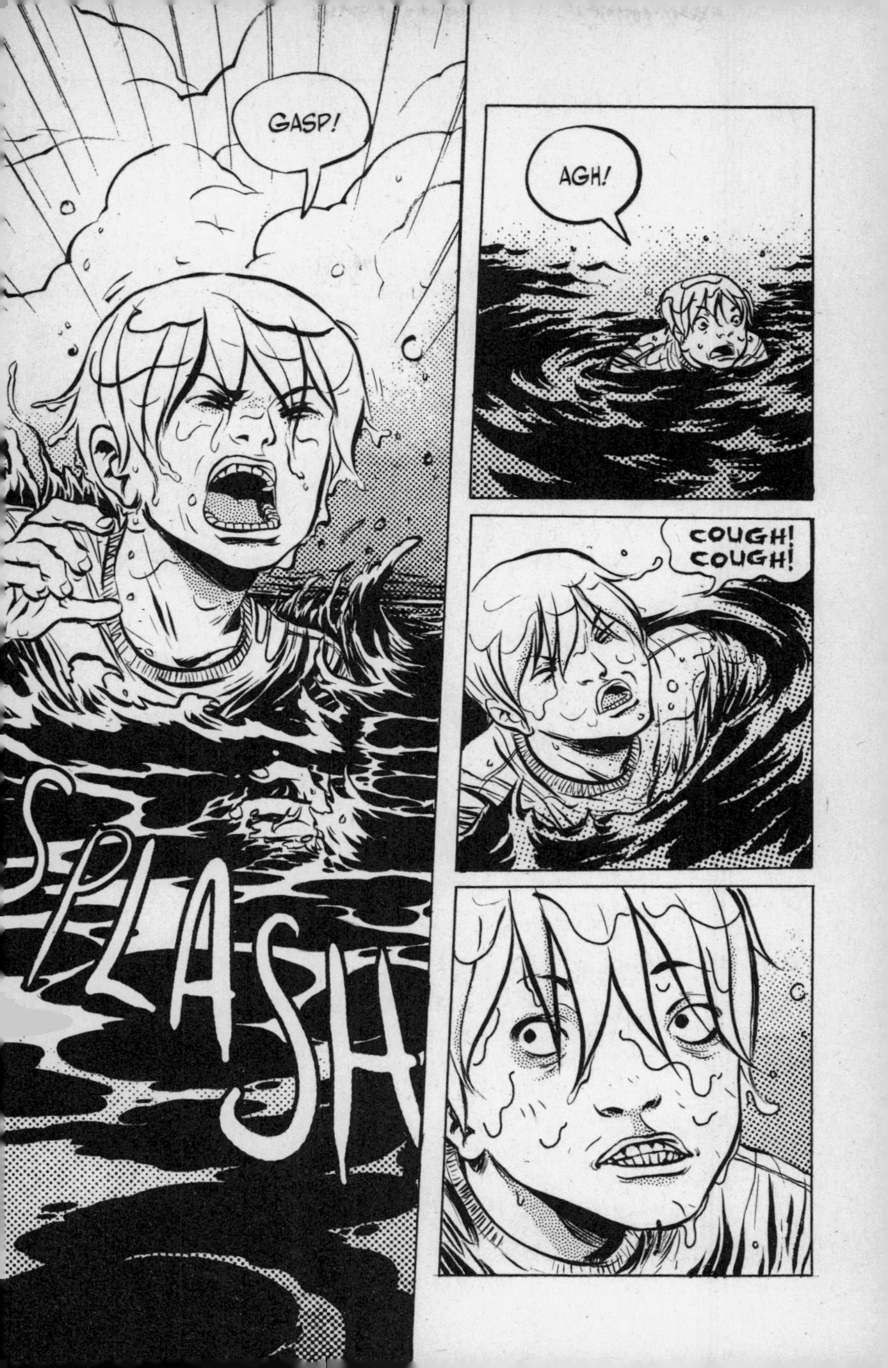
GASP!
SPLASH
AGH!
COUGH! COUGH!

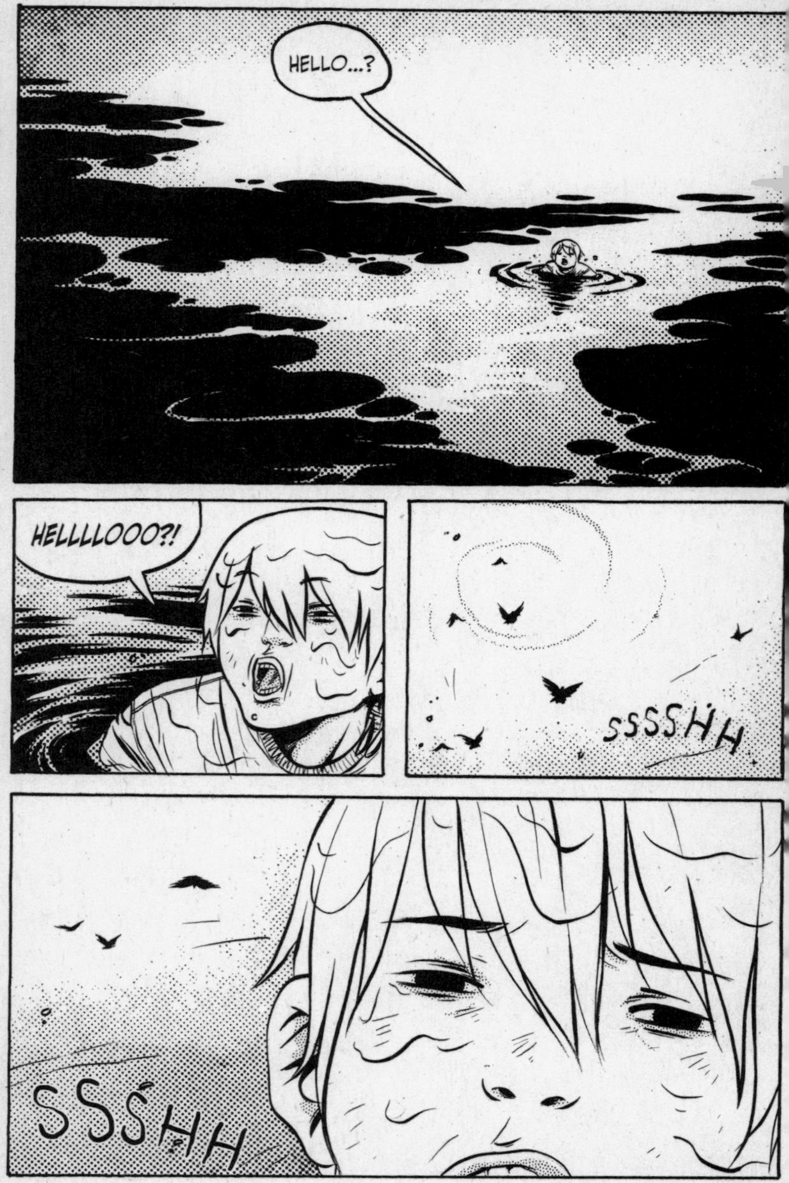
HELLO...?
HELLLLOOO?!
SSSSHH
SSSHH

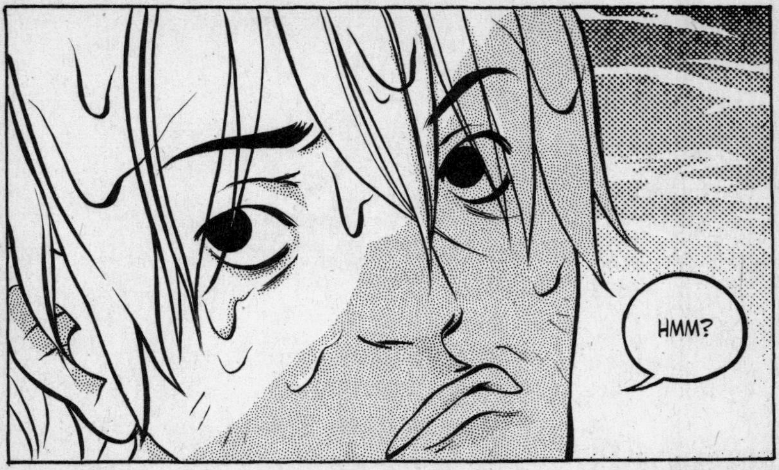
HMM?

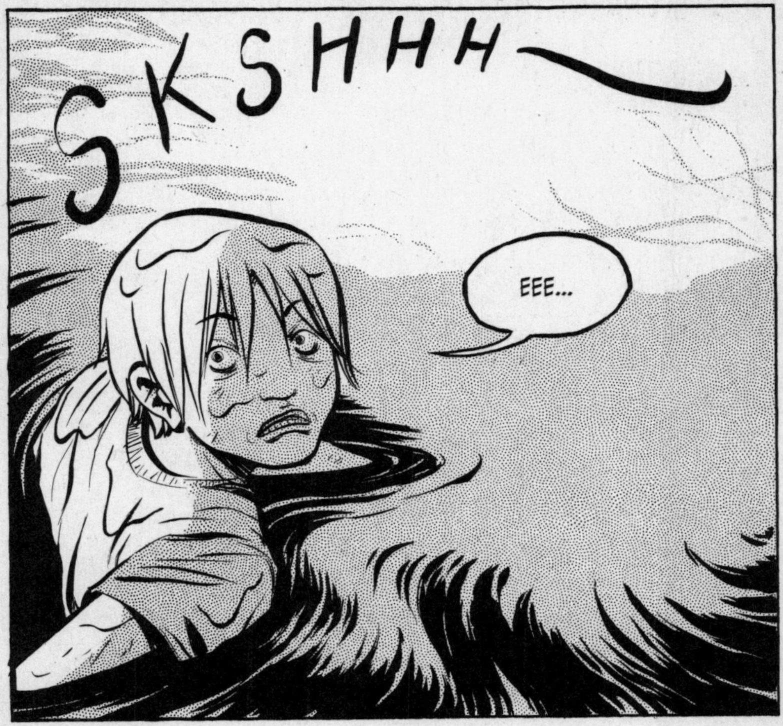
SKSHHH
EEE...

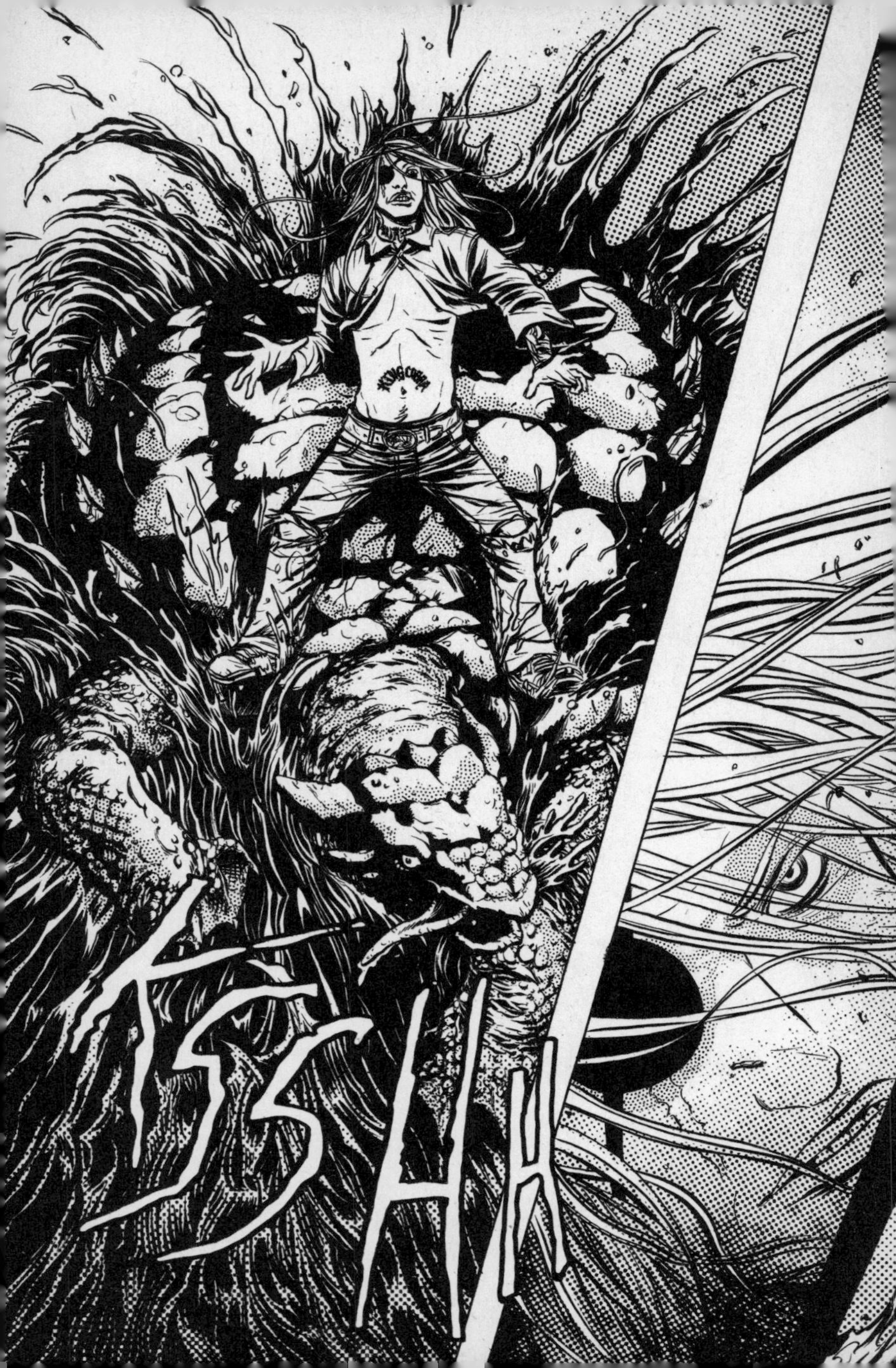
KING COBRA
TSSHH

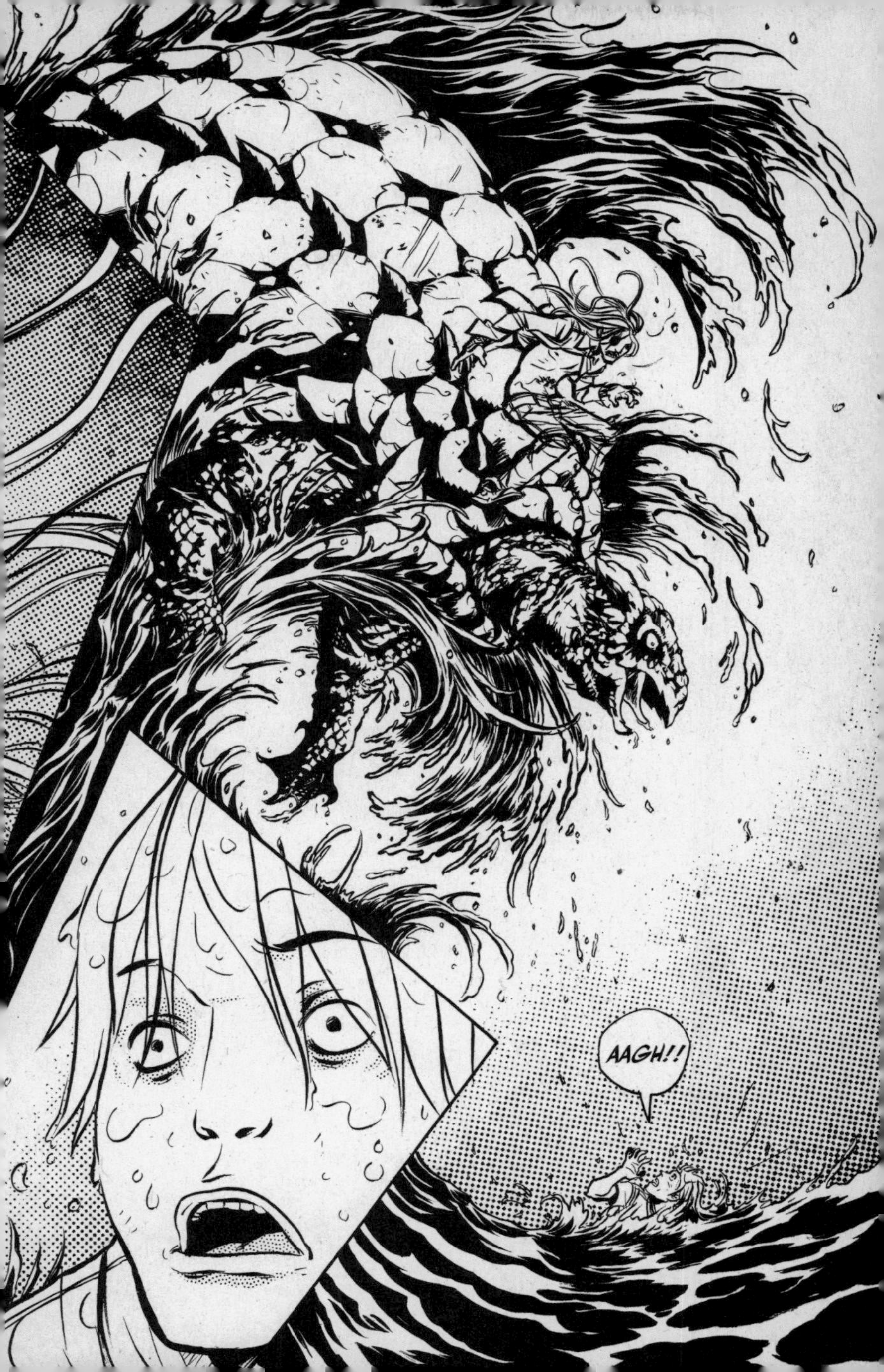
AAGH!!

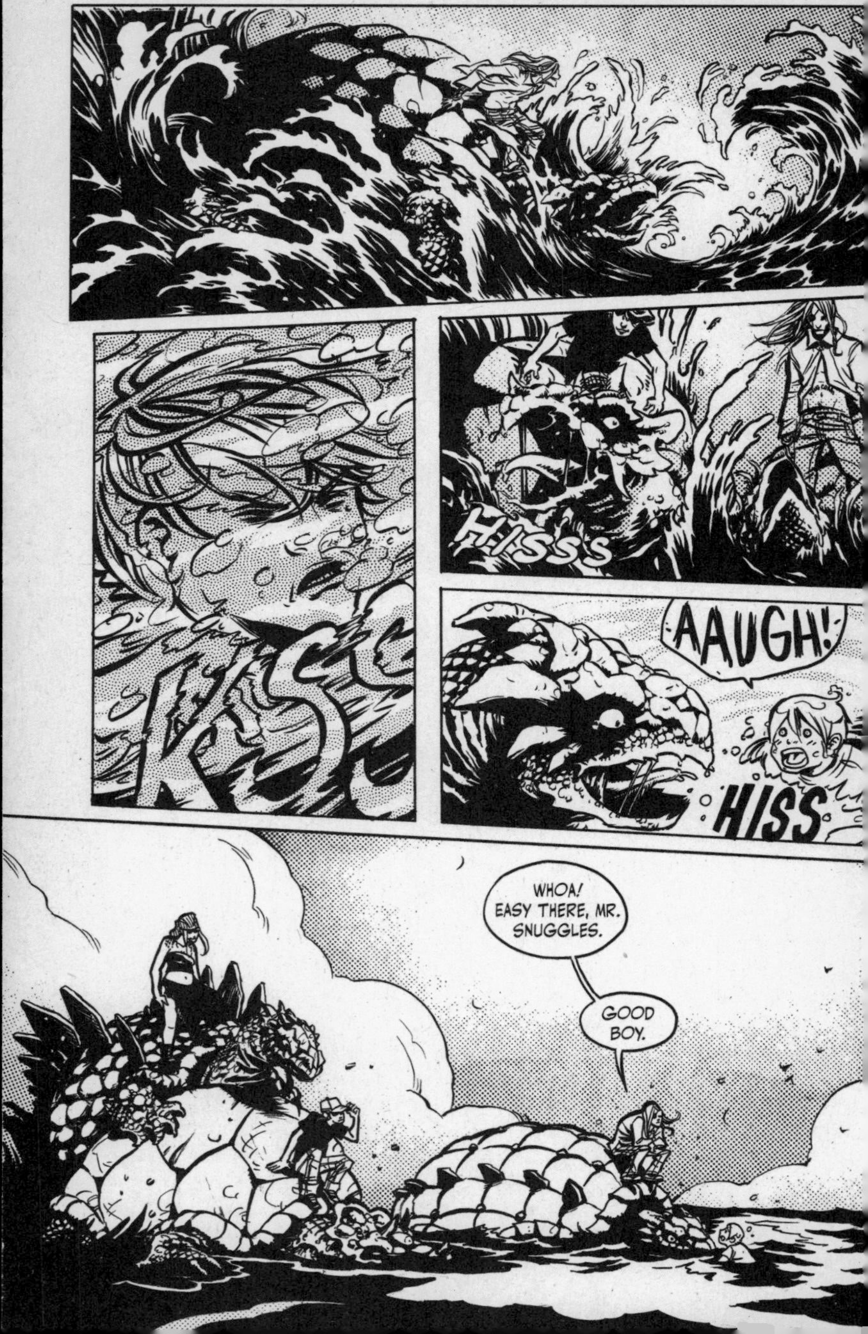
HISSS
AAUGH!
HISS
WHOA! EASY THERE, MR. SNUGGLES.
GOOD BOY.

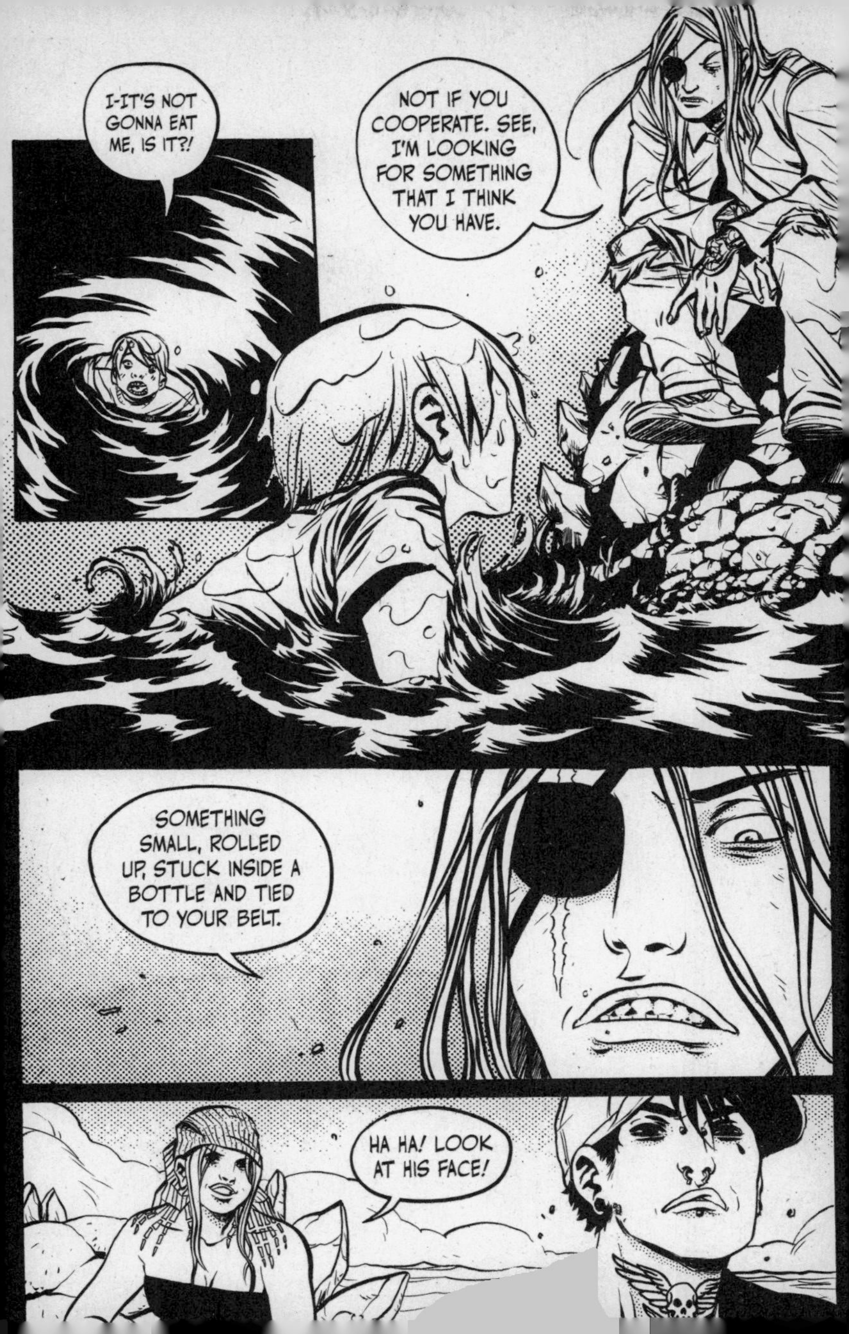
I-IT'S NOT GONNA EAT ME, IS IT?!
NOT IF YOU COOPERATE. SEE, I'M LOOKING FOR SOMETHING THAT I THINK YOU HAVE.
SOMETHING SMALL, ROLLED UP, STUCK INSIDE A BOTTLE AND TIED TO YOUR BELT.
HA HA! LOOK AT HIS FACE!

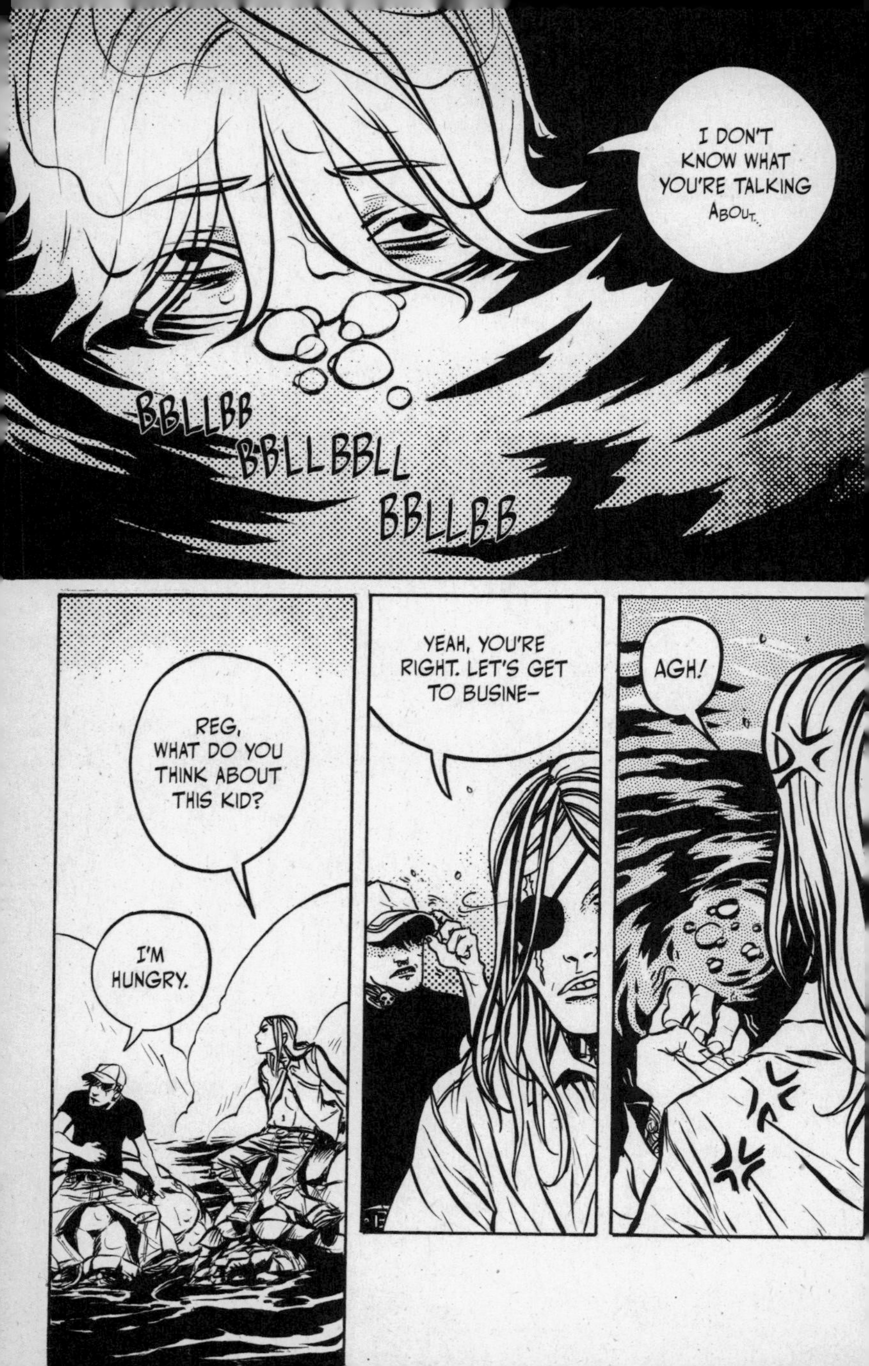
I DON'T KNOW WHAT YOU'RE TALKING ABOUT...
BBLLBB BBLLBBLL BBLLBB
REG, WHAT DO YOU THINK ABOUT THIS KID?
I'M HUNGRY.
YEAH, YOU'RE RIGHT. LET'S GET TO BUSINE-
AGH!

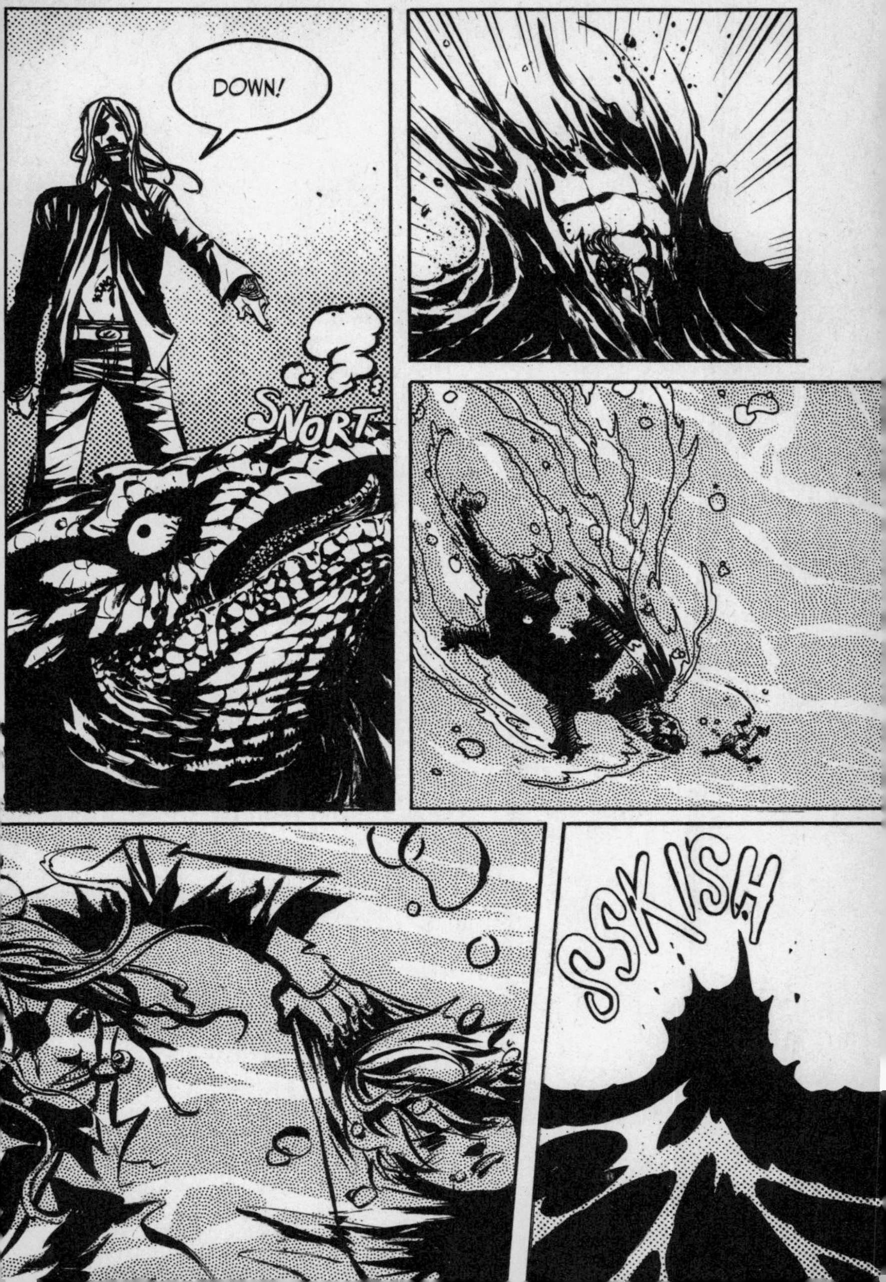
DOWN!
SNORT
SSKISH

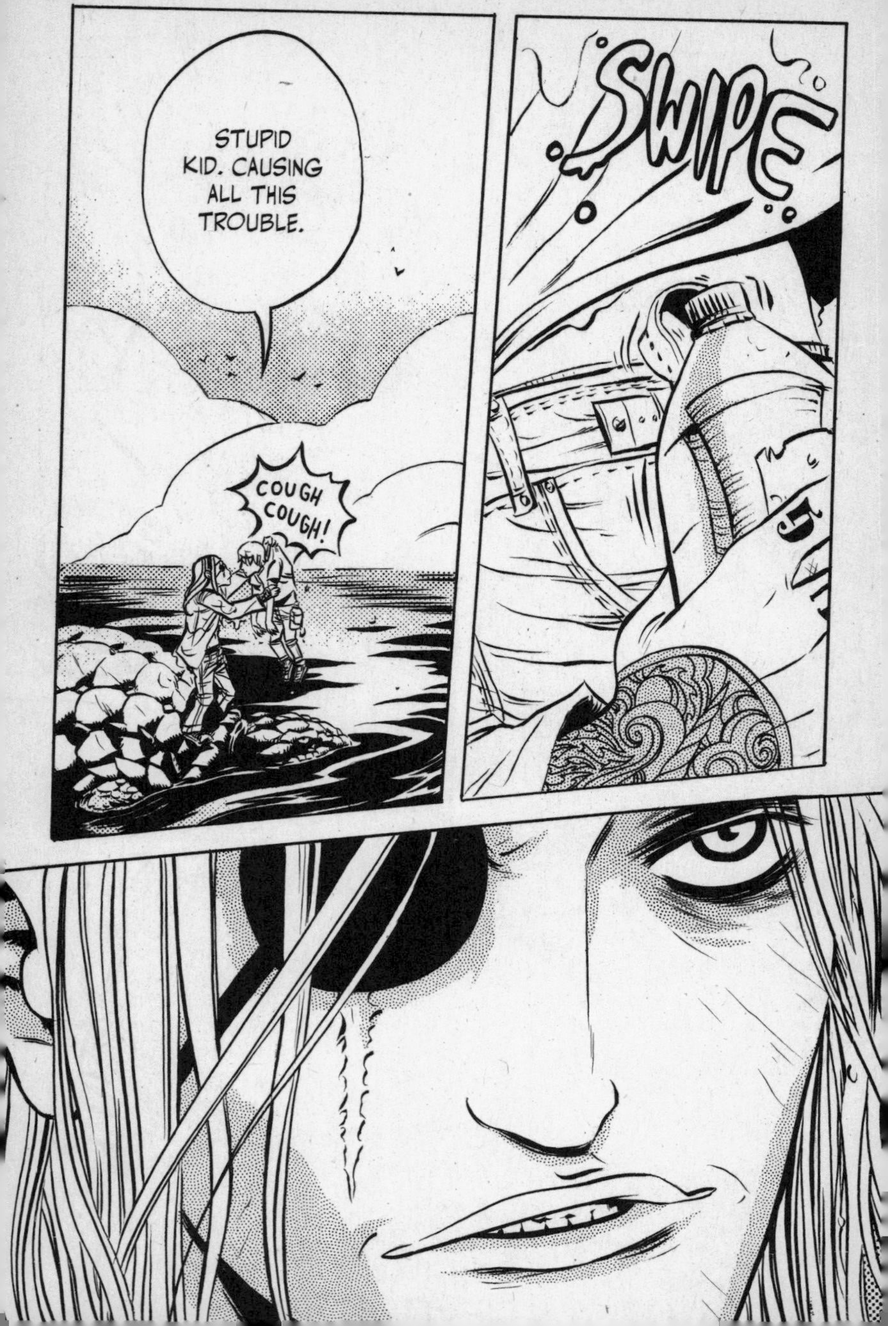
STUPID KID. CAUSING ALL THIS TROUBLE.
COUGH COUGH!
SWIPE

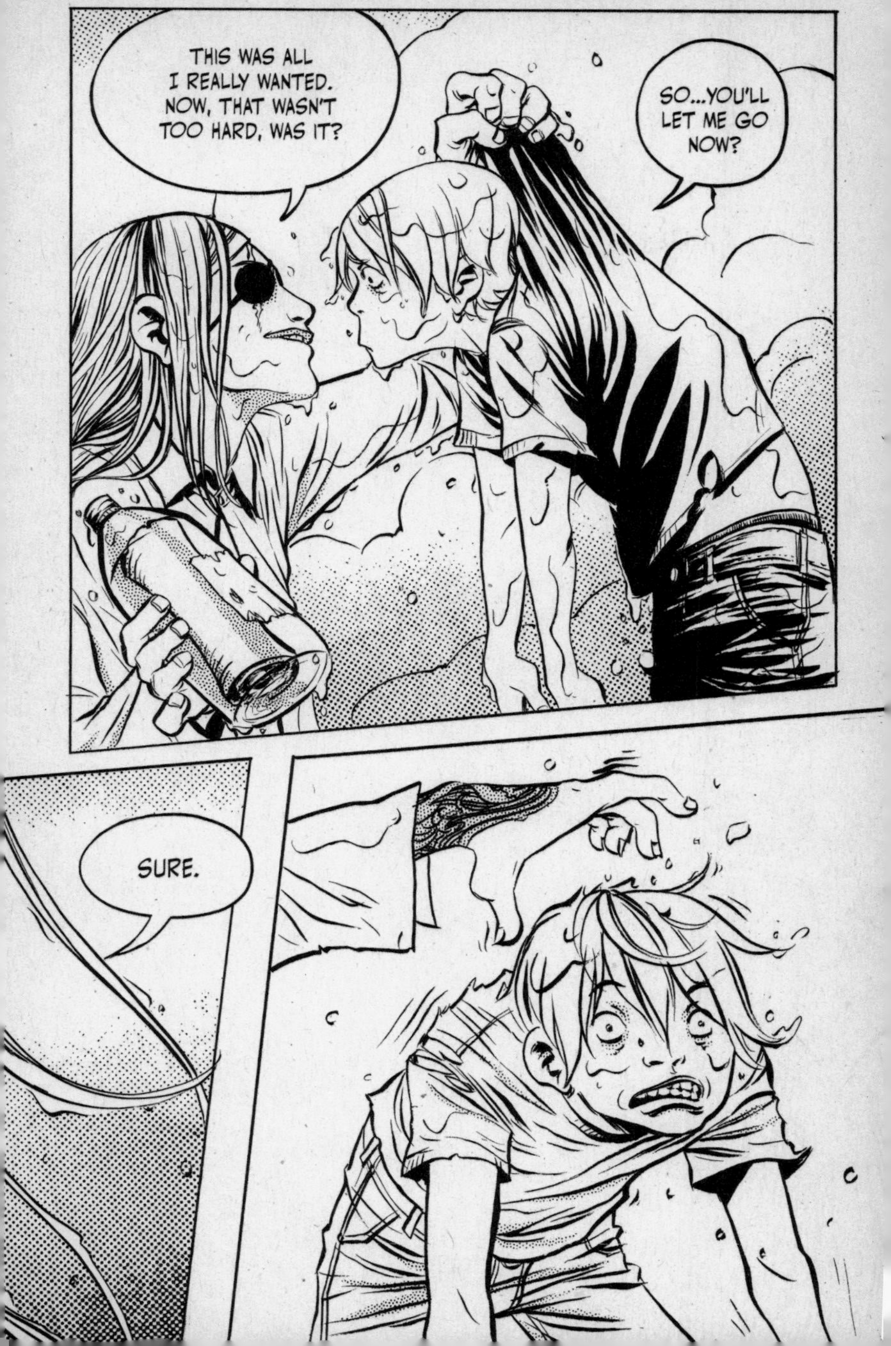
THIS WAS ALL I REALLY WANTED. NOW, THAT WASN'T TOO HARD, WAS IT?
SO...YOU'LL LET ME GO NOW?
SURE.

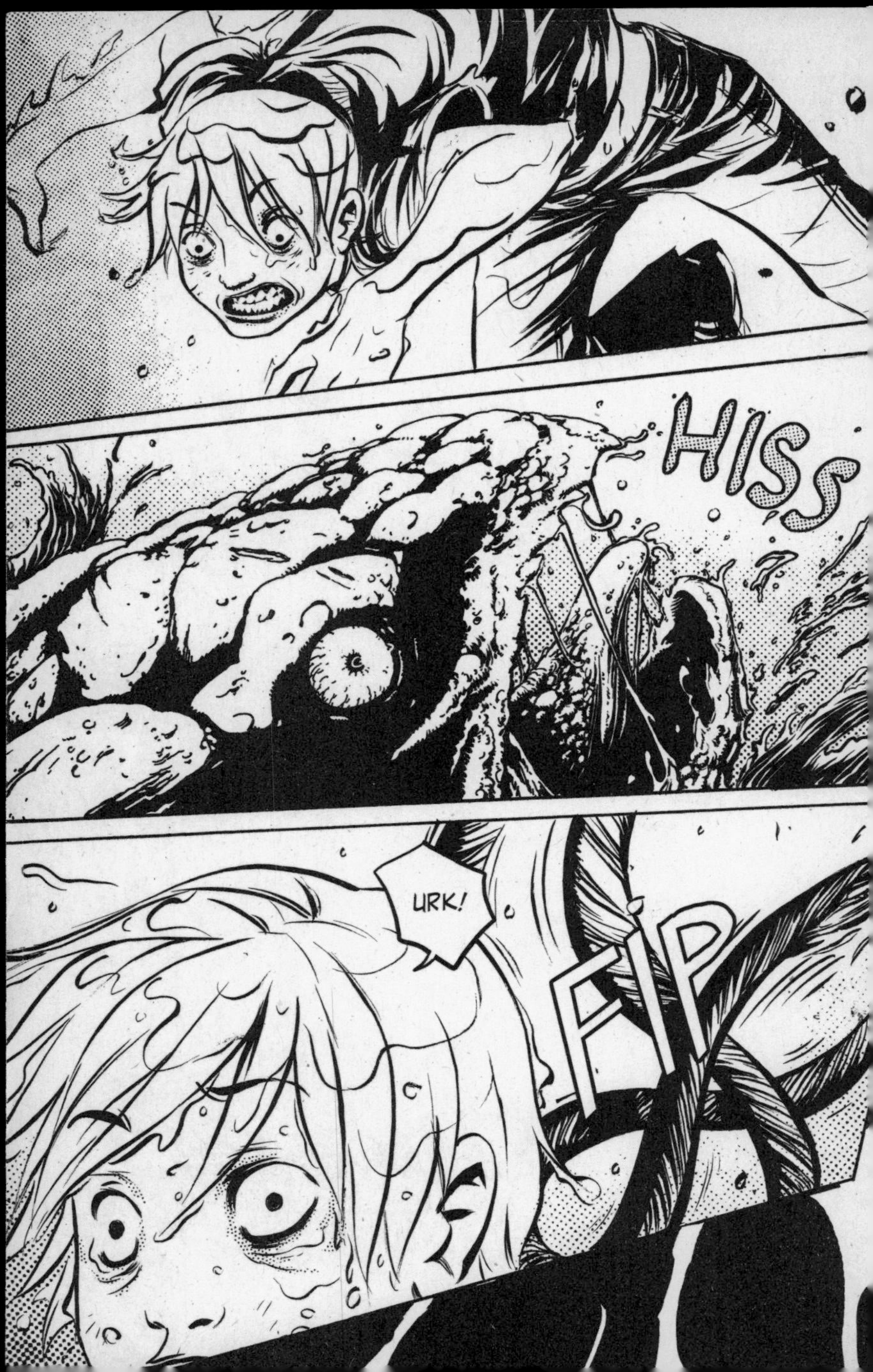
HISS
URK!
FIP

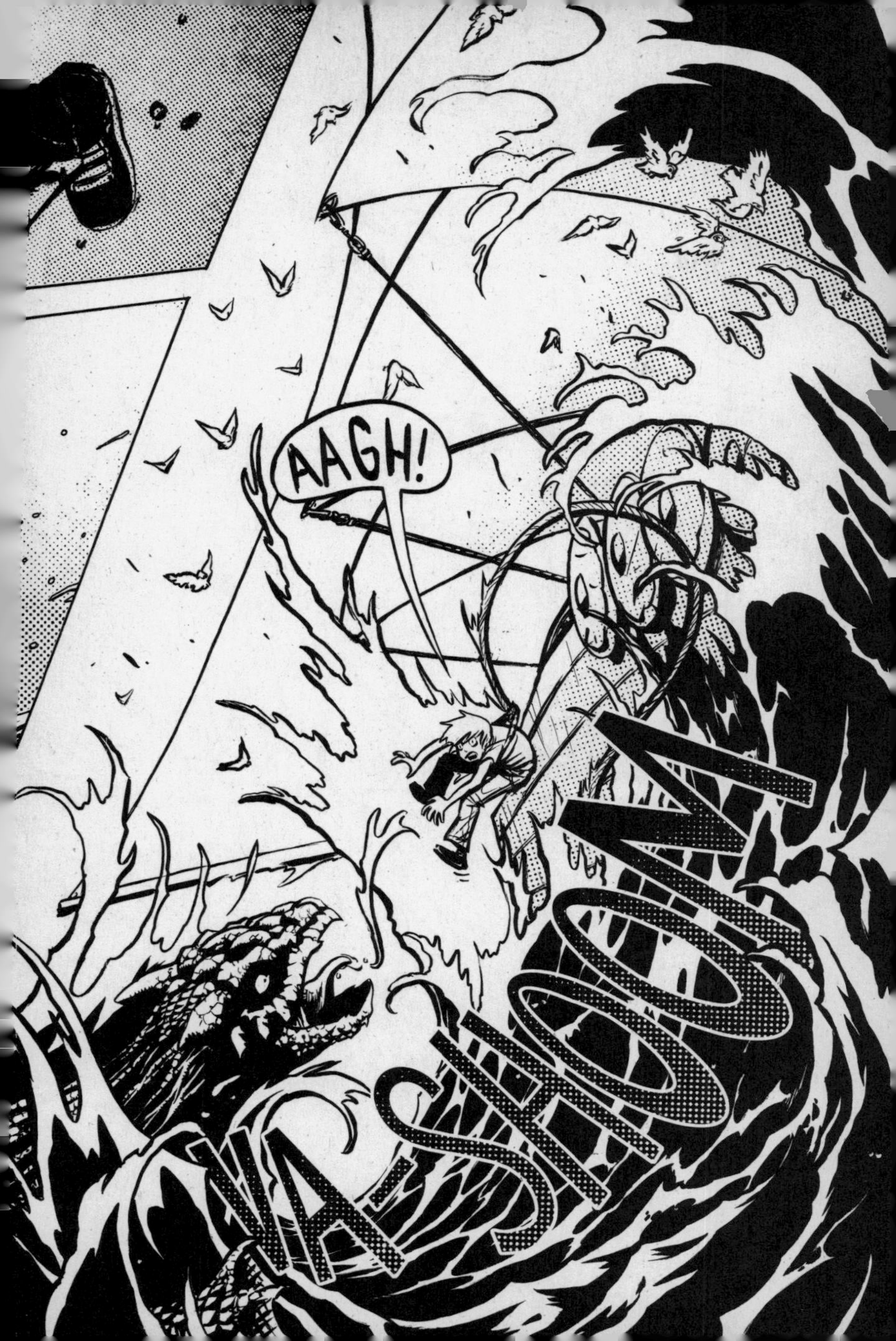

AAGH!
KA-SHOOOM!

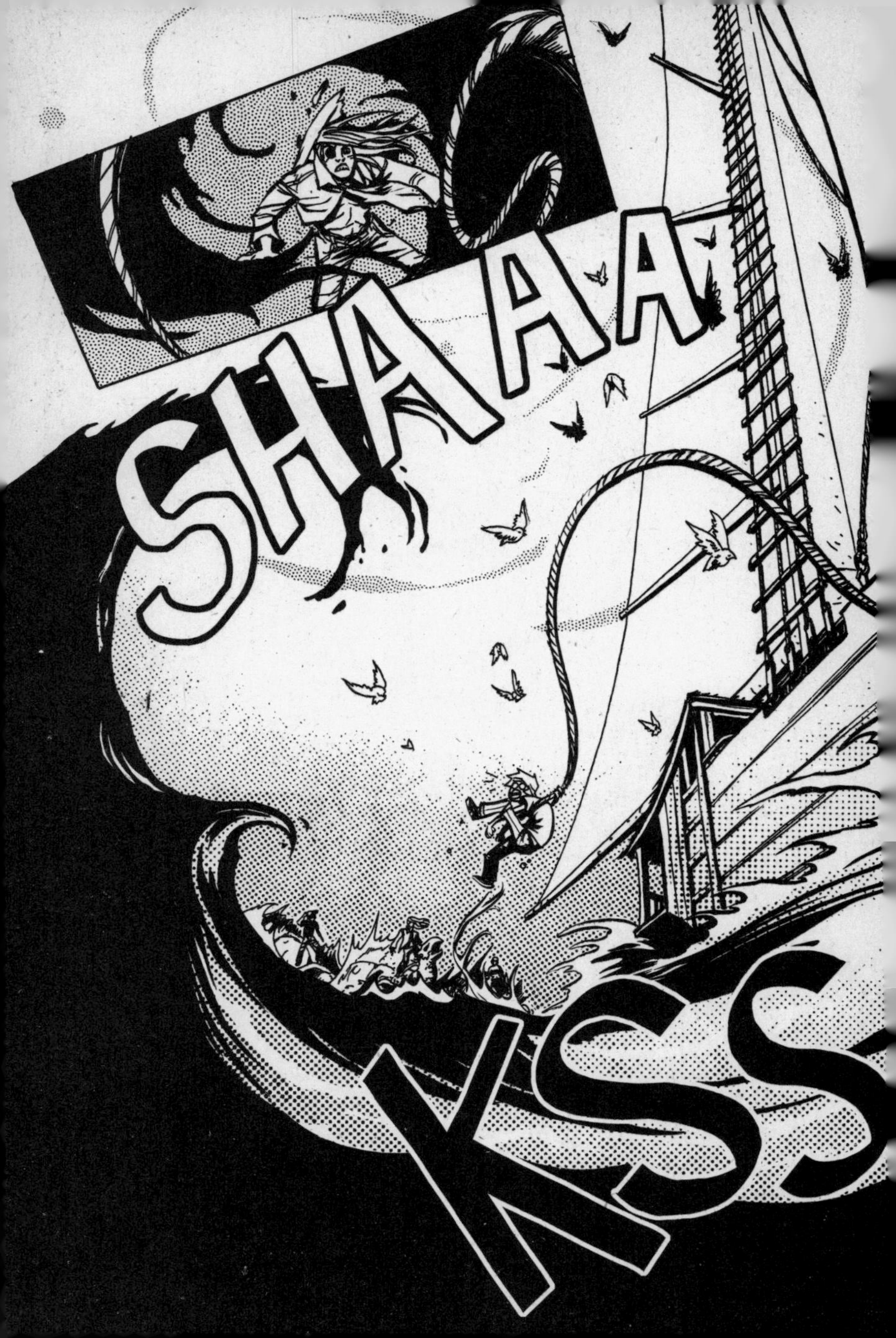
SHAAAA
KSSS

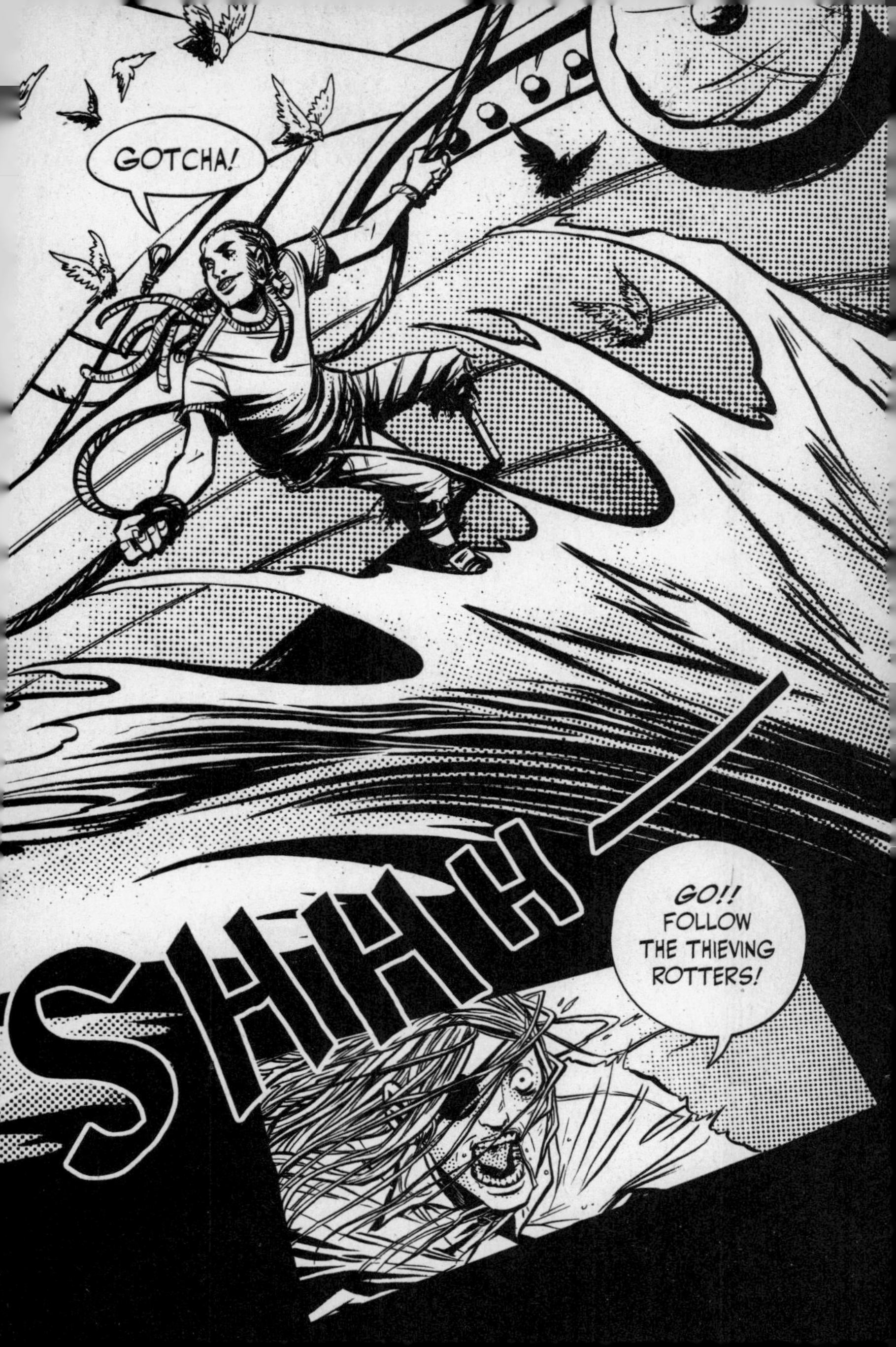
GOTCHA!
SHHHH
GO!! FOLLOW THE THIEVING ROTTERS!

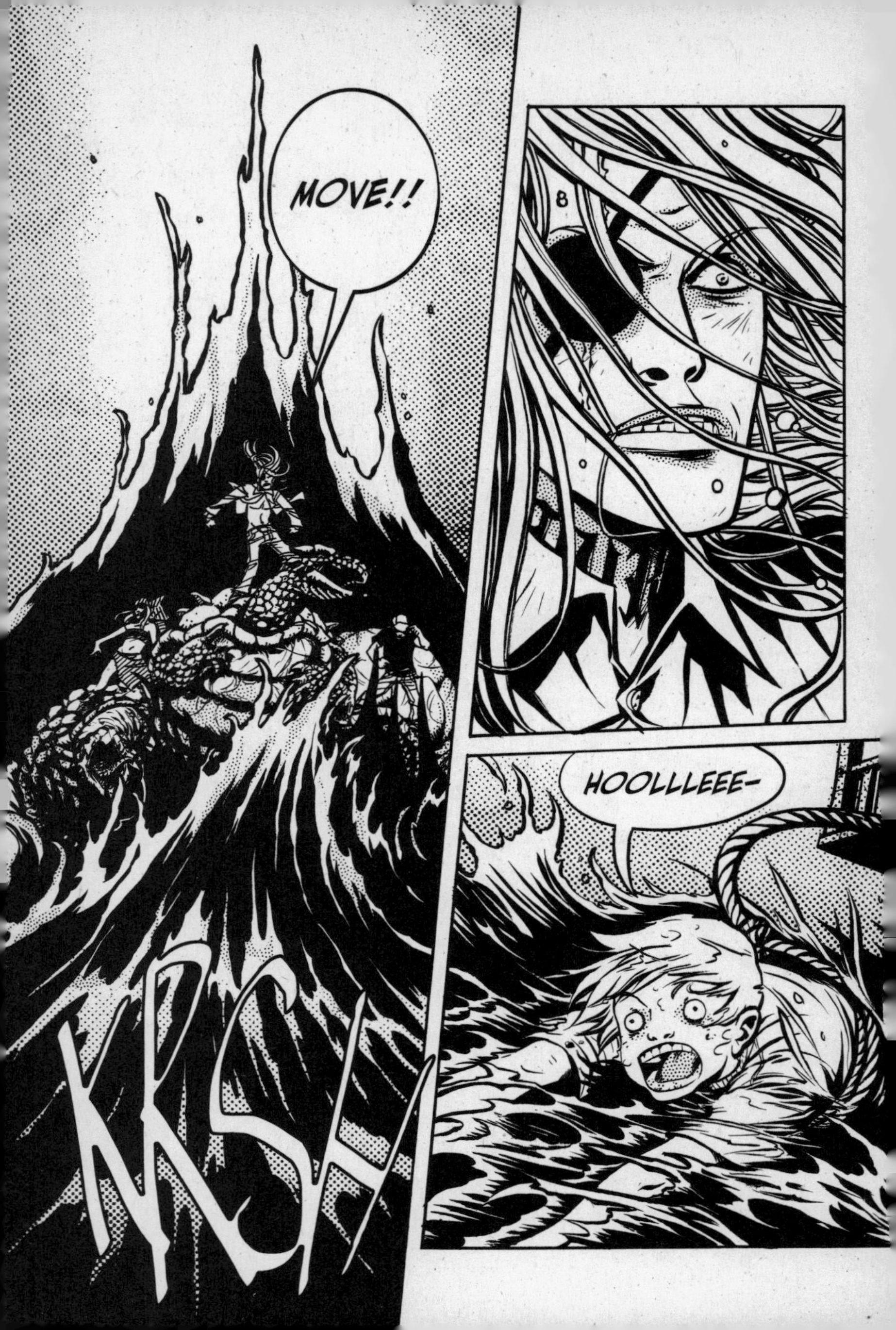
MOVE!!
KRSH
HOOLLLEEE-

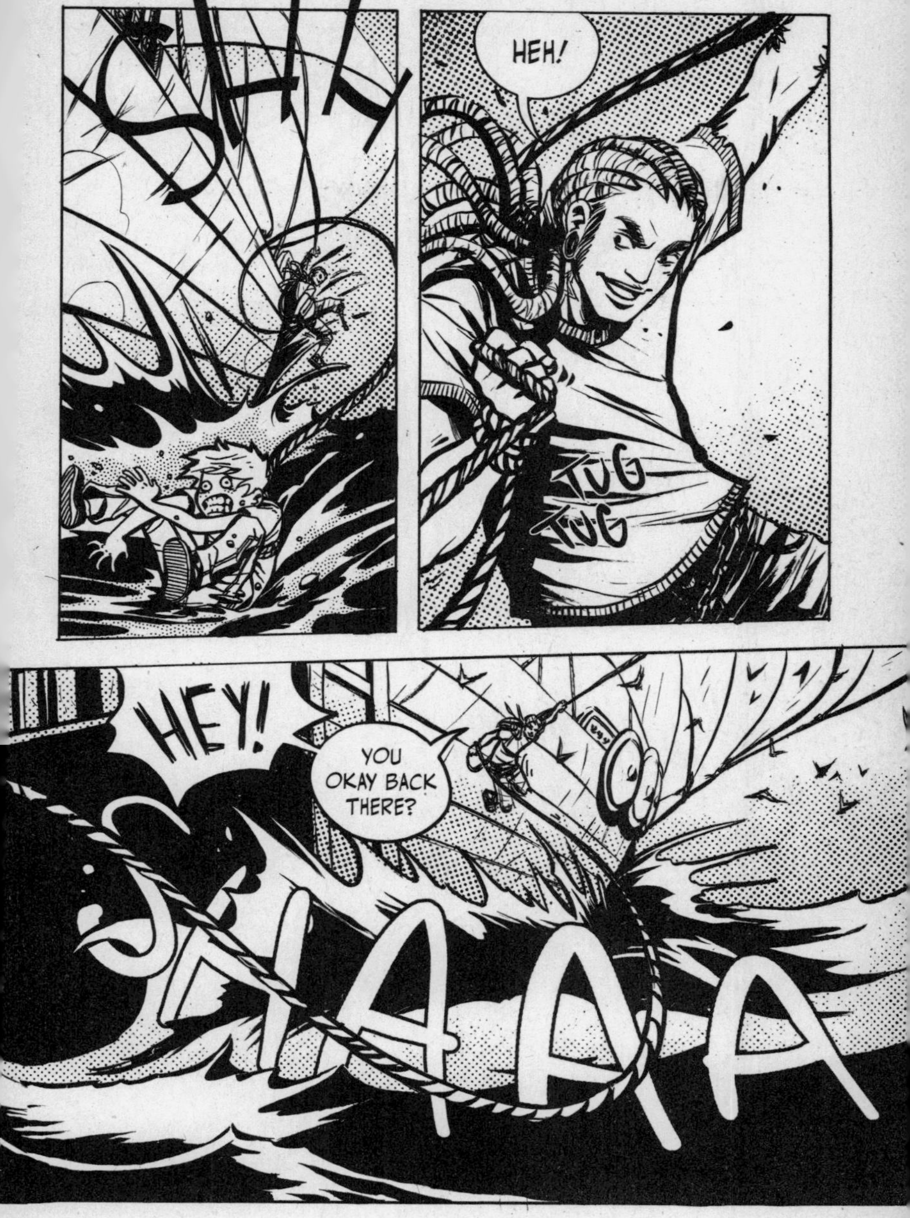
HEH!
TUG
TUG
HEY!
YOU OKAY BACK THERE?
SHAAA

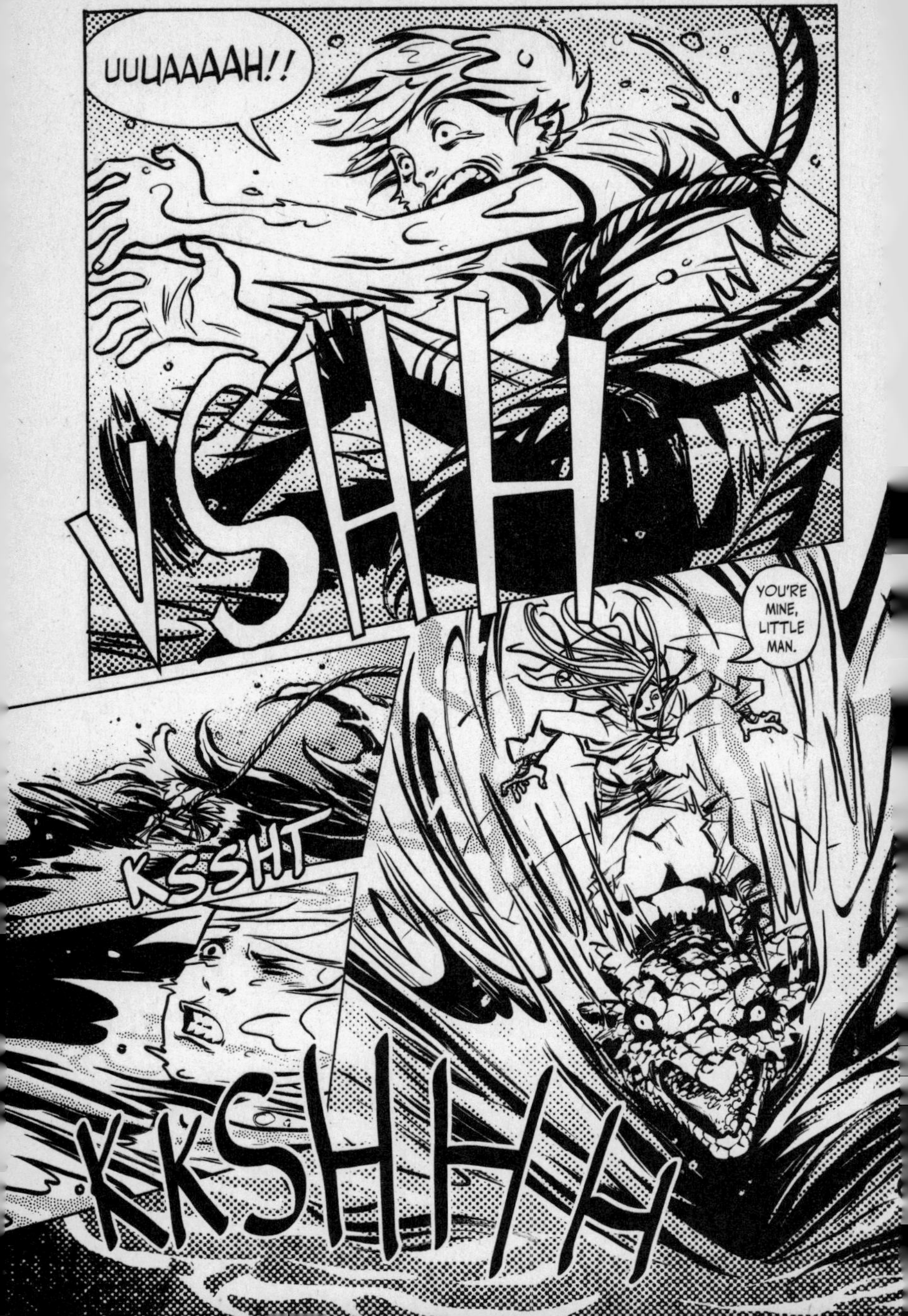
UUUAAAAH!!
VSHHH
YOU'RE MINE, LITTLE MAN.
KSSHT
KKSHHHH

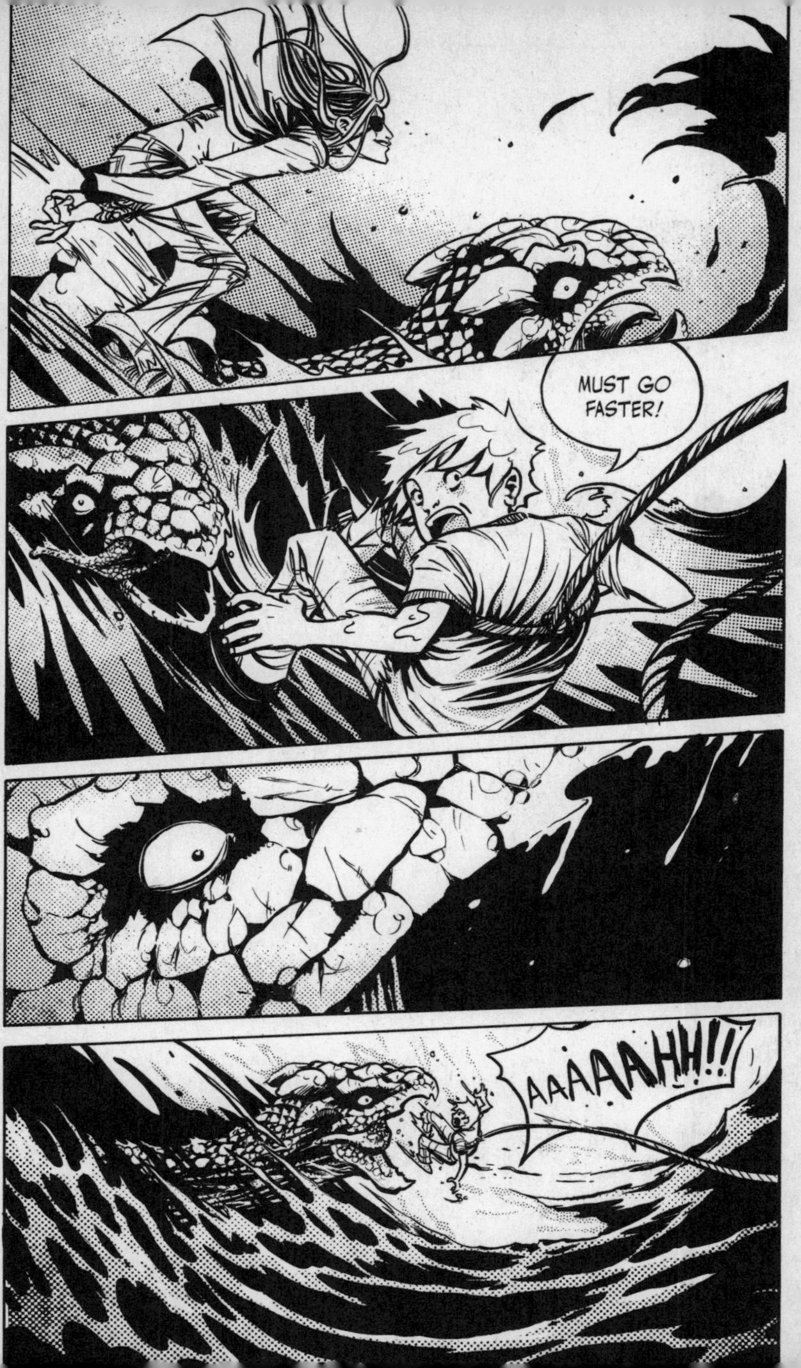
MUST GO FASTER!
AAAAAHH!!!

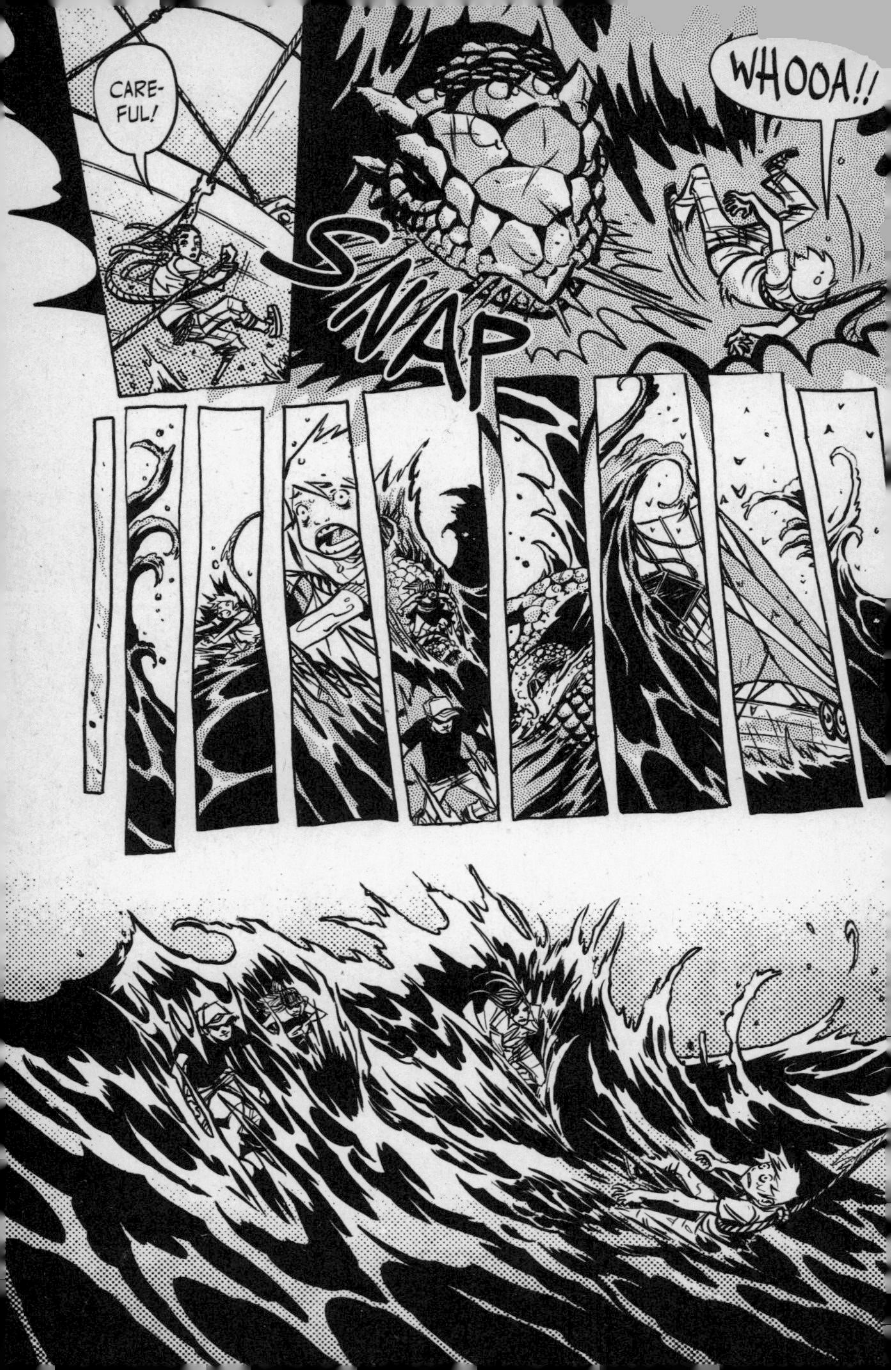
CARE-
FUL!
SNAP
WHOOA!!

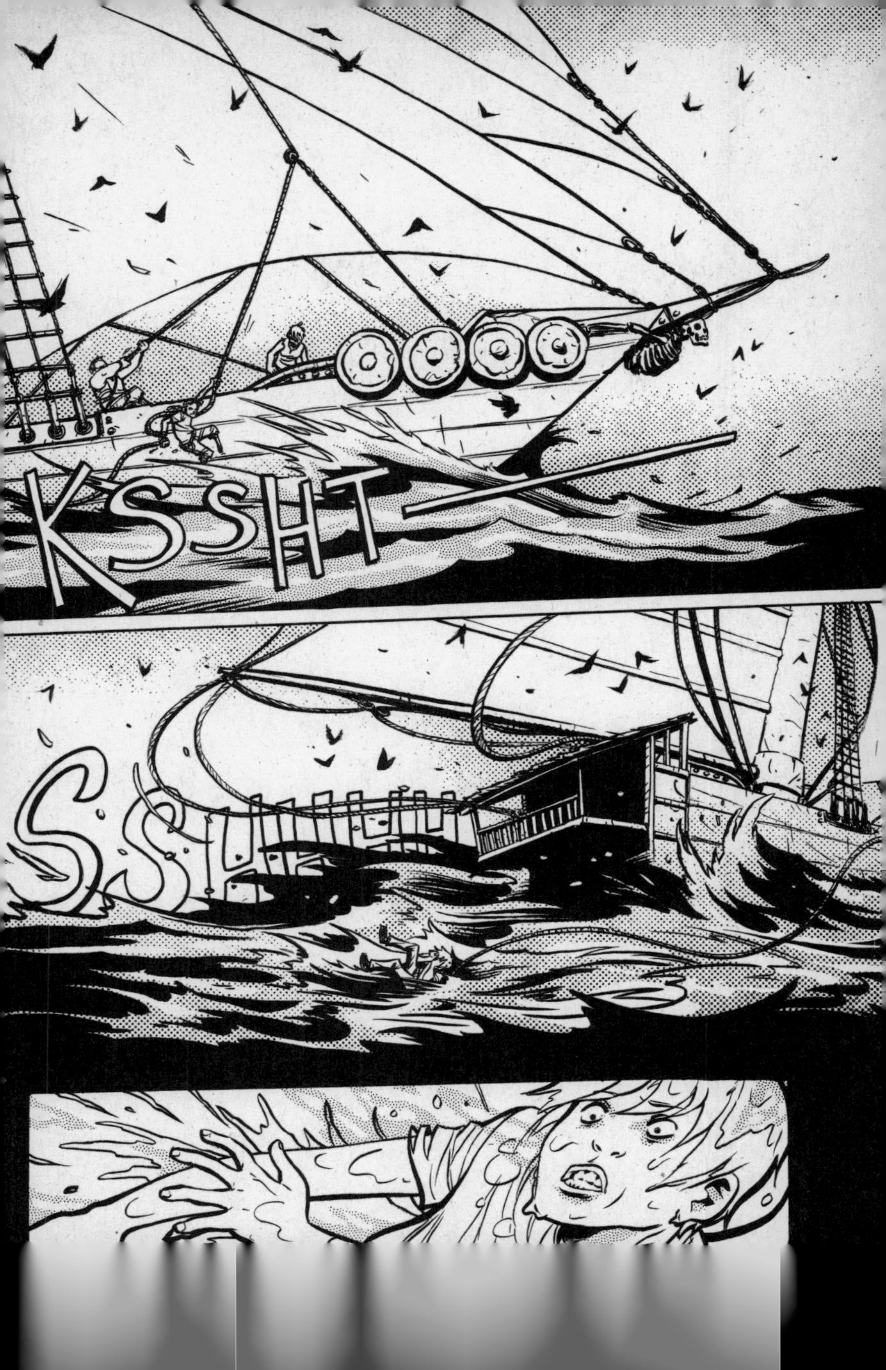
KSSHT

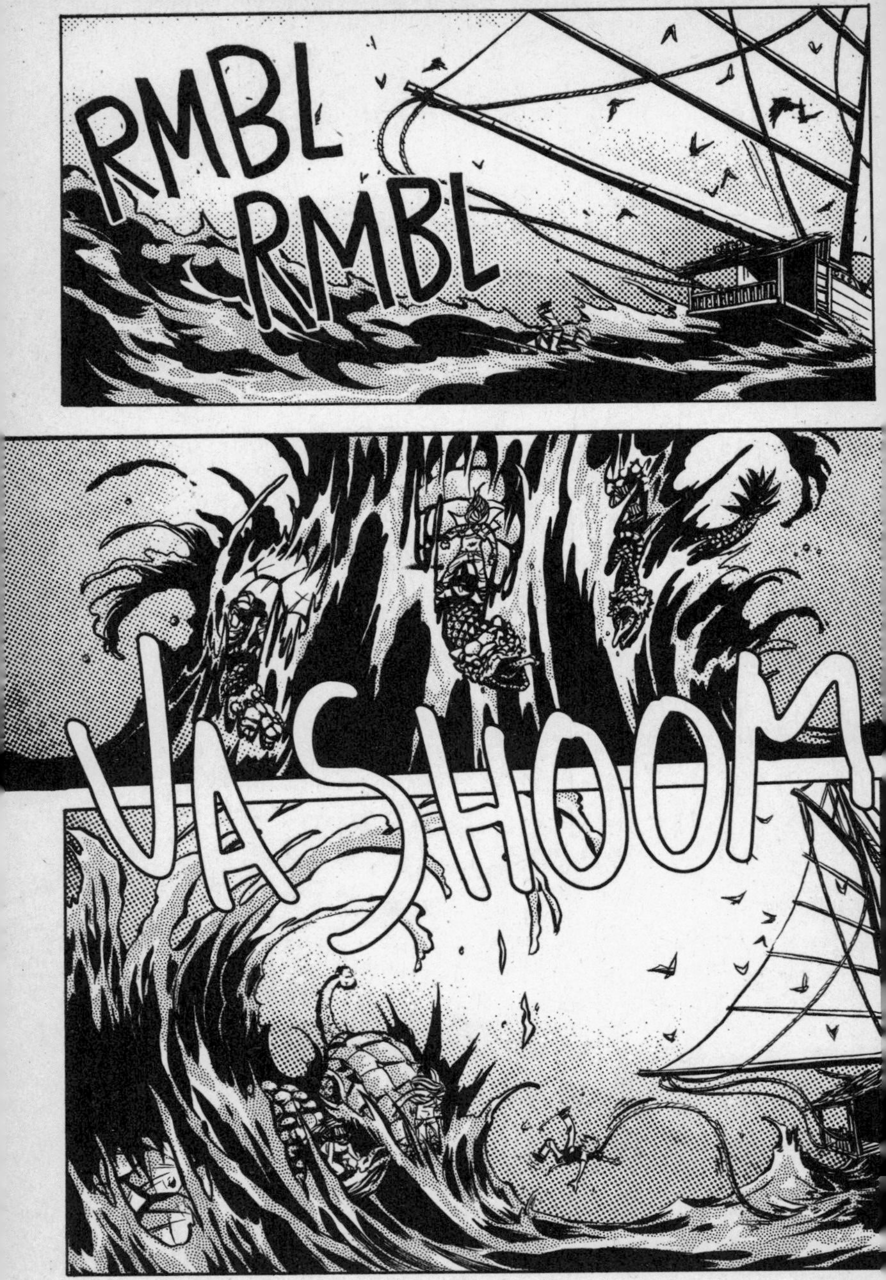
RMBL RMBL
VASHOOM

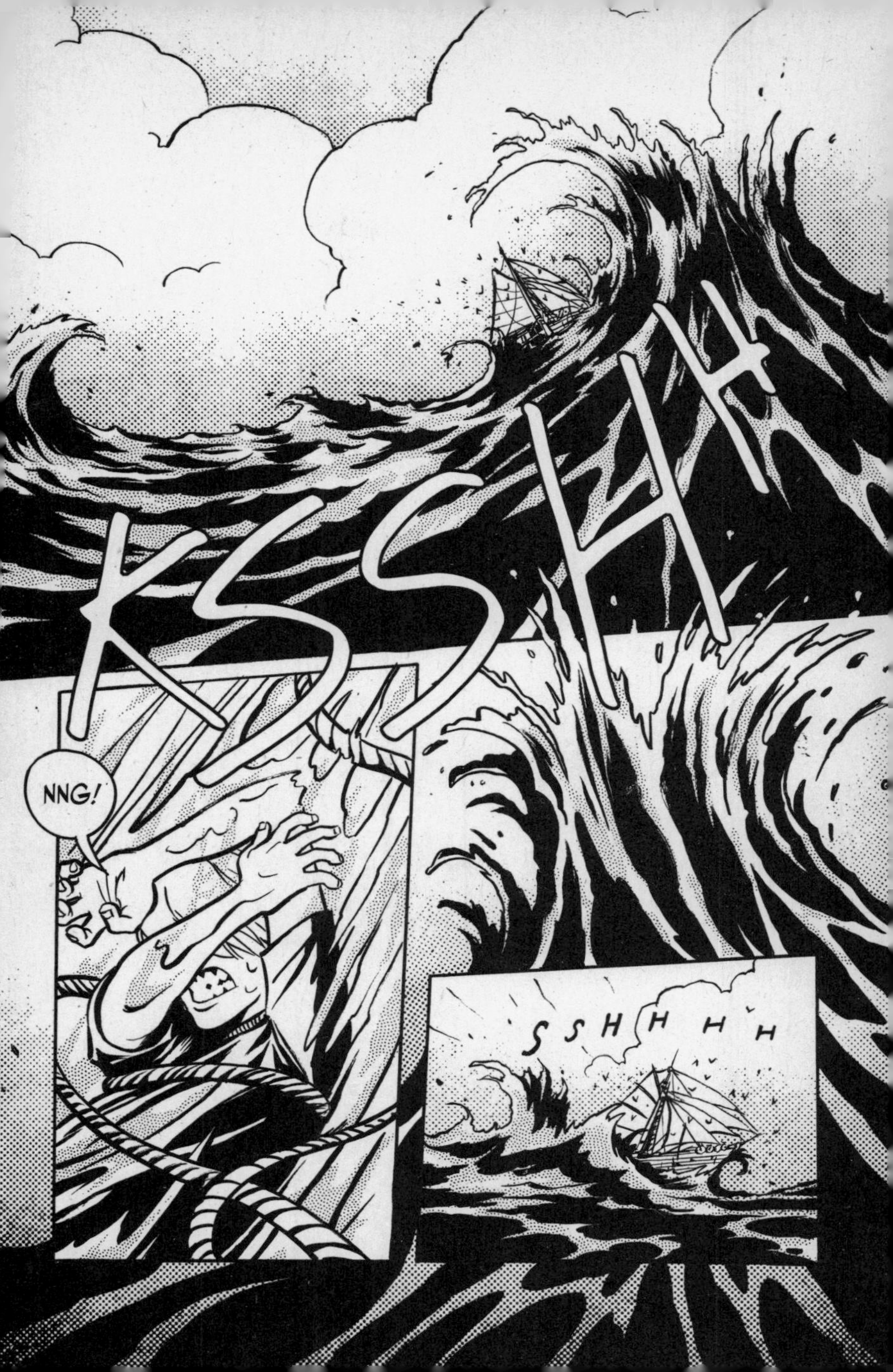
KSSHH
NNG!
SSHHHH

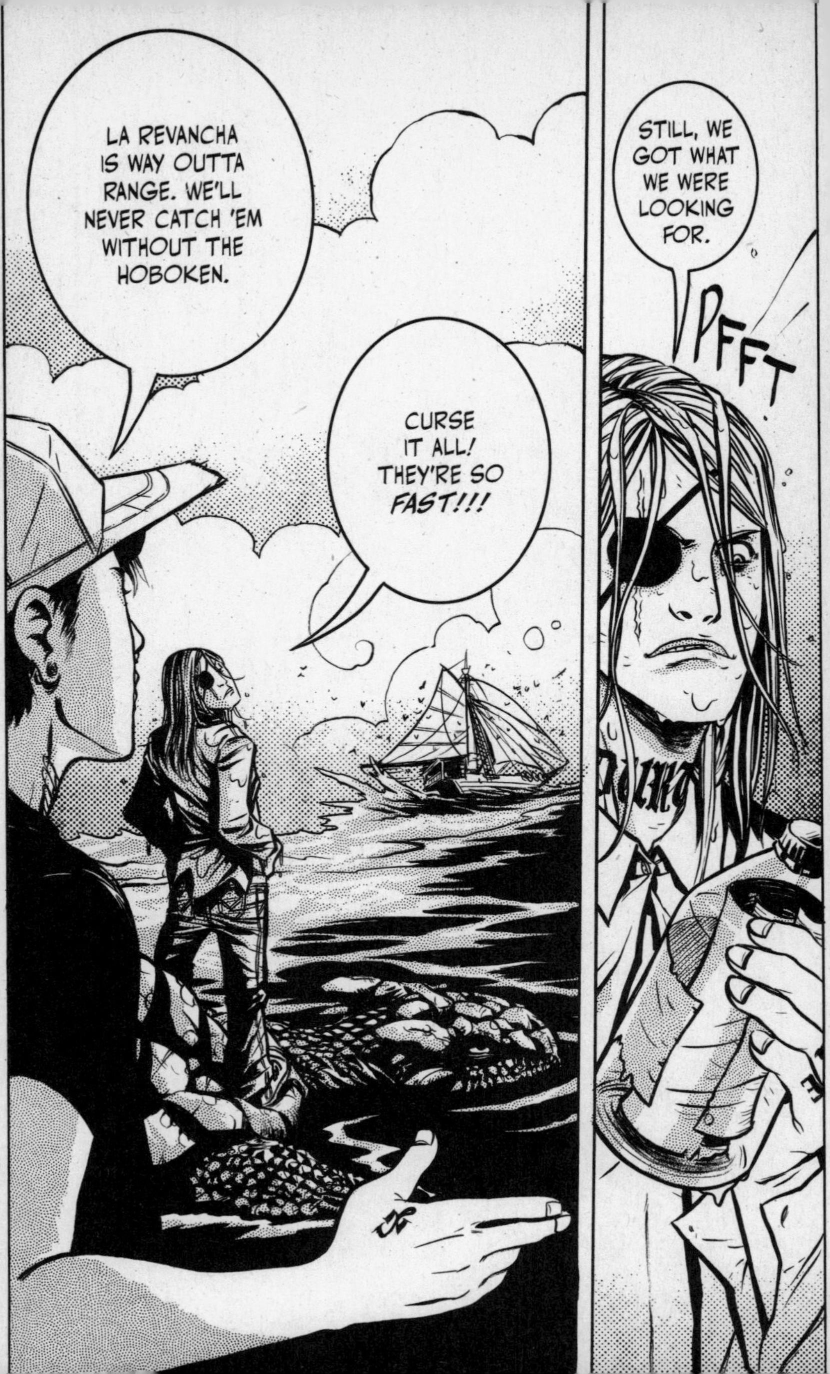
LA REVANCHA IS WAY OUTTA RANGE. WE'LL NEVER CATCH 'EM WITHOUT THE HOBOKEN.
CURSE IT ALL! THEY'RE SO *FAST!!!*
STILL, WE GOT WHAT WE WERE LOOKING FOR.
PFFT

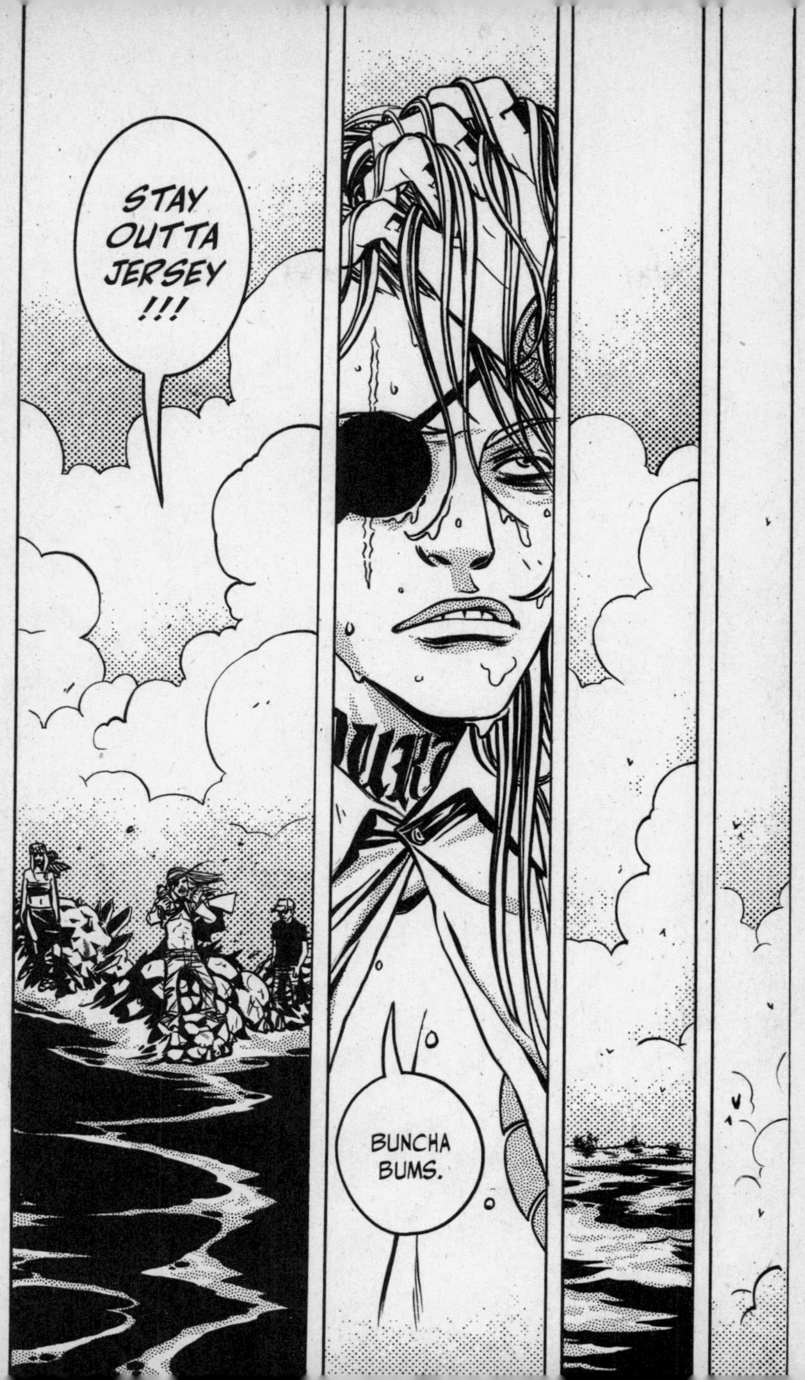
STAY OUTTA JERSEY !!!
BUNCHA BUMS.

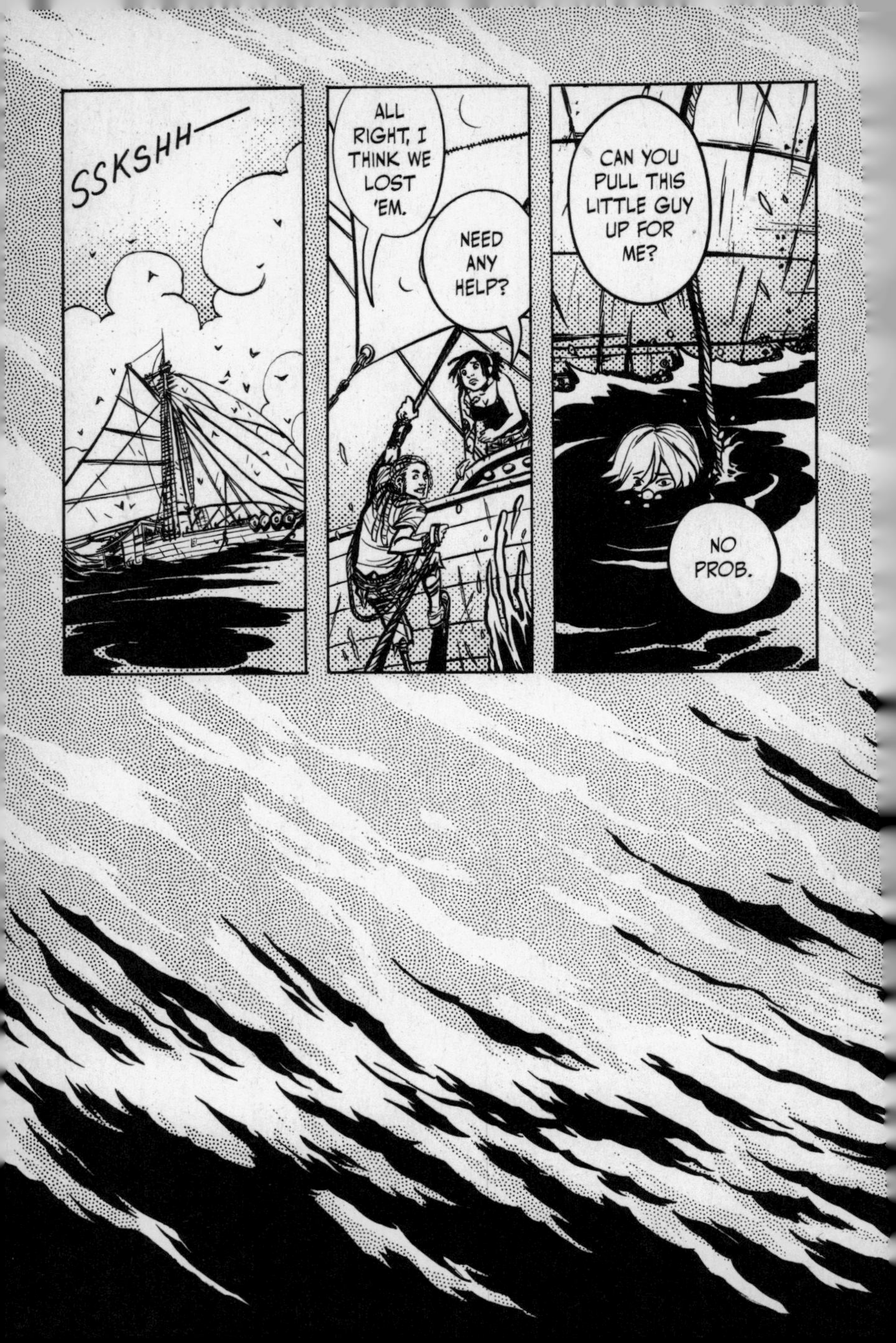
SSKSHH—
ALL RIGHT, I THINK WE LOST 'EM.
NEED ANY HELP?
CAN YOU PULL THIS LITTLE GUY UP FOR ME?
NO PROB.

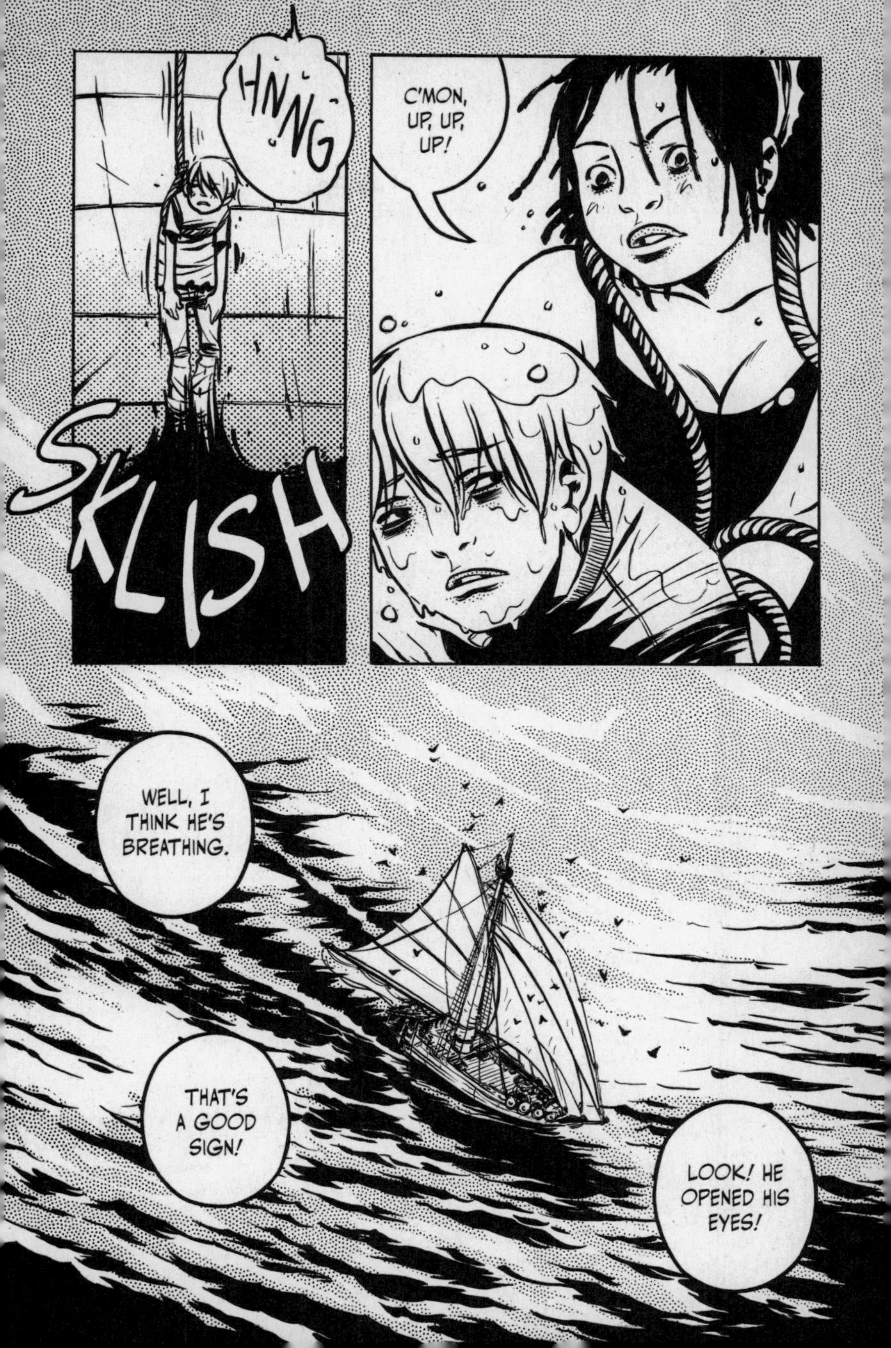
HNNG
SKLISH
C'MON, UP, UP, UP!
WELL, I THINK HE'S BREATHING.
THAT'S A GOOD SIGN!
LOOK! HE OPENED HIS EYES!

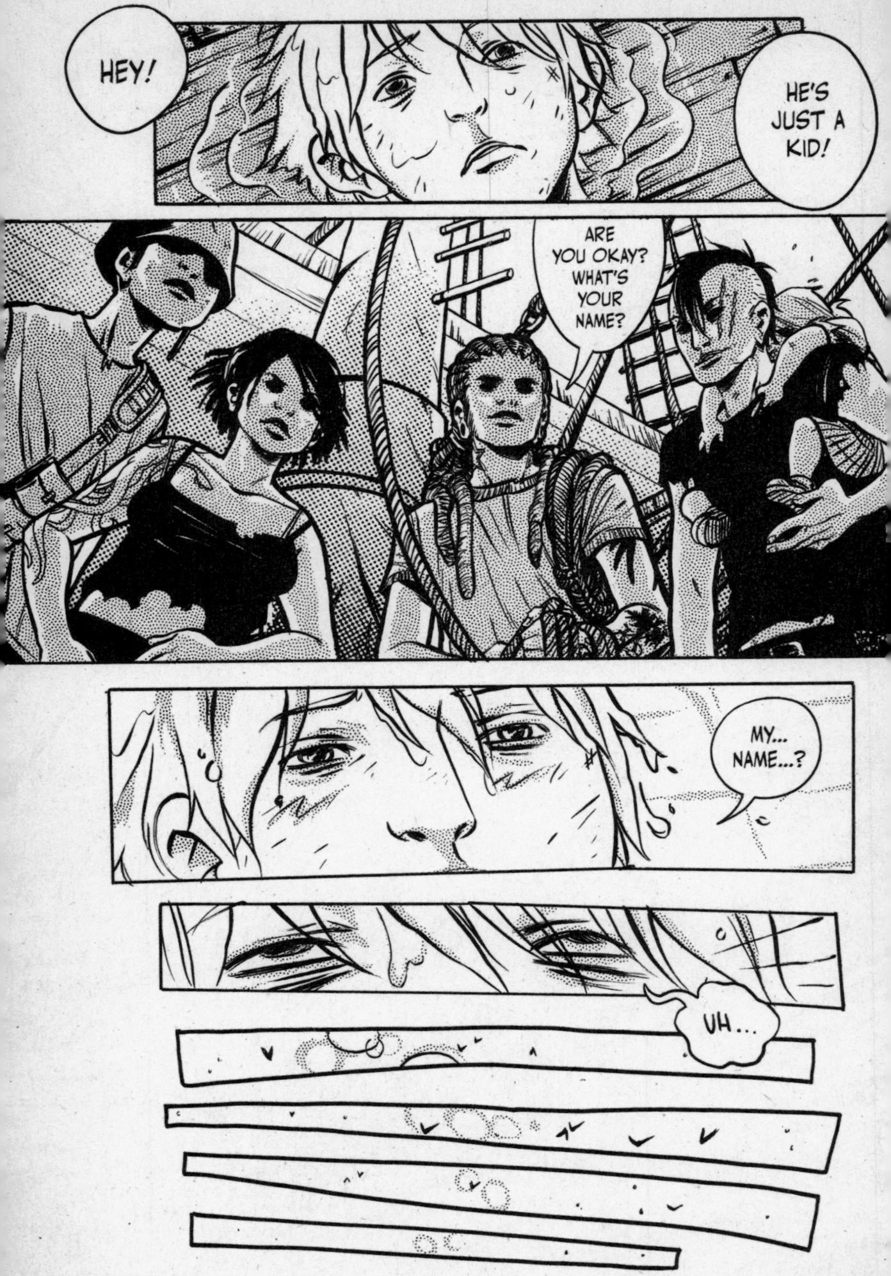
HEY!
HE'S JUST A KID!
ARE YOU OKAY? WHAT'S YOUR NAME?
MY... NAME...?
UH...

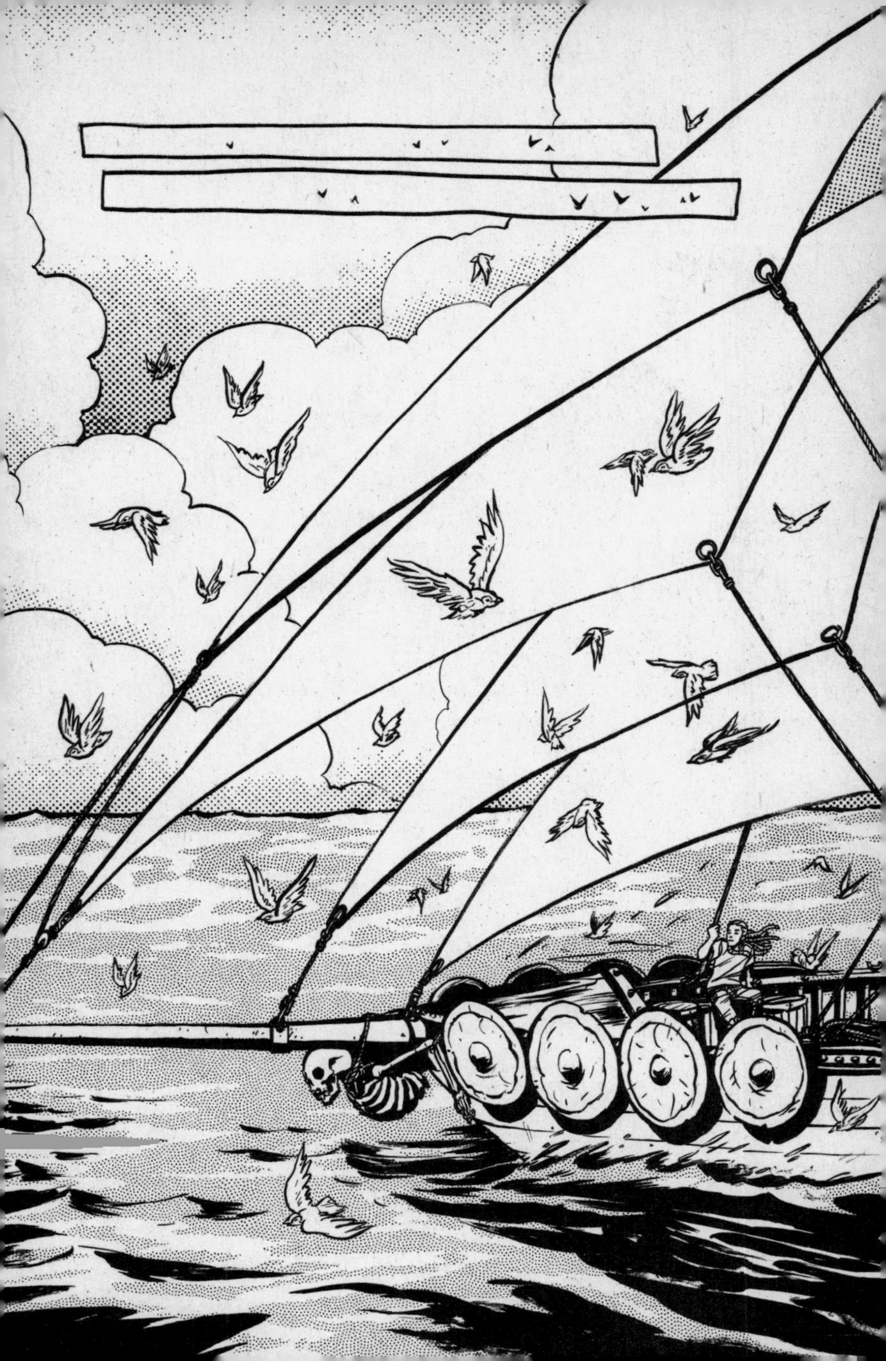

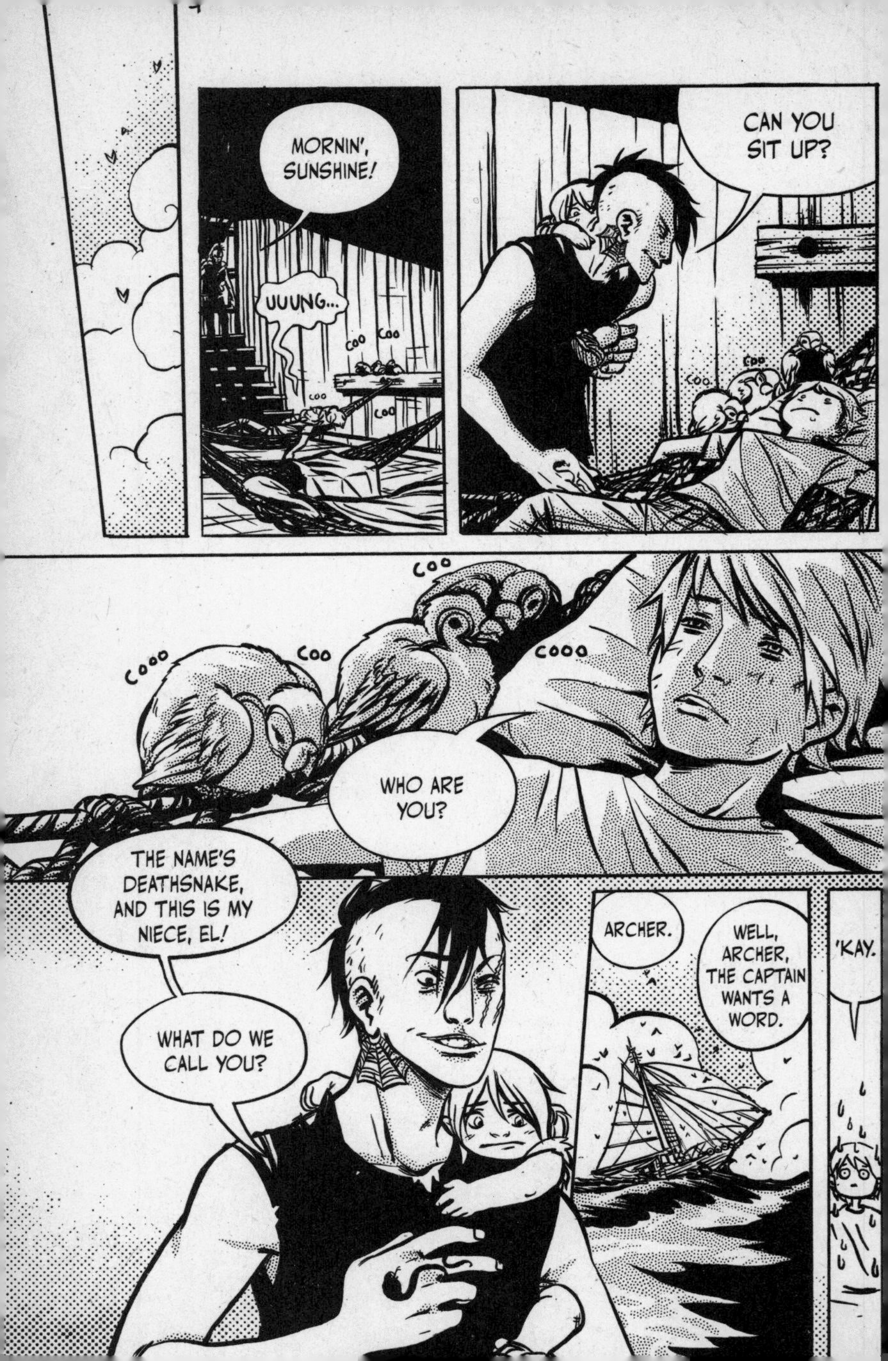
MORNIN', SUNSHINE!
UUUNG...
COO COO
COO
COO
CAN YOU SIT UP?
COO
COO.
COOO
COO
COO
COOO
WHO ARE YOU?
THE NAME'S DEATHSNAKE, AND THIS IS MY NIECE, EL!
WHAT DO WE CALL YOU?
ARCHER.
WELL, ARCHER, THE CAPTAIN WANTS A WORD.
'KAY.

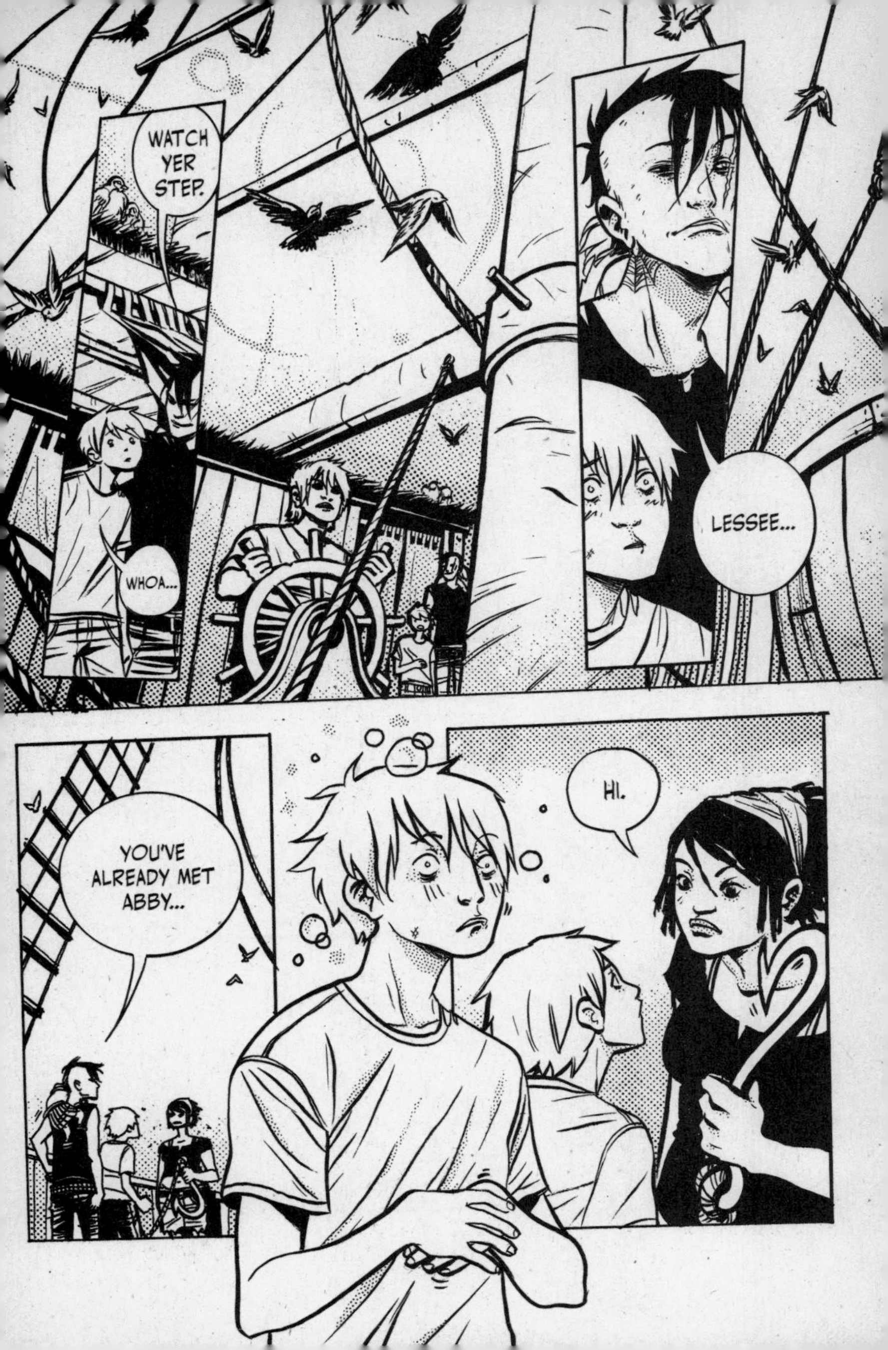
WATCH YER STEP.
WHOA...
LESSEE...
YOU'VE ALREADY MET ABBY...
HI.

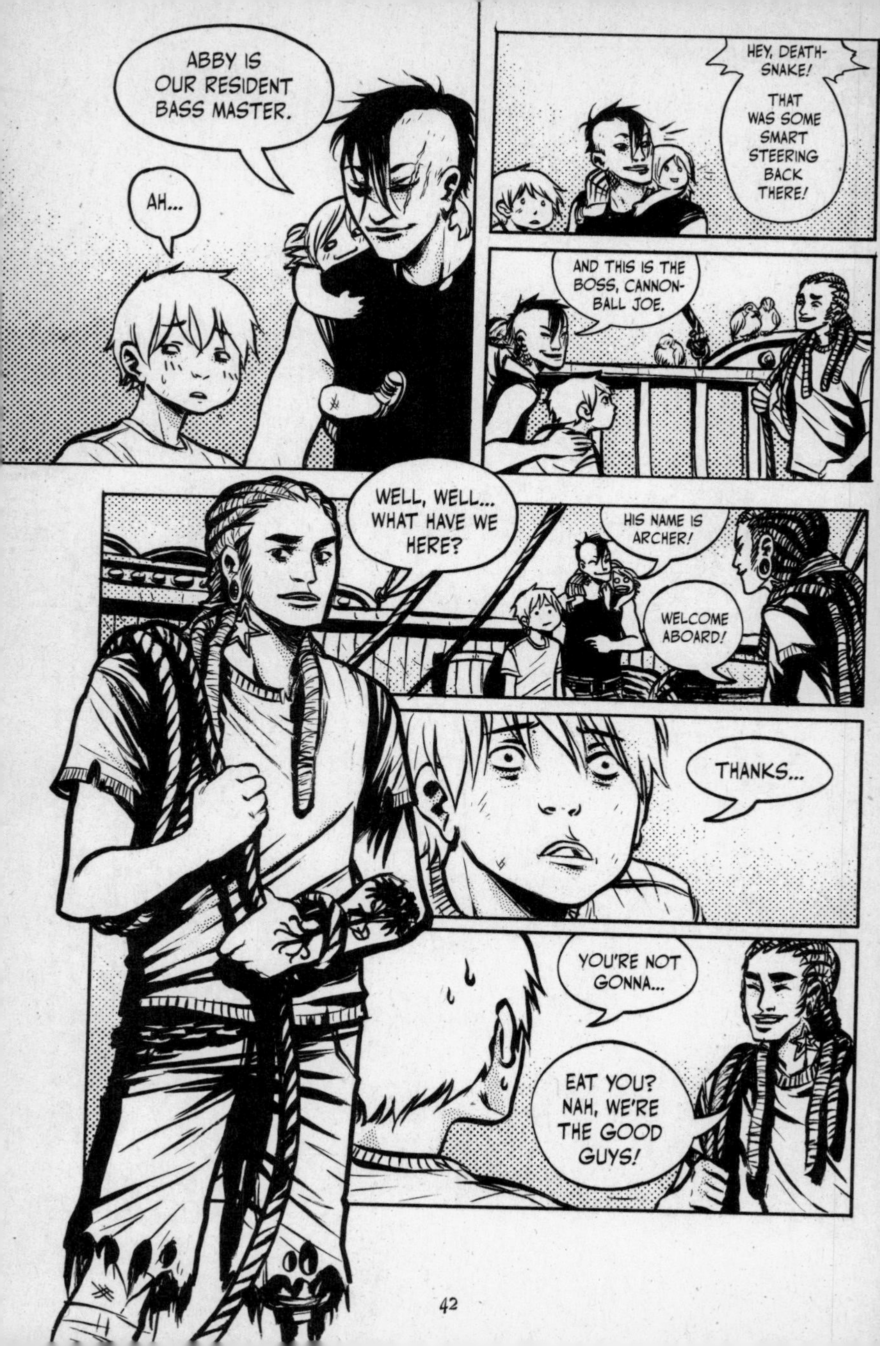
ABBY IS OUR RESIDENT BASS MASTER.
AH...
HEY, DEATH-SNAKE!
THAT WAS SOME SMART STEERING BACK THERE!
AND THIS IS THE BOSS, CANNON-BALL JOE.
WELL, WELL... WHAT HAVE WE HERE?
HIS NAME IS ARCHER!
WELCOME ABOARD!
THANKS...
YOU'RE NOT GONNA...
EAT YOU? NAH, WE'RE THE GOOD GUYS!

TELL YOU WHAT. LET ME KNOW WHAT YOUR DESTINATION WAS AND WE'LL TAKE YOU THERE AFTER OUR NEXT DROP-OFF.

...

JERSEY CAN BE A DANGEROUS PLACE...

I'M SORRY ABOUT WHAT HAPPENED TO YOUR CREWMATES.

BUT-BUT WHY CAN'T I JUST SAIL WITH YOU GUYS? I CAN PULL MY WEIGHT!! I CAN!

UM...

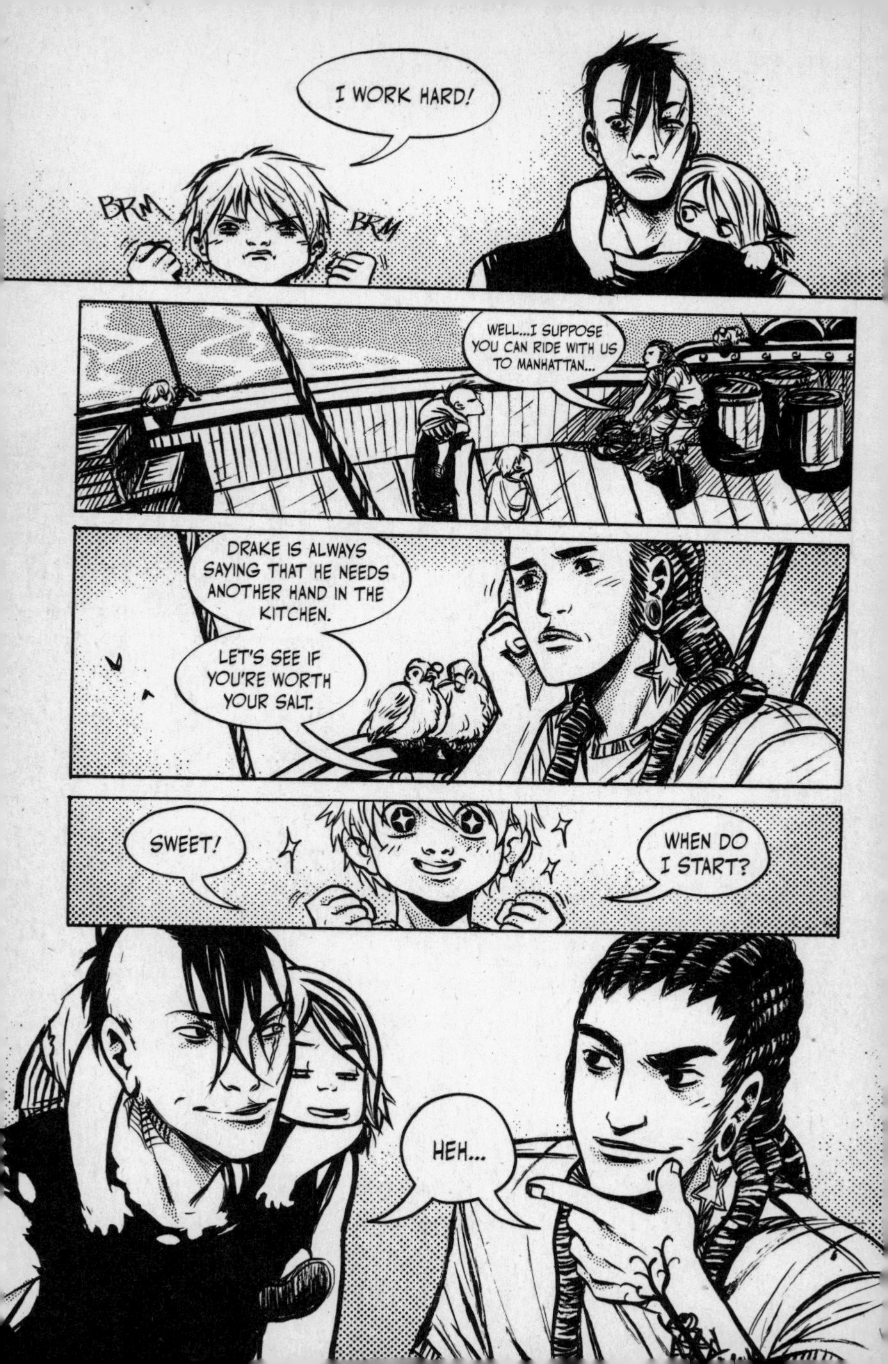
I WORK HARD!
BRM
BRM
WELL...I SUPPOSE YOU CAN RIDE WITH US TO MANHATTAN...
DRAKE IS ALWAYS SAYING THAT HE NEEDS ANOTHER HAND IN THE KITCHEN.
LET'S SEE IF YOU'RE WORTH YOUR SALT.
SWEET!
WHEN DO I START?
HEH...

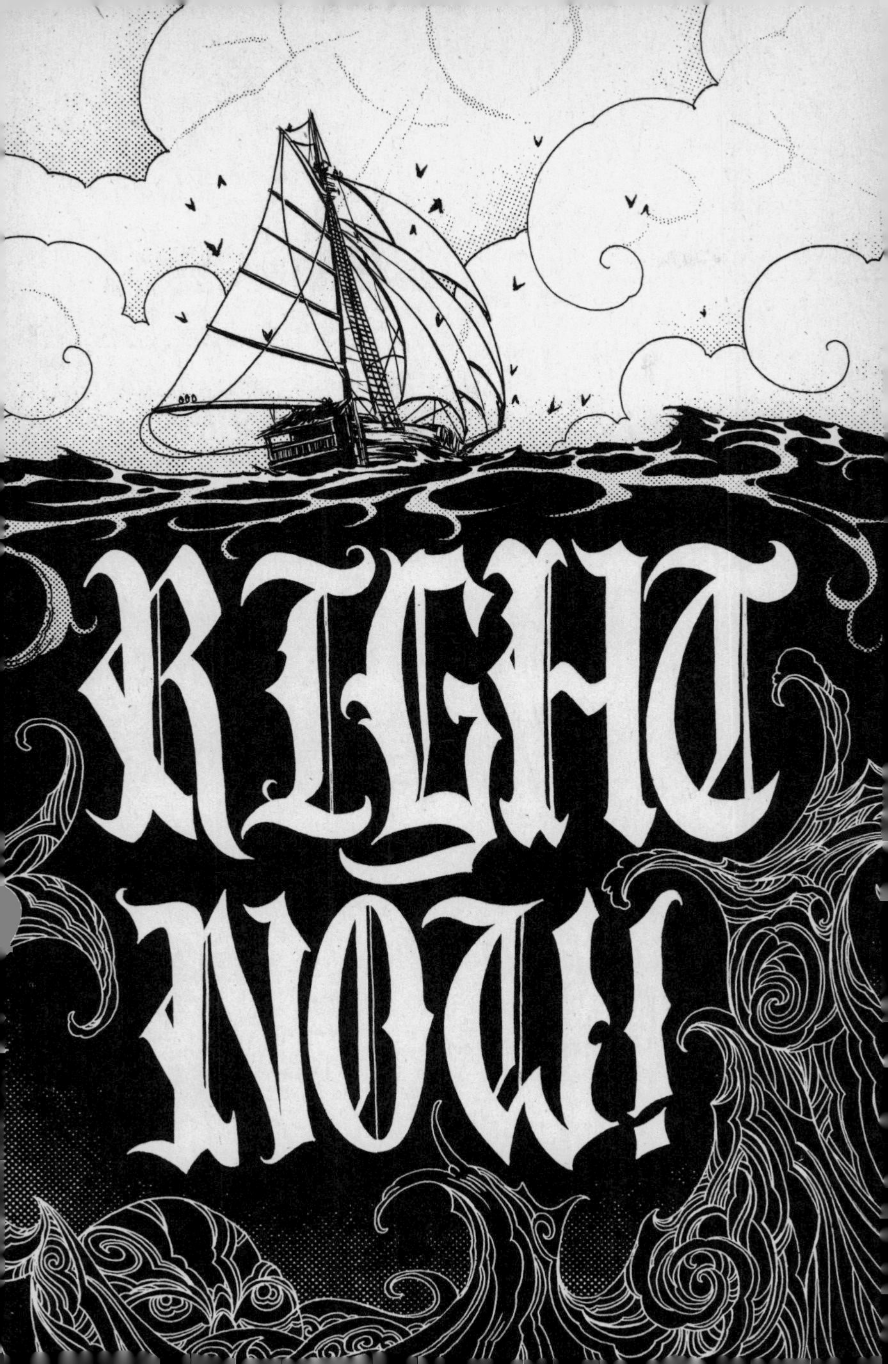
RIGHT
NOW!

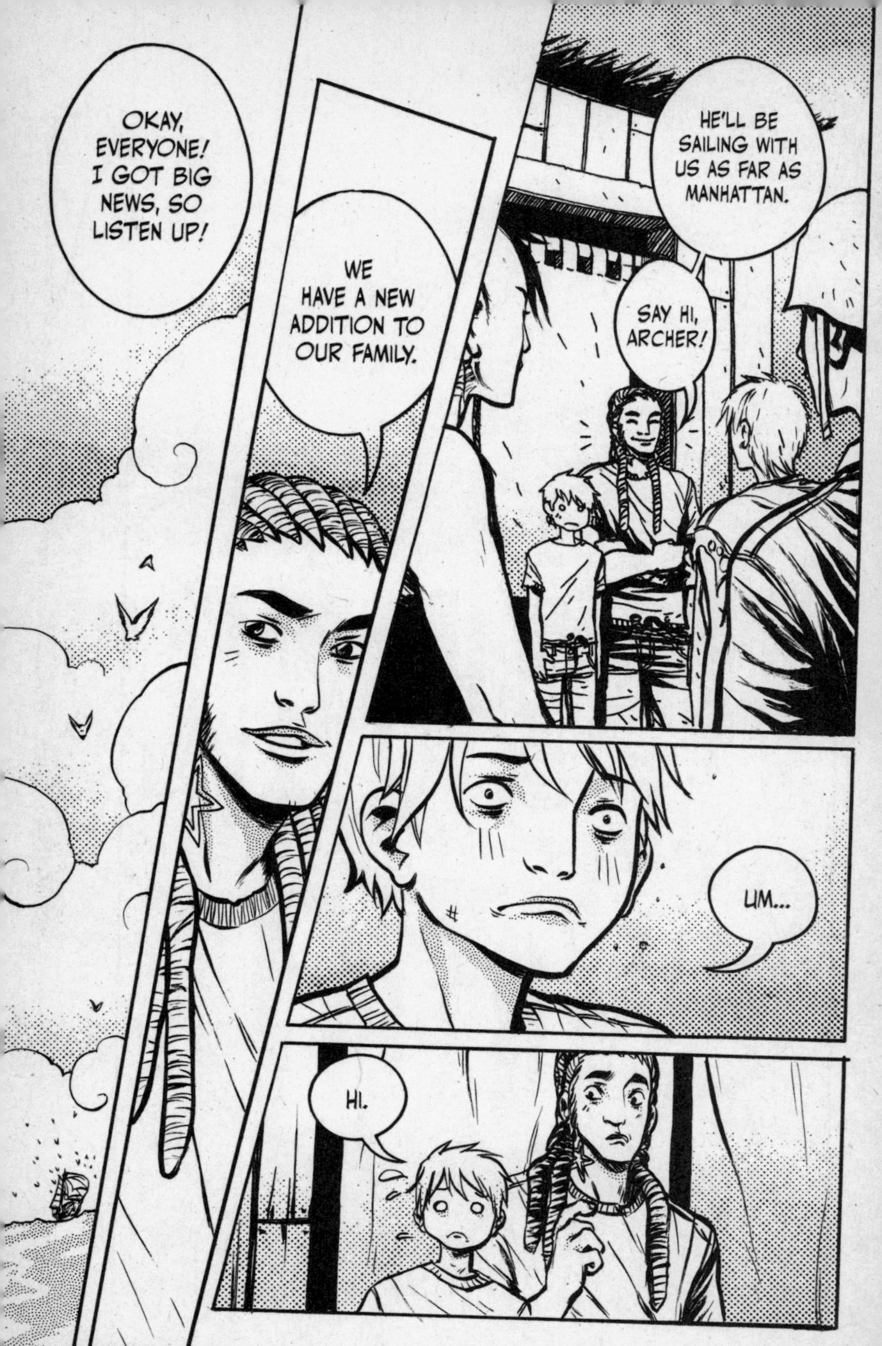
OKAY, EVERYONE! I GOT BIG NEWS, SO LISTEN UP!
WE HAVE A NEW ADDITION TO OUR FAMILY.
HE'LL BE SAILING WITH US AS FAR AS MANHATTAN.
SAY HI, ARCHER!
UM...
HI.

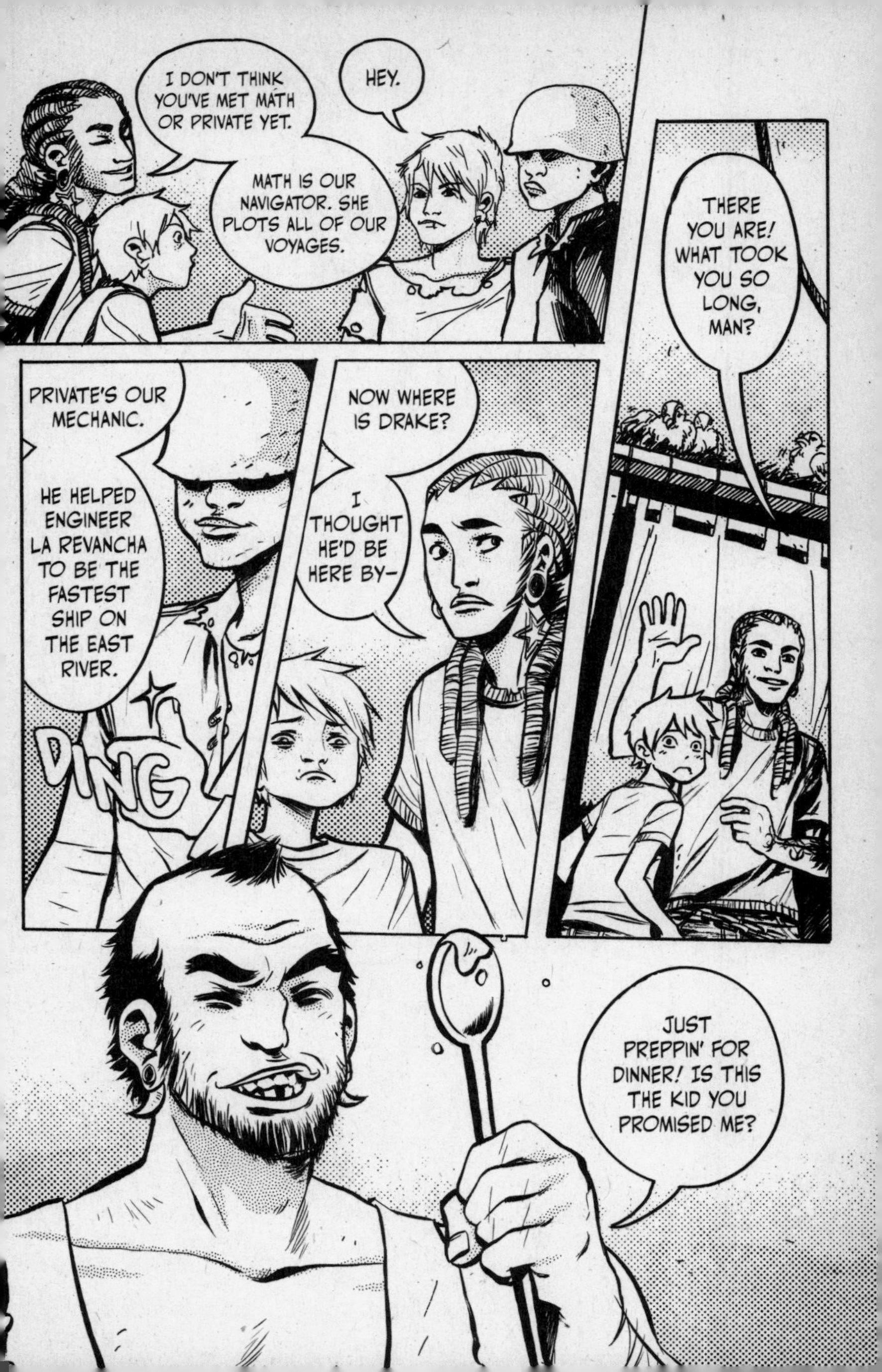
I DON'T THINK YOU'VE MET MATH OR PRIVATE YET.
HEY.
MATH IS OUR NAVIGATOR. SHE PLOTS ALL OF OUR VOYAGES.
PRIVATE'S OUR MECHANIC.
HE HELPED ENGINEER LA REVANCHA TO BE THE FASTEST SHIP ON THE EAST RIVER.
DING
NOW WHERE IS DRAKE?
I THOUGHT HE'D BE HERE BY–
THERE YOU ARE! WHAT TOOK YOU SO LONG, MAN?
JUST PREPPIN' FOR DINNER! IS THIS THE KID YOU PROMISED ME?

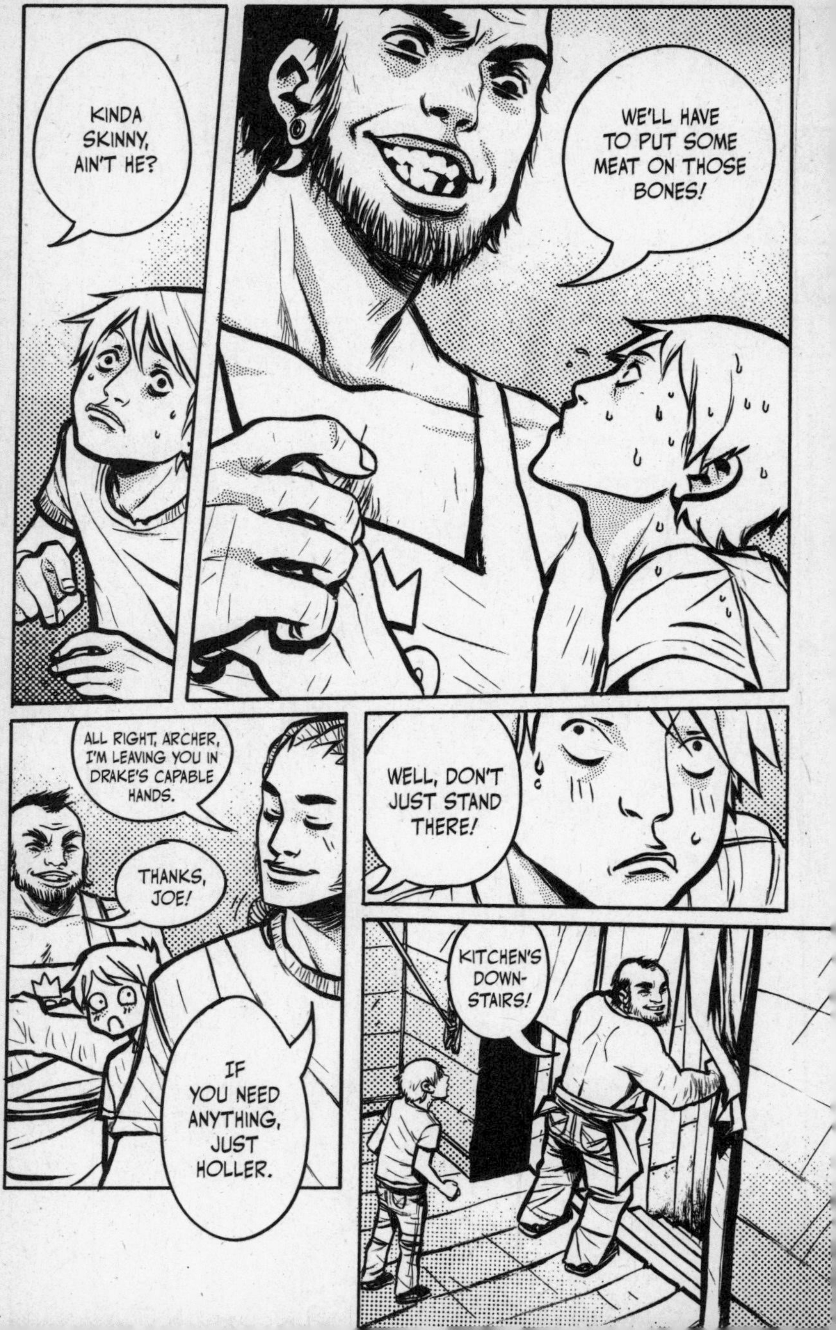
KINDA SKINNY, AIN'T HE?
WE'LL HAVE TO PUT SOME MEAT ON THOSE BONES!
ALL RIGHT, ARCHER, I'M LEAVING YOU IN DRAKE'S CAPABLE HANDS.
THANKS, JOE!
IF YOU NEED ANYTHING, JUST HOLLER.
WELL, DON'T JUST STAND THERE!
KITCHEN'S DOWN-STAIRS!

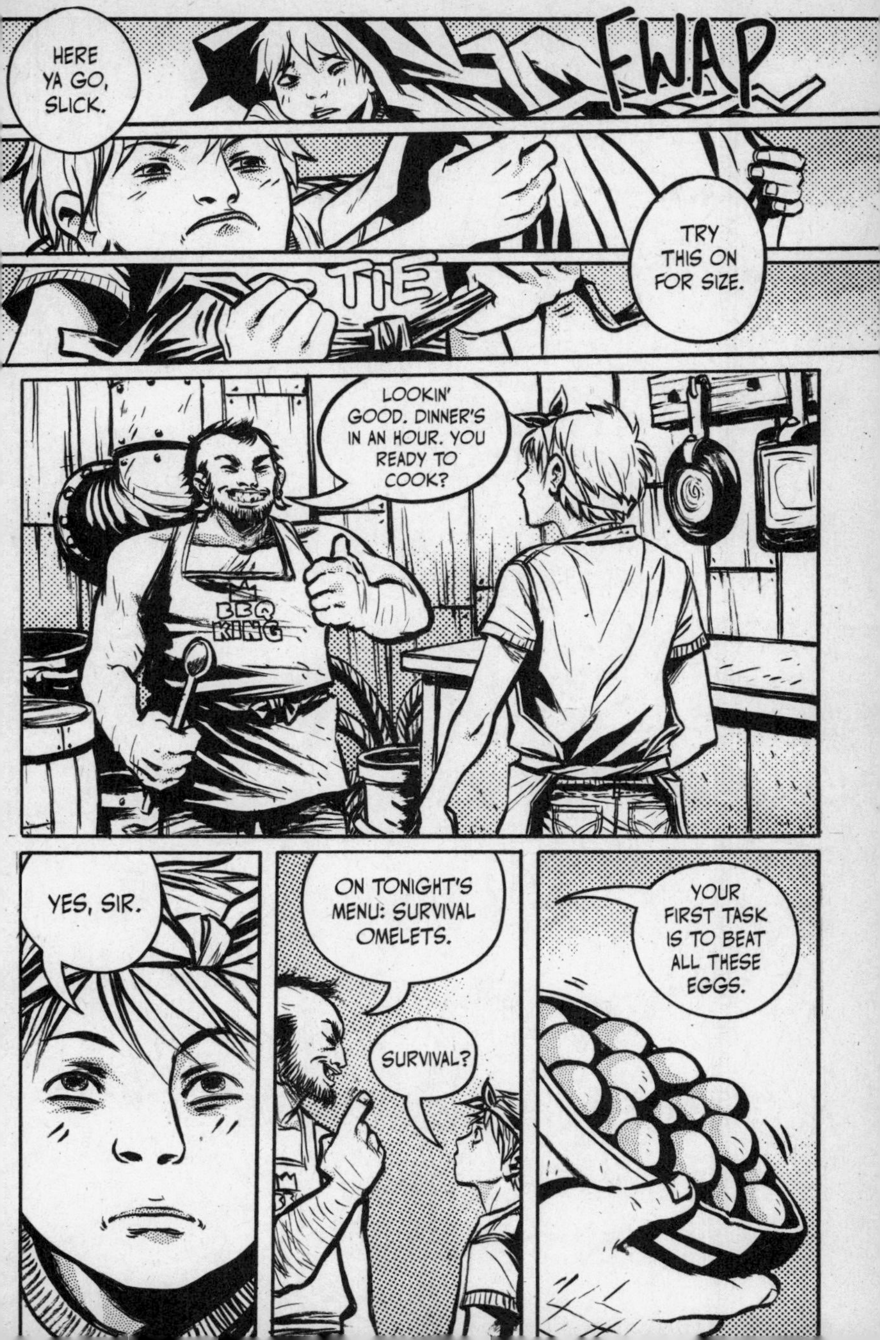
HERE YA GO, SLICK.
FWAP
TRY THIS ON FOR SIZE.
TIE
LOOKIN' GOOD. DINNER'S IN AN HOUR. YOU READY TO COOK?
BBQ KING
YES, SIR.
ON TONIGHT'S MENU: SURVIVAL OMELETS.
SURVIVAL?
YOUR FIRST TASK IS TO BEAT ALL THESE EGGS.

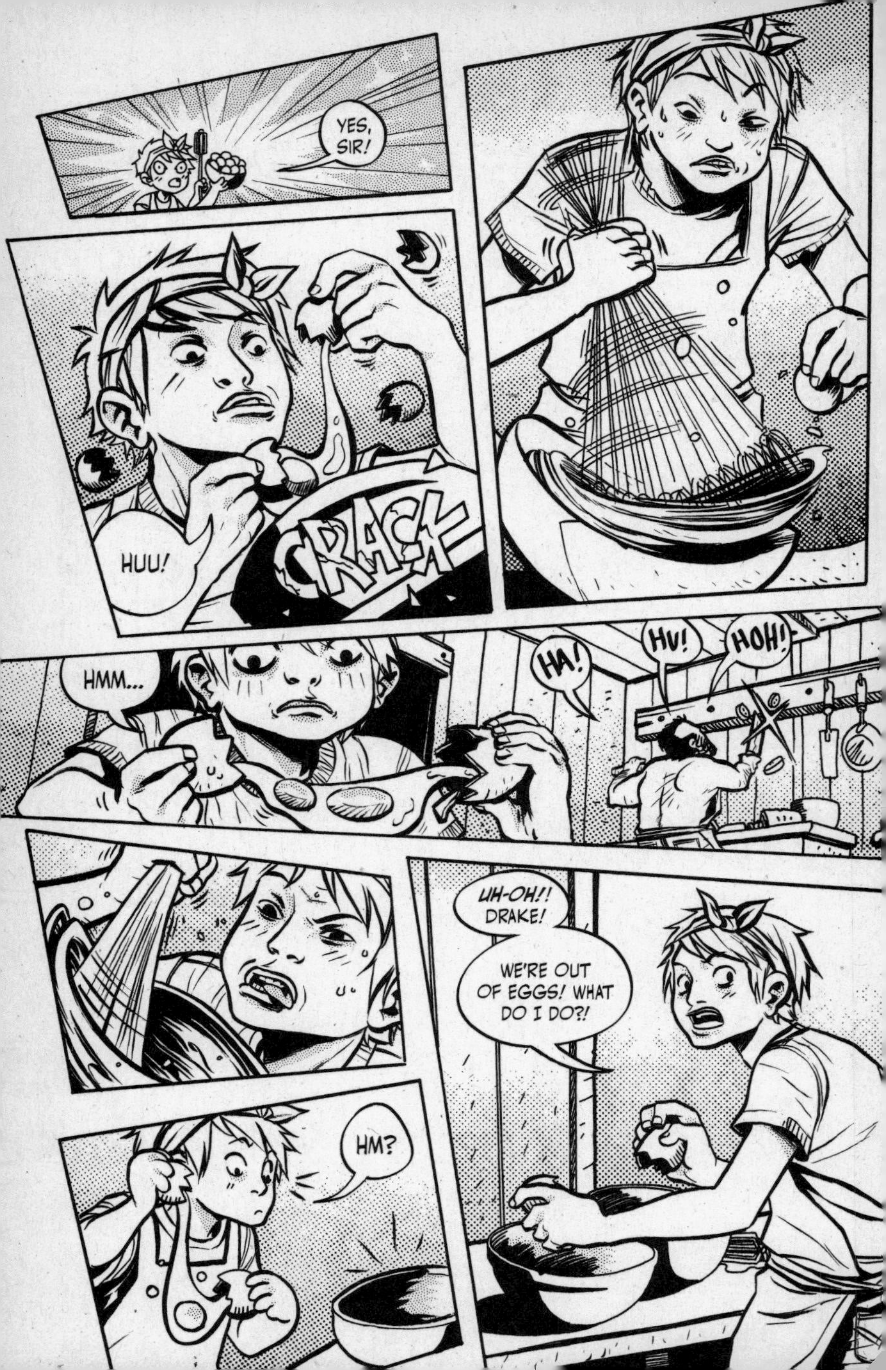
YES, SIR!
HUU!
CRACK
HMM...
HA!
HU!
HOH!
UH-OH!! DRAKE!
WE'RE OUT OF EGGS! WHAT DO I DO?!
HM?

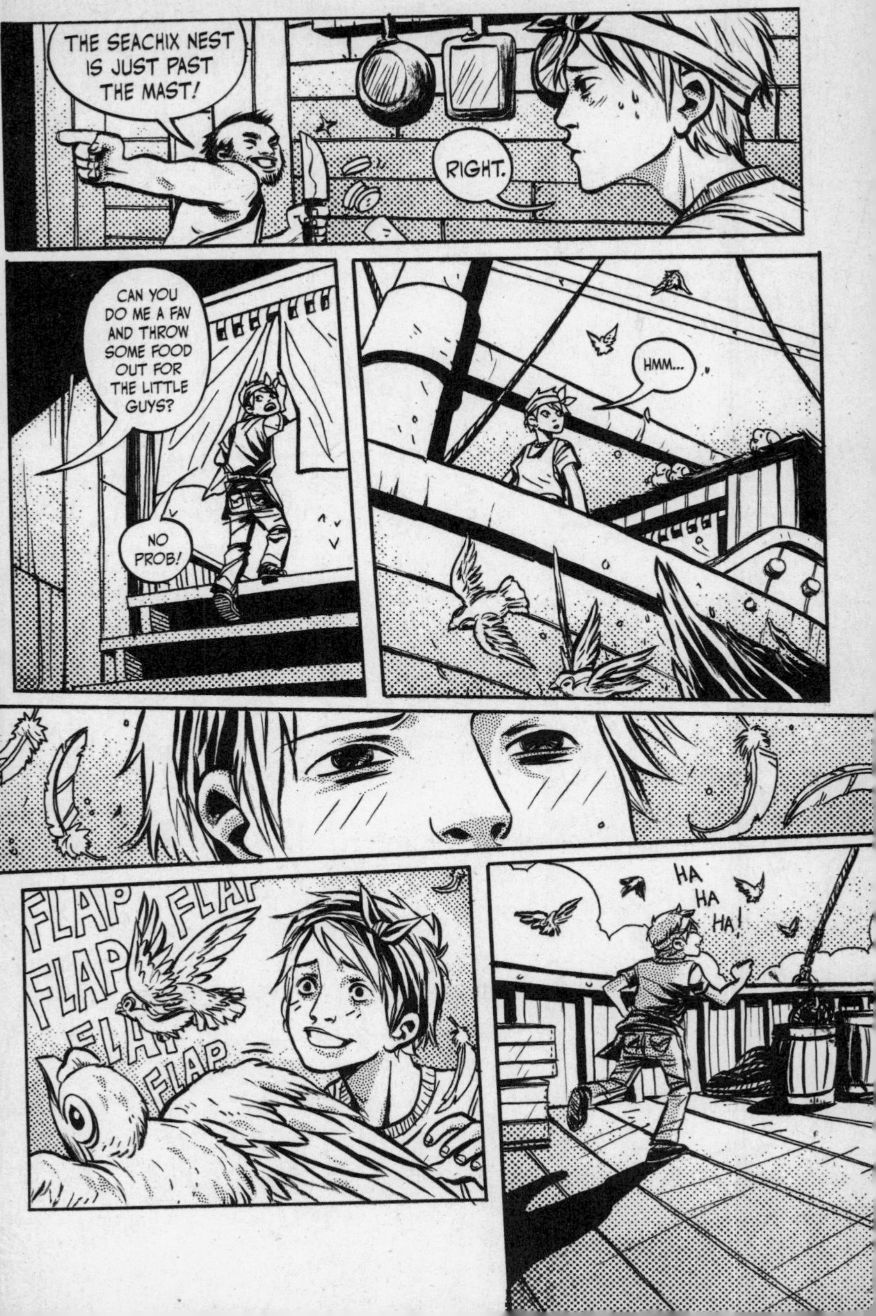
THE SEACHIX NEST IS JUST PAST THE MAST!
RIGHT.
CAN YOU DO ME A FAV AND THROW SOME FOOD OUT FOR THE LITTLE GUYS?
NO PROB!
HMM...
FLAP FLAP FLAP FLAP FLAP
HA HA HA!

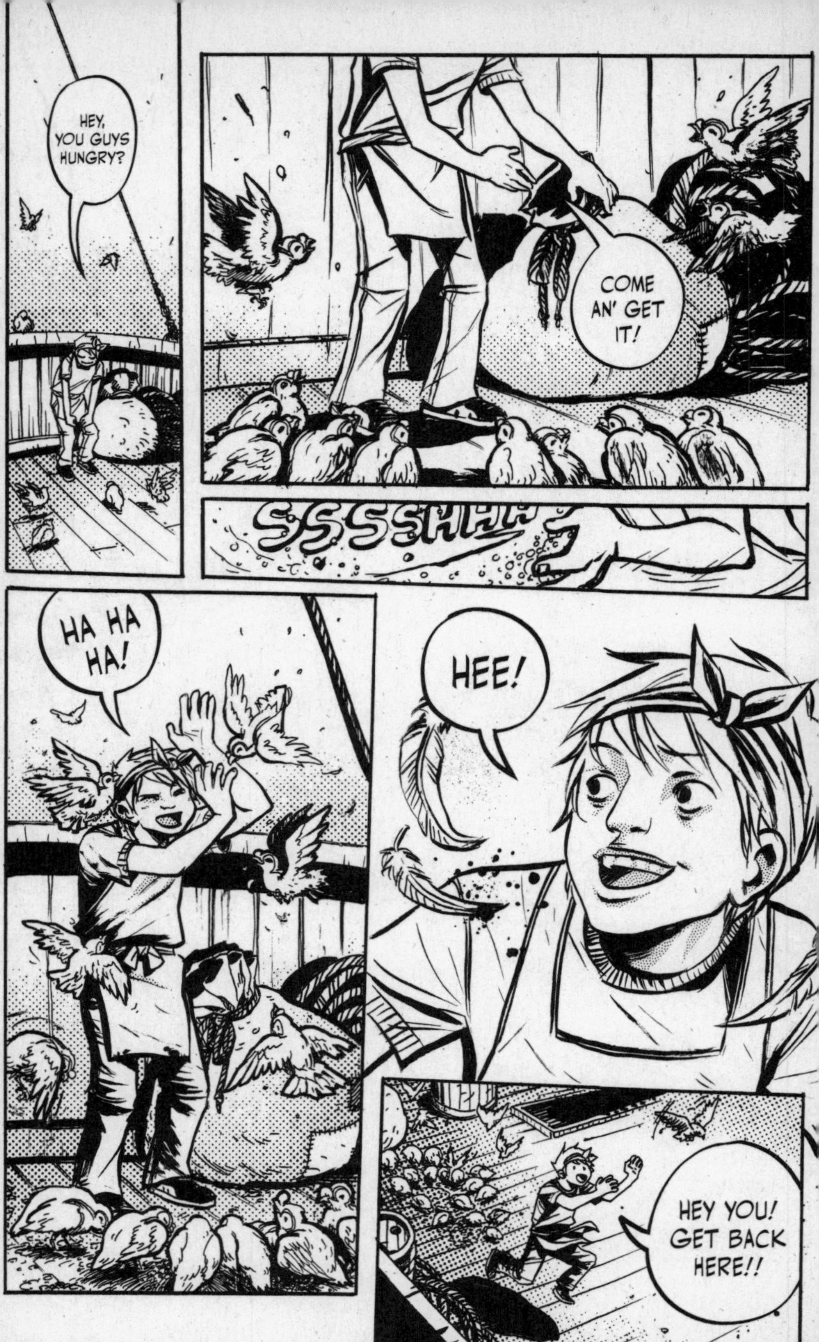
HEY, YOU GUYS HUNGRY?
COME AN' GET IT!
SSSSHHH
HA HA HA!
HEE!
HEY YOU! GET BACK HERE!!

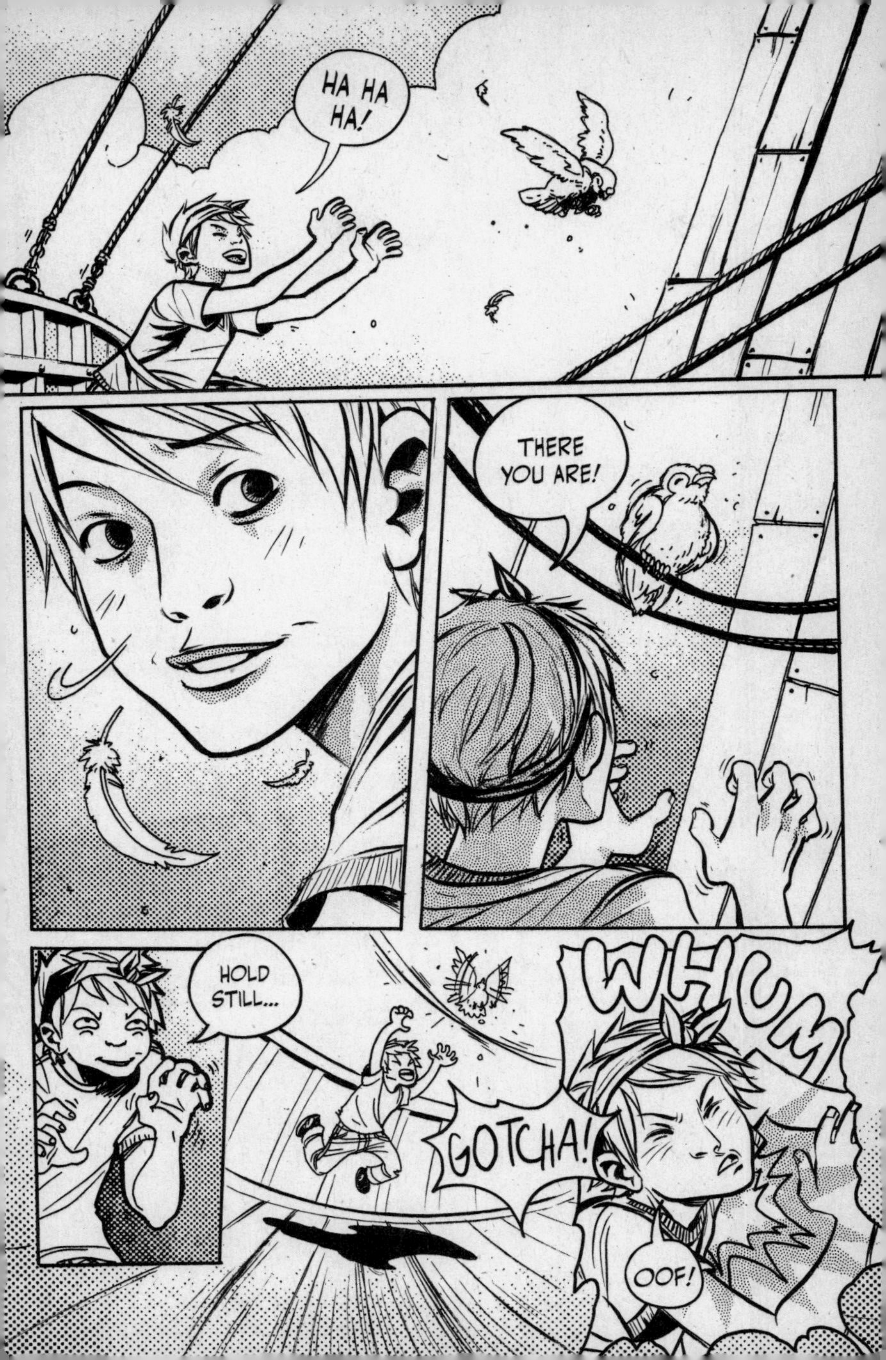
HA HA HA!
THERE YOU ARE!
HOLD STILL...
GOTCHA!
WHUM
OOF!

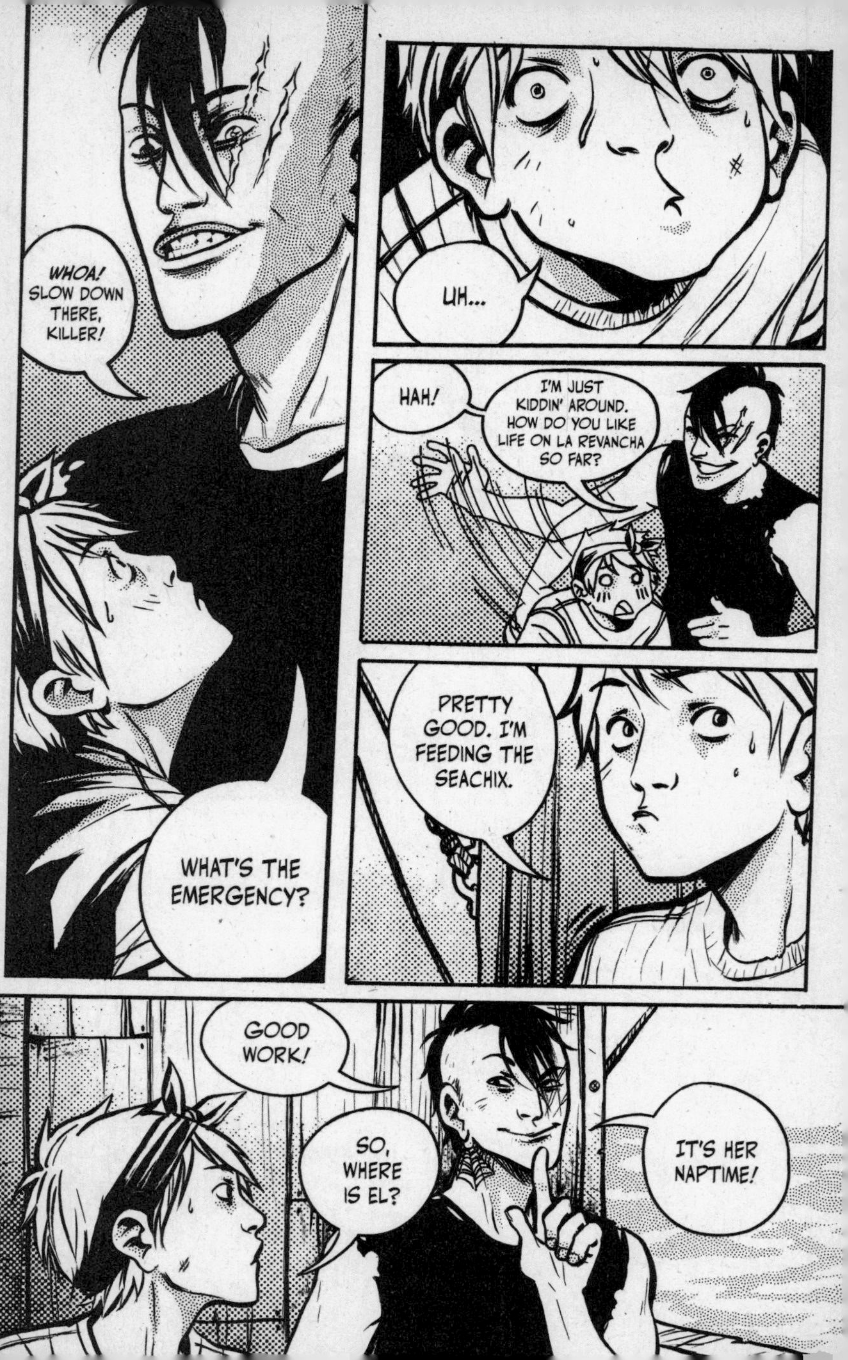
WHOA! SLOW DOWN THERE, KILLER!
WHAT'S THE EMERGENCY?
UH...
HAH!
I'M JUST KIDDIN' AROUND. HOW DO YOU LIKE LIFE ON LA REVANCHA SO FAR?
PRETTY GOOD. I'M FEEDING THE SEACHIX.
GOOD WORK!
SO, WHERE IS EL?
IT'S HER NAPTIME!

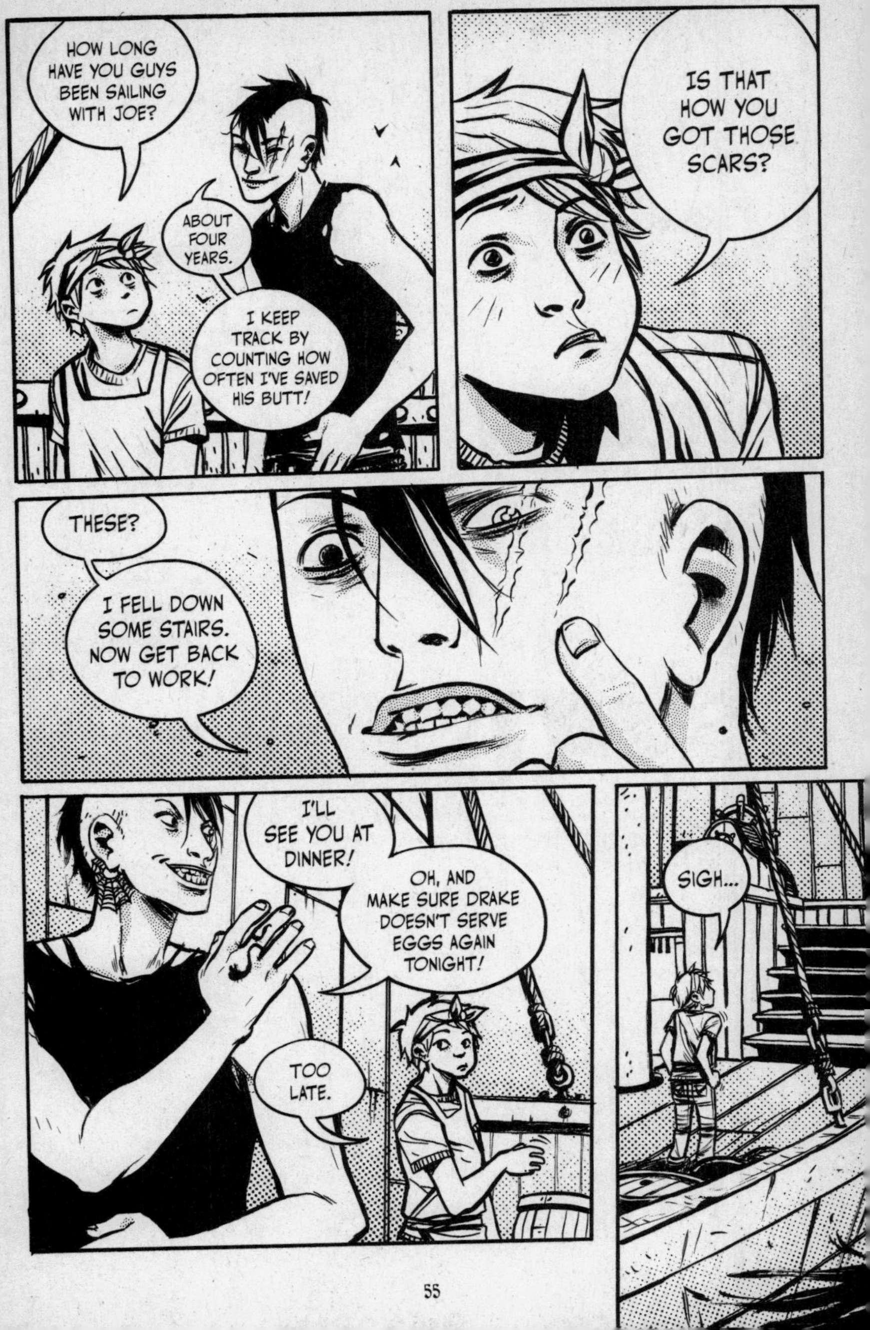
HOW LONG HAVE YOU GUYS BEEN SAILING WITH JOE?
ABOUT FOUR YEARS.
I KEEP TRACK BY COUNTING HOW OFTEN I'VE SAVED HIS BUTT!
IS THAT HOW YOU GOT THOSE SCARS?
THESE?
I FELL DOWN SOME STAIRS. NOW GET BACK TO WORK!
I'LL SEE YOU AT DINNER!
OH, AND MAKE SURE DRAKE DOESN'T SERVE EGGS AGAIN TONIGHT!
TOO LATE.
SIGH...

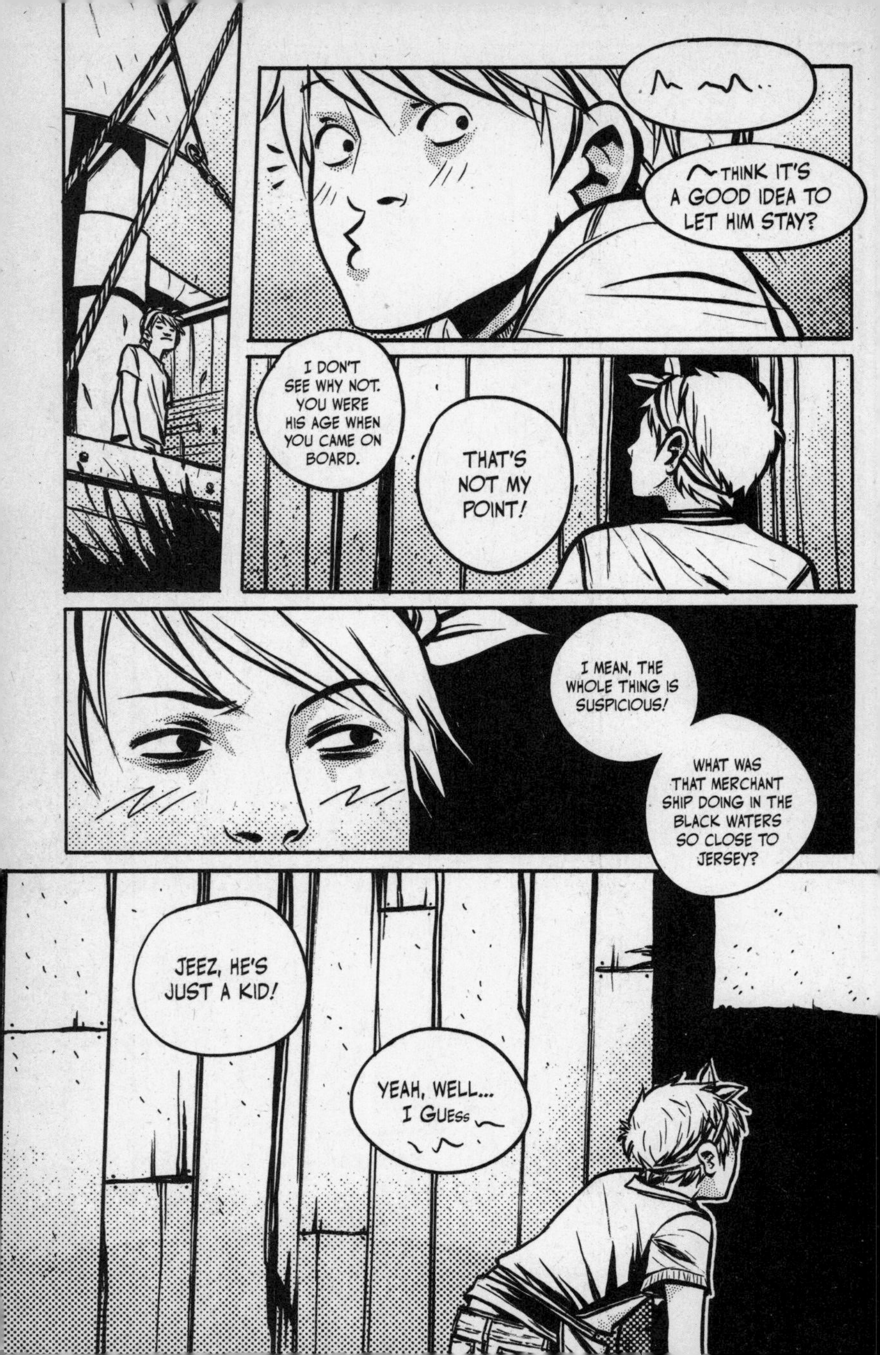
~THINK IT'S A GOOD IDEA TO LET HIM STAY?
I DON'T SEE WHY NOT. YOU WERE HIS AGE WHEN YOU CAME ON BOARD.
THAT'S NOT MY POINT!
I MEAN, THE WHOLE THING IS SUSPICIOUS!
WHAT WAS THAT MERCHANT SHIP DOING IN THE BLACK WATERS SO CLOSE TO JERSEY?
JEEZ, HE'S JUST A KID!
YEAH, WELL... I GUESS

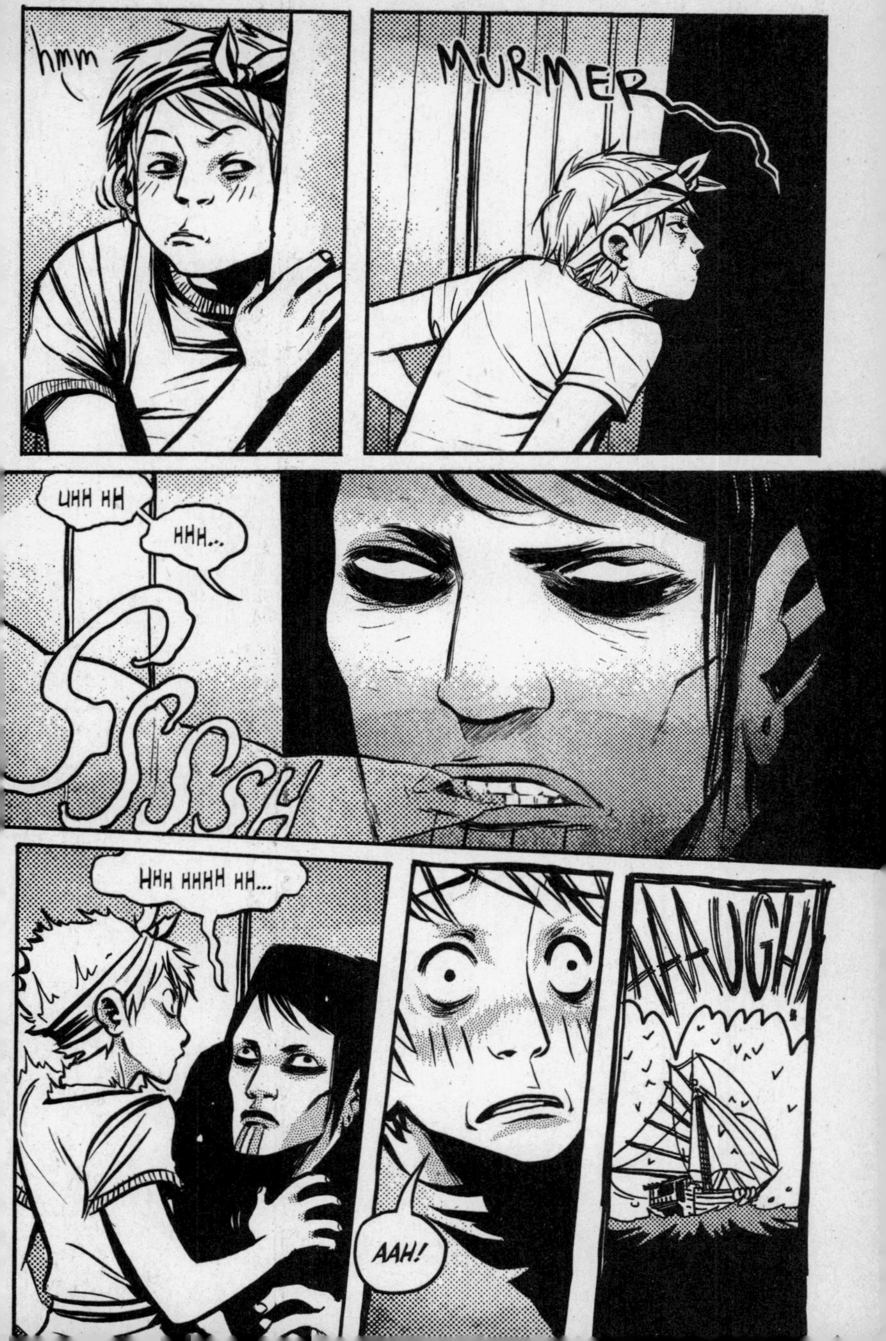
hmm
MURMER
UHH HH
HHH...
SSSSH
HHH HHHH HH...
AAH!
AAAUGH!

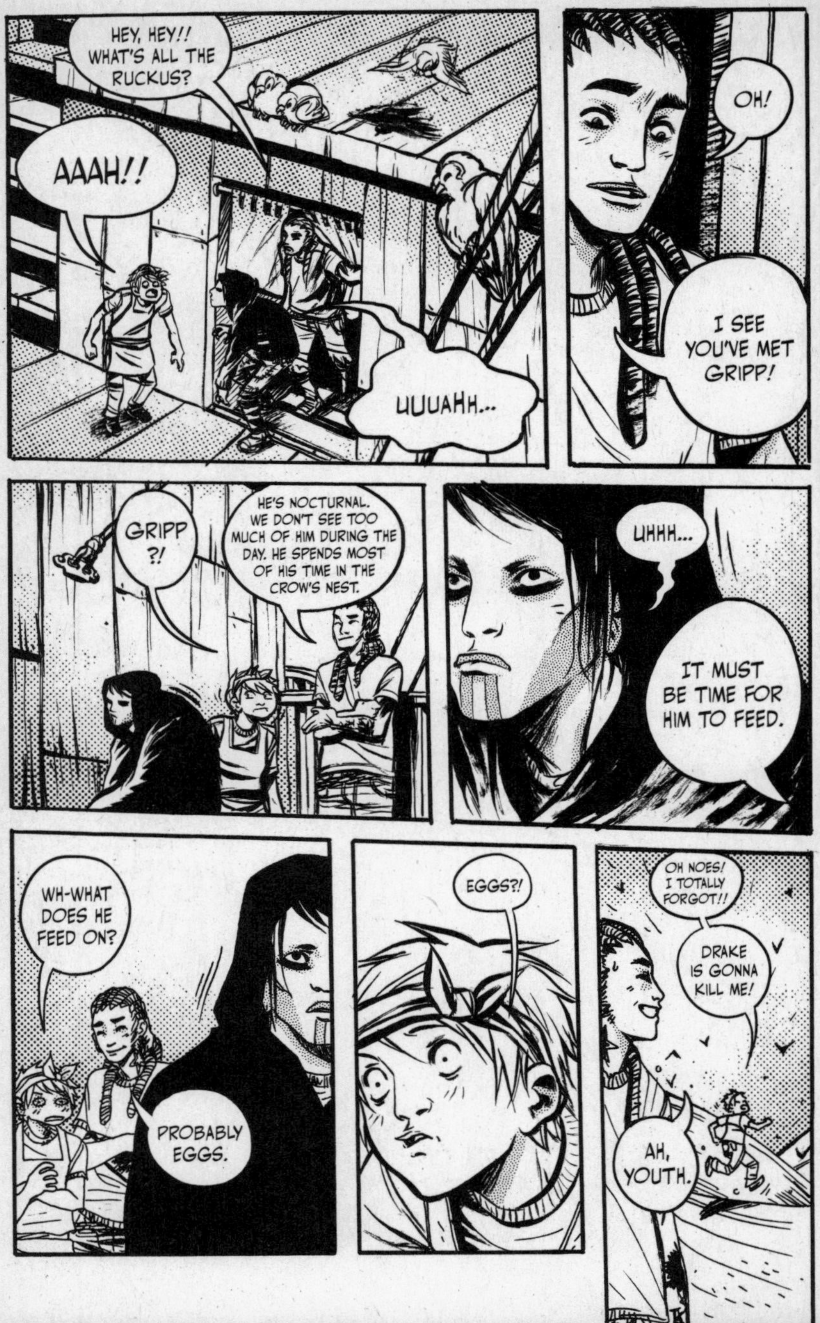
HEY, HEY!! WHAT'S ALL THE RUCKUS?
AAAH!!
UUUAHH...
OH!
I SEE YOU'VE MET GRIPP!
GRIPP ?!
HE'S NOCTURNAL. WE DON'T SEE TOO MUCH OF HIM DURING THE DAY. HE SPENDS MOST OF HIS TIME IN THE CROW'S NEST.
UHHH...
IT MUST BE TIME FOR HIM TO FEED.
WH-WHAT DOES HE FEED ON?
PROBABLY EGGS.
EGGS?!
OH NOES! I TOTALLY FORGOT!!
DRAKE IS GONNA KILL ME!
AH, YOUTH.

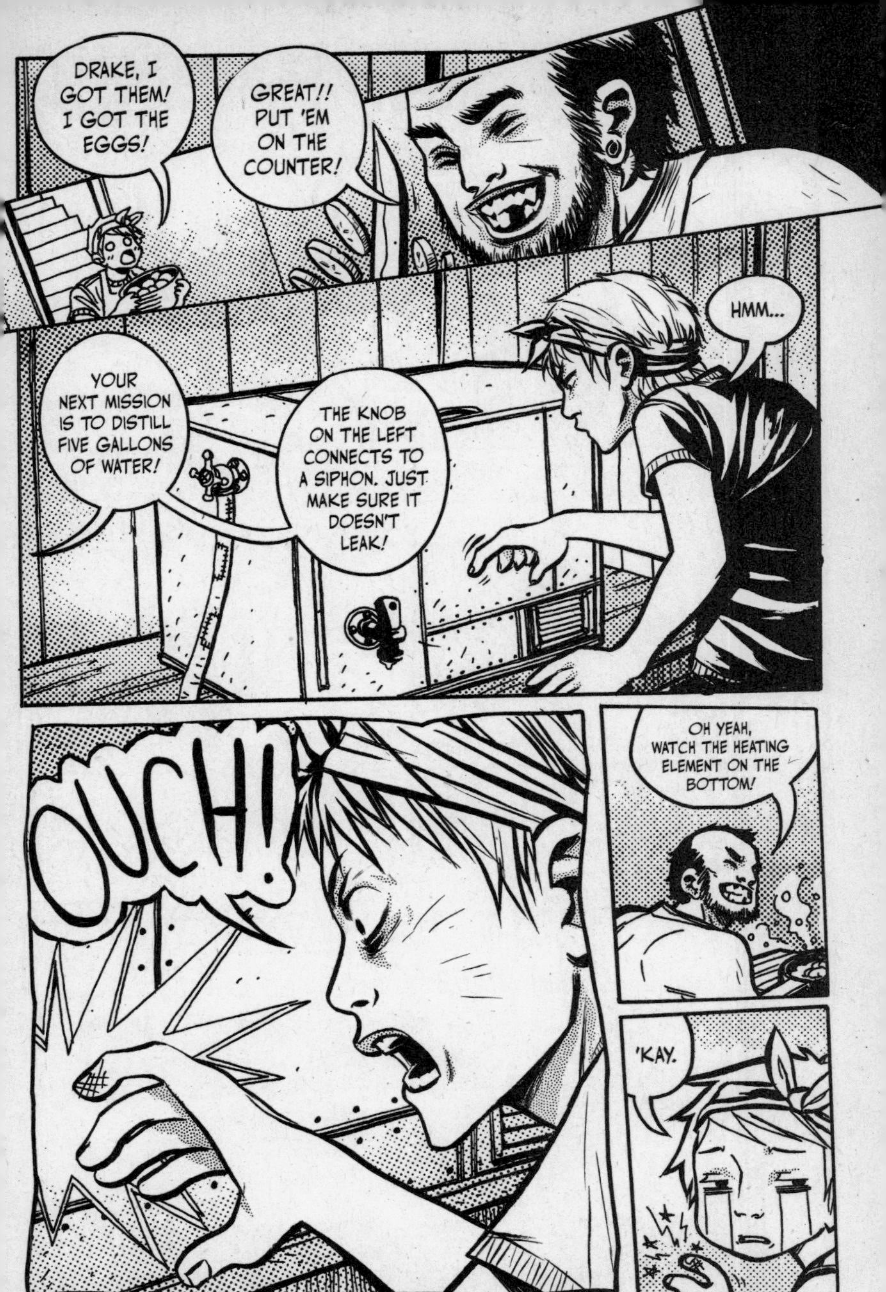
DRAKE, I GOT THEM! I GOT THE EGGS!
GREAT!! PUT 'EM ON THE COUNTER!
HMM...
YOUR NEXT MISSION IS TO DISTILL FIVE GALLONS OF WATER!
THE KNOB ON THE LEFT CONNECTS TO A SIPHON. JUST MAKE SURE IT DOESN'T LEAK!
OUCH!!
OH YEAH, WATCH THE HEATING ELEMENT ON THE BOTTOM!
'KAY.

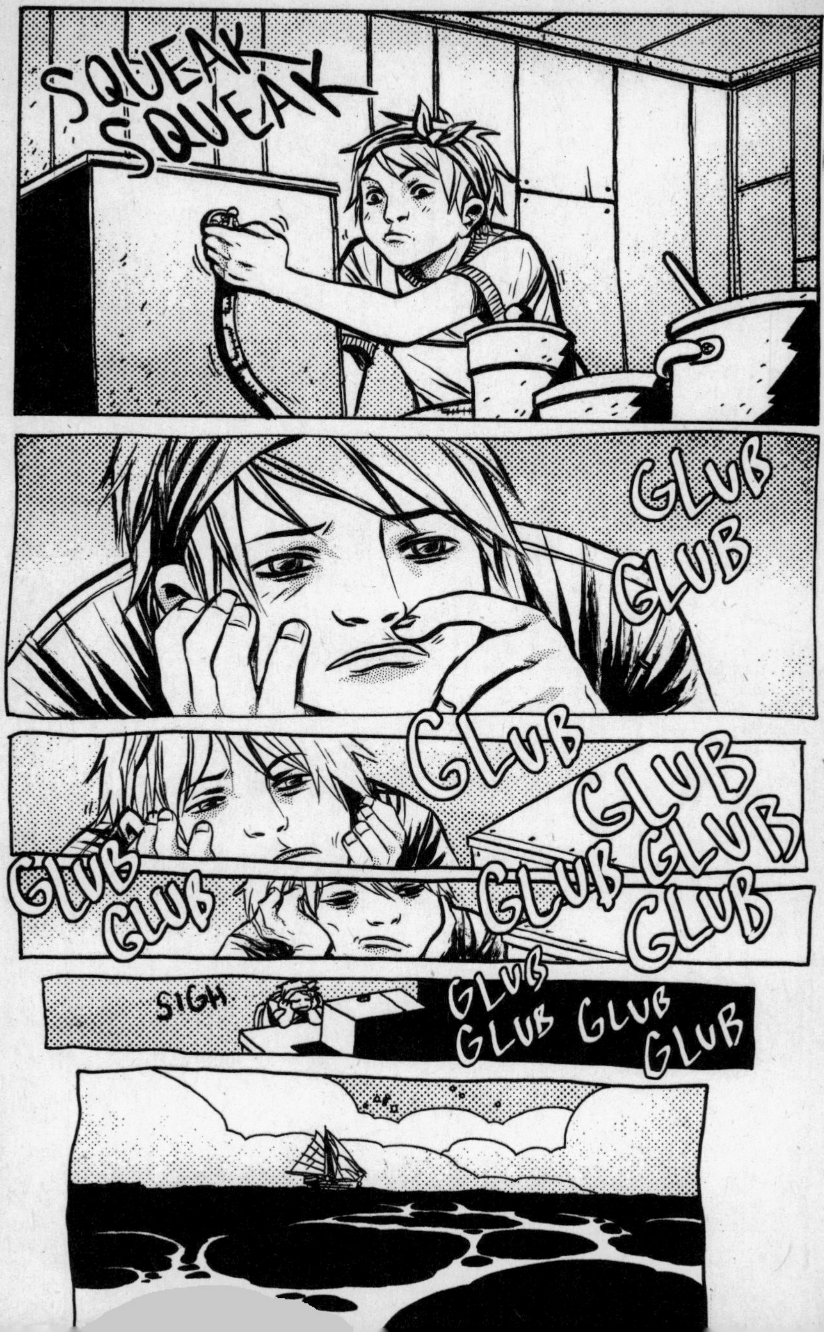
SQUEAK SQUEAK
GLUB GLUB
GLUB
GLUB GLUB GLUB
GLUB GLUB
GLUB GLUB
SIGH
GLUB GLUB GLUB GLUB

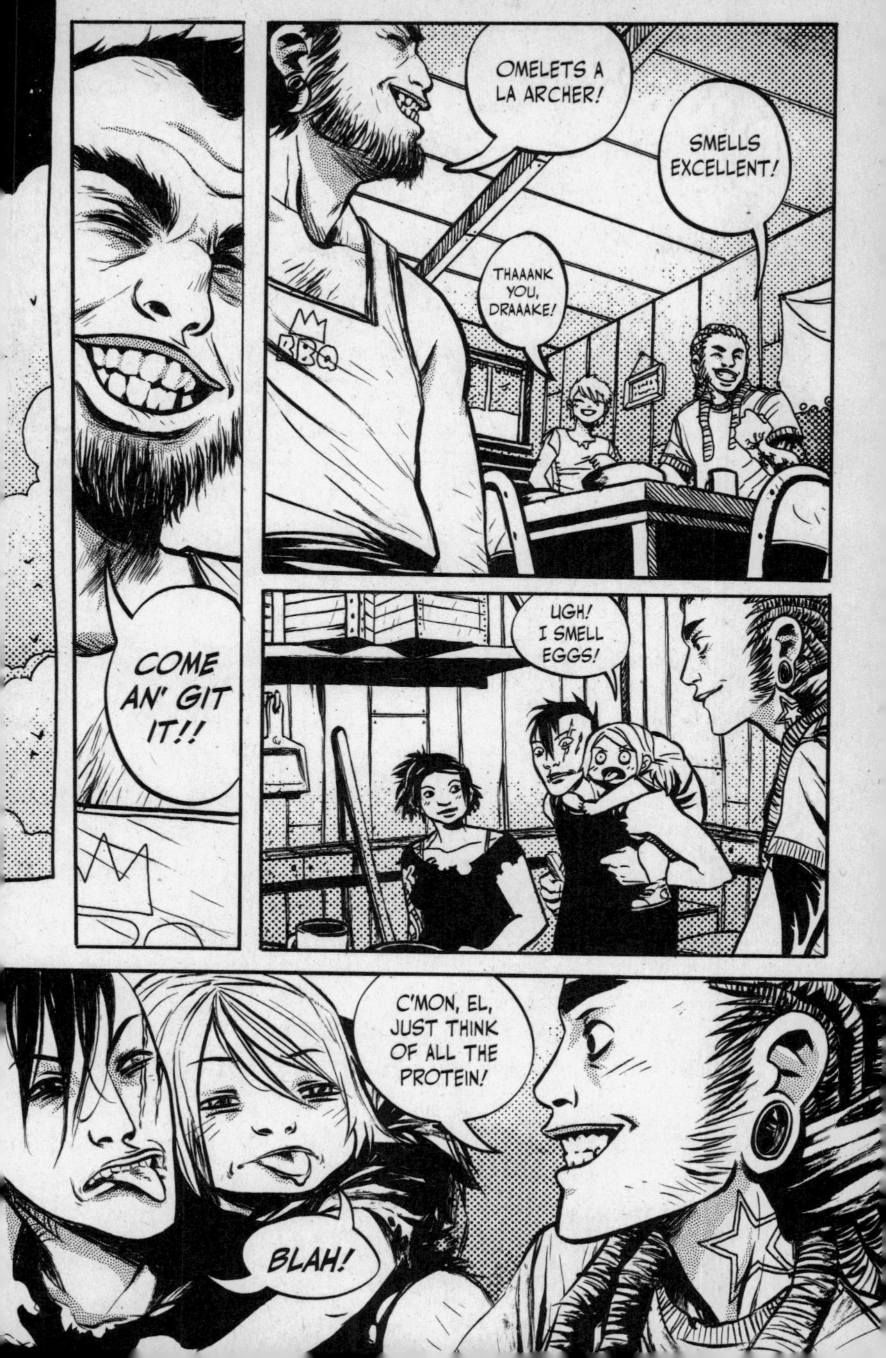
COME AN' GIT IT!!
OMELETS A LA ARCHER!
SMELLS EXCELLENT!
THAAANK YOU, DRAAAKE!
UGH! I SMELL EGGS!
C'MON, EL, JUST THINK OF ALL THE PROTEIN!
BLAH!

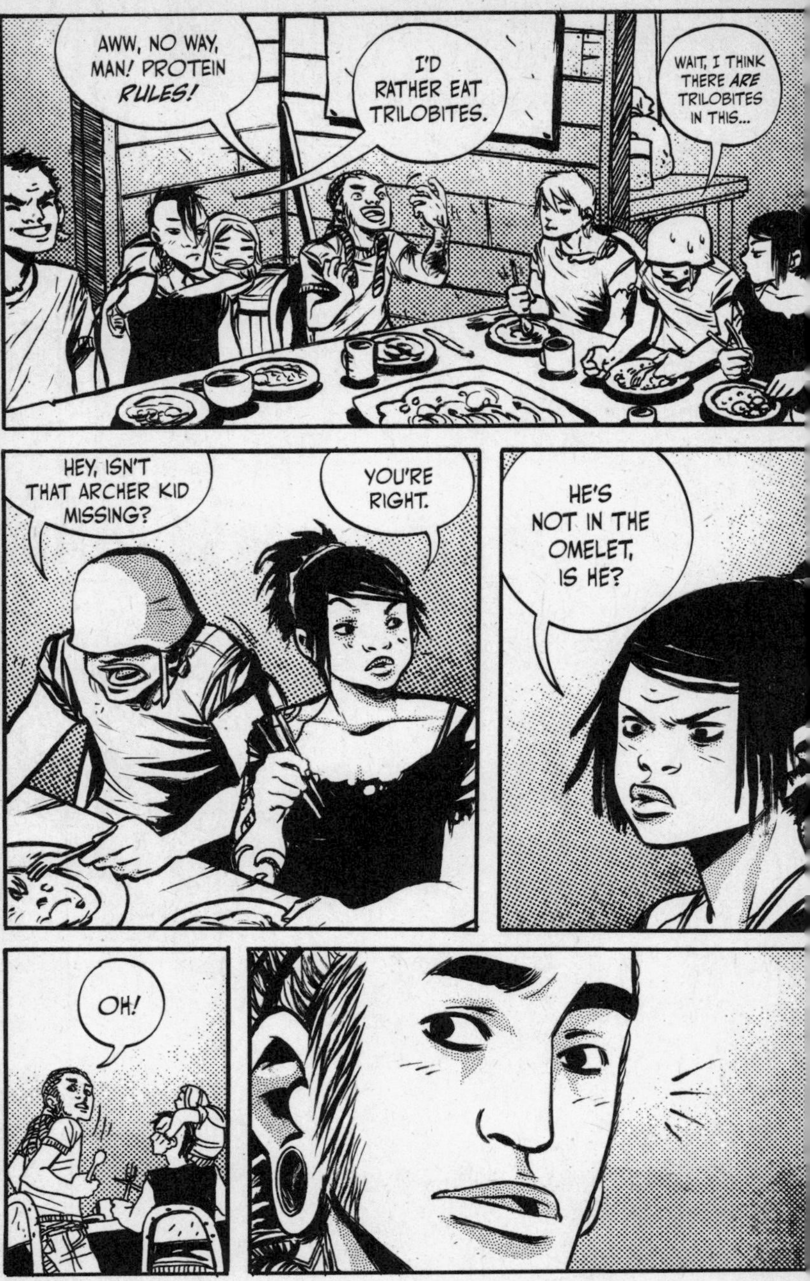
AWW, NO WAY, MAN! PROTEIN *RULES!*
I'D RATHER EAT TRILOBITES.
WAIT, I THINK THERE *ARE* TRILOBITES IN THIS...
HEY, ISN'T THAT ARCHER KID MISSING?
YOU'RE RIGHT.
HE'S NOT IN THE OMELET, IS HE?
OH!

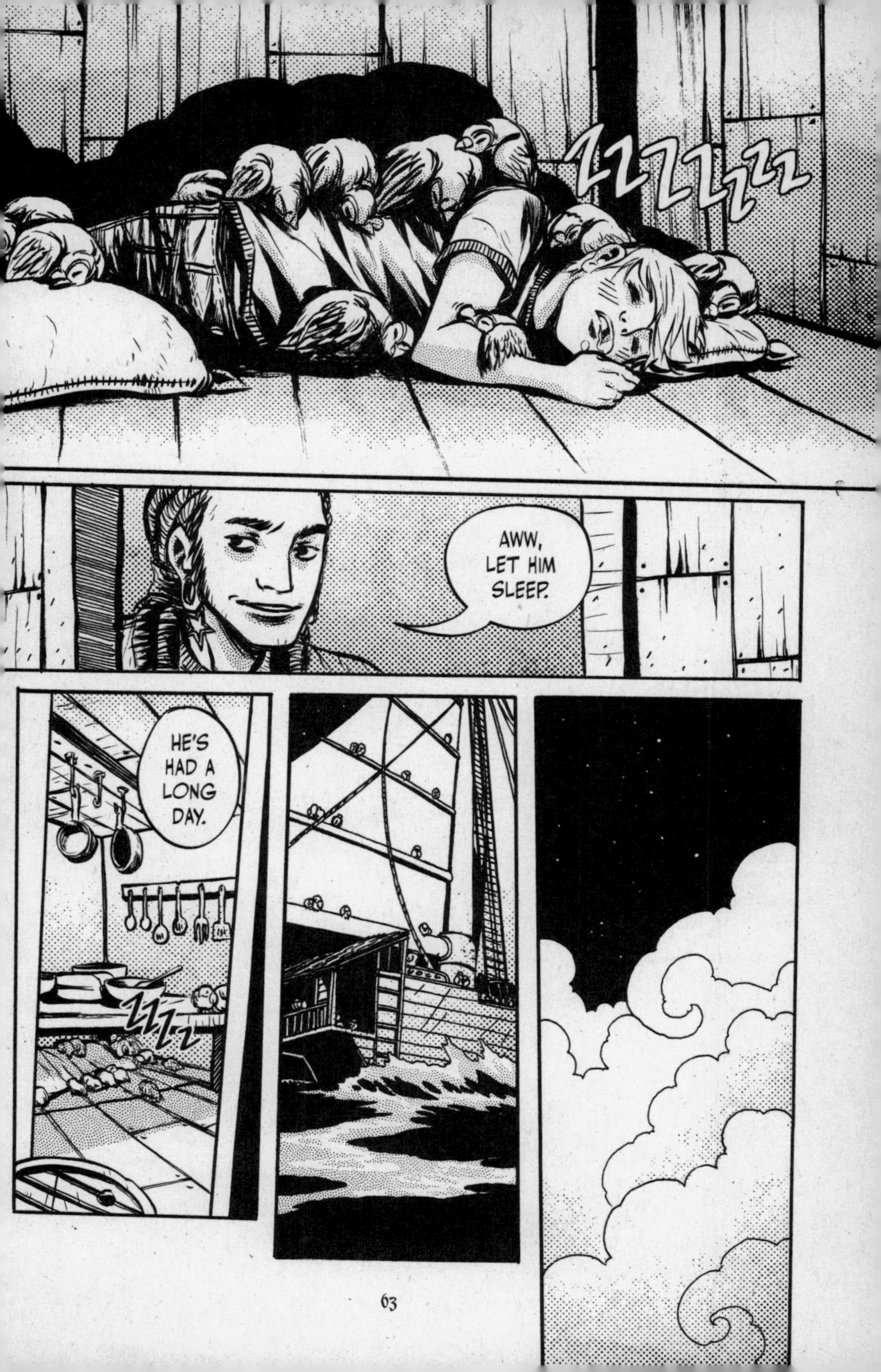
ZZZZZZZZ
AWW, LET HIM SLEEP.
HE'S HAD A LONG DAY.
ZZZZ

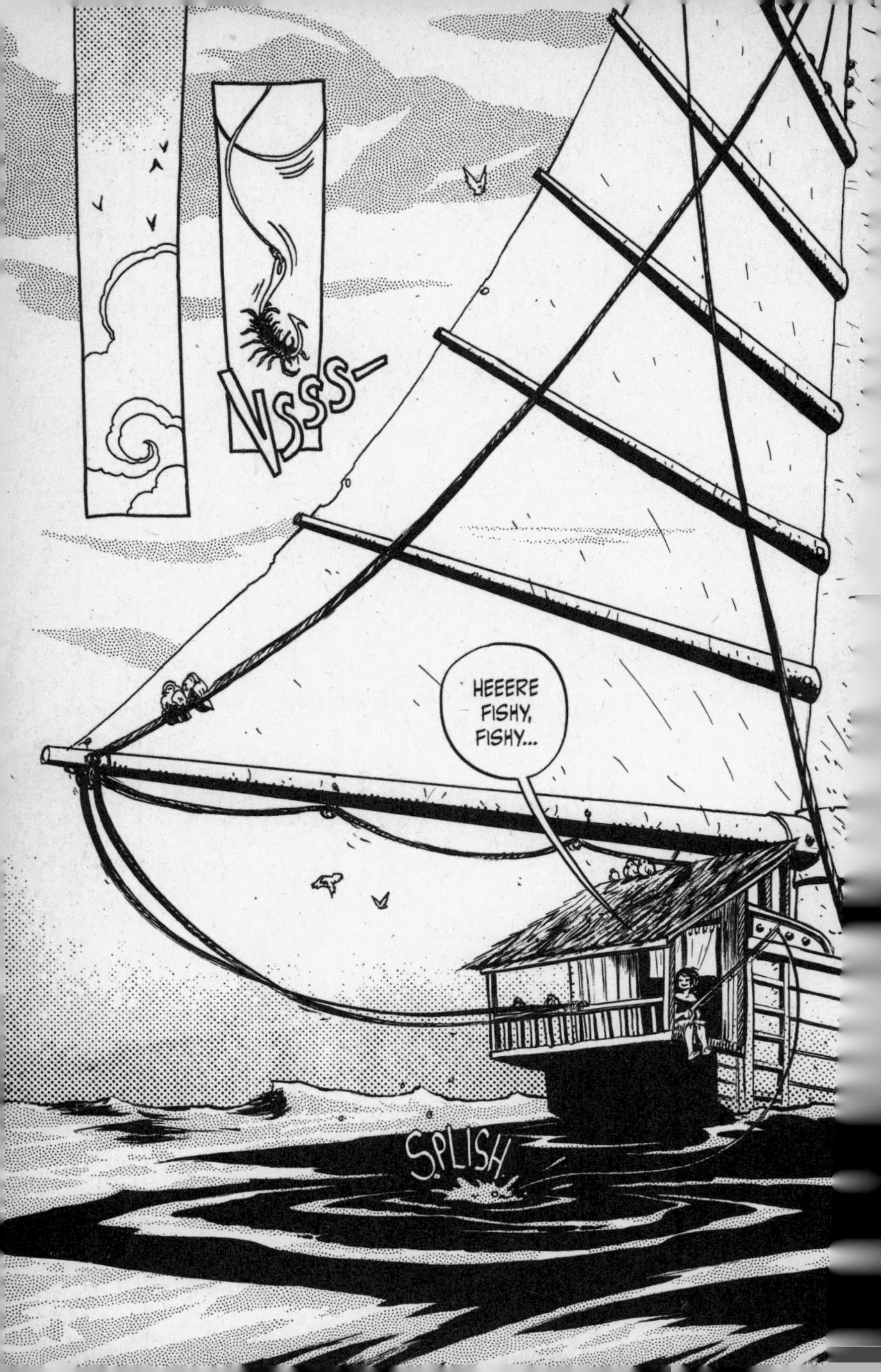
VSSS-
HEEERE FISHY, FISHY...
SPLISH

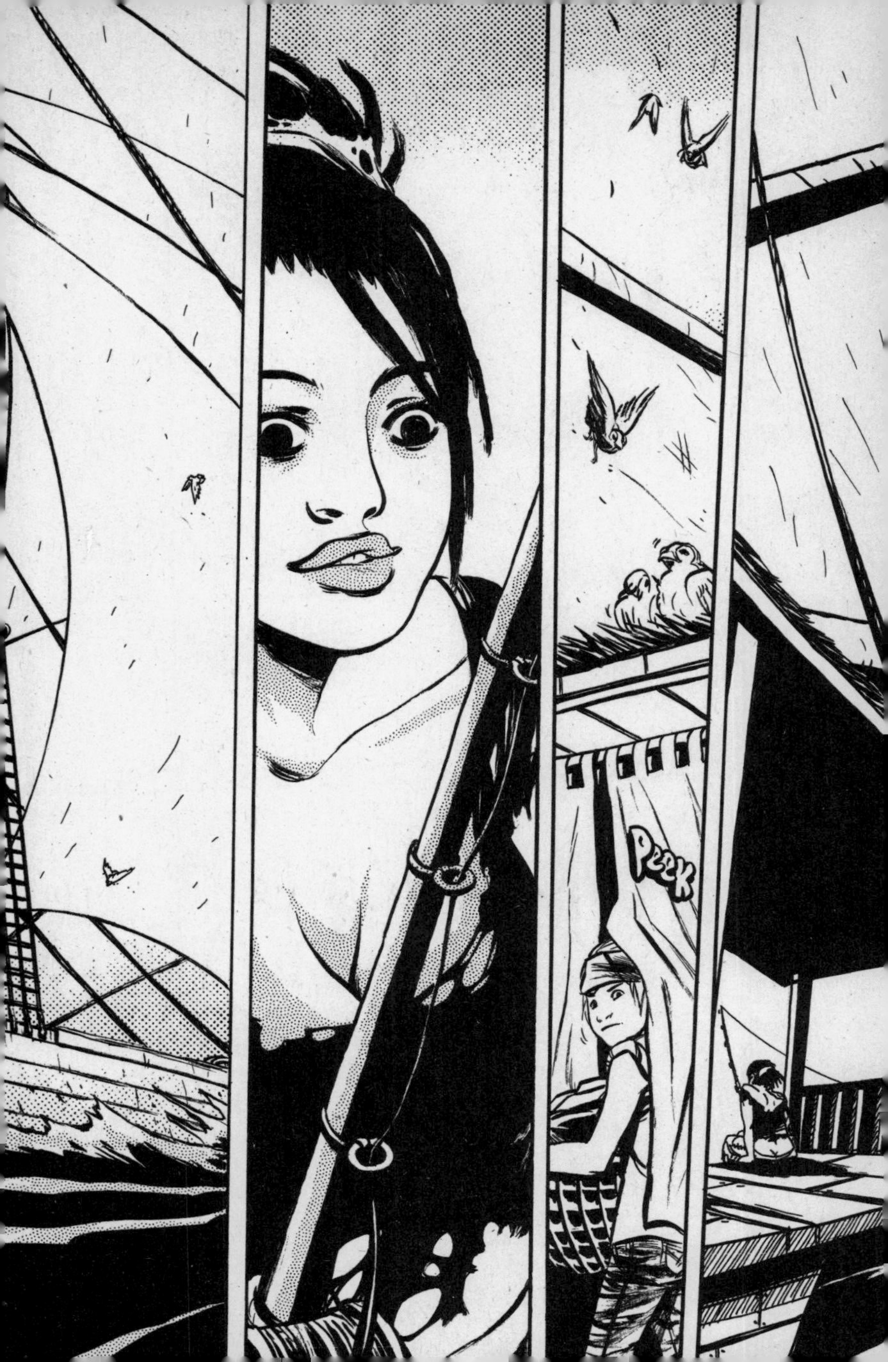
PEEK

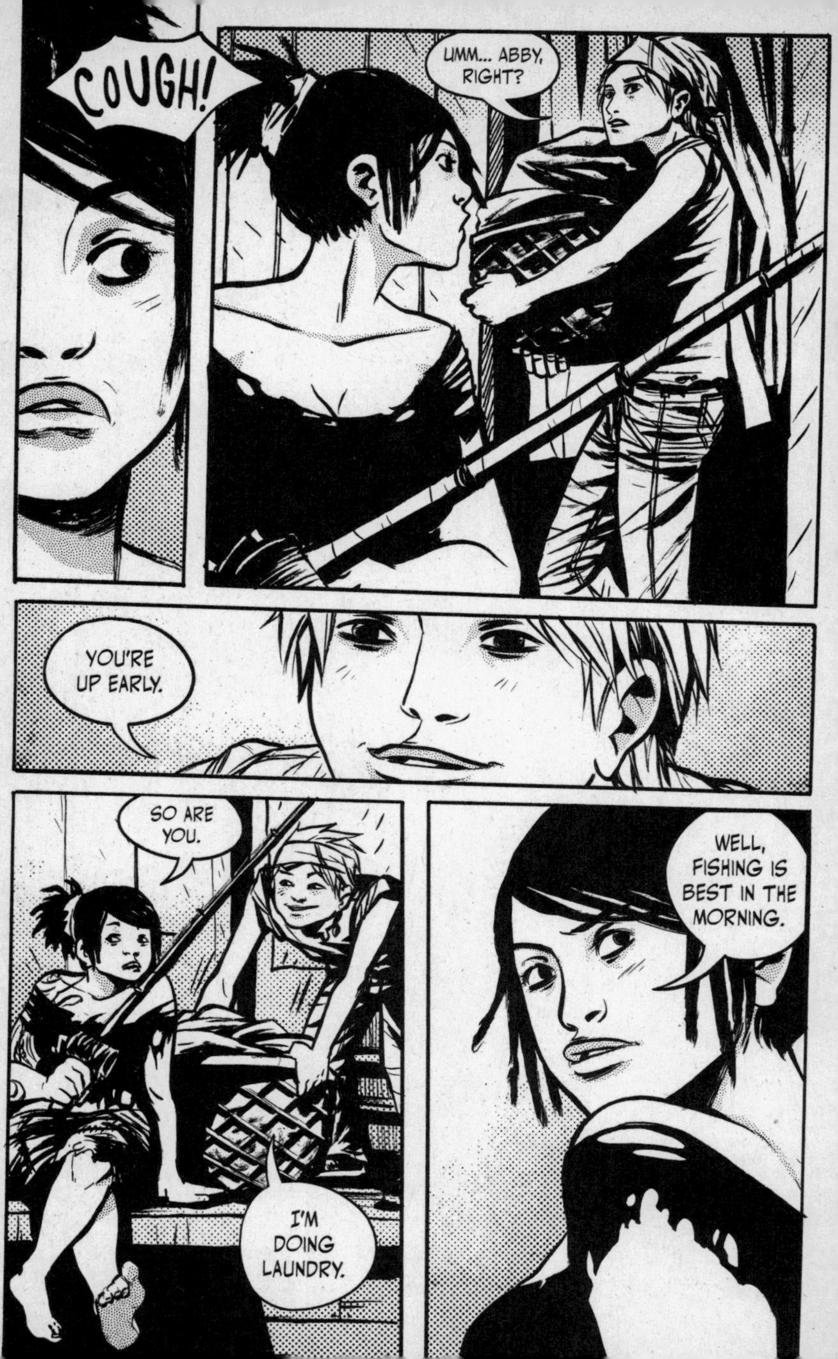
COUGH!
UMM... ABBY, RIGHT?
YOU'RE UP EARLY.
SO ARE YOU.
I'M DOING LAUNDRY.
WELL, FISHING IS BEST IN THE MORNING.

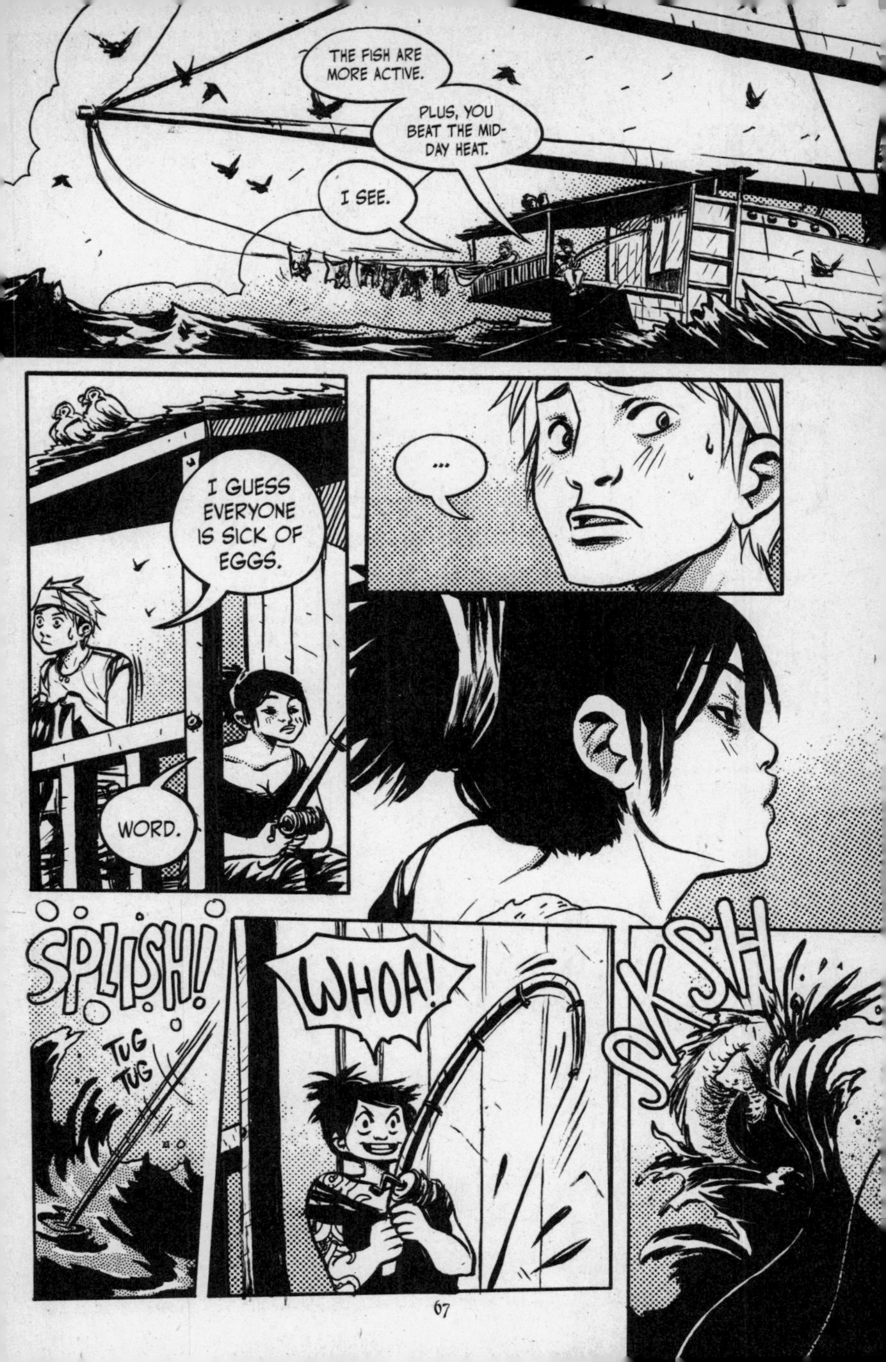
THE FISH ARE MORE ACTIVE.
PLUS, YOU BEAT THE MID-DAY HEAT.
I SEE.
I GUESS EVERYONE IS SICK OF EGGS.
WORD.
...
SPLISH!
TUG TUG
WHOA!
SKSH

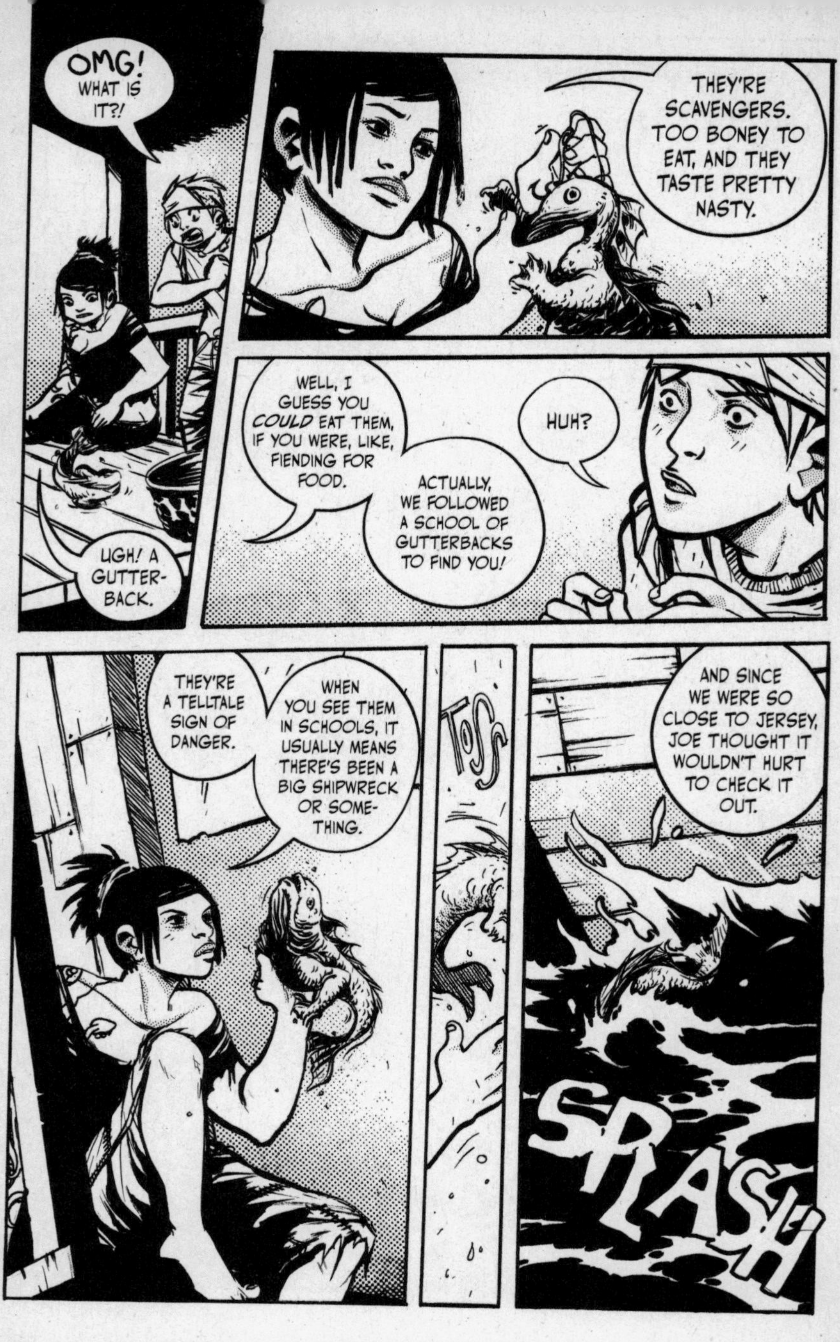
OMG! WHAT IS IT?!
UGH! A GUTTER-BACK.
THEY'RE SCAVENGERS. TOO BONEY TO EAT, AND THEY TASTE PRETTY NASTY.
WELL, I GUESS YOU COULD EAT THEM, IF YOU WERE, LIKE, FIENDING FOR FOOD.
ACTUALLY, WE FOLLOWED A SCHOOL OF GUTTERBACKS TO FIND YOU!
HUH?
THEY'RE A TELLTALE SIGN OF DANGER.
WHEN YOU SEE THEM IN SCHOOLS, IT USUALLY MEANS THERE'S BEEN A BIG SHIPWRECK OR SOME-THING.
TOSS
AND SINCE WE WERE SO CLOSE TO JERSEY, JOE THOUGHT IT WOULDN'T HURT TO CHECK IT OUT.
SPLASH

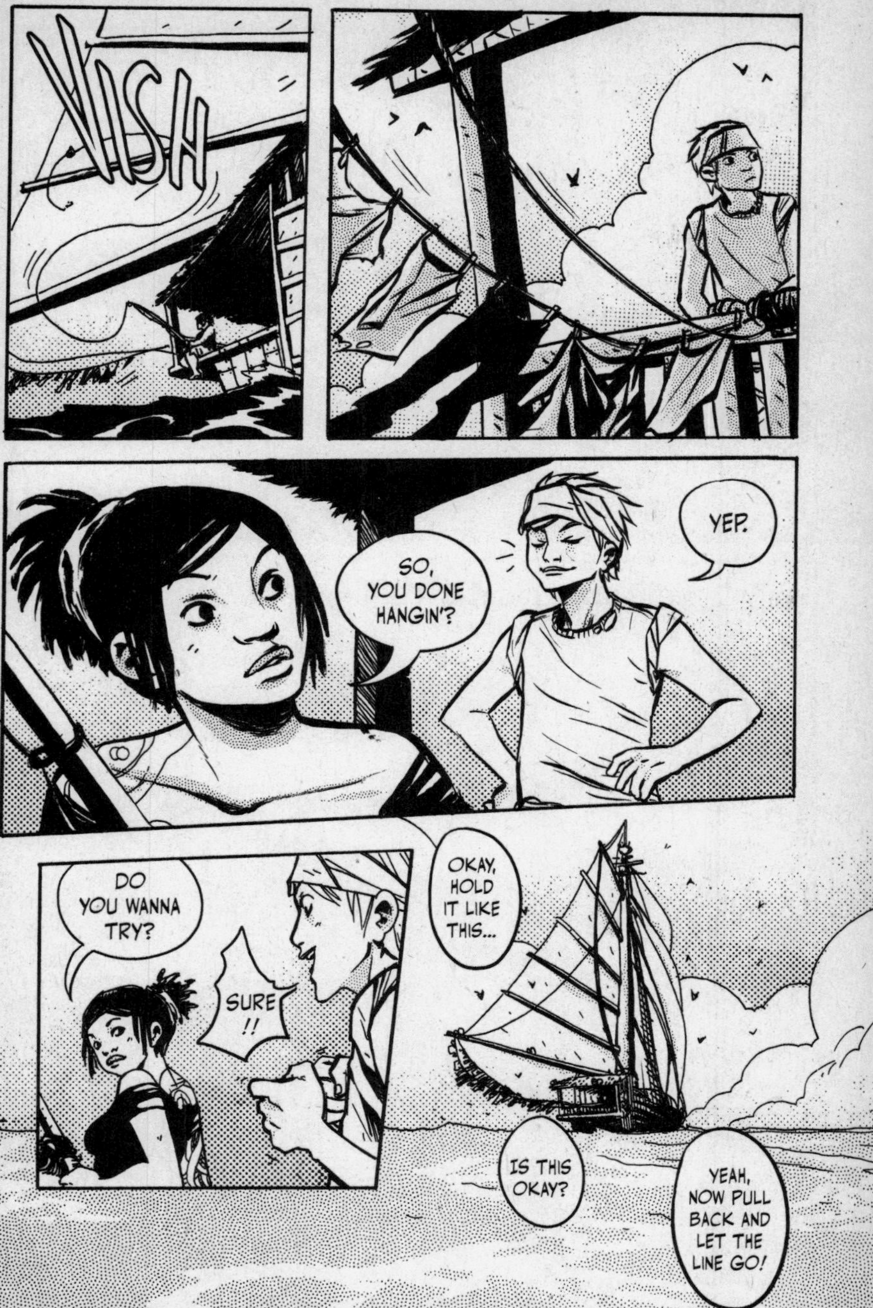
VISH
SO, YOU DONE HANGIN'?
YEP.
DO YOU WANNA TRY?
SURE !!
OKAY, HOLD IT LIKE THIS...
IS THIS OKAY?
YEAH, NOW PULL BACK AND LET THE LINE GO!

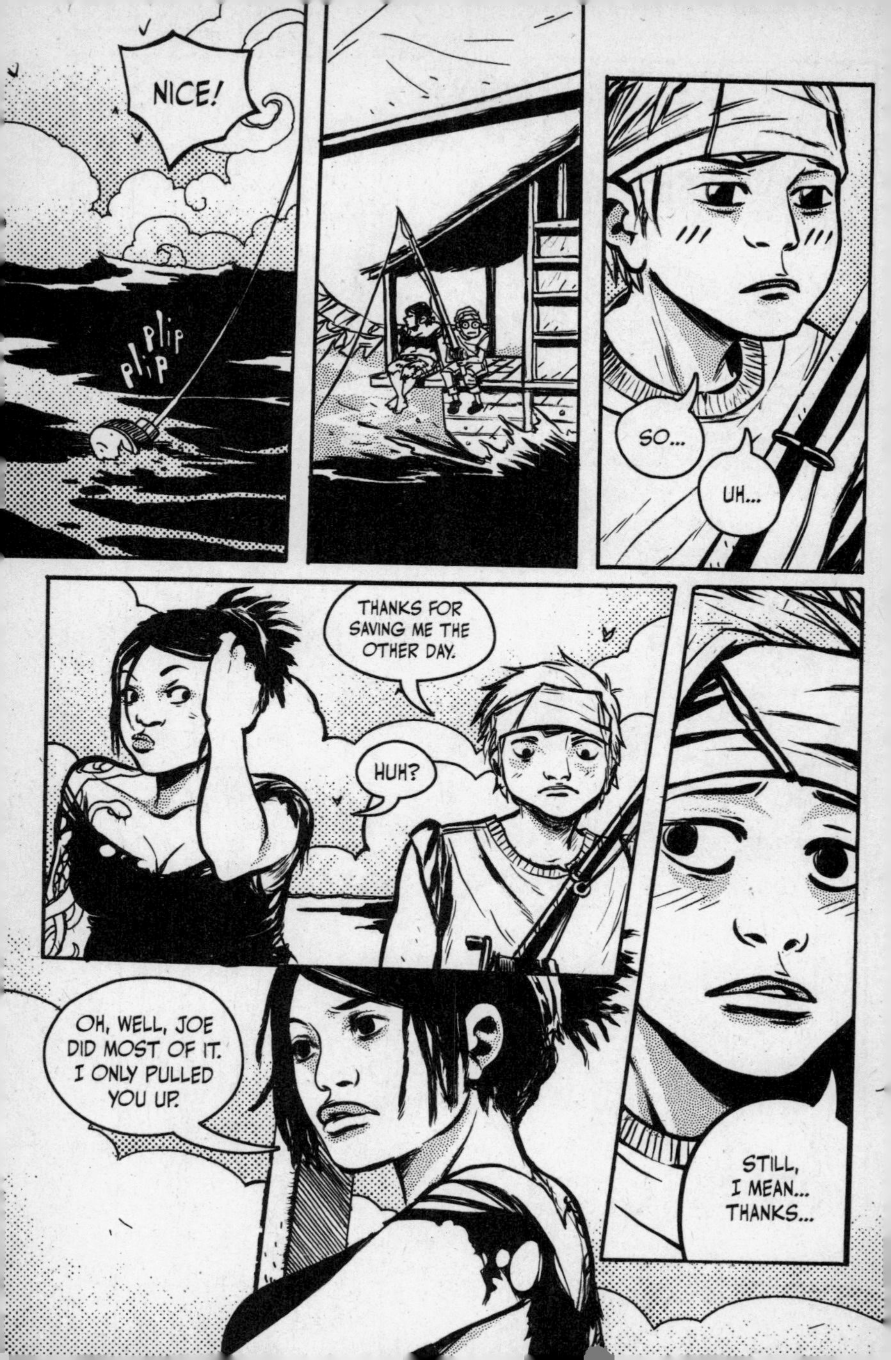

NICE!
plip plip
SO...
UH...
THANKS FOR SAVING ME THE OTHER DAY.
HUH?
OH, WELL, JOE DID MOST OF IT. I ONLY PULLED YOU UP.
STILL, I MEAN... THANKS...

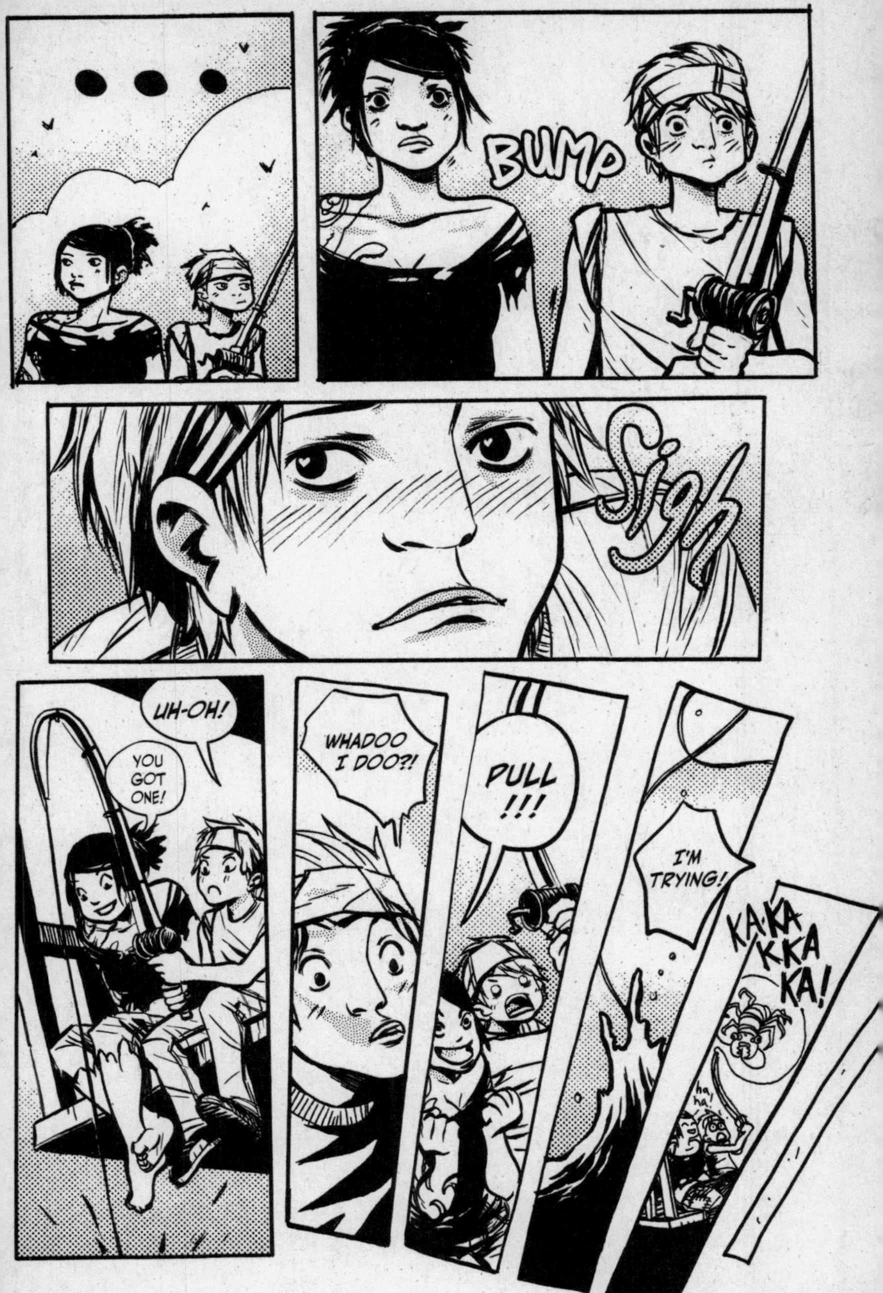

...
BUMP
Sigh
UH-OH!
YOU GOT ONE!
WHADOO I DOO?!
PULL !!!
I'M TRYING!
KA-KA KKA KA!
ha! ha!

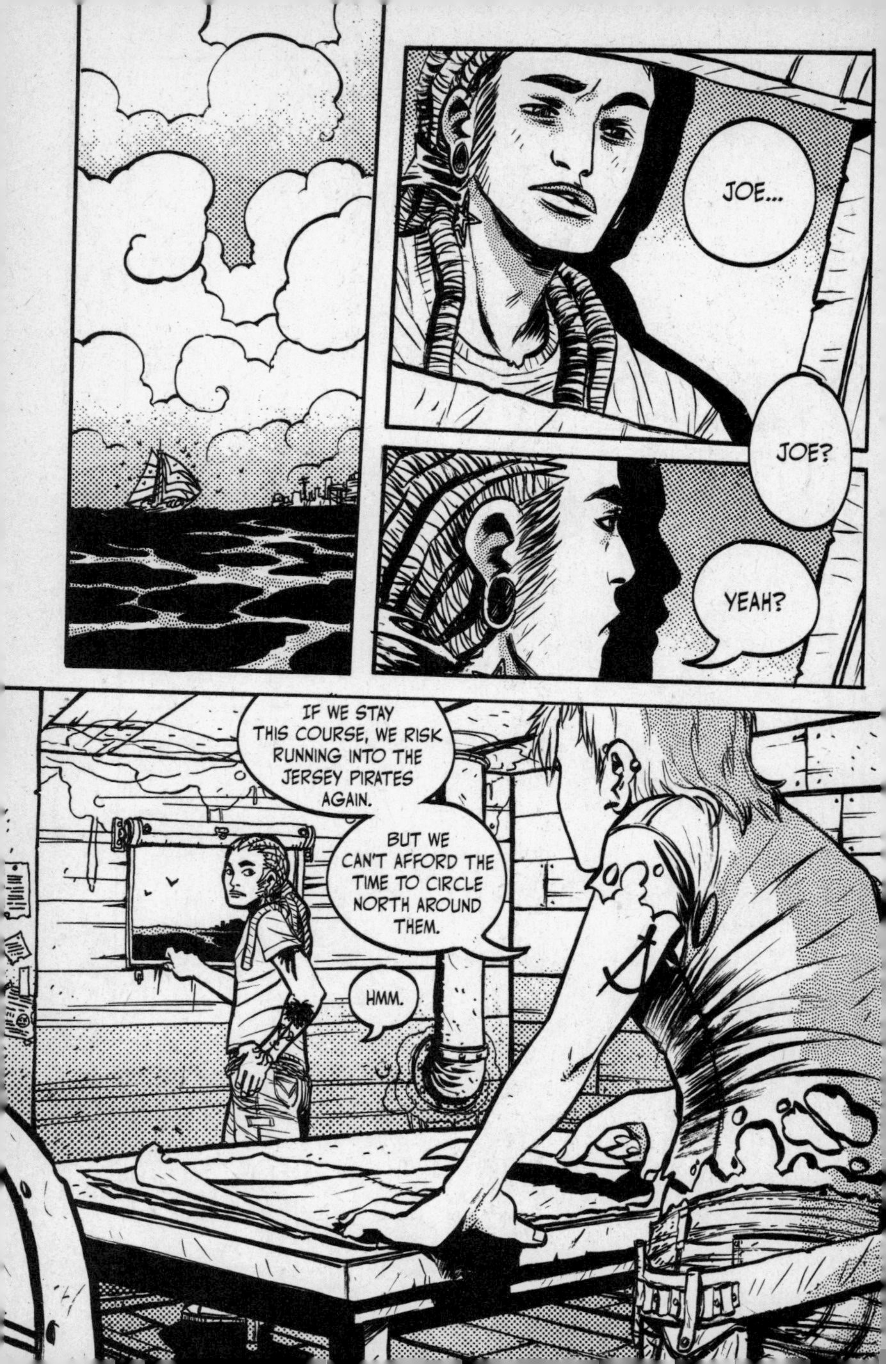
JOE...
JOE?
YEAH?
IF WE STAY THIS COURSE, WE RISK RUNNING INTO THE JERSEY PIRATES AGAIN.
BUT WE CAN'T AFFORD THE TIME TO CIRCLE NORTH AROUND THEM.
HMM.

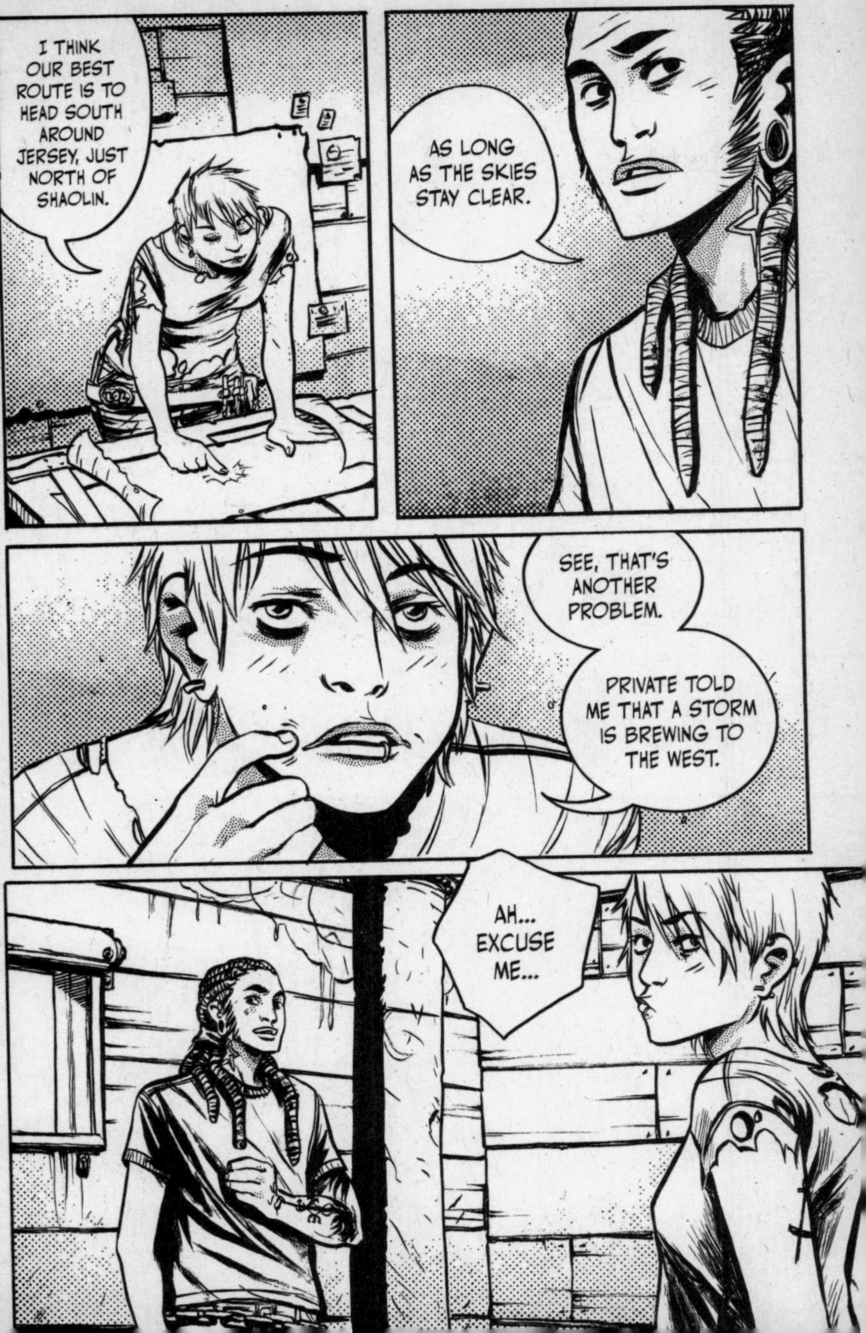
I THINK OUR BEST ROUTE IS TO HEAD SOUTH AROUND JERSEY, JUST NORTH OF SHAOLIN.
AS LONG AS THE SKIES STAY CLEAR.
SEE, THAT'S ANOTHER PROBLEM.
PRIVATE TOLD ME THAT A STORM IS BREWING TO THE WEST.
AH... EXCUSE ME...

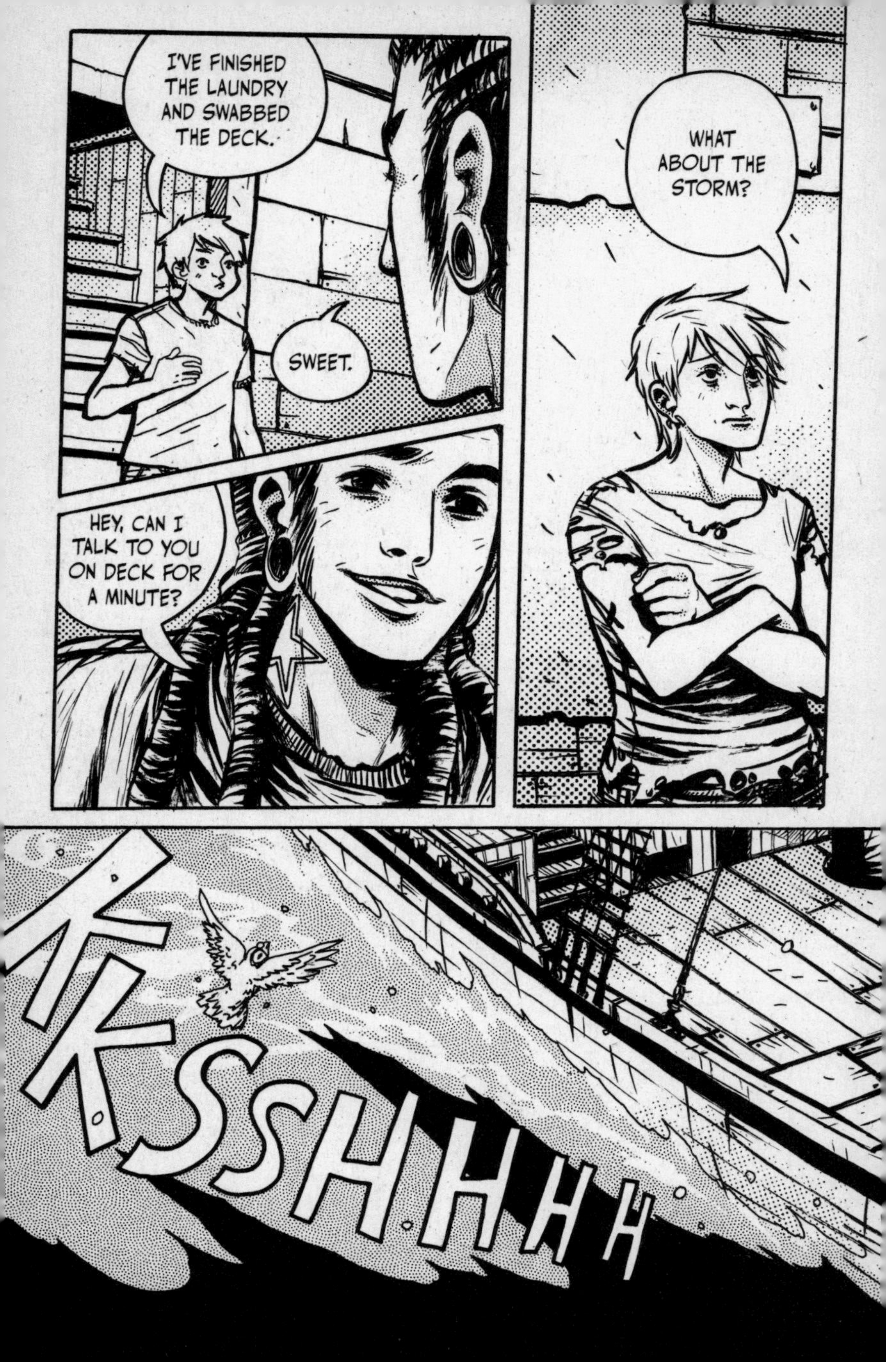
I'VE FINISHED THE LAUNDRY AND SWABBED THE DECK.
SWEET.
WHAT ABOUT THE STORM?
HEY, CAN I TALK TO YOU ON DECK FOR A MINUTE?
KKSSHHHHH

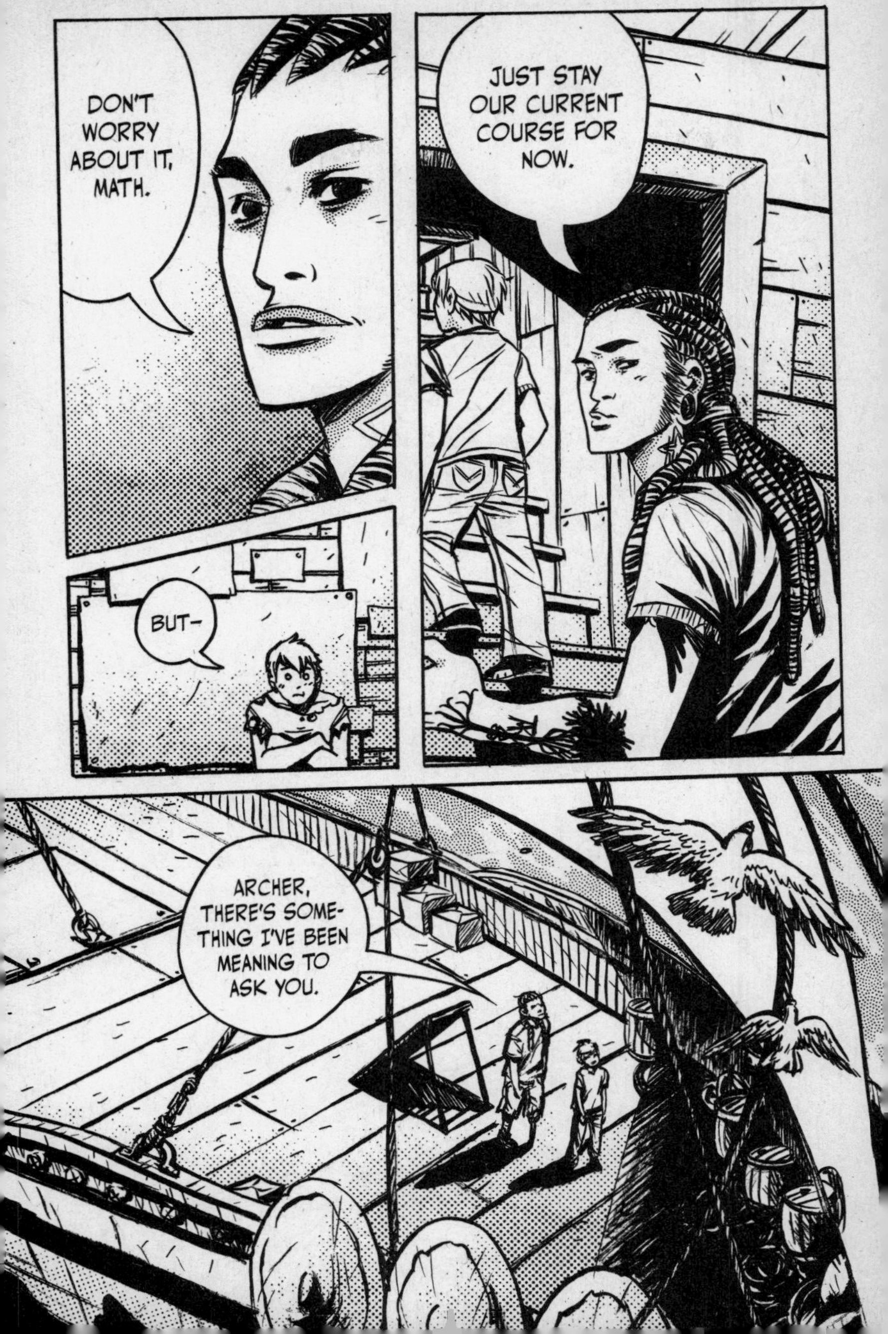
DON'T WORRY ABOUT IT, MATH.
BUT-
JUST STAY OUR CURRENT COURSE FOR NOW.
ARCHER, THERE'S SOME-THING I'VE BEEN MEANING TO ASK YOU.

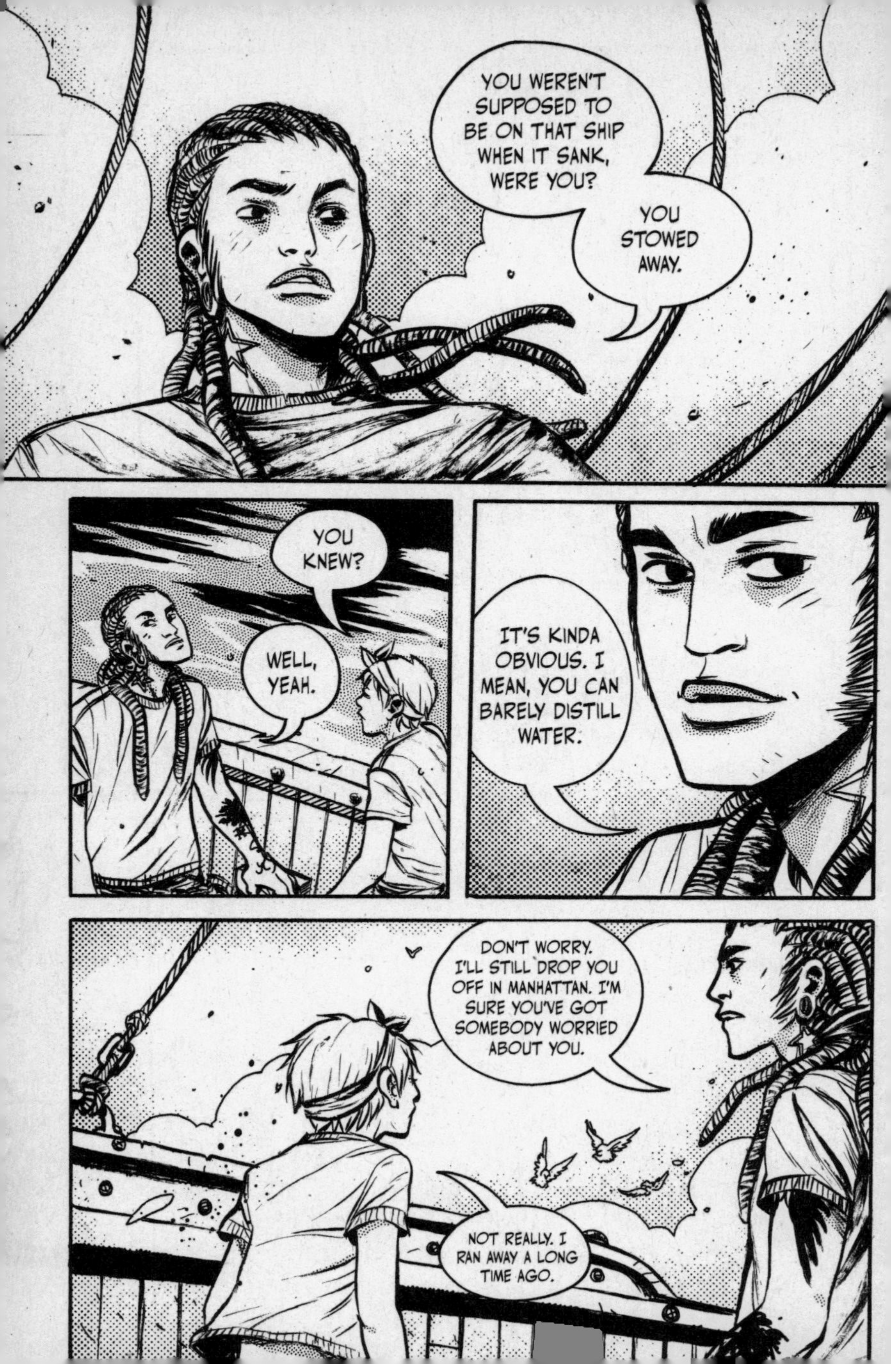
YOU WEREN'T SUPPOSED TO BE ON THAT SHIP WHEN IT SANK, WERE YOU?
YOU STOWED AWAY.
YOU KNEW?
WELL, YEAH.
IT'S KINDA OBVIOUS. I MEAN, YOU CAN BARELY DISTILL WATER.
DON'T WORRY. I'LL STILL DROP YOU OFF IN MANHATTAN. I'M SURE YOU'VE GOT SOMEBODY WORRIED ABOUT YOU.
NOT REALLY. I RAN AWAY A LONG TIME AGO.

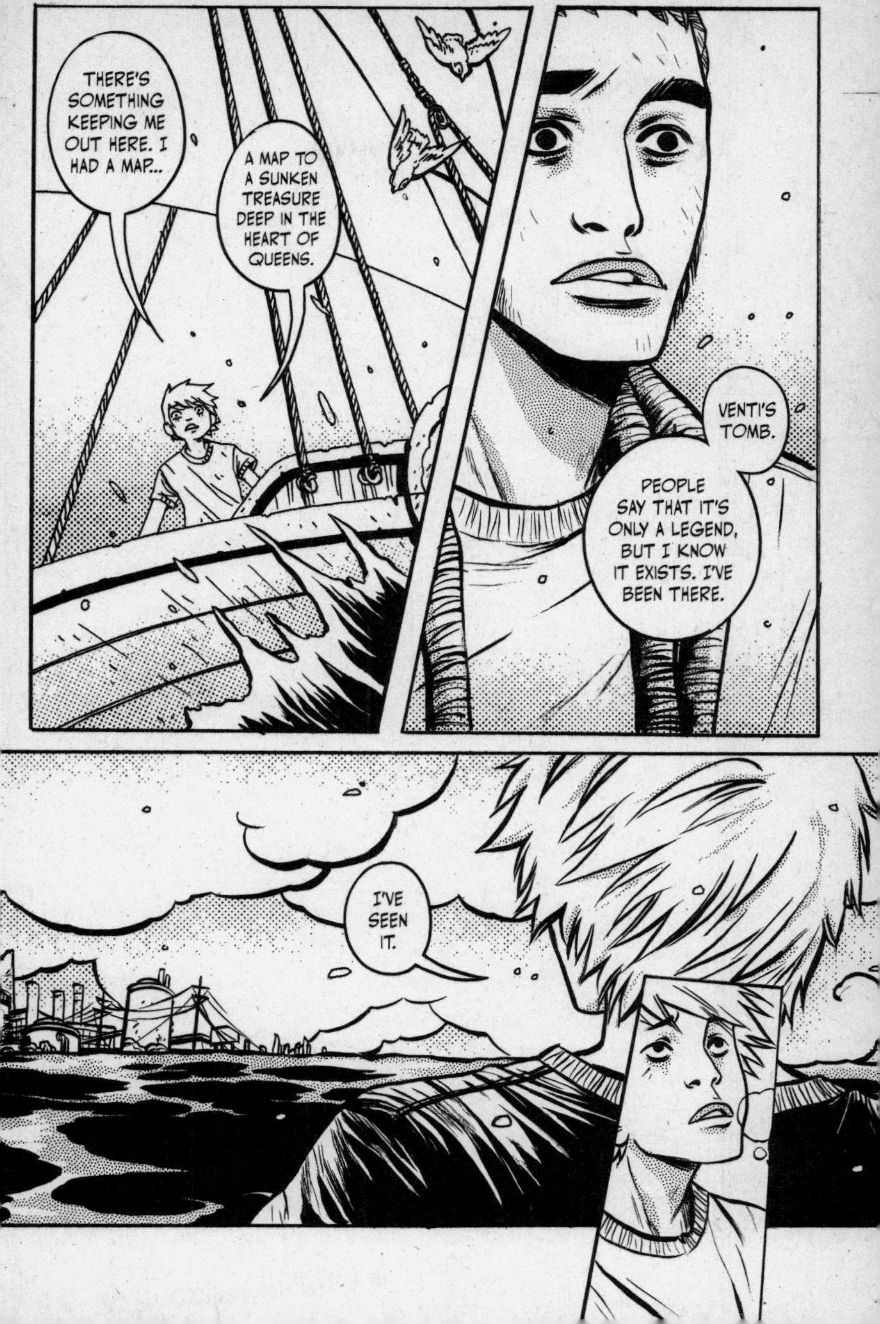
THERE'S SOMETHING KEEPING ME OUT HERE. I HAD A MAP...
A MAP TO A SUNKEN TREASURE DEEP IN THE HEART OF QUEENS.
VENTI'S TOMB.
PEOPLE SAY THAT IT'S ONLY A LEGEND, BUT I KNOW IT EXISTS. I'VE BEEN THERE.
I'VE SEEN IT.

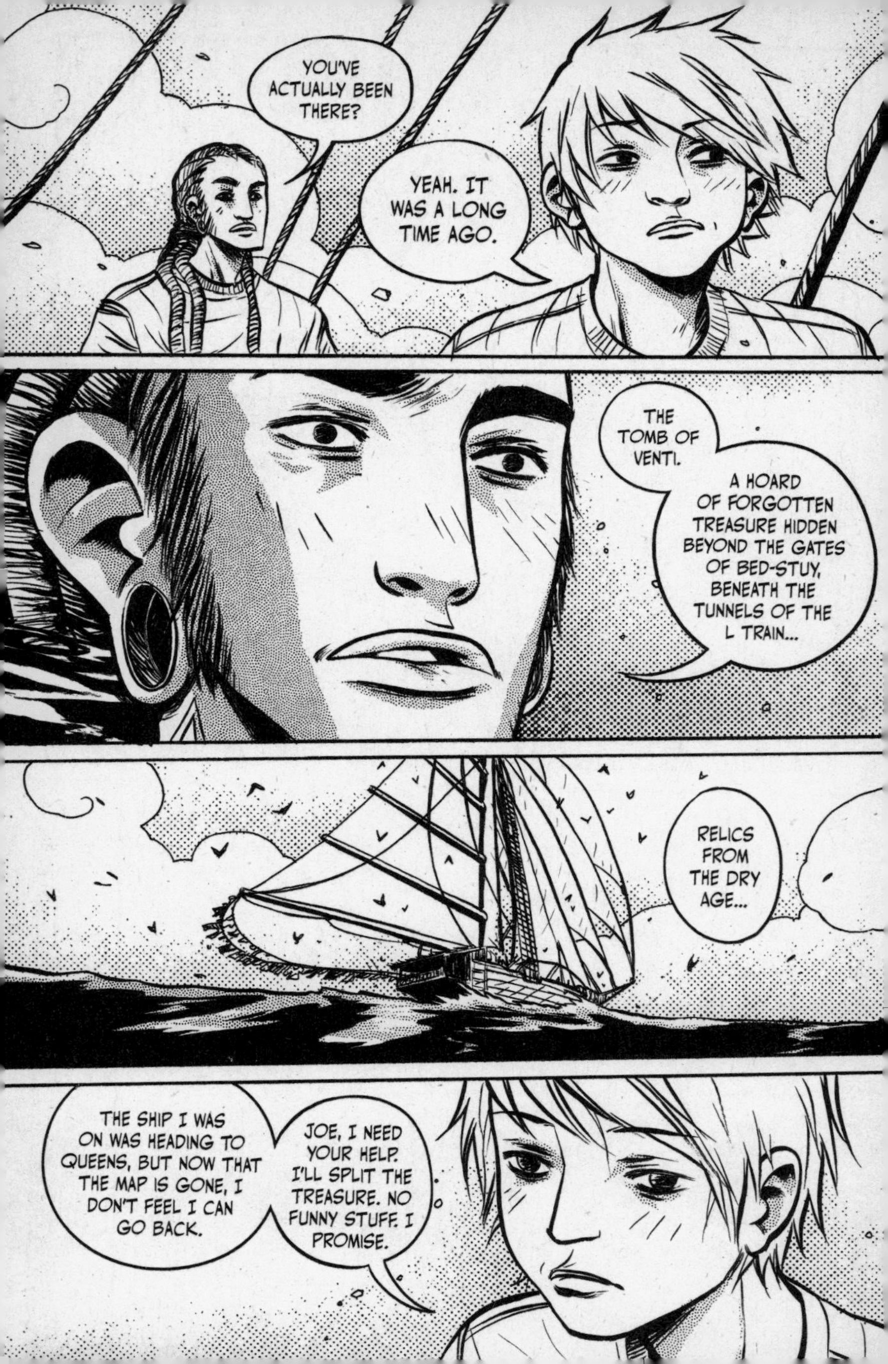
YOU'VE ACTUALLY BEEN THERE?
YEAH. IT WAS A LONG TIME AGO.
THE TOMB OF VENTI.
A HOARD OF FORGOTTEN TREASURE HIDDEN BEYOND THE GATES OF BED-STUY, BENEATH THE TUNNELS OF THE L TRAIN...
RELICS FROM THE DRY AGE...
THE SHIP I WAS ON WAS HEADING TO QUEENS, BUT NOW THAT THE MAP IS GONE, I DON'T FEEL I CAN GO BACK.
JOE, I NEED YOUR HELP. I'LL SPLIT THE TREASURE. NO FUNNY STUFF. I PROMISE.

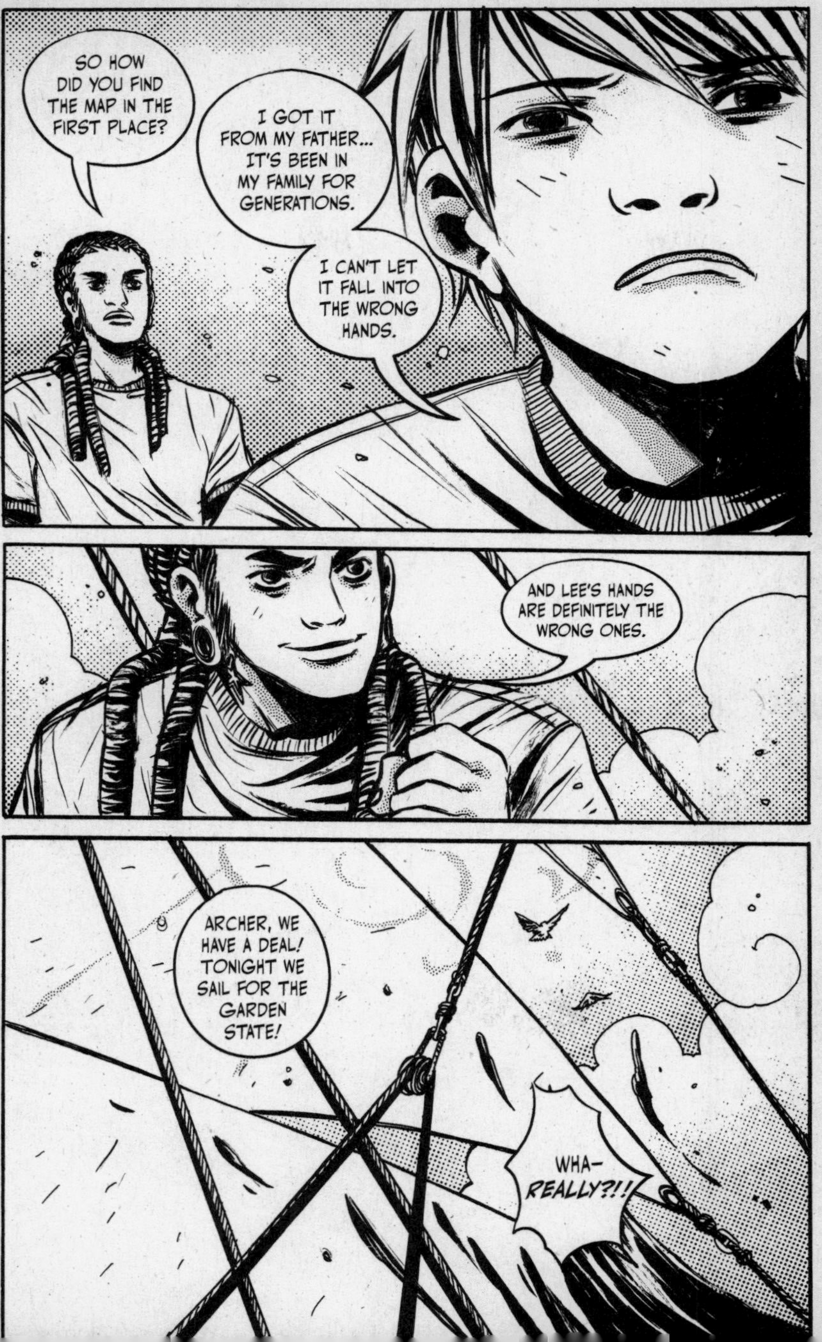
SO HOW DID YOU FIND THE MAP IN THE FIRST PLACE?
I GOT IT FROM MY FATHER... IT'S BEEN IN MY FAMILY FOR GENERATIONS.
I CAN'T LET IT FALL INTO THE WRONG HANDS.
AND LEE'S HANDS ARE DEFINITELY THE WRONG ONES.
ARCHER, WE HAVE A DEAL! TONIGHT WE SAIL FOR THE GARDEN STATE!
WHA- REALLY?!!

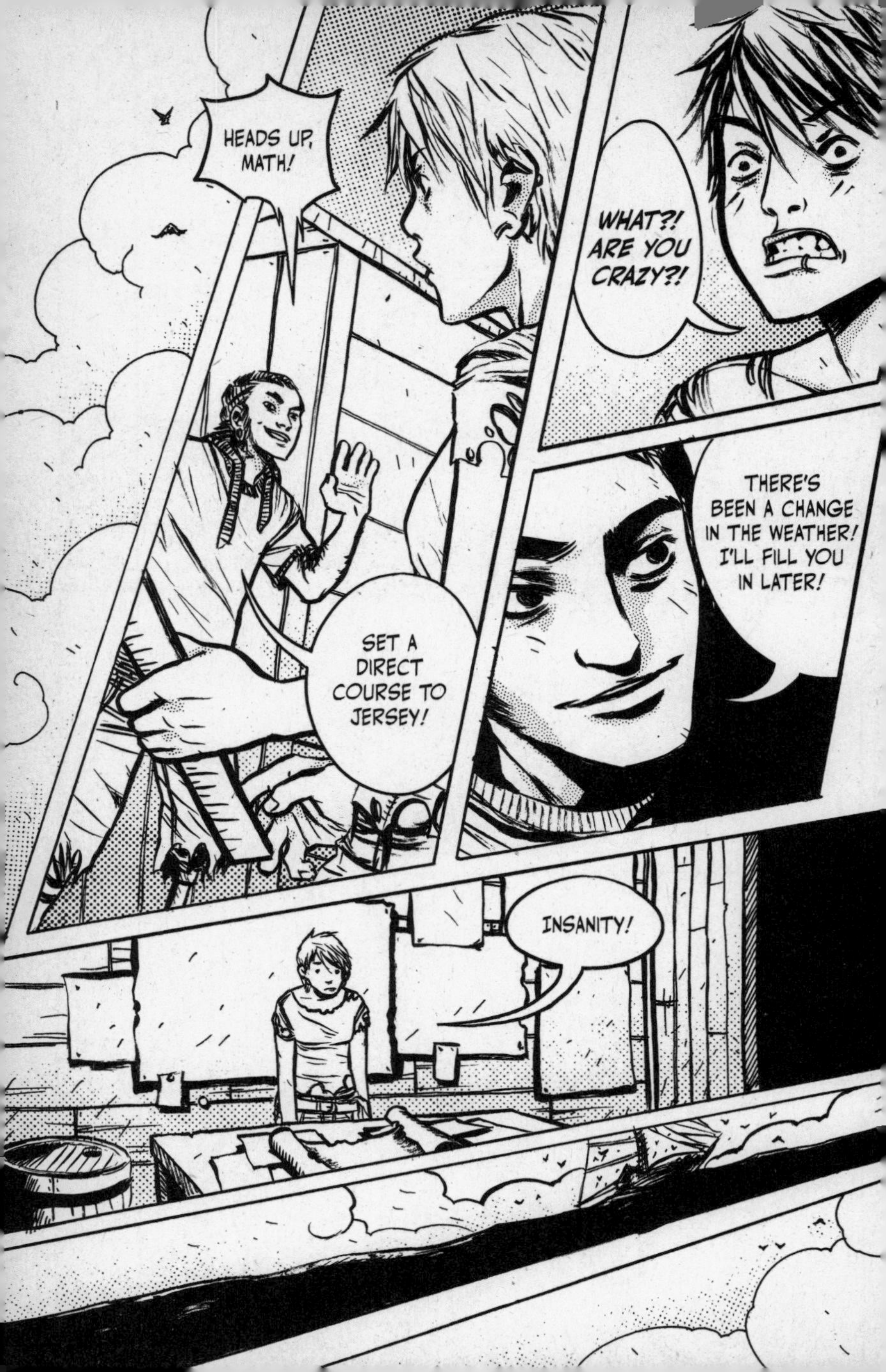
HEADS UP, MATH!
SET A DIRECT COURSE TO JERSEY!
WHAT?! ARE YOU CRAZY?!
THERE'S BEEN A CHANGE IN THE WEATHER! I'LL FILL YOU IN LATER!
INSANITY!

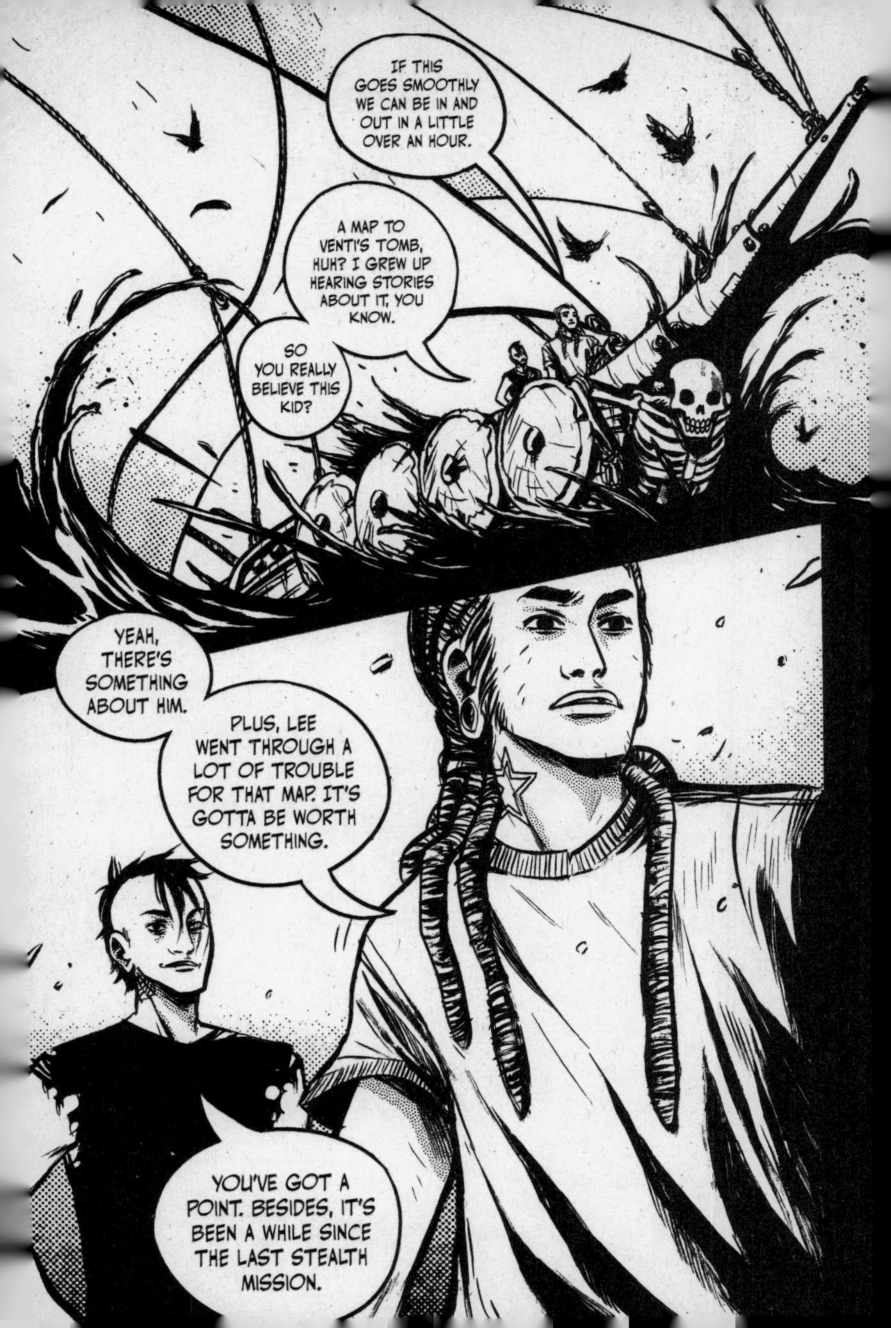
IF THIS GOES SMOOTHLY WE CAN BE IN AND OUT IN A LITTLE OVER AN HOUR.
A MAP TO VENTI'S TOMB, HUH? I GREW UP HEARING STORIES ABOUT IT, YOU KNOW.
SO YOU REALLY BELIEVE THIS KID?
YEAH, THERE'S SOMETHING ABOUT HIM.
PLUS, LEE WENT THROUGH A LOT OF TROUBLE FOR THAT MAP. IT'S GOTTA BE WORTH SOMETHING.
YOU'VE GOT A POINT. BESIDES, IT'S BEEN A WHILE SINCE THE LAST STEALTH MISSION.

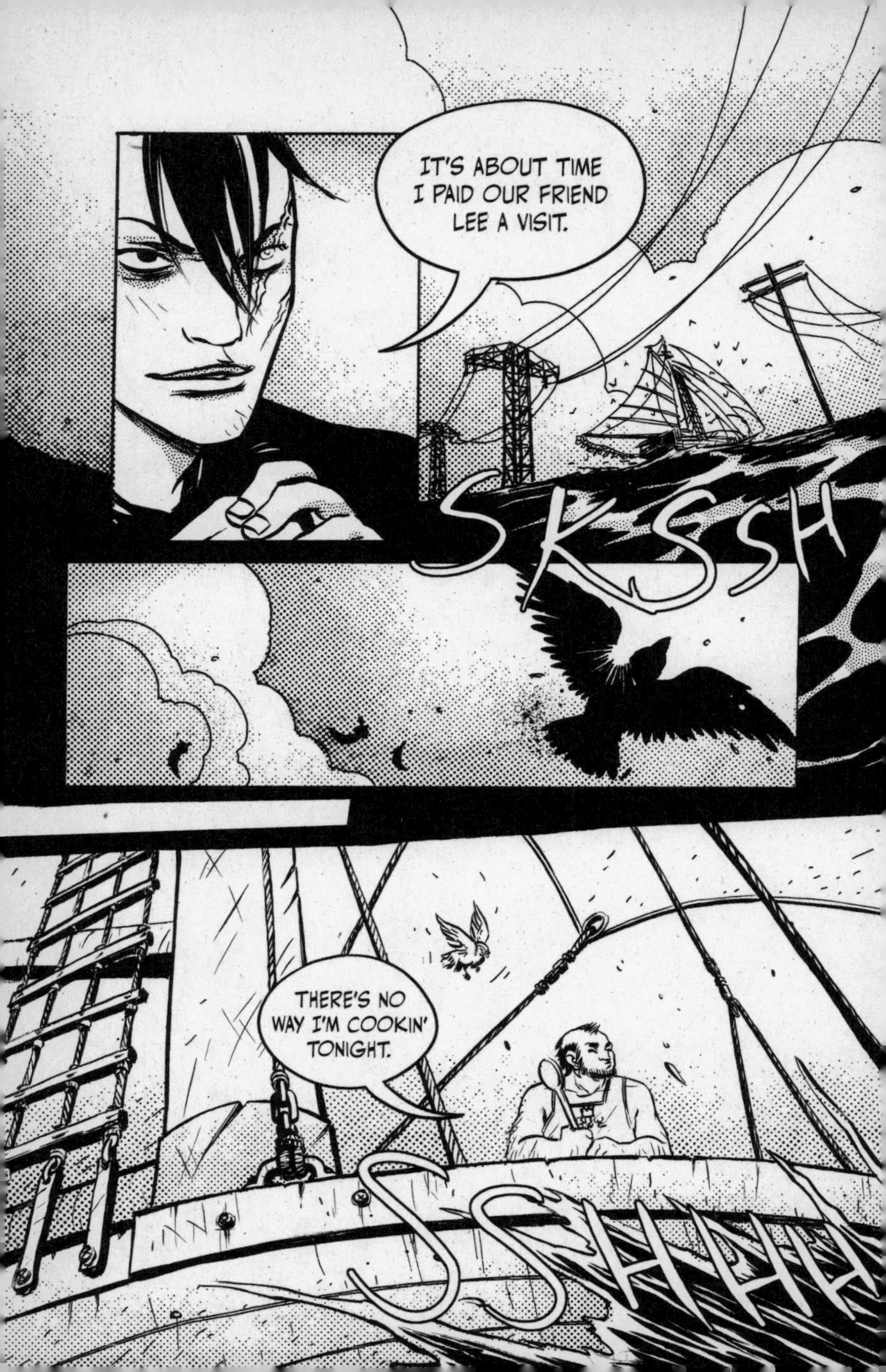
IT'S ABOUT TIME I PAID OUR FRIEND LEE A VISIT.
SKSSH
THERE'S NO WAY I'M COOKIN' TONIGHT.
SSHHH

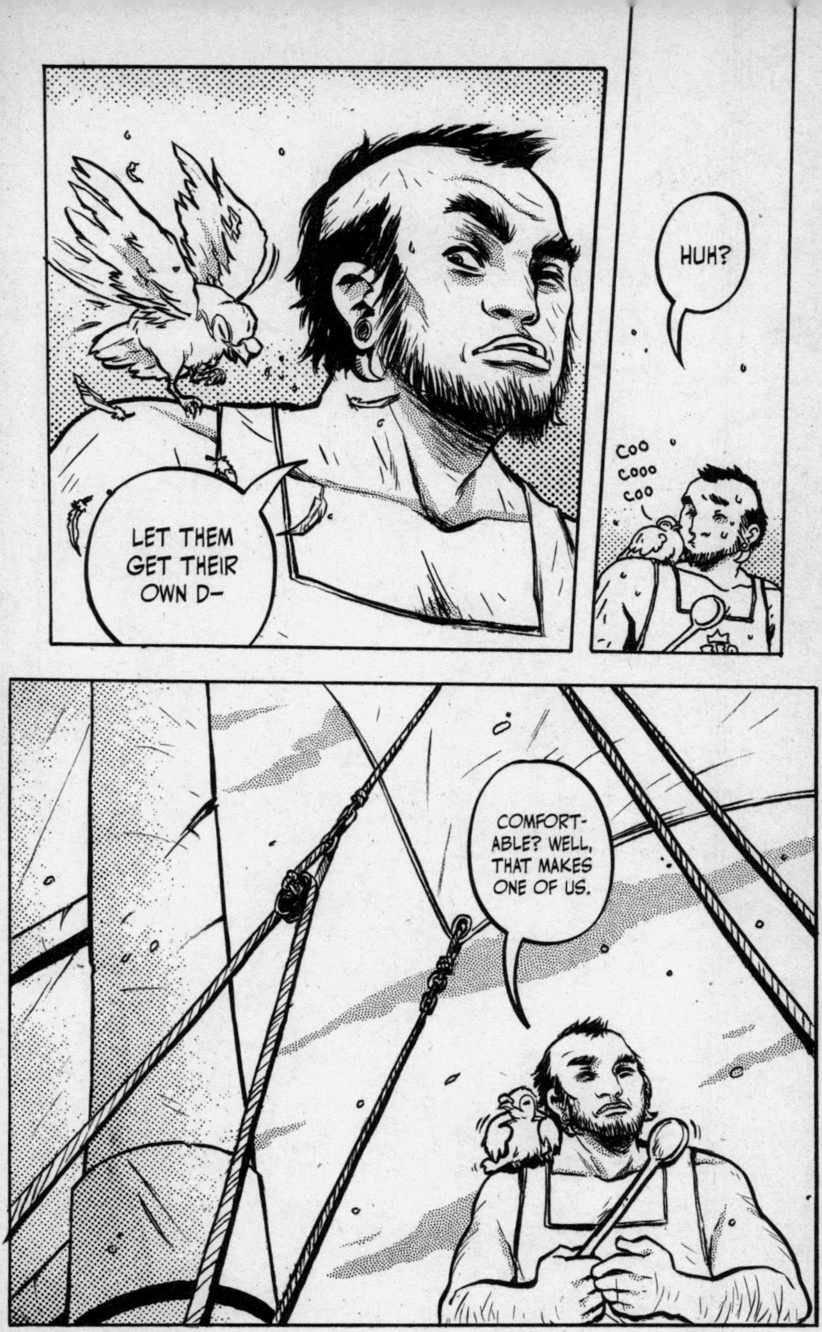
LET THEM GET THEIR OWN D–
HUH?
COO COOO COO
COMFORT-ABLE? WELL, THAT MAKES ONE OF US.

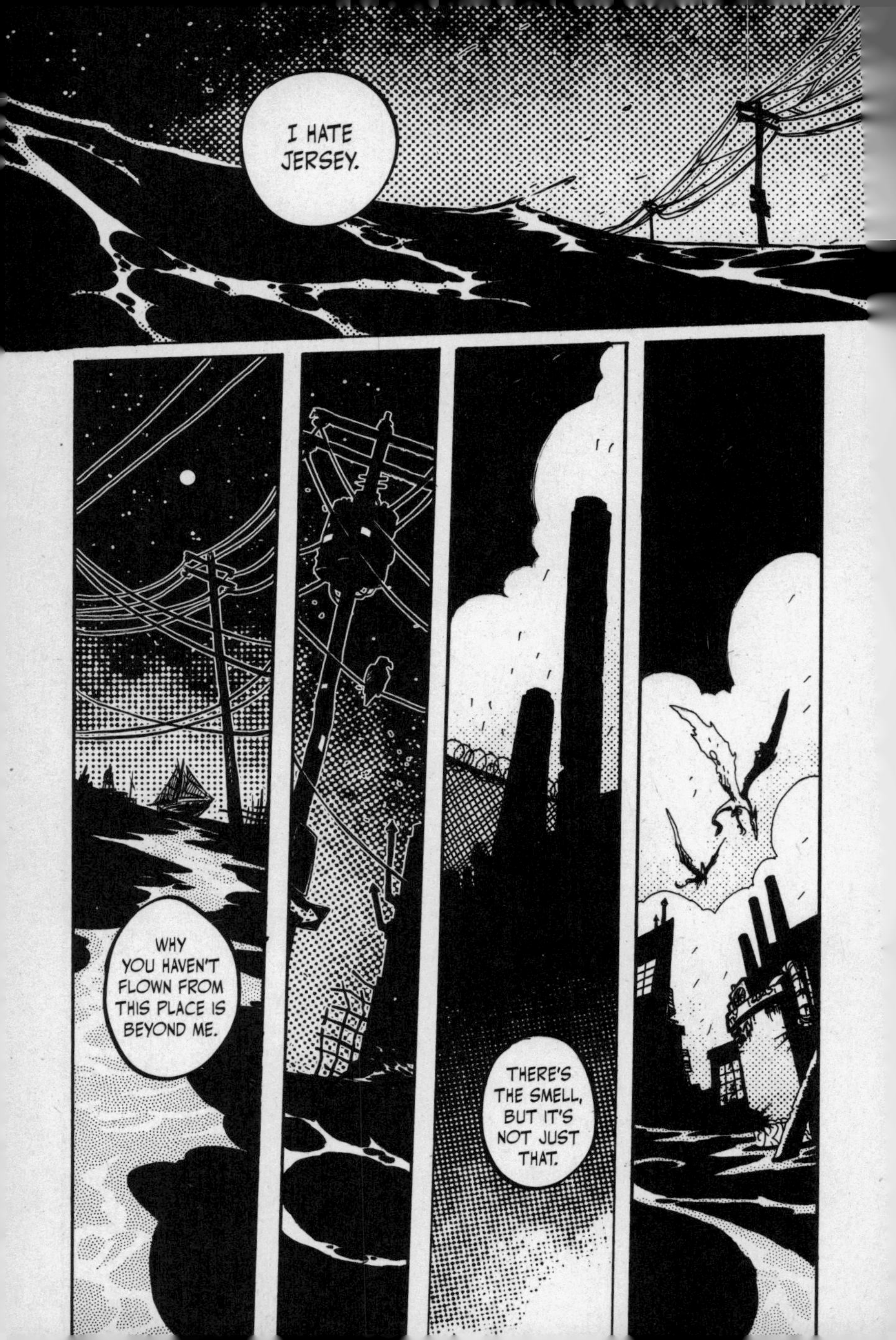
I HATE JERSEY.
WHY YOU HAVEN'T FLOWN FROM THIS PLACE IS BEYOND ME.
THERE'S THE SMELL, BUT IT'S NOT JUST THAT.

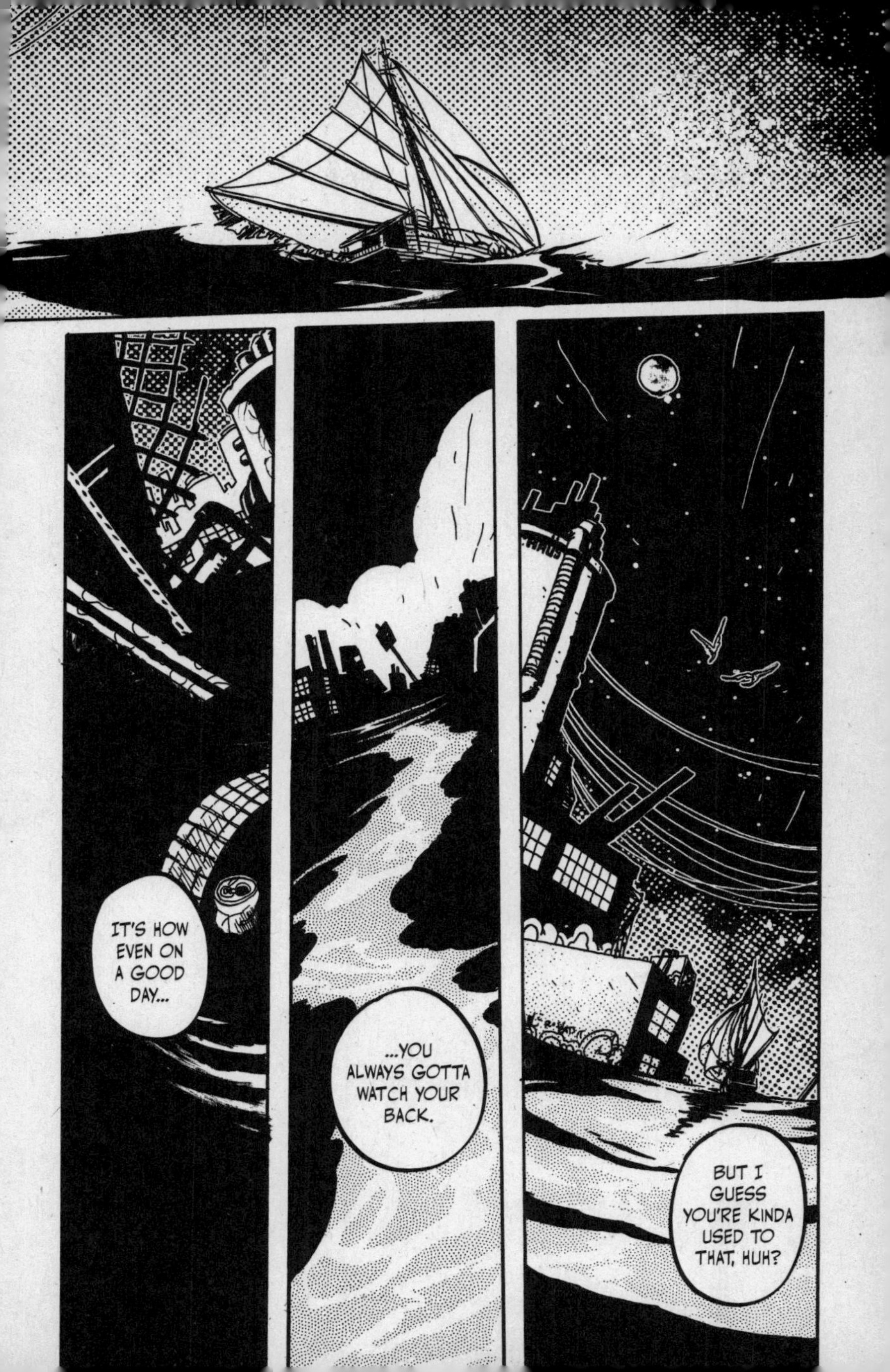
IT'S HOW EVEN ON A GOOD DAY...
...YOU ALWAYS GOTTA WATCH YOUR BACK.
BUT I GUESS YOU'RE KINDA USED TO THAT, HUH?

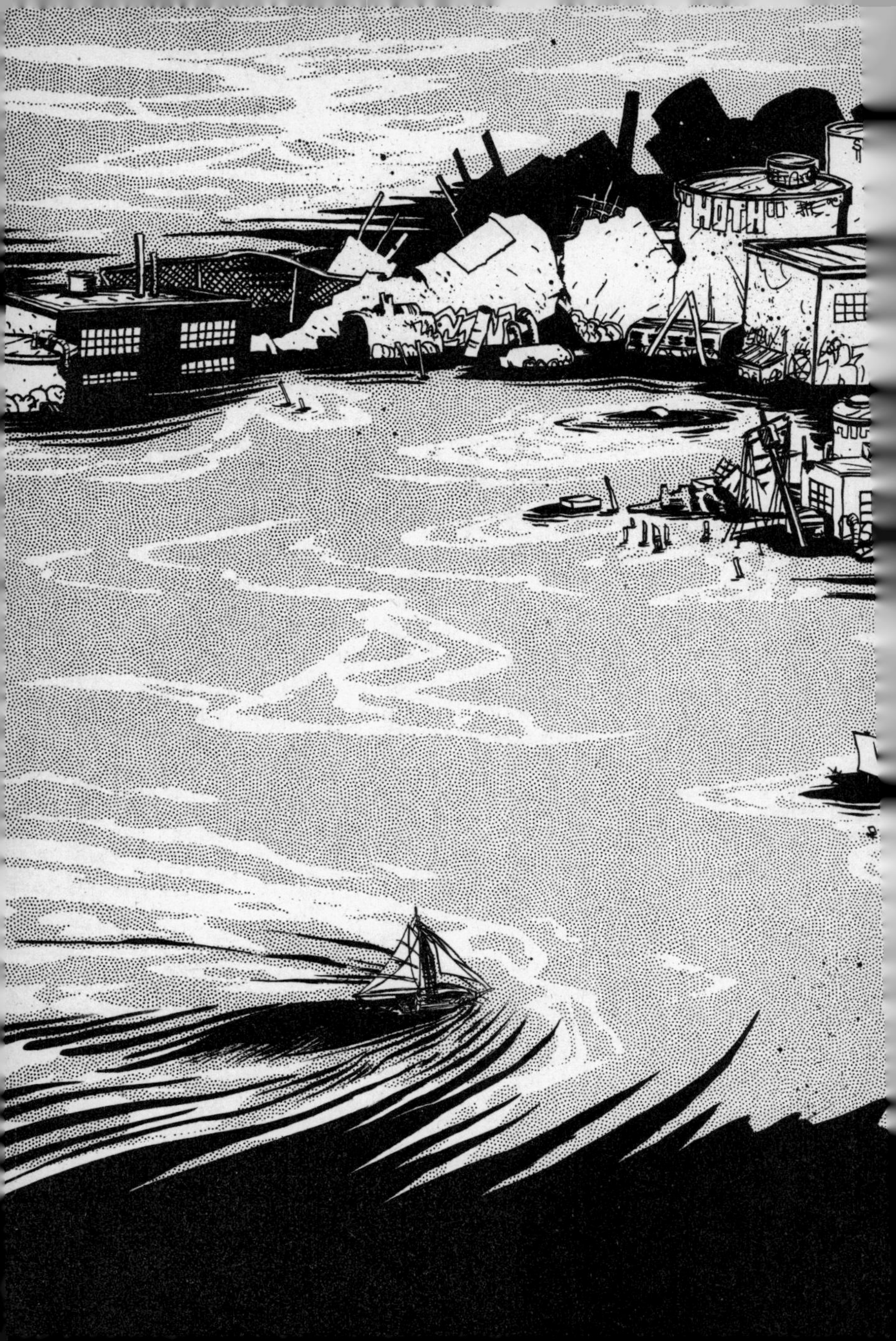
HOTH

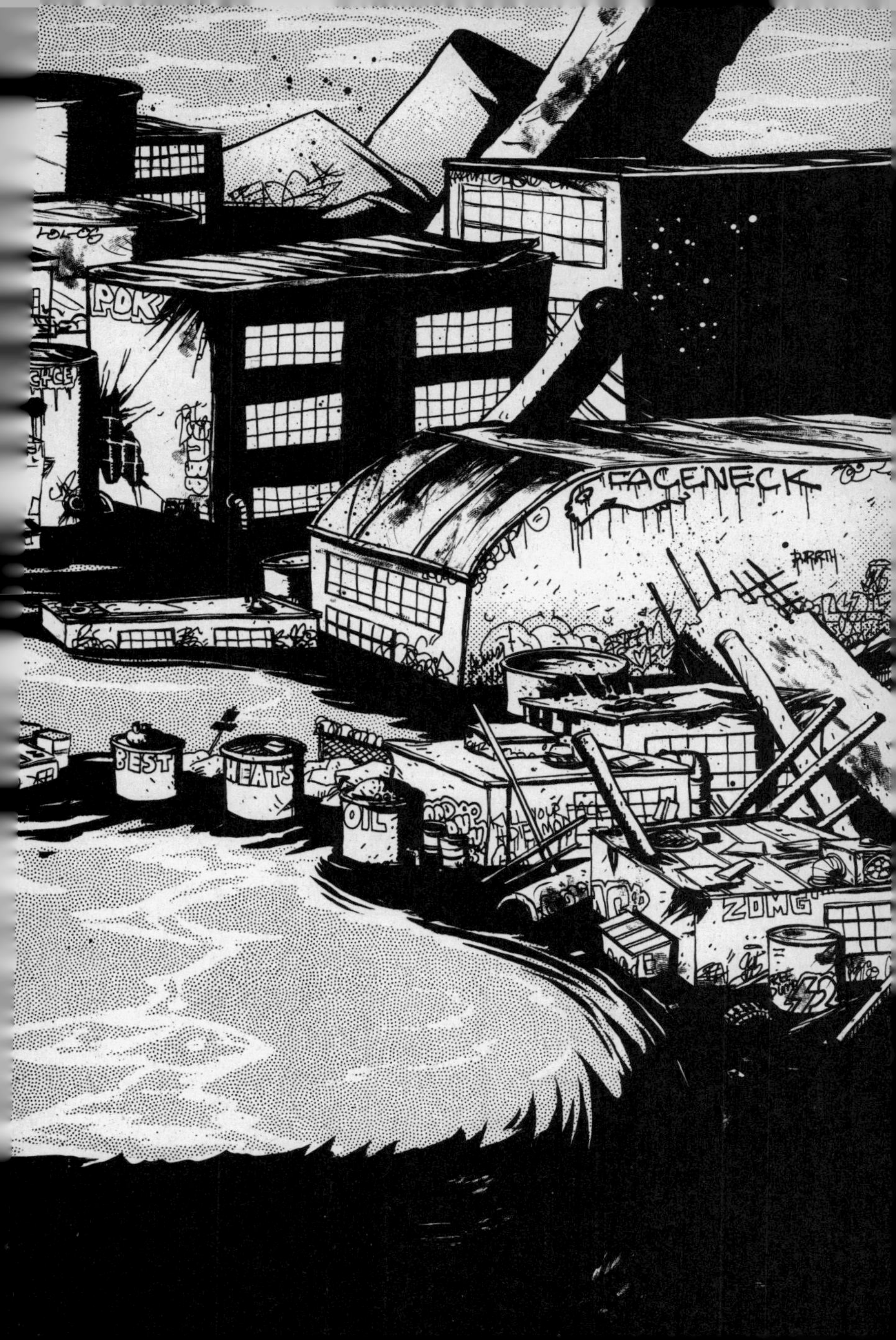
FACENECK
BEST
HEATS
OIL
ZOMG

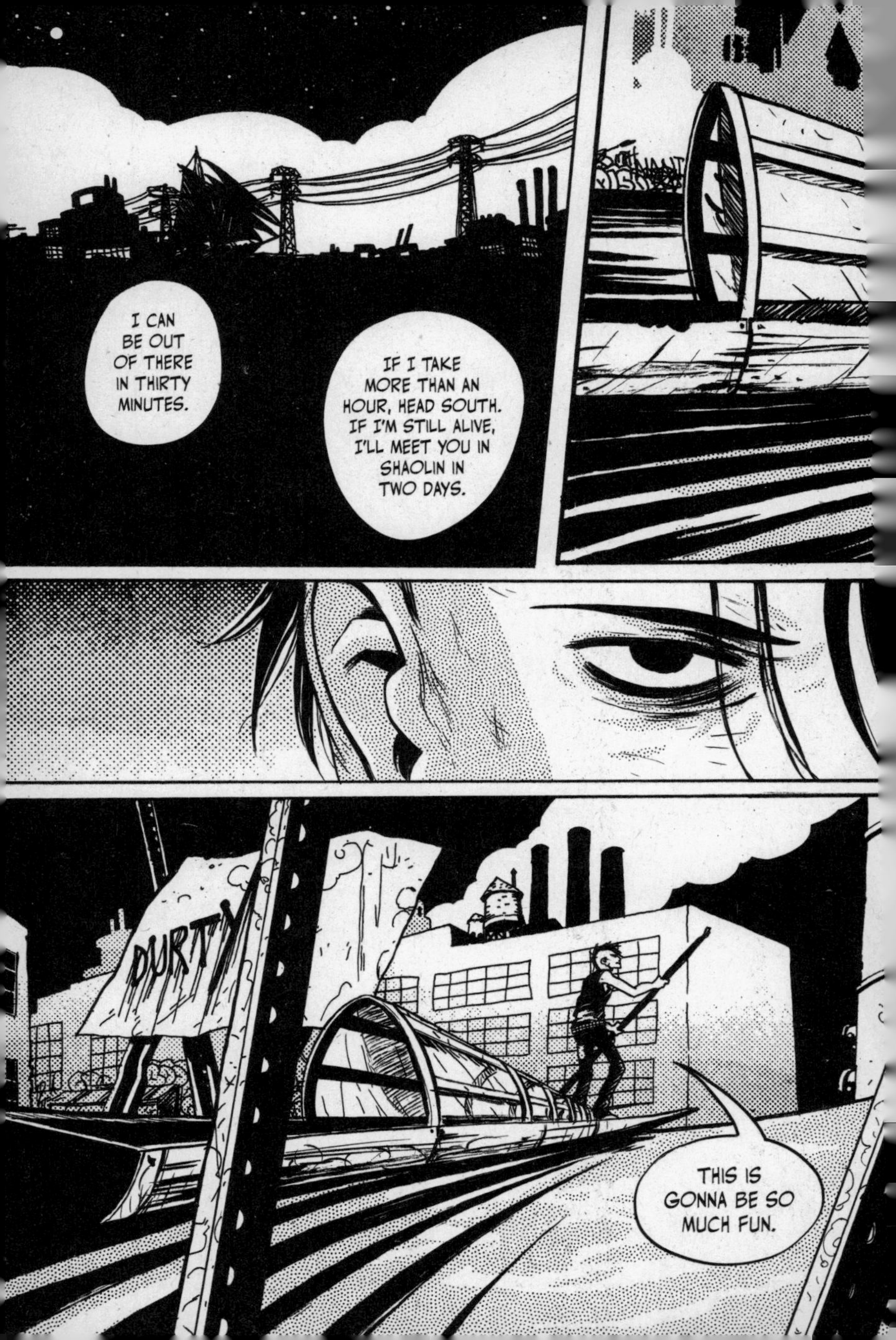
I CAN BE OUT OF THERE IN THIRTY MINUTES.
IF I TAKE MORE THAN AN HOUR, HEAD SOUTH. IF I'M STILL ALIVE, I'LL MEET YOU IN SHAOLIN IN TWO DAYS.
DURTY
THIS IS GONNA BE SO MUCH FUN.

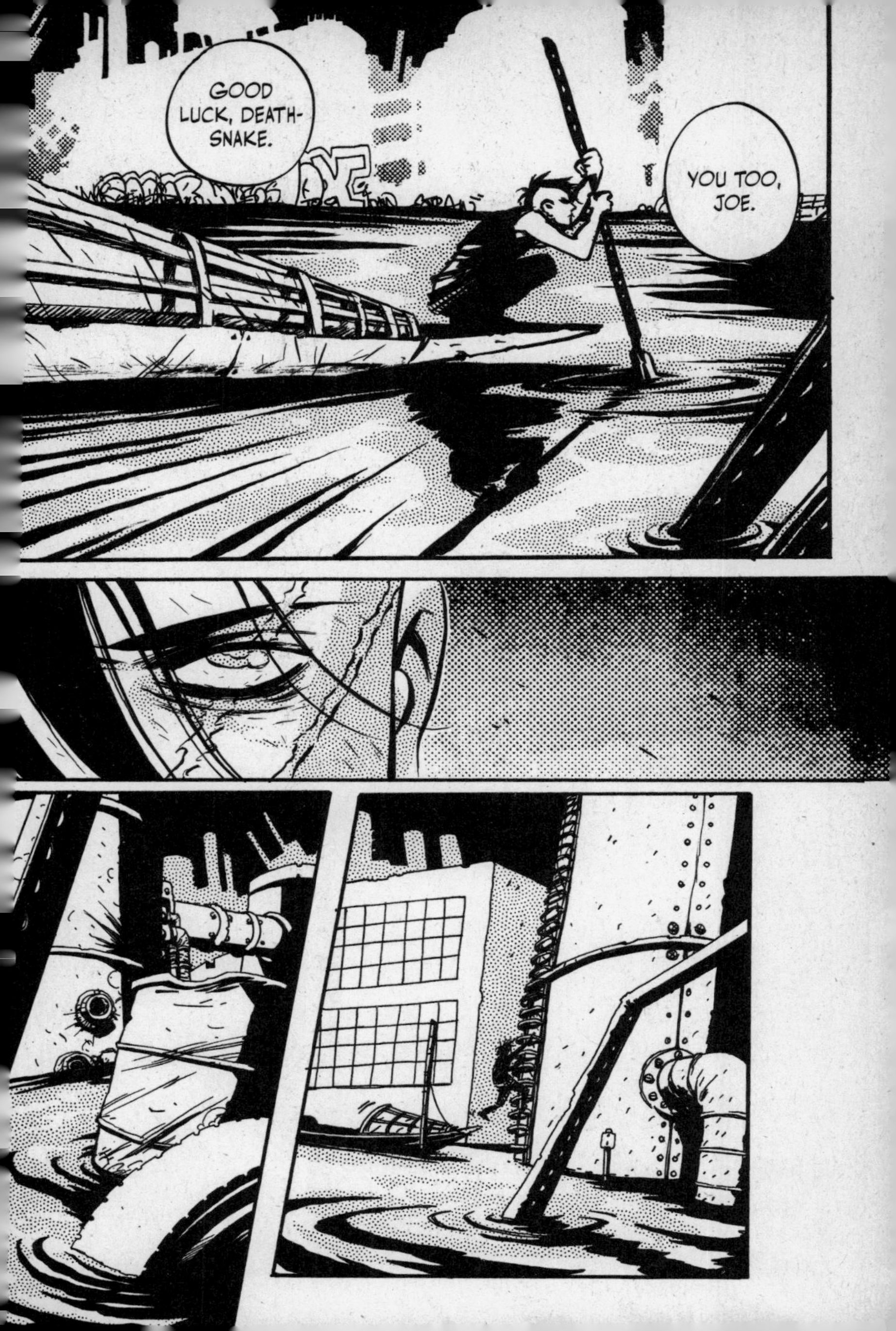
GOOD LUCK, DEATH-SNAKE.
YOU TOO, JOE.

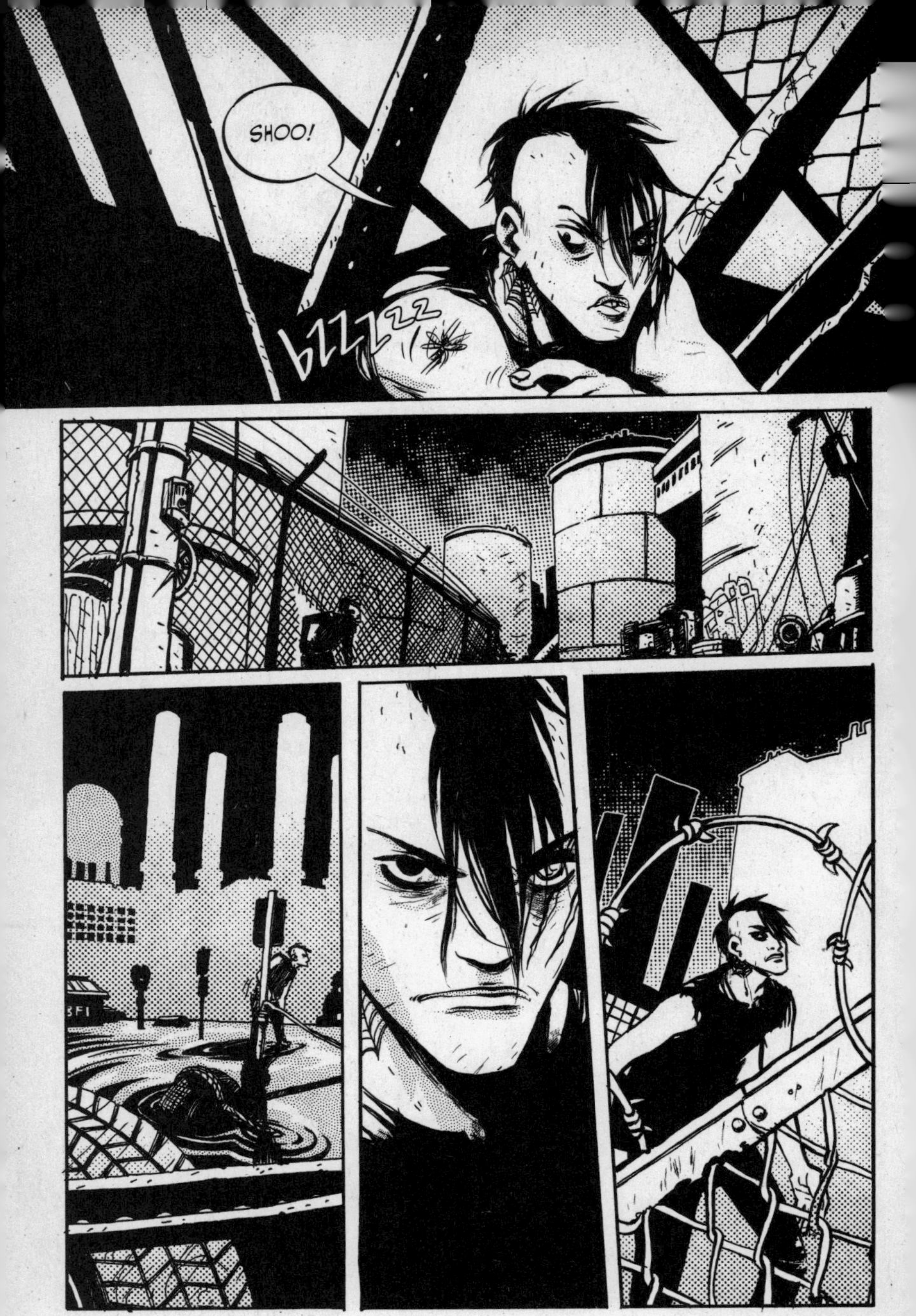
SHOO!
bzzzzz

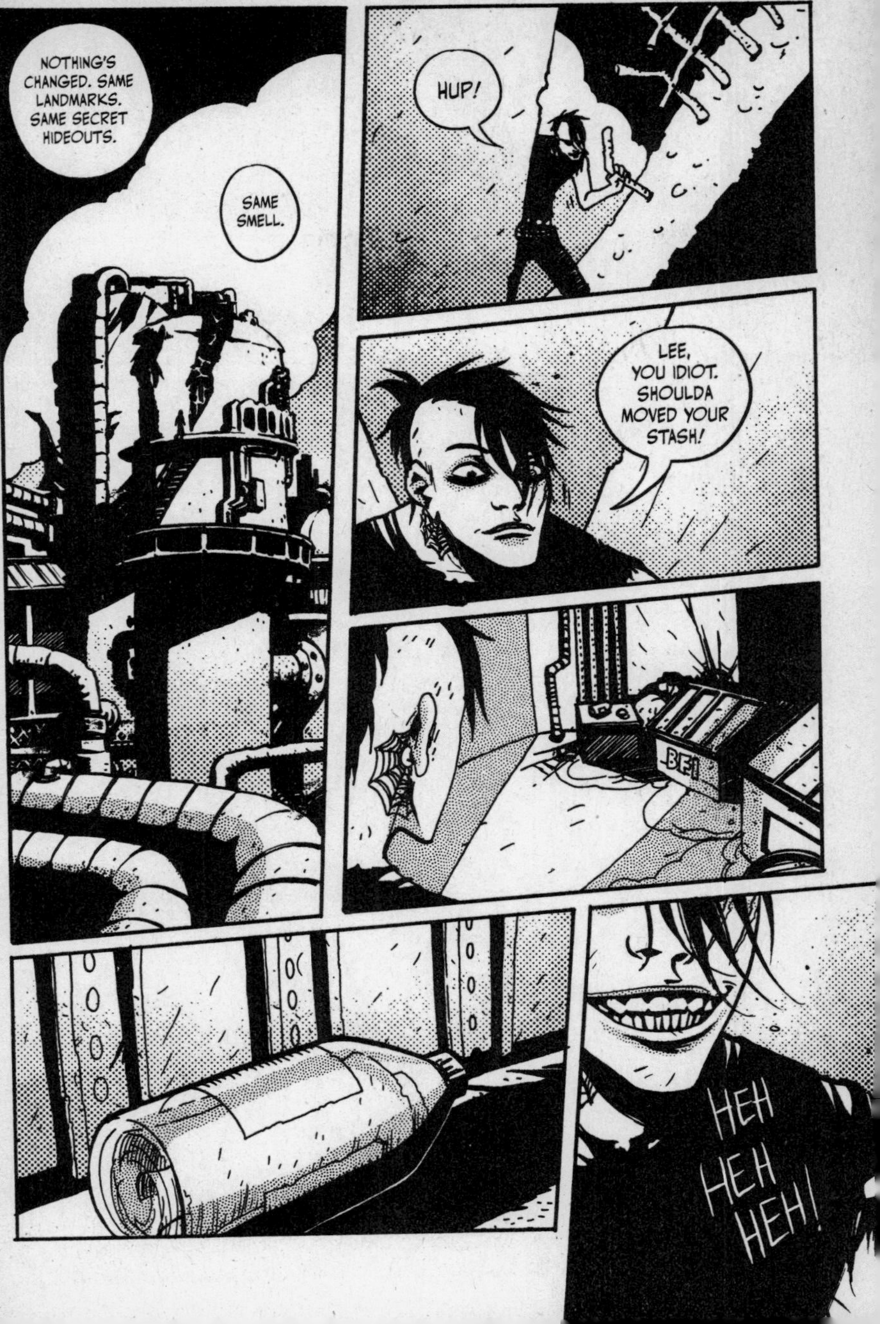
NOTHING'S CHANGED. SAME LANDMARKS. SAME SECRET HIDEOUTS.
SAME SMELL.
HUP!
LEE, YOU IDIOT. SHOULDA MOVED YOUR STASH!
HEH HEH HEH!

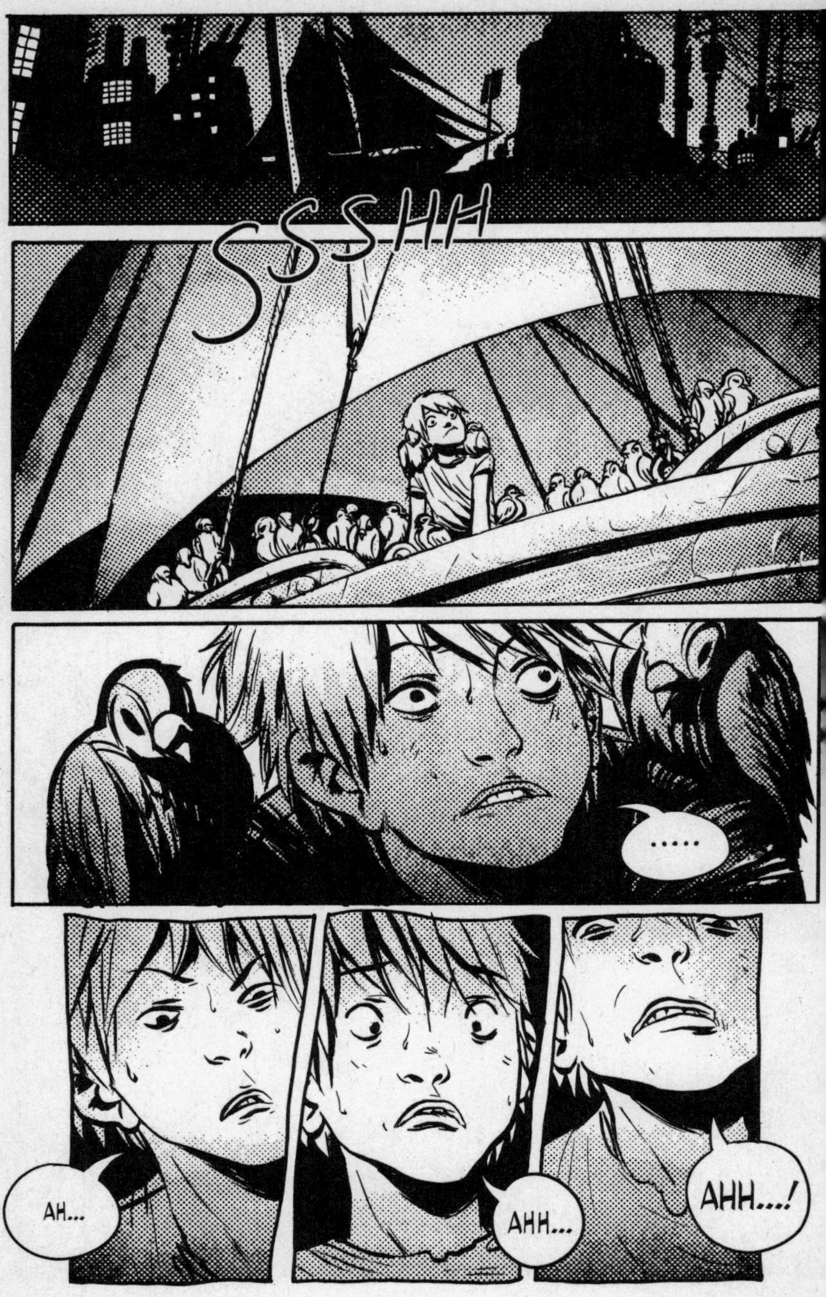
SSSHH
......
AH...
AHH...
AHH...!

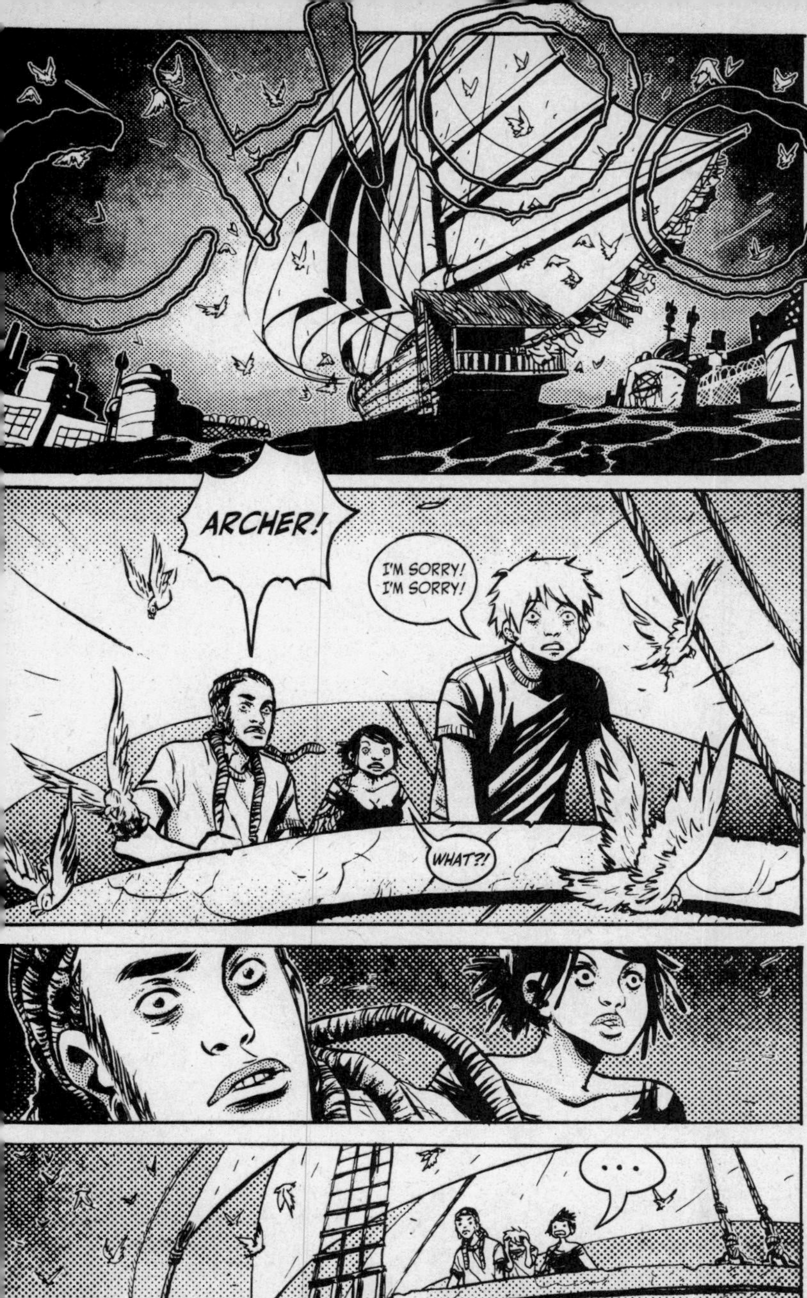
ARCHER!
I'M SORRY! I'M SORRY!
WHAT?!
...

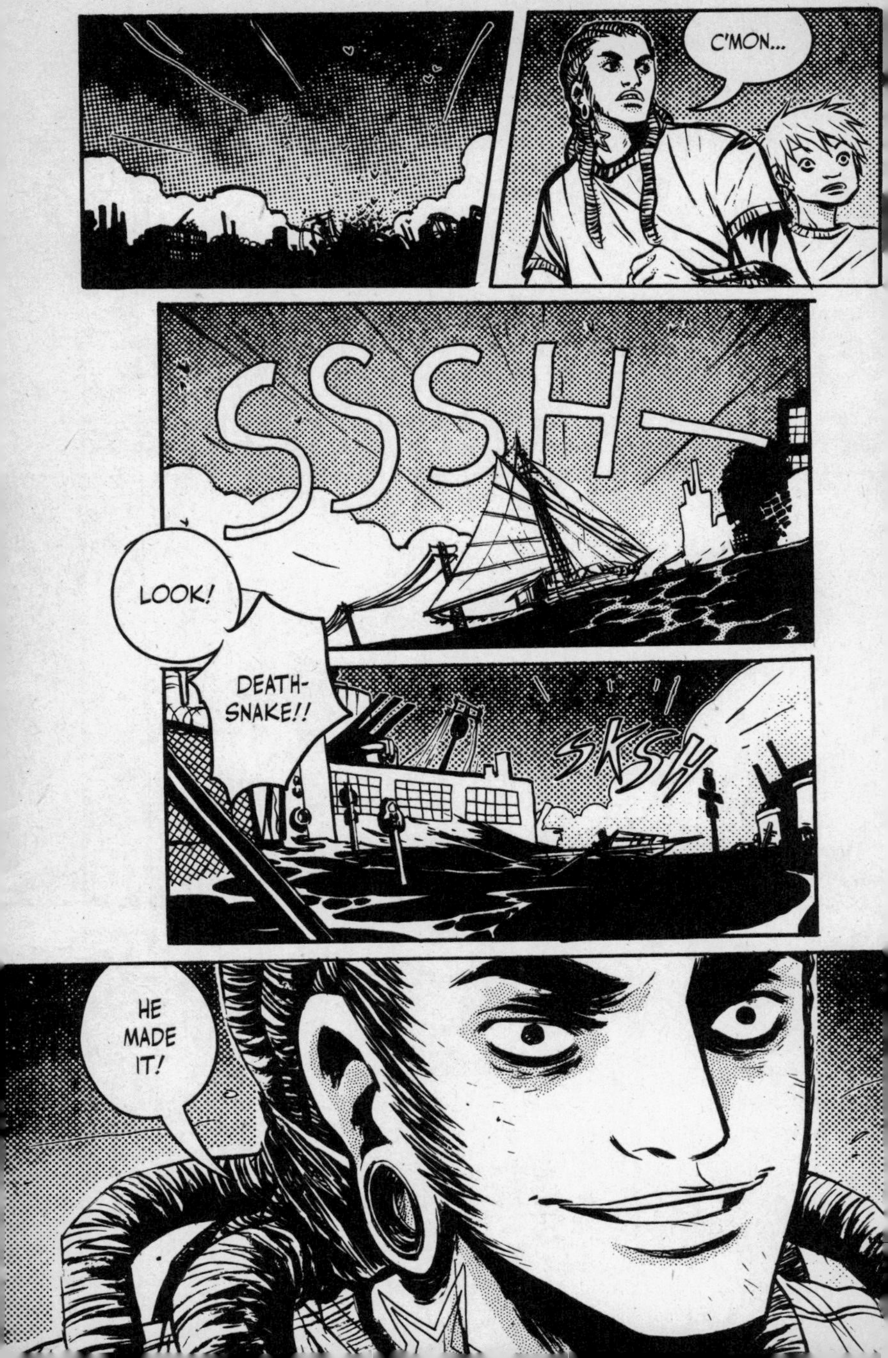
C'MON...
SSSH--
LOOK!
DEATH-SNAKE!!
SKSH
HE MADE IT!

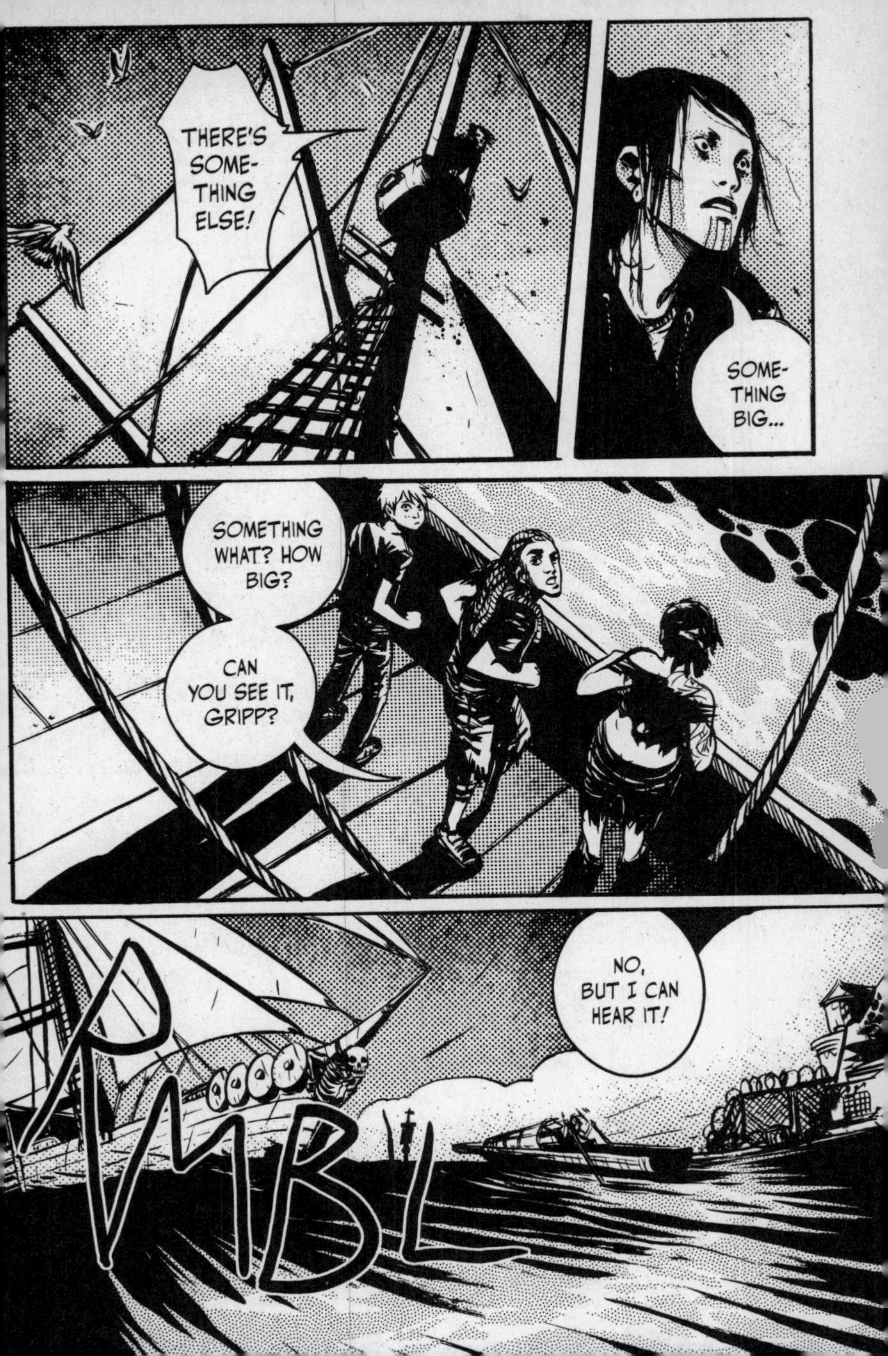
THERE'S SOME-THING ELSE!
SOME-THING BIG...
SOMETHING WHAT? HOW BIG?
CAN YOU SEE IT, GRIPP?
NO, BUT I CAN HEAR IT!
RMBL

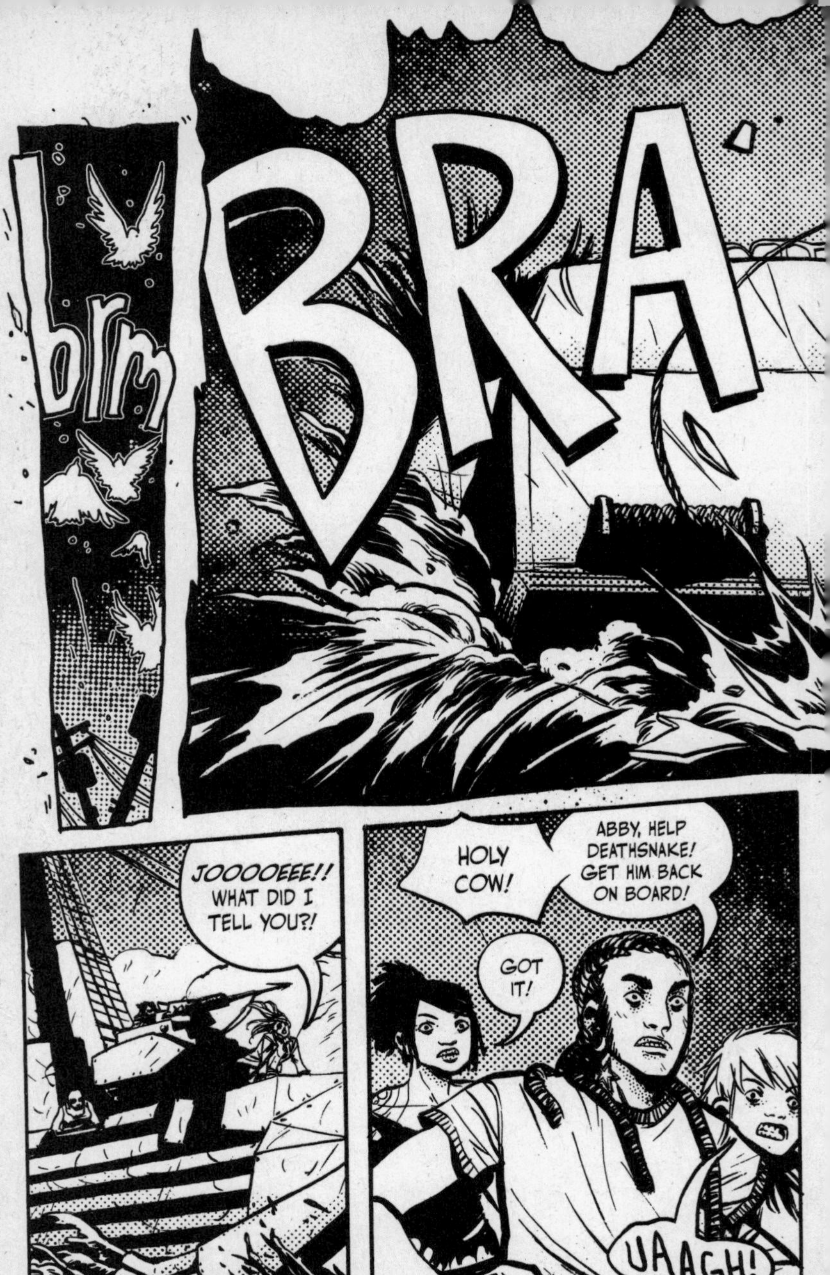
brm
BRA
JOOOOEEE!! WHAT DID I TELL YOU?!
HOLY COW!
ABBY, HELP DEATHSNAKE! GET HIM BACK ON BOARD!
GOT IT!
UAAGH!

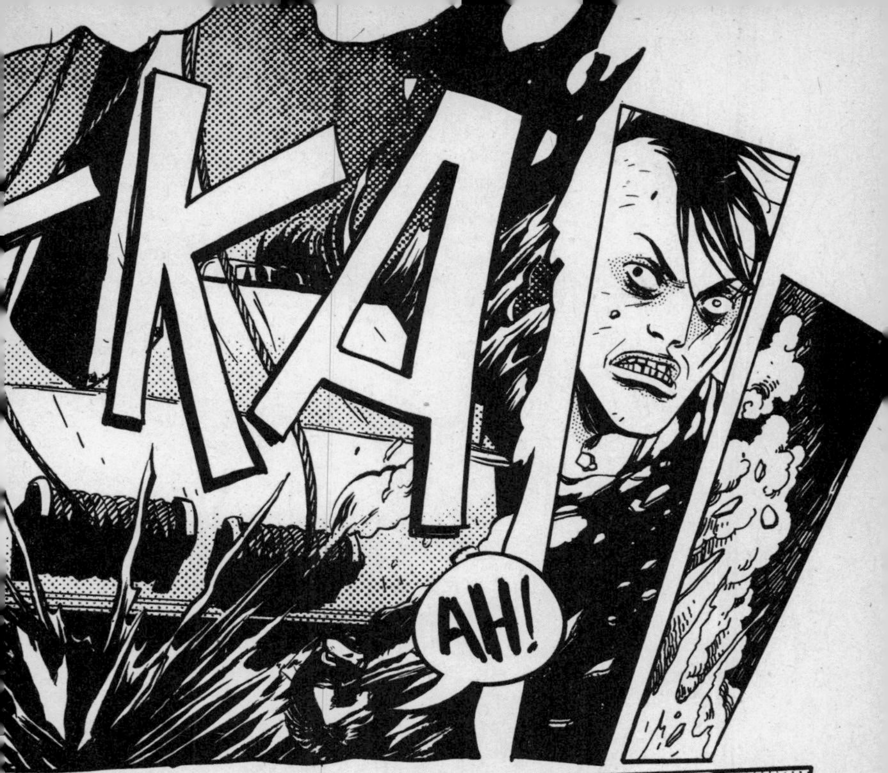
KA
AH!

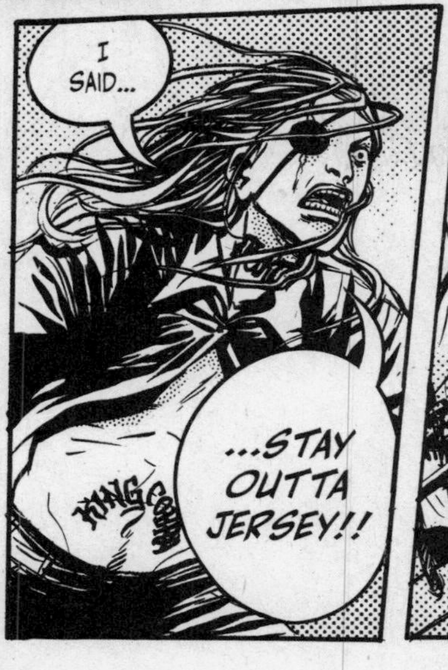
I SAID...
...STAY OUTTA JERSEY!!
KING COBRA

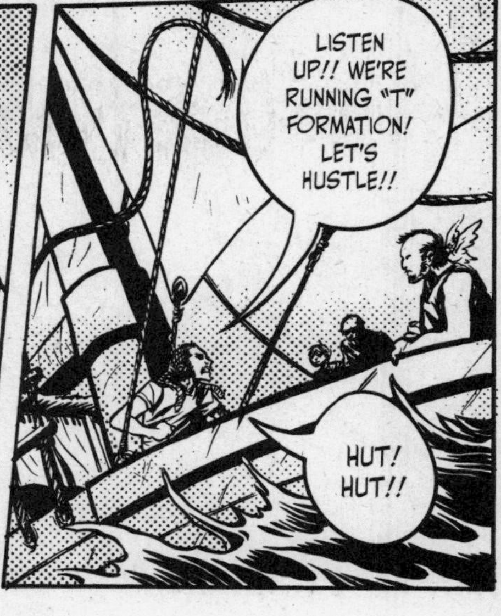
LISTEN UP!! WE'RE RUNNING "T" FORMATION! LET'S HUSTLE!!
HUT! HUT!!

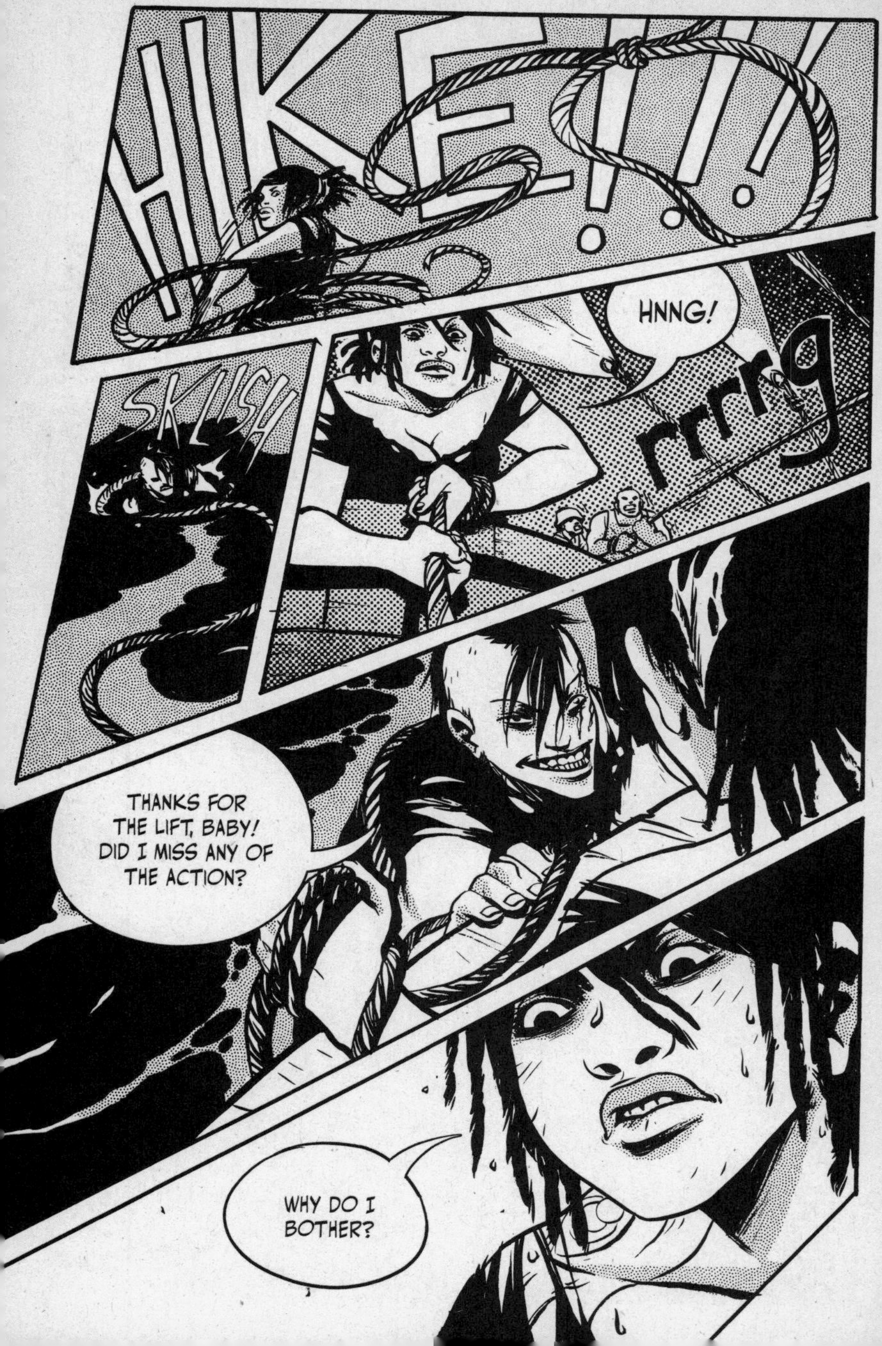
HIKE!!!
SKLISH
HNNG!
rrrrg
THANKS FOR THE LIFT, BABY! DID I MISS ANY OF THE ACTION?
WHY DO I BOTHER?

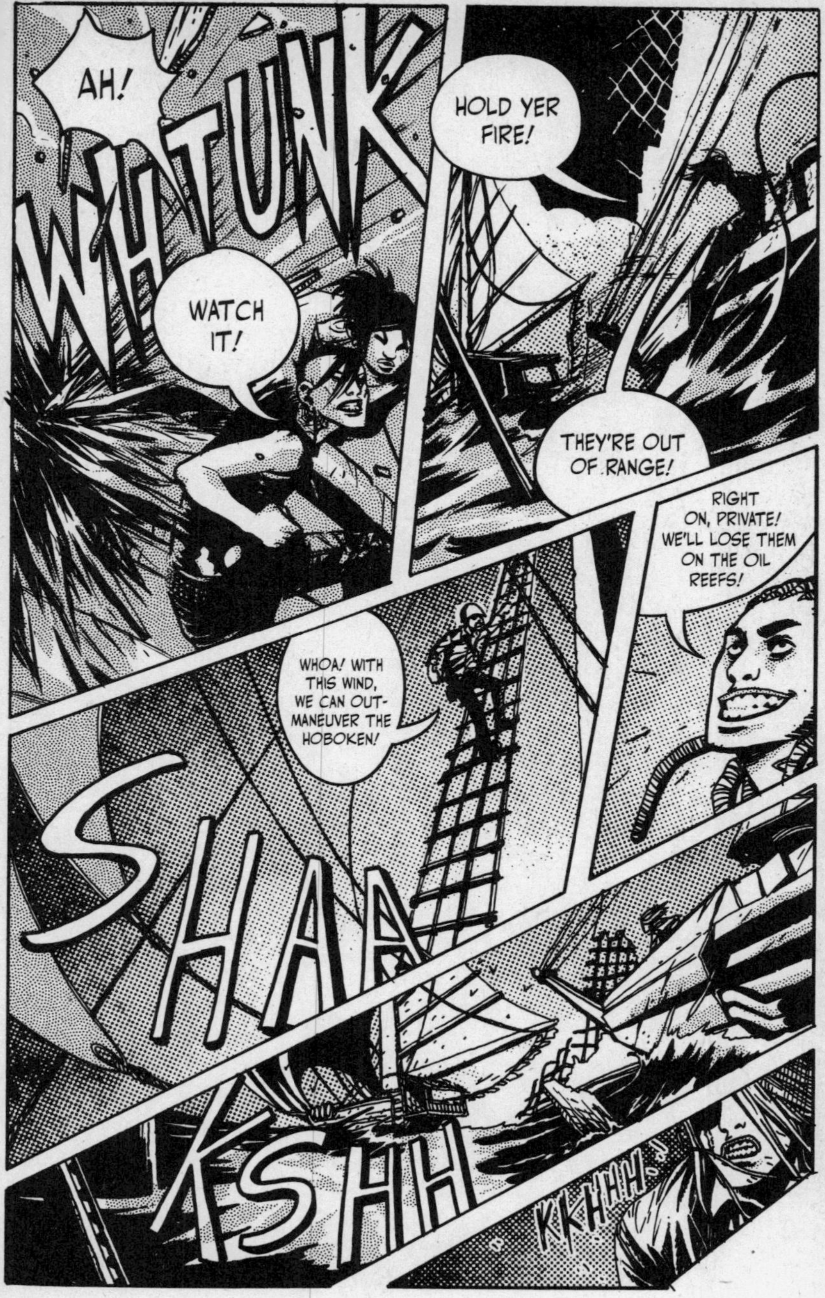
AH!
WHTUNK
HOLD YER FIRE!
WATCH IT!
THEY'RE OUT OF RANGE!
WHOA! WITH THIS WIND, WE CAN OUT-MANEUVER THE HOBOKEN!
SHAA
RIGHT ON, PRIVATE! WE'LL LOSE THEM ON THE OIL REEFS!
KSHH
KKHHH

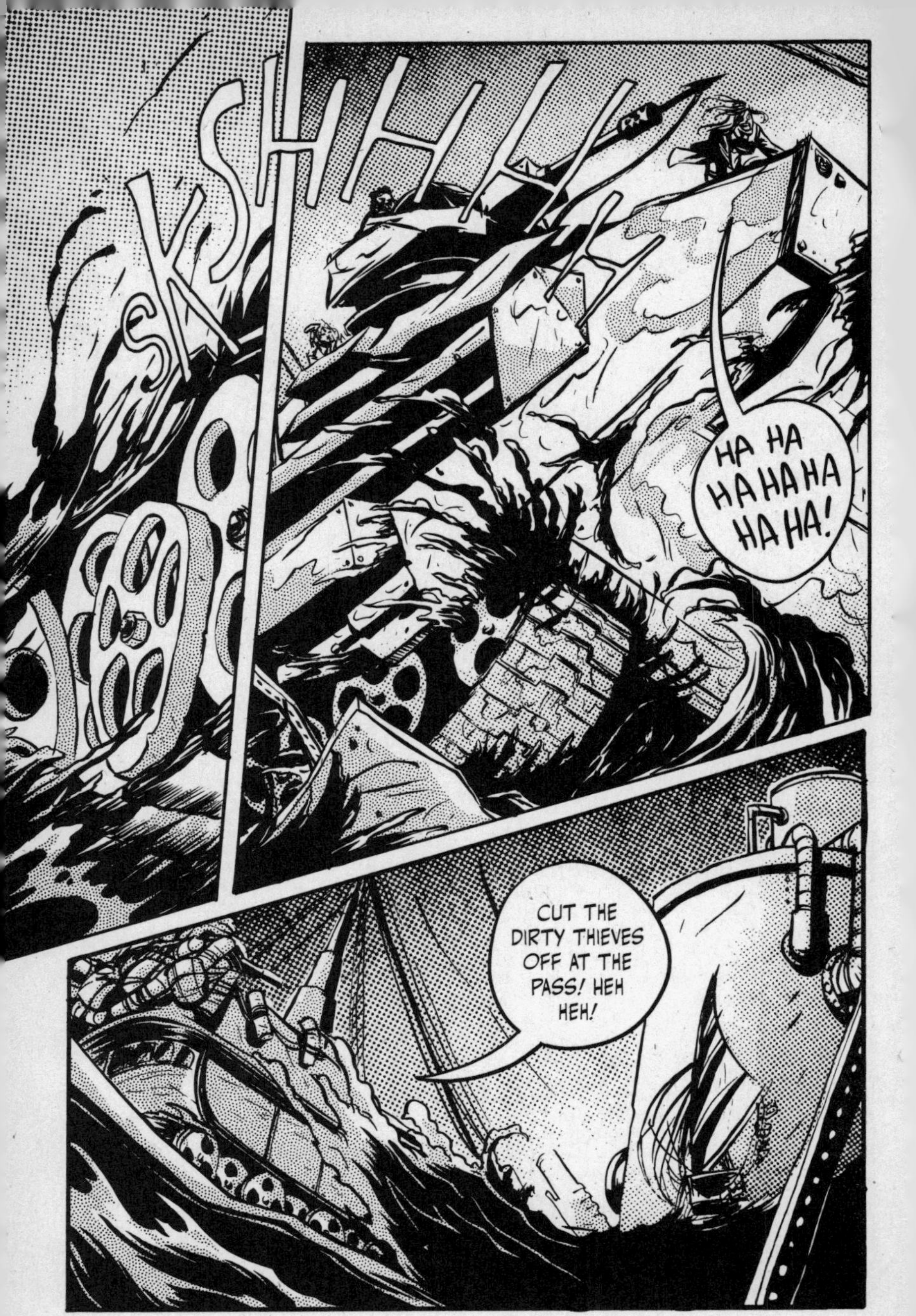
SKSSHHHHHHH
HA HA HA HA HA HA HA!
CUT THE DIRTY THIEVES OFF AT THE PASS! HEH HEH!

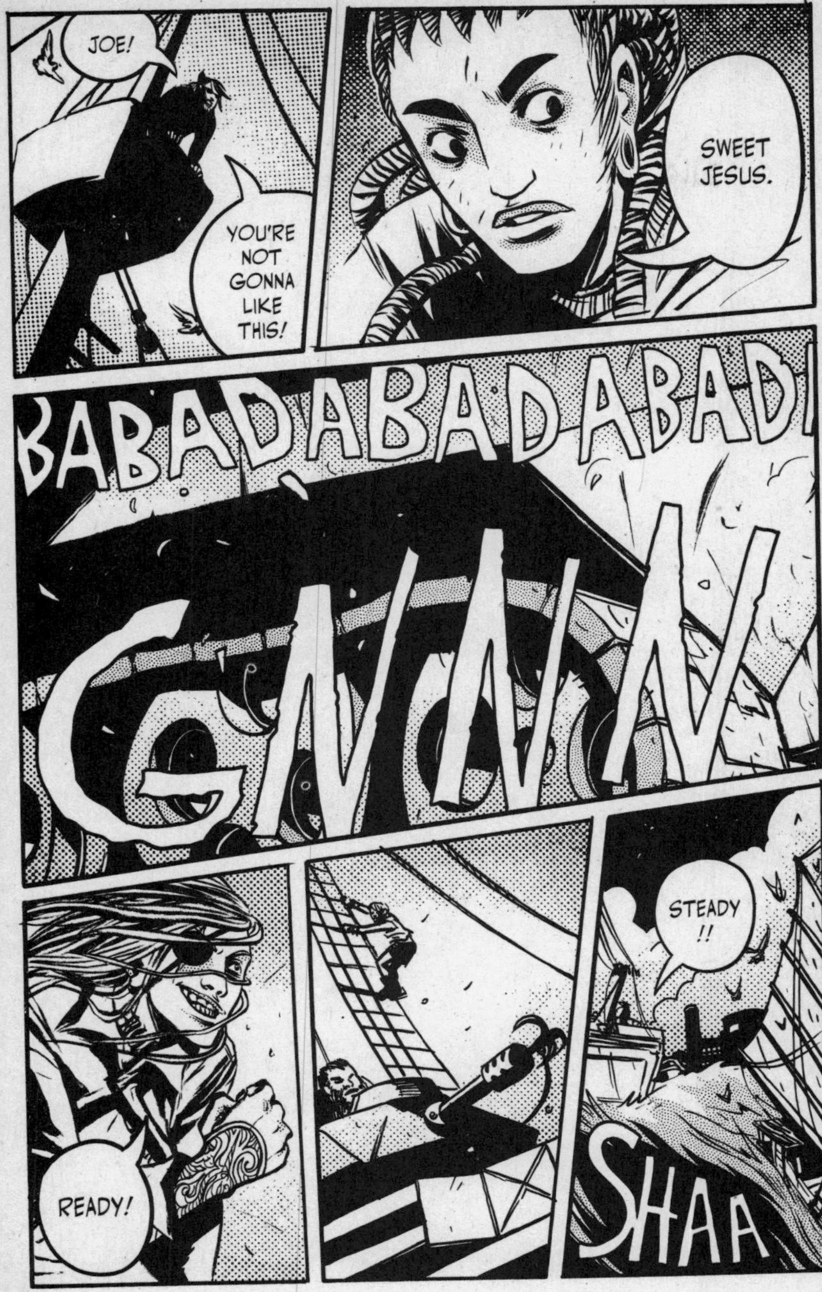
JOE!
YOU'RE NOT GONNA LIKE THIS!
SWEET JESUS.
BABADABADABADI
GWW
READY!
STEADY !!
SHAA

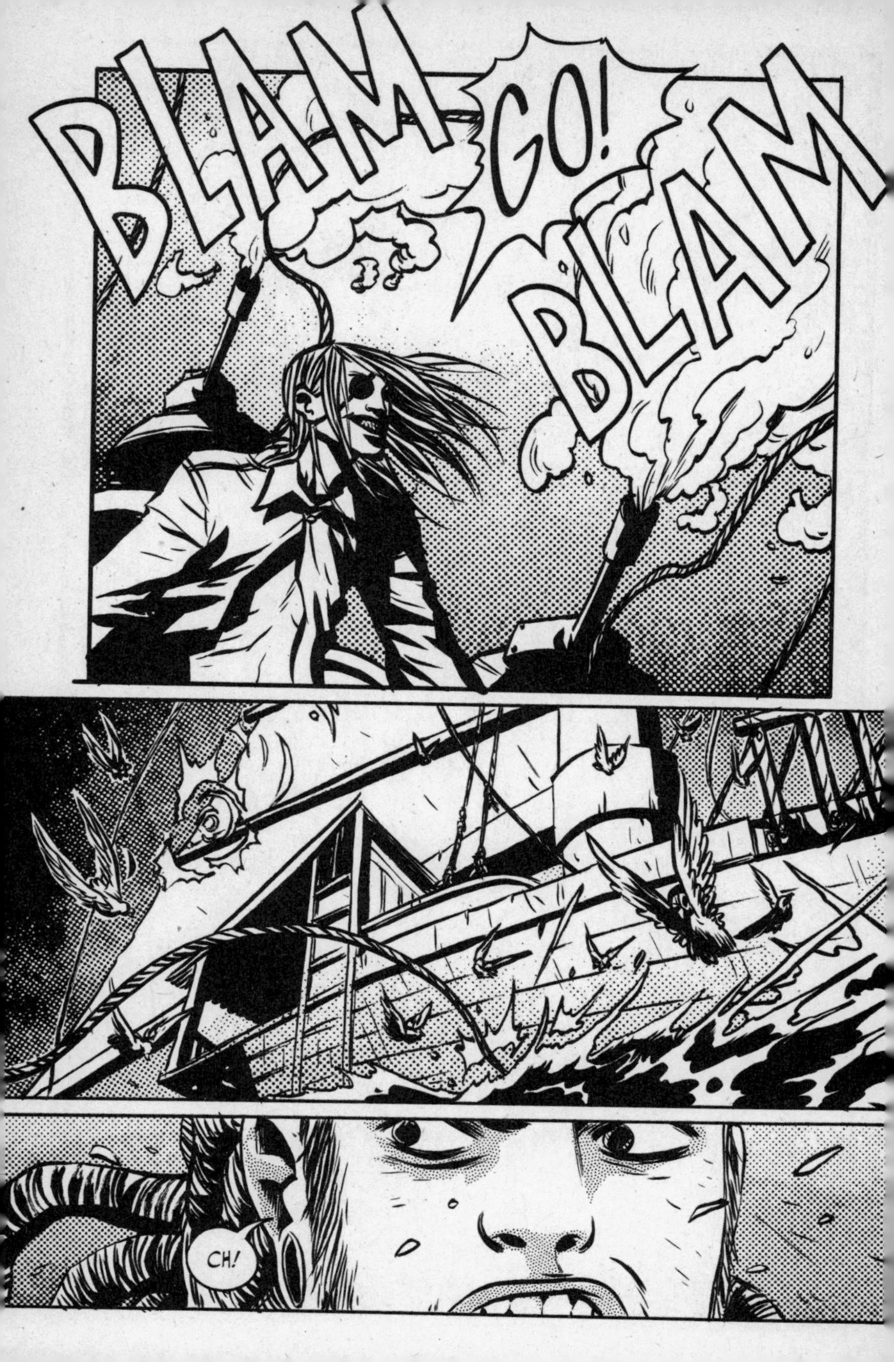
BLAM
GO!
BLAM
CH!

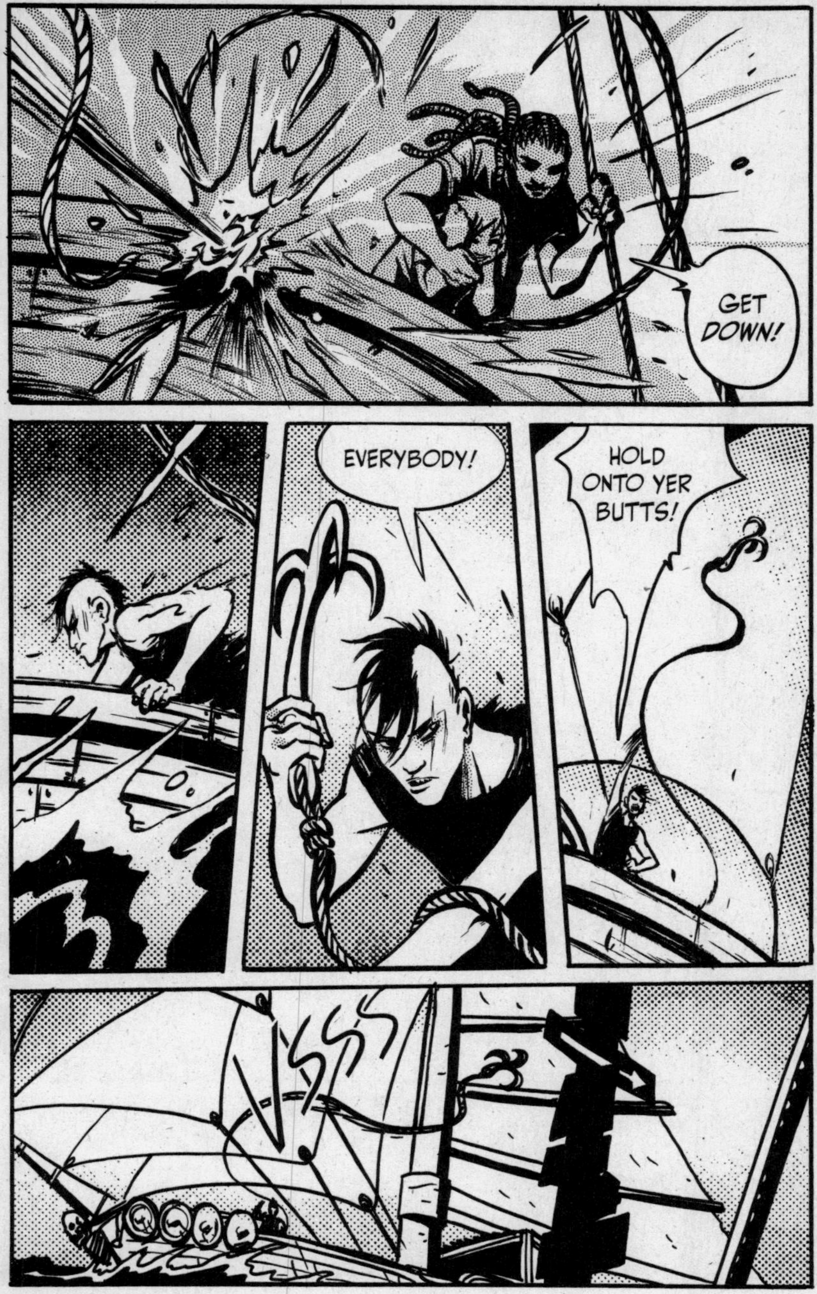
GET DOWN!
EVERYBODY!
HOLD ONTO YER BUTTS!
VSSS

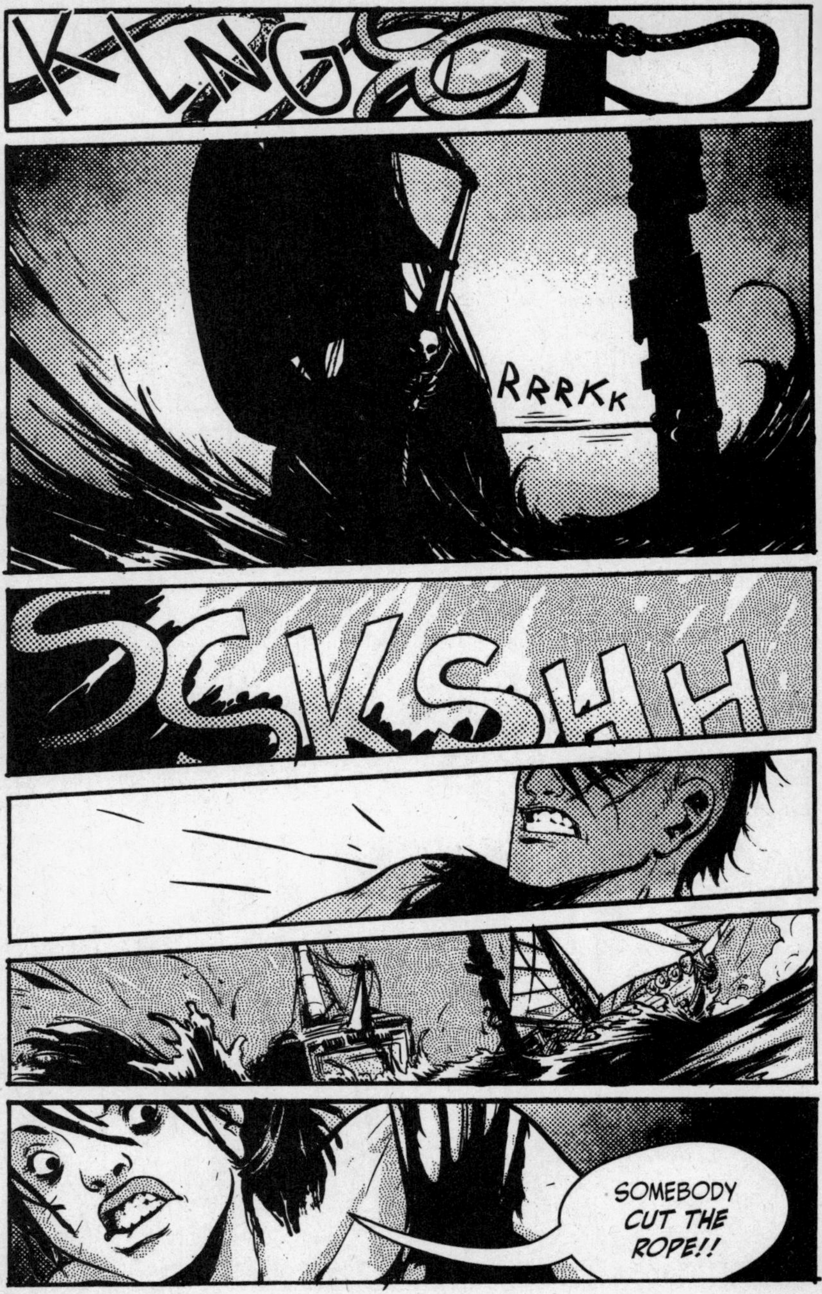
KLNG
RRRKk
SCKSHH
SOMEBODY CUT THE ROPE!!

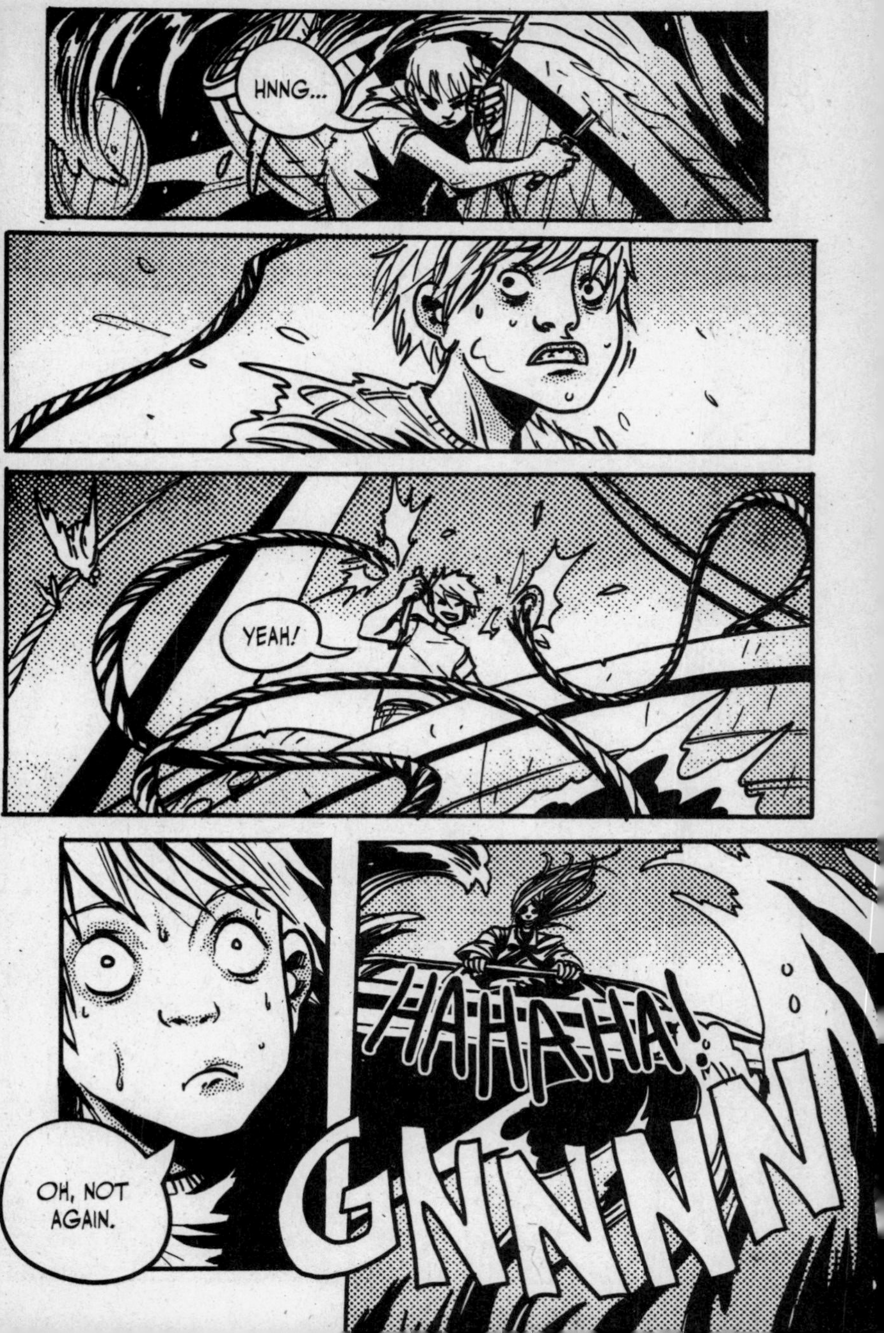
HNNG...
YEAH!
OH, NOT AGAIN.
HAHAHA!
GNNNN

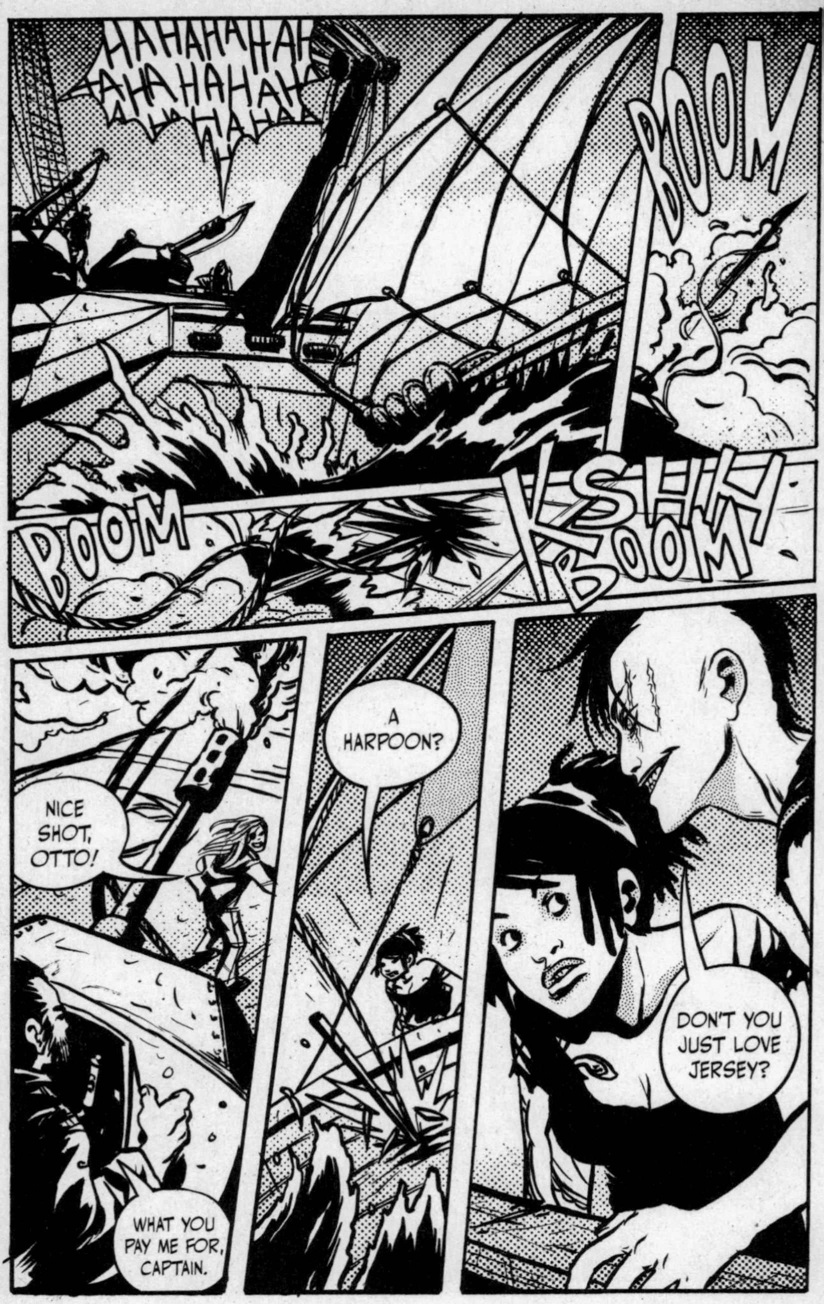

HAHAHAHAHAH
AHAHAHAHAH
BOOM
BOOM
KSHH
BOOM
NICE SHOT, OTTO!
WHAT YOU PAY ME FOR, CAPTAIN.
A HARPOON?
DON'T YOU JUST LOVE JERSEY?

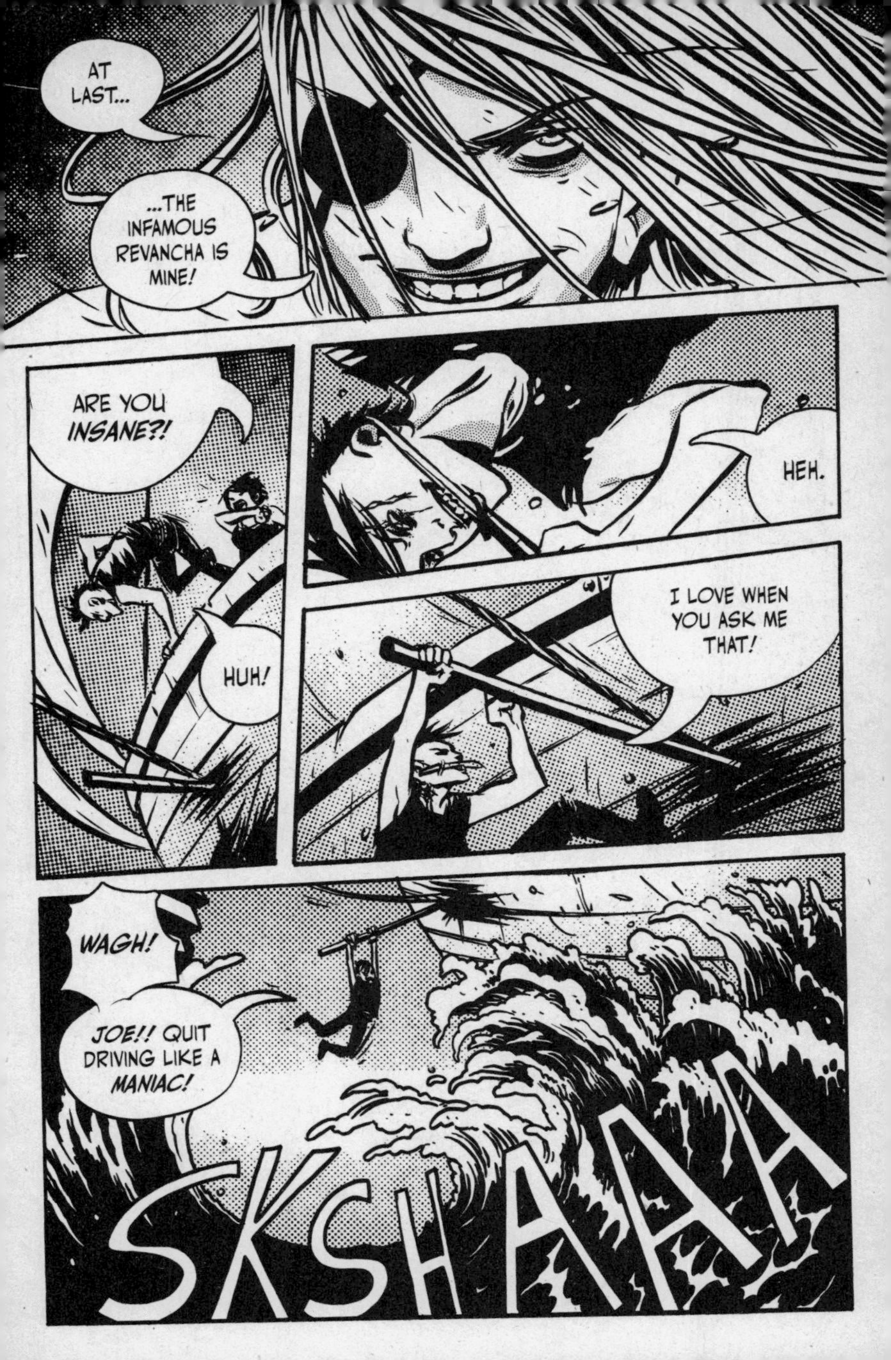
AT LAST...
...THE INFAMOUS REVANCHA IS MINE!
ARE YOU INSANE?!
HUH!
HEH.
I LOVE WHEN YOU ASK ME THAT!
WAGH!
JOE!! QUIT DRIVING LIKE A MANIAC!
SKSHAAAA

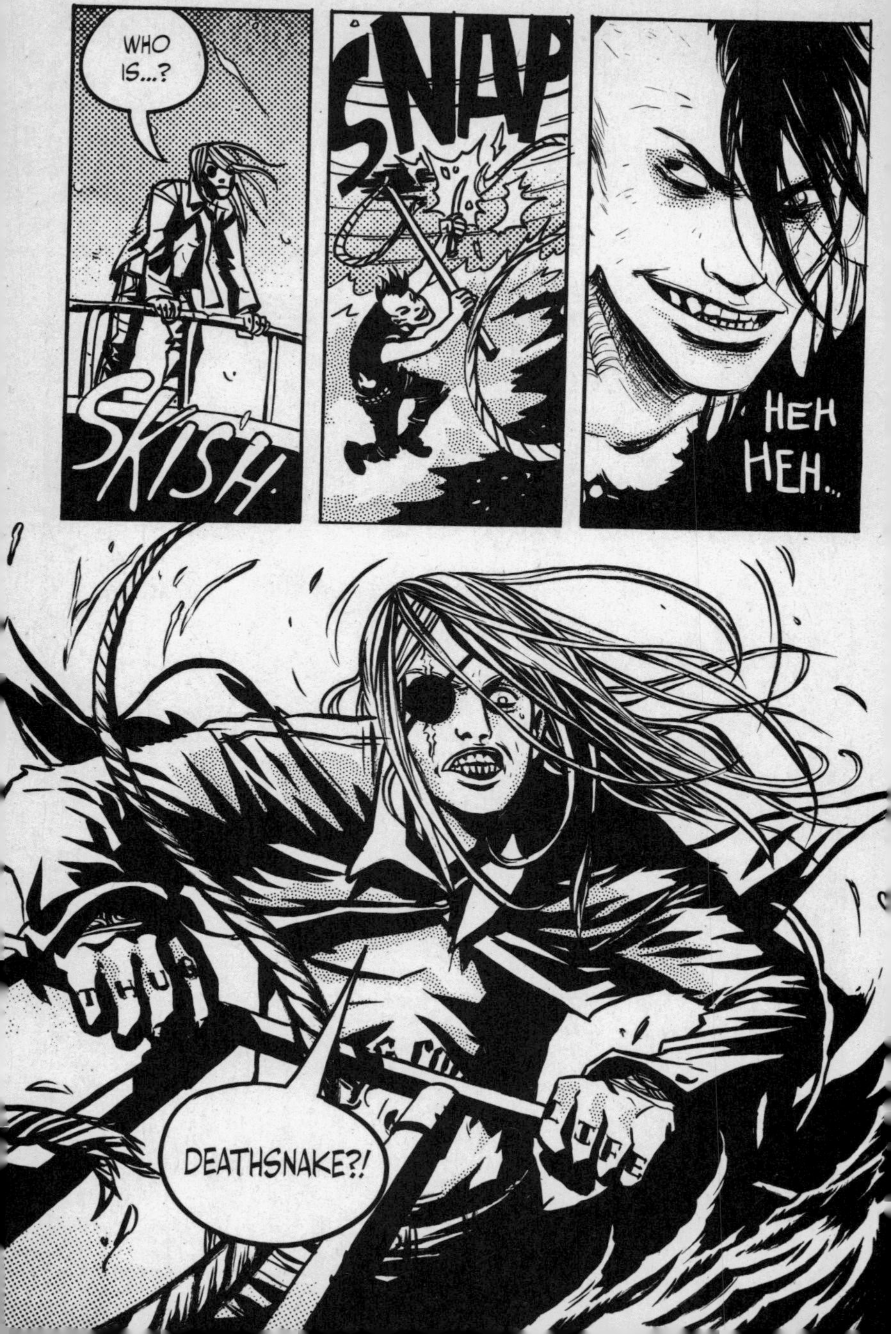
WHO IS...?
SKISH
SNAP
HEH HEH...
DEATHSNAKE?!

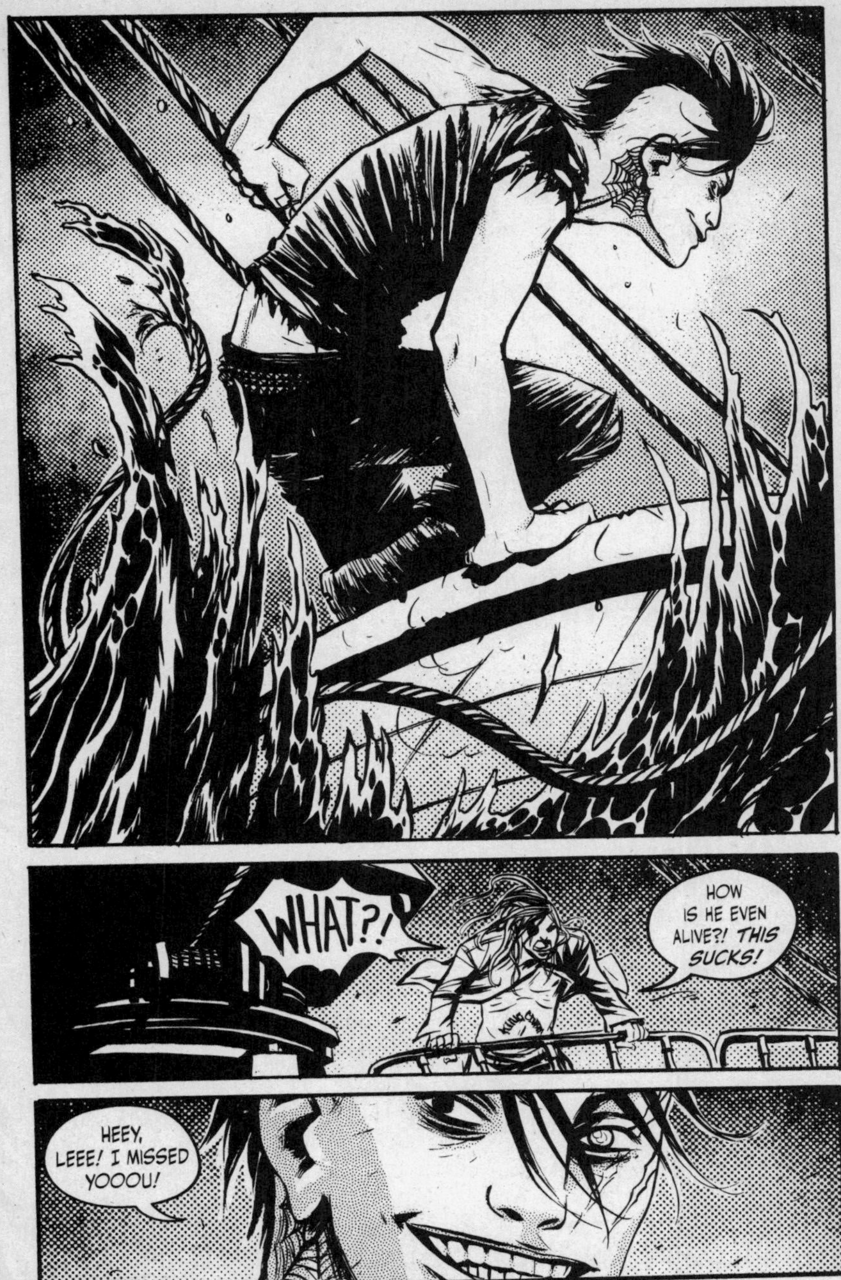
WHAT?!
HOW IS HE EVEN ALIVE?! THIS SUCKS!
HEEY, LEEE! I MISSED YOOOU!

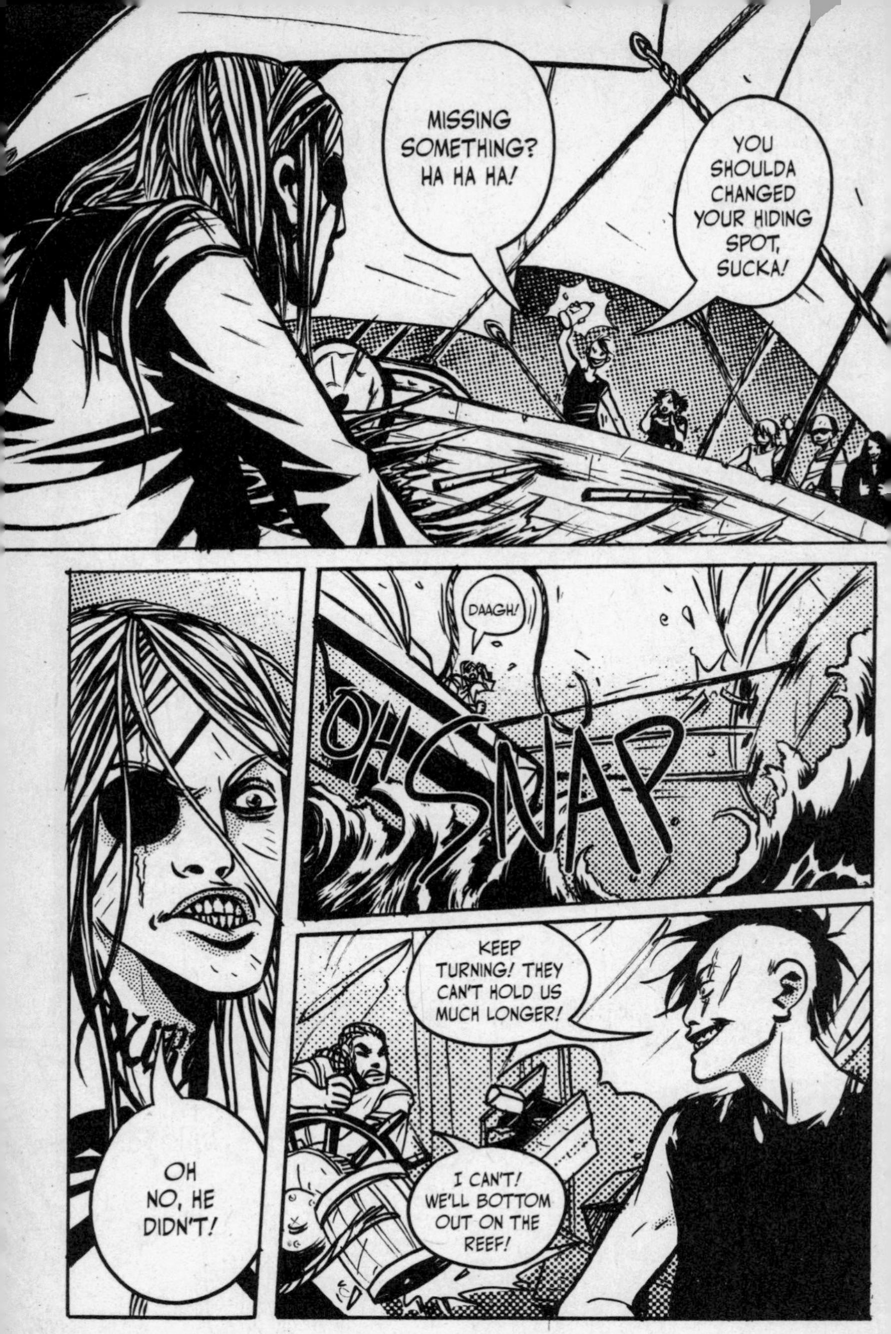
MISSING SOMETHING? HA HA HA!
YOU SHOULDA CHANGED YOUR HIDING SPOT, SUCKA!
OH NO, HE DIDN'T!
DAAGH!
OH SNAP
KEEP TURNING! THEY CAN'T HOLD US MUCH LONGER!
I CAN'T! WE'LL BOTTOM OUT ON THE REEF!

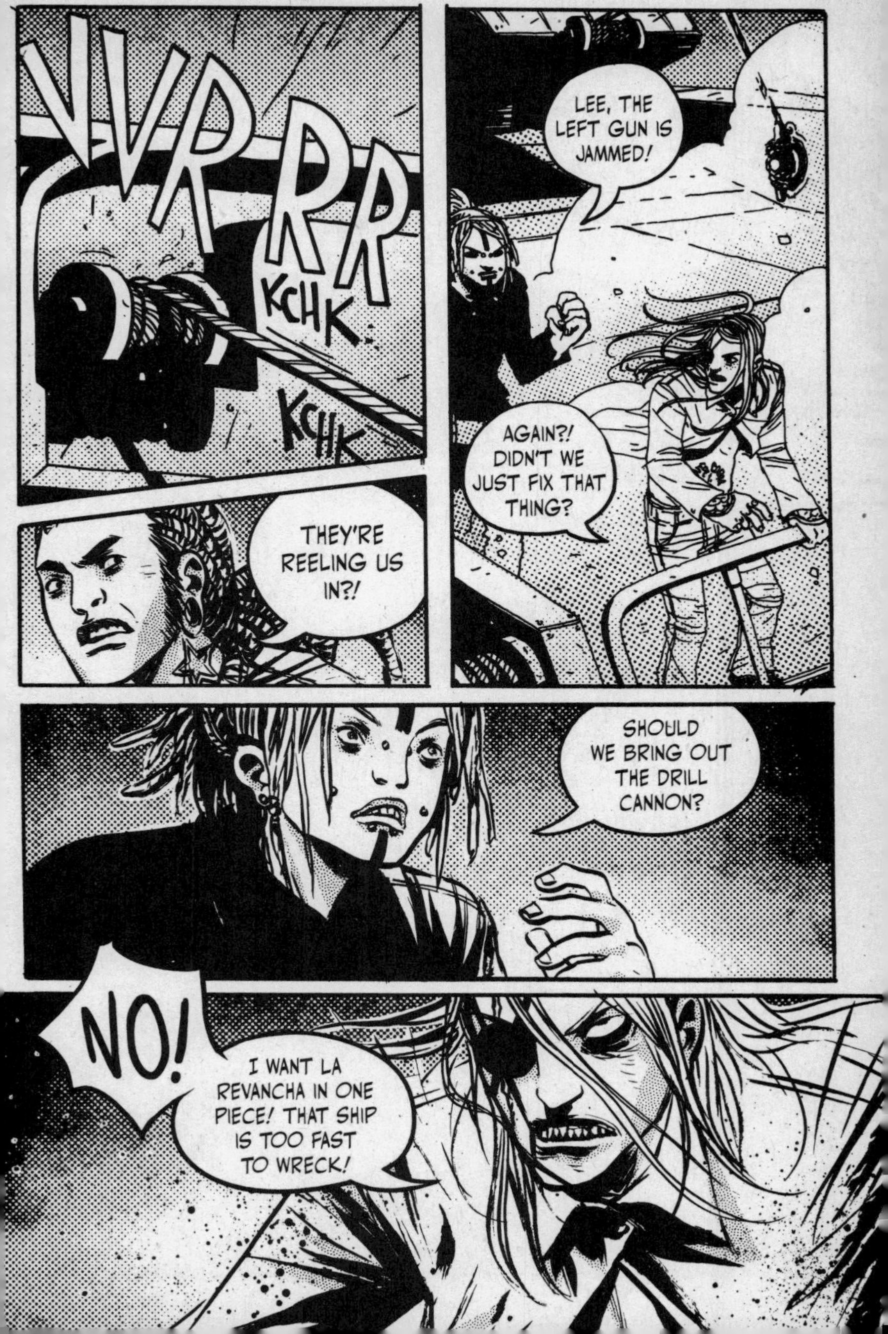
VVRRR
KCHK
KCHK
THEY'RE REELING US IN?!
LEE, THE LEFT GUN IS JAMMED!
AGAIN?! DIDN'T WE JUST FIX THAT THING?
SHOULD WE BRING OUT THE DRILL CANNON?
NO!
I WANT LA REVANCHA IN ONE PIECE! THAT SHIP IS TOO FAST TO WRECK!

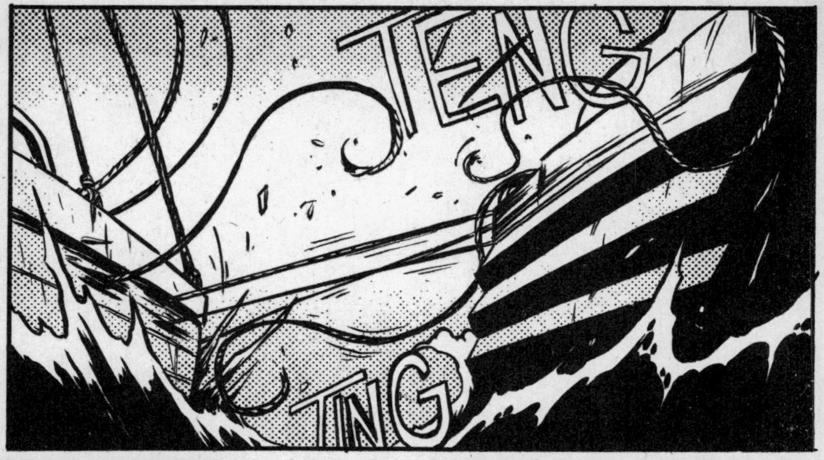
TENG
TNG

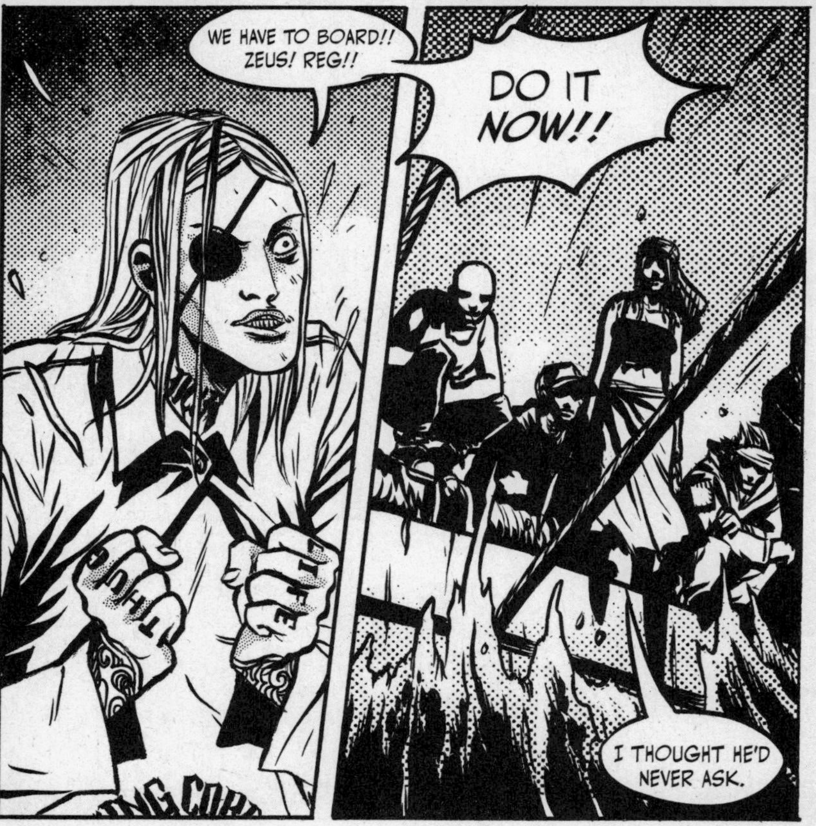
WE HAVE TO BOARD!! ZEUS! REG!!
DO IT NOW!!
I THOUGHT HE'D NEVER ASK.

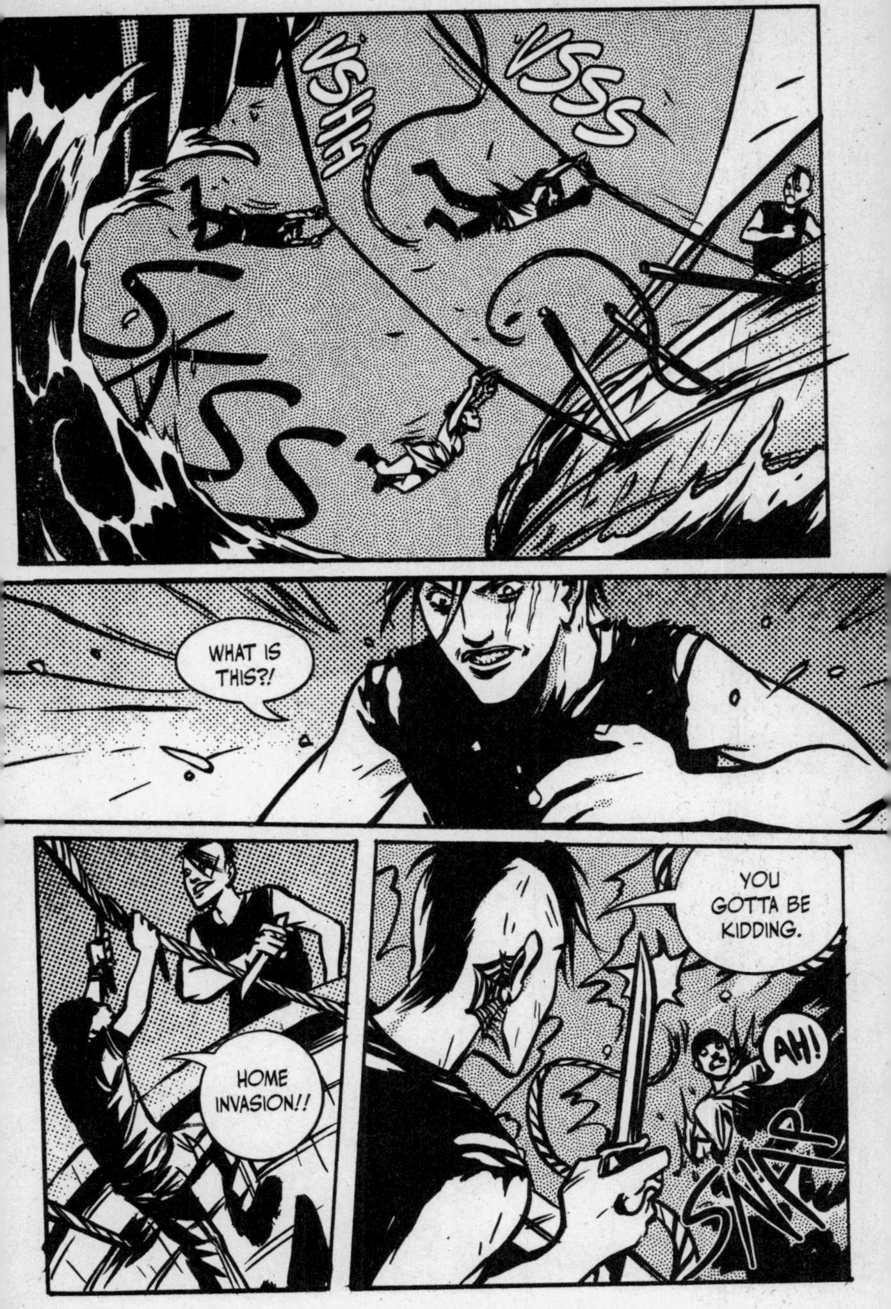
VSHH
VSSS
SSS
WHAT IS THIS?!
HOME INVASION!!
YOU GOTTA BE KIDDING.
AH!
SNAP

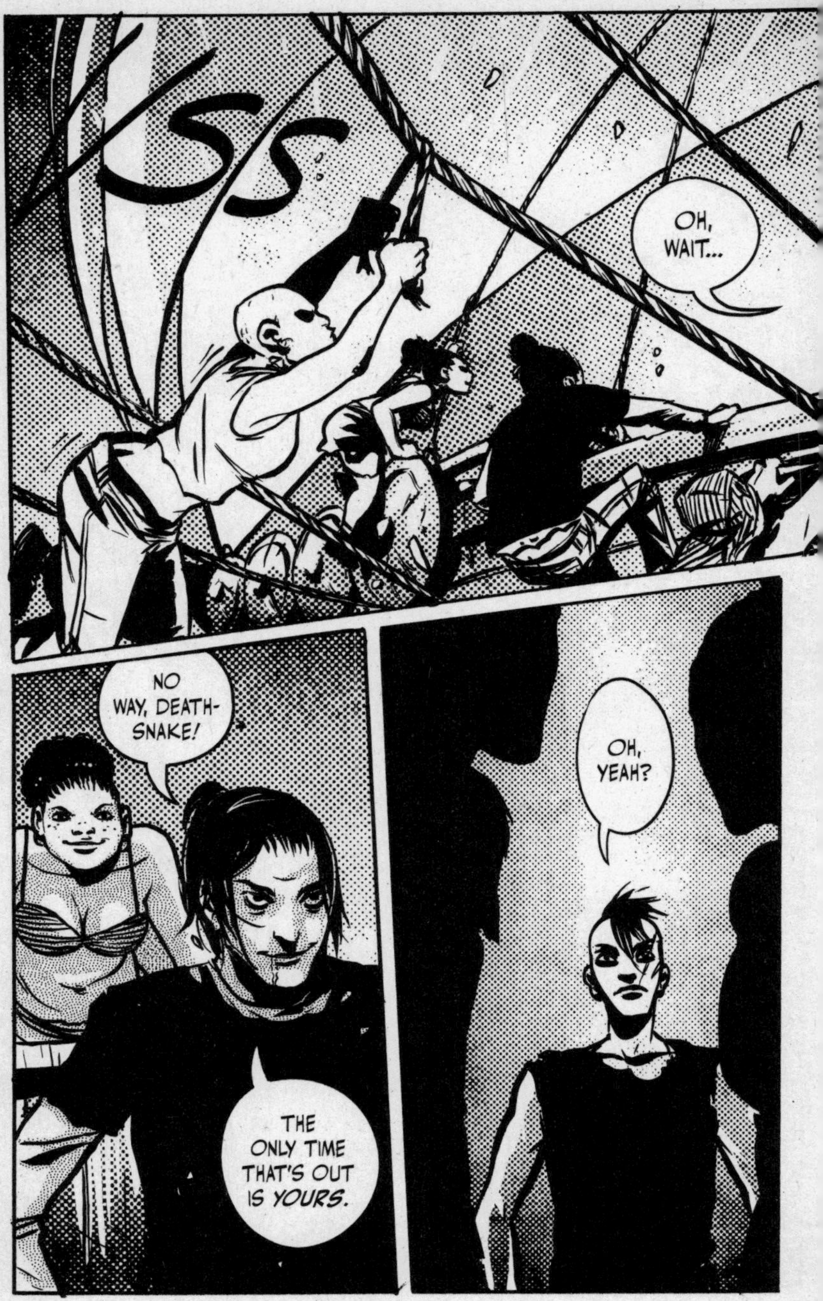
SS
OH, WAIT...
NO WAY, DEATH-SNAKE!
THE ONLY TIME THAT'S OUT IS *YOURS*.
OH, YEAH?

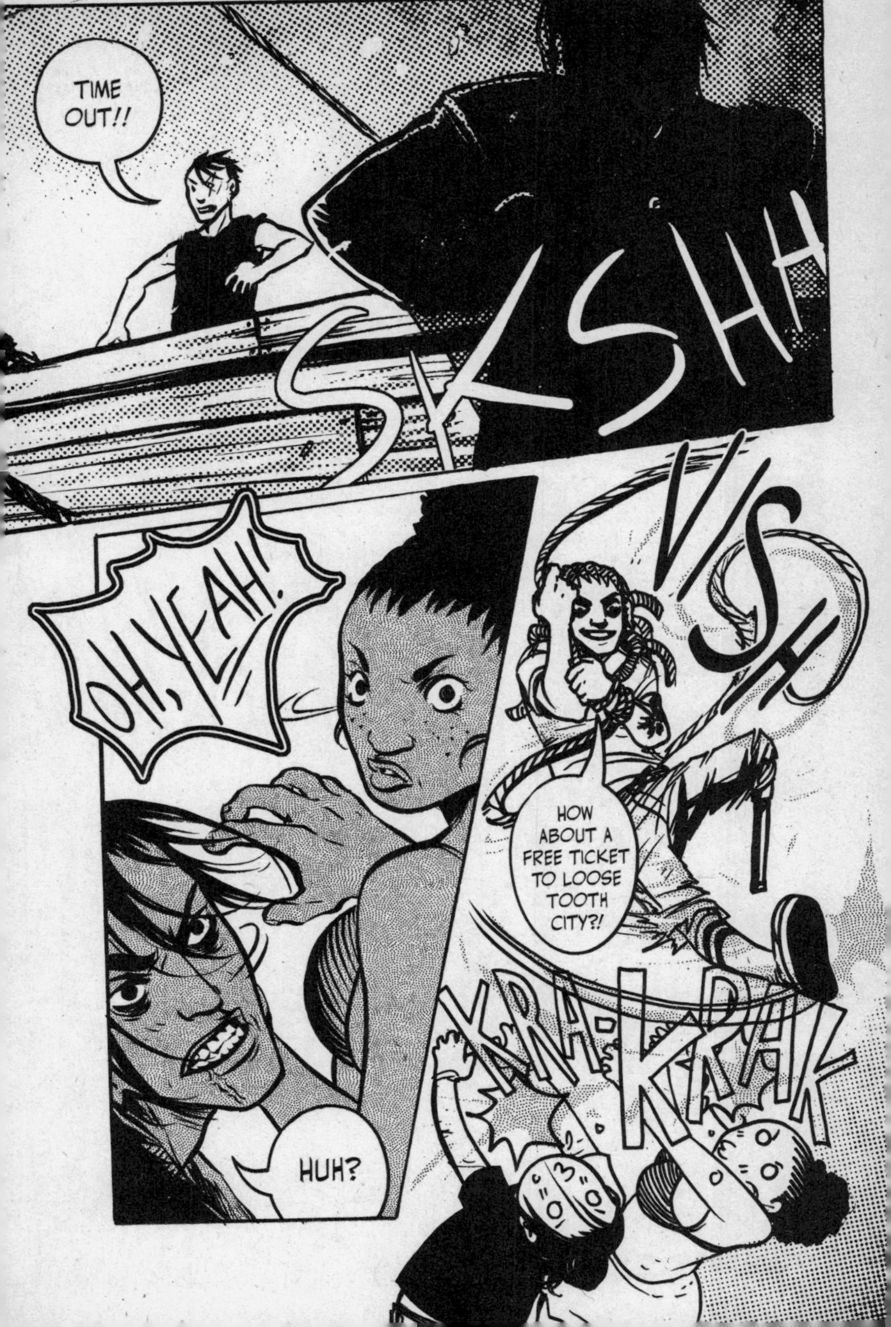
TIME OUT!!
SKSHH
OH, YEAH!
HUH?
VISH
HOW ABOUT A FREE TICKET TO LOOSE TOOTH CITY?!
KRAK-KRAK

ALL RIGHT! WHO WANTS SOME?!

THEY'RE MULTIPLYING!

LORDA MERCY! LEE HAS A CLONING MACHINE?

WAIT A MINUTE! THERE'S LIKE A MILLION OF THEM!

HAHA

HA! IMAGINE LITTLE LEES RUNNING AROUND!

WHAT A NIGHTMARE!

AH!

WHUD

HUH?

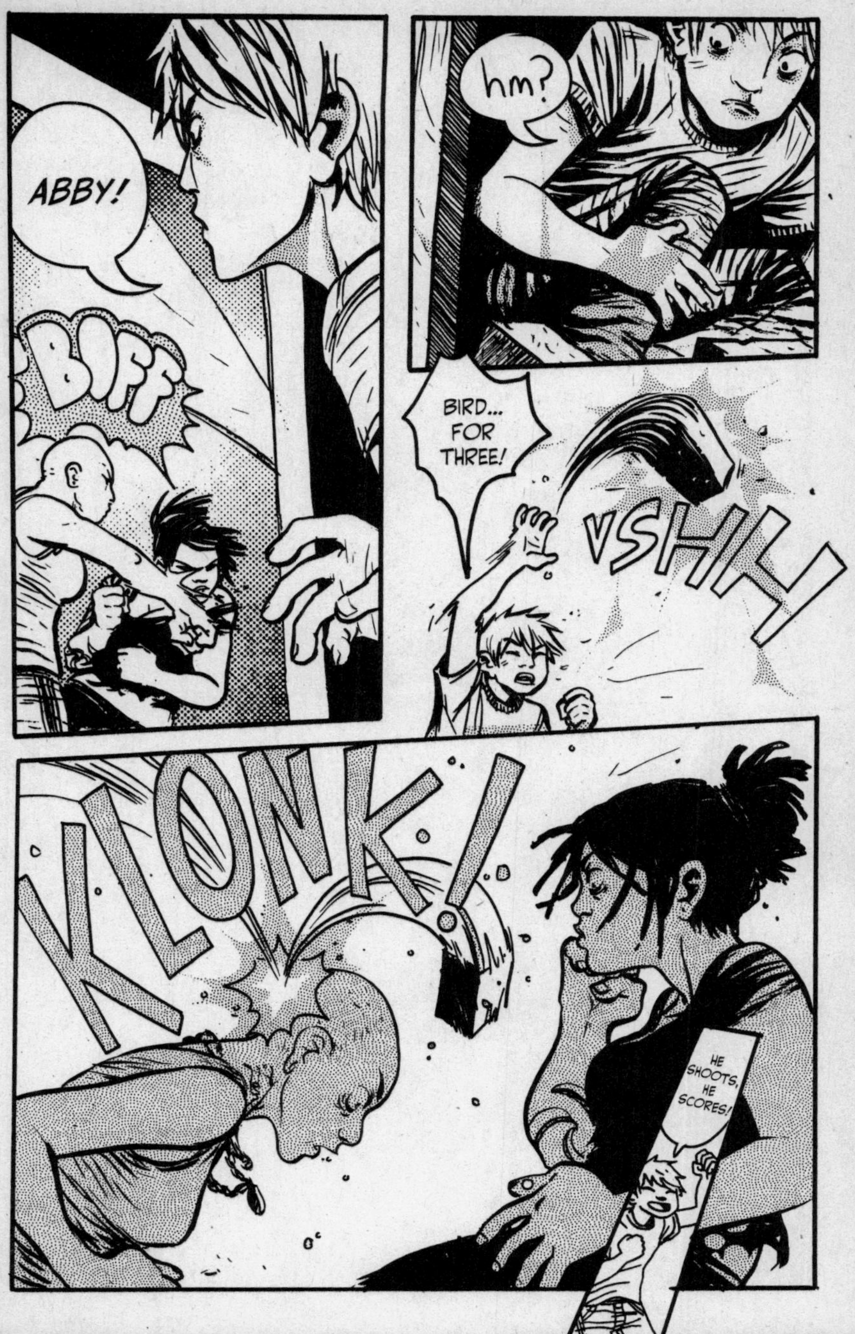
ABBY!
BIFF
hm?
BIRD... FOR THREE!
VSHHH
KLONK!
HE SHOOTS, HE SCORES!

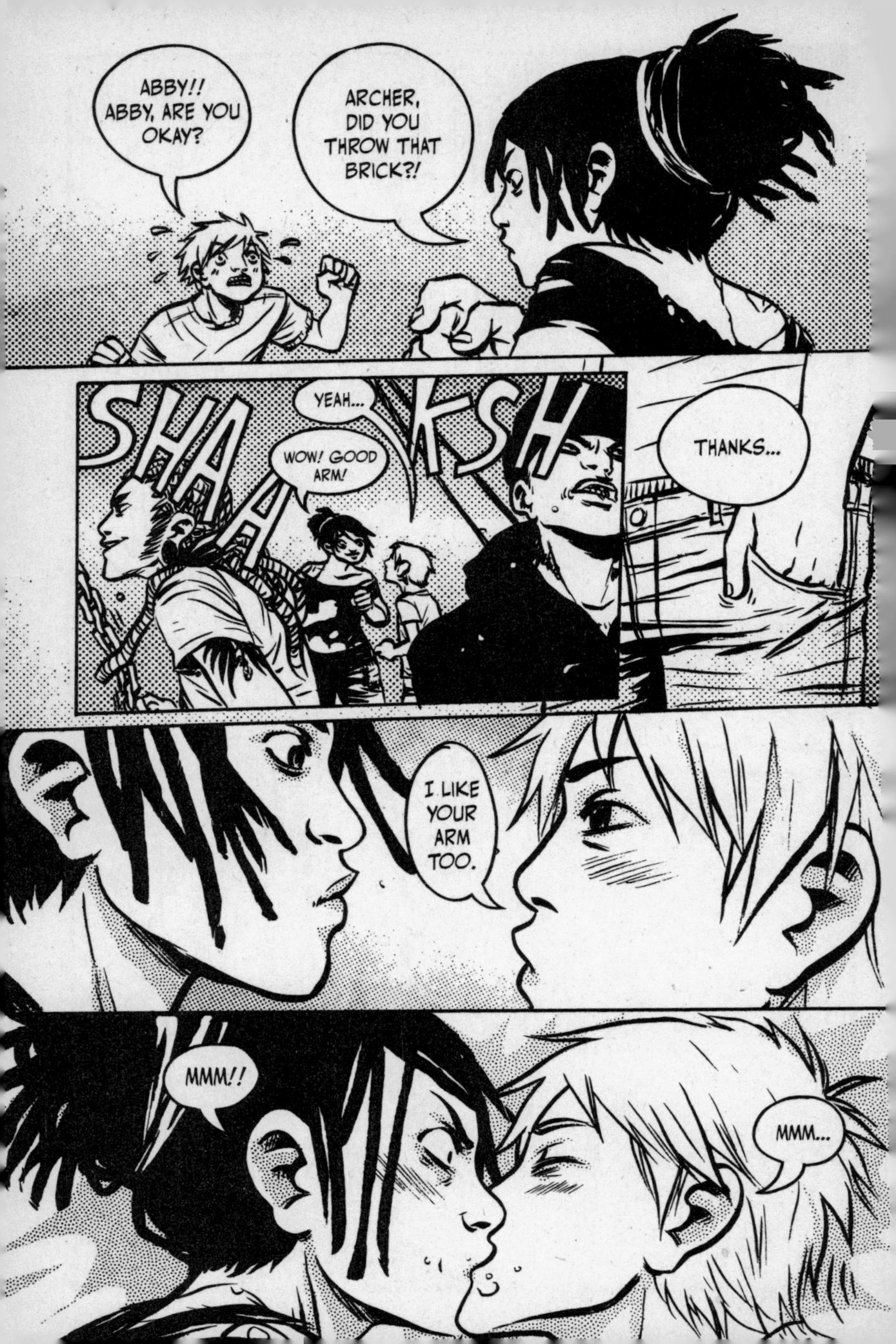
ABBY!! ABBY, ARE YOU OKAY?
ARCHER, DID YOU THROW THAT BRICK?!
SHAAAKSH
YEAH...
WOW! GOOD ARM!
THANKS...
I LIKE YOUR ARM TOO.
MMM!!
MMM...

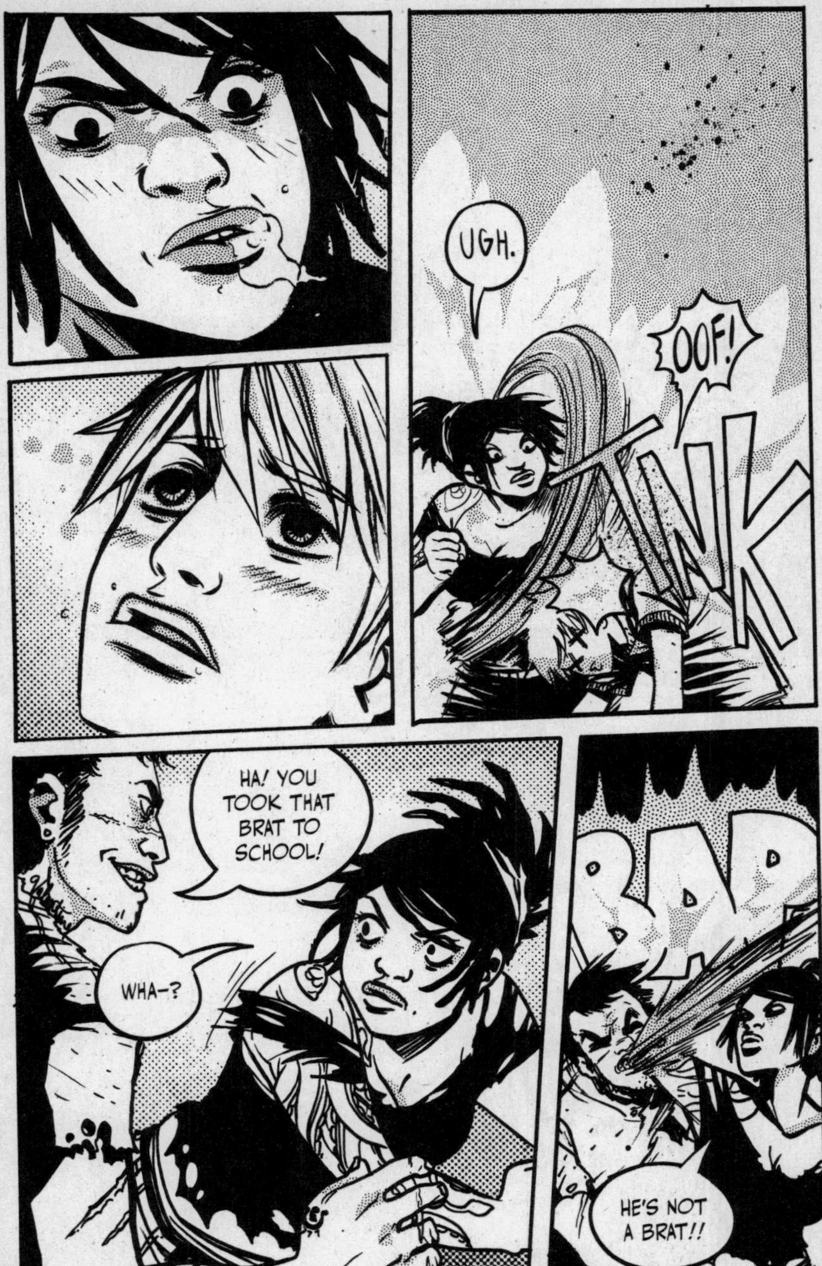
UGH.
OOF!
TINK
HA! YOU TOOK THAT BRAT TO SCHOOL!
WHA-?
HE'S NOT A BRAT!!

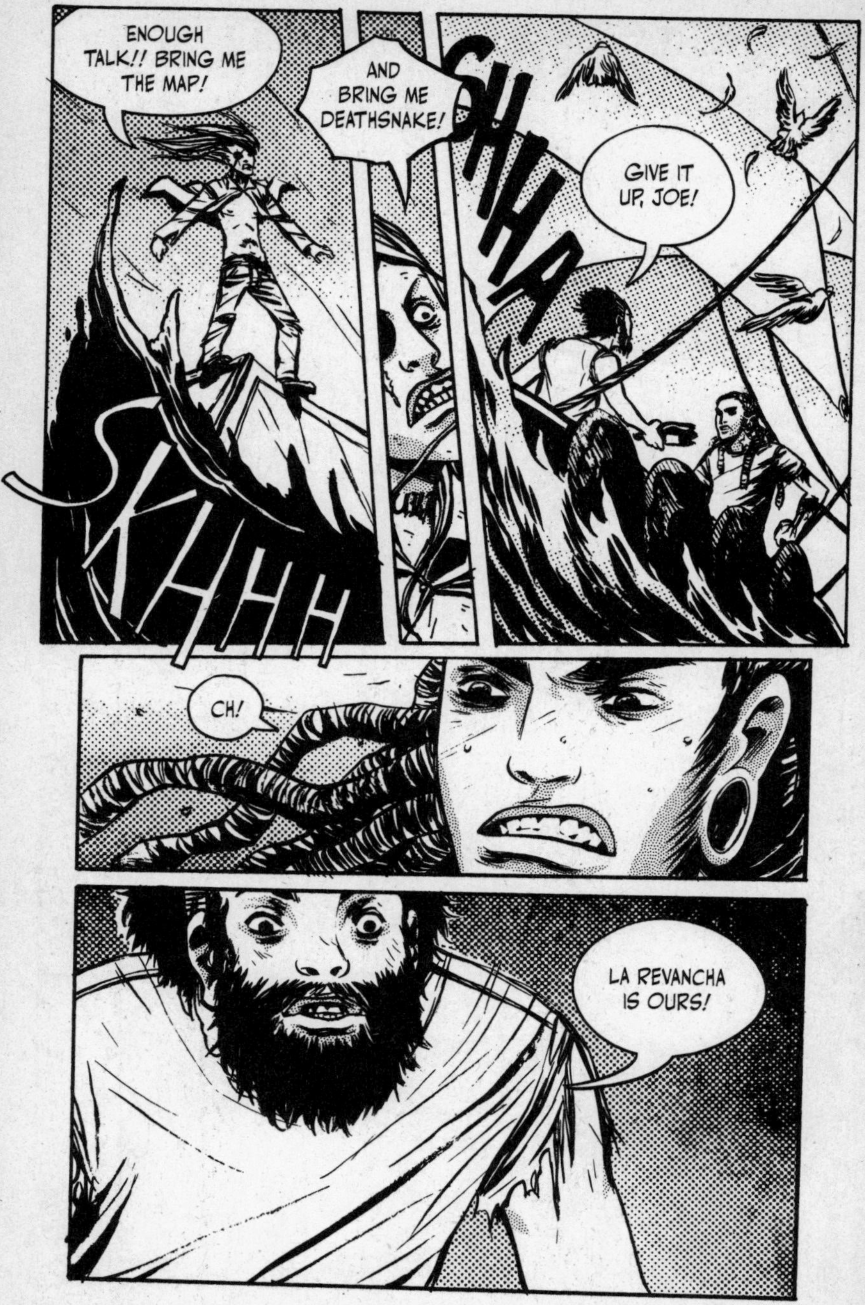
ENOUGH TALK!! BRING ME THE MAP!
SKHHH
AND BRING ME DEATHSNAKE!
SHHA
GIVE IT UP, JOE!
CH!
LA REVANCHA IS OURS!

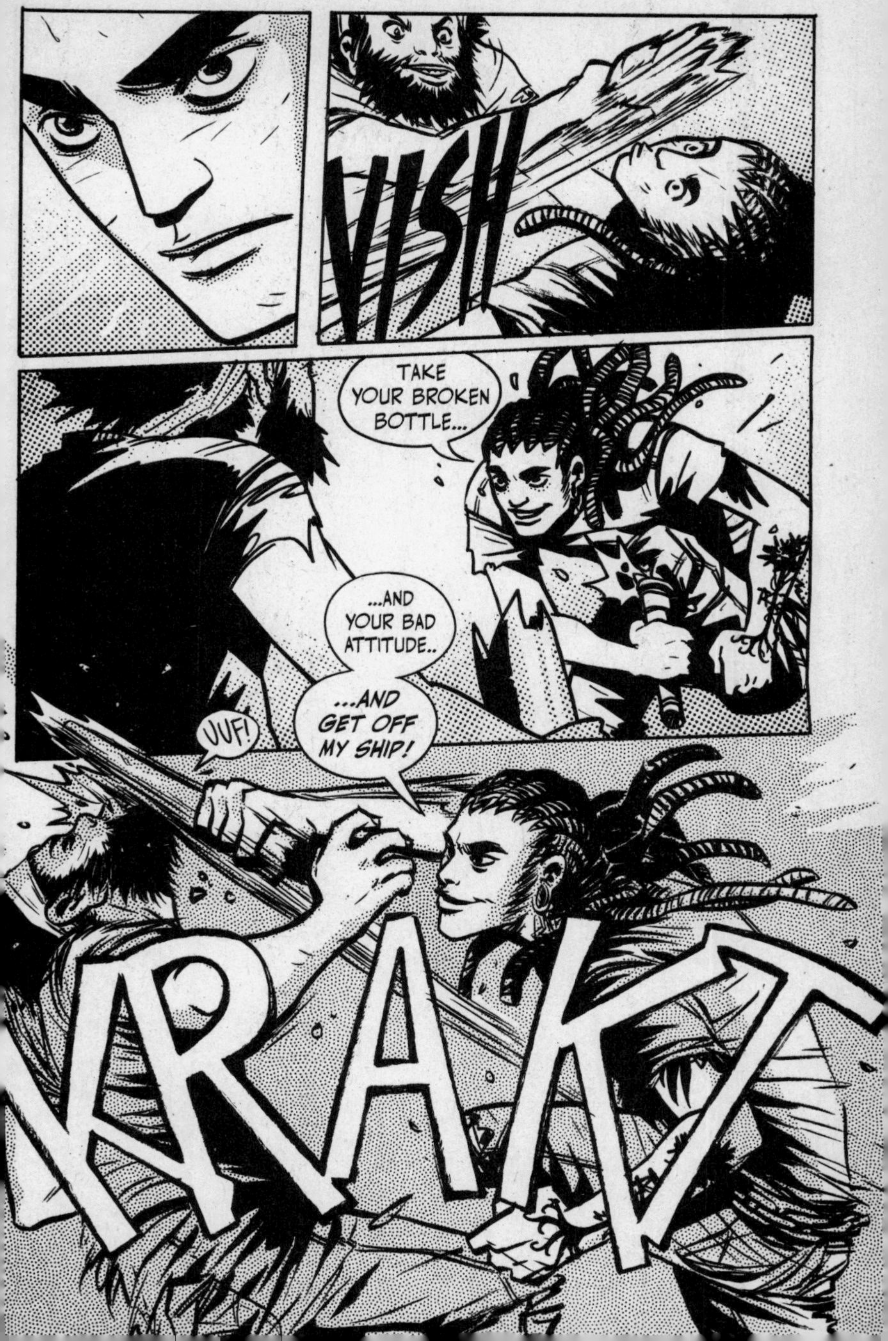
VISH
TAKE YOUR BROKEN BOTTLE...
...AND YOUR BAD ATTITUDE..
UUF!
...AND GET OFF MY SHIP!
KRAKT

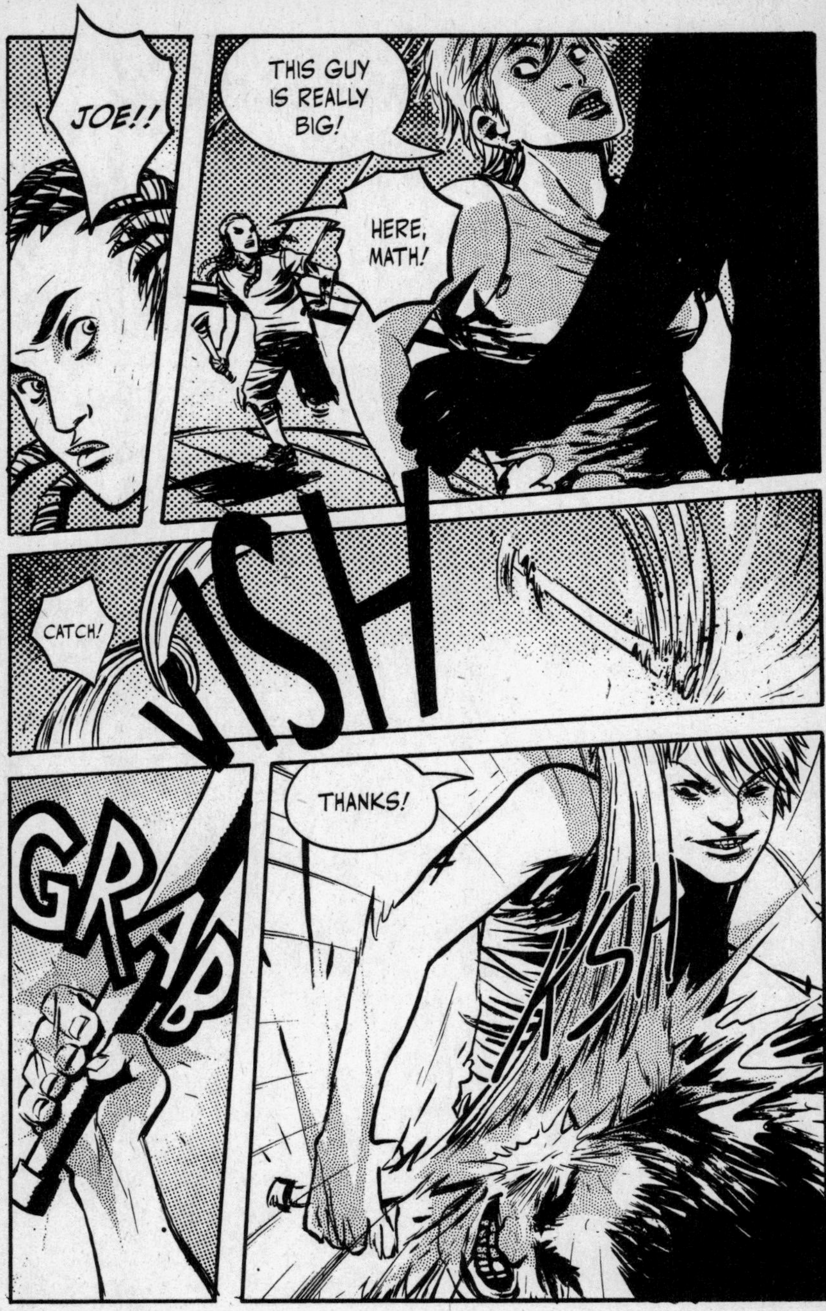
JOE!!
THIS GUY IS REALLY BIG!
HERE, MATH!
CATCH!
VISH
GRAB
THANKS!
KSH

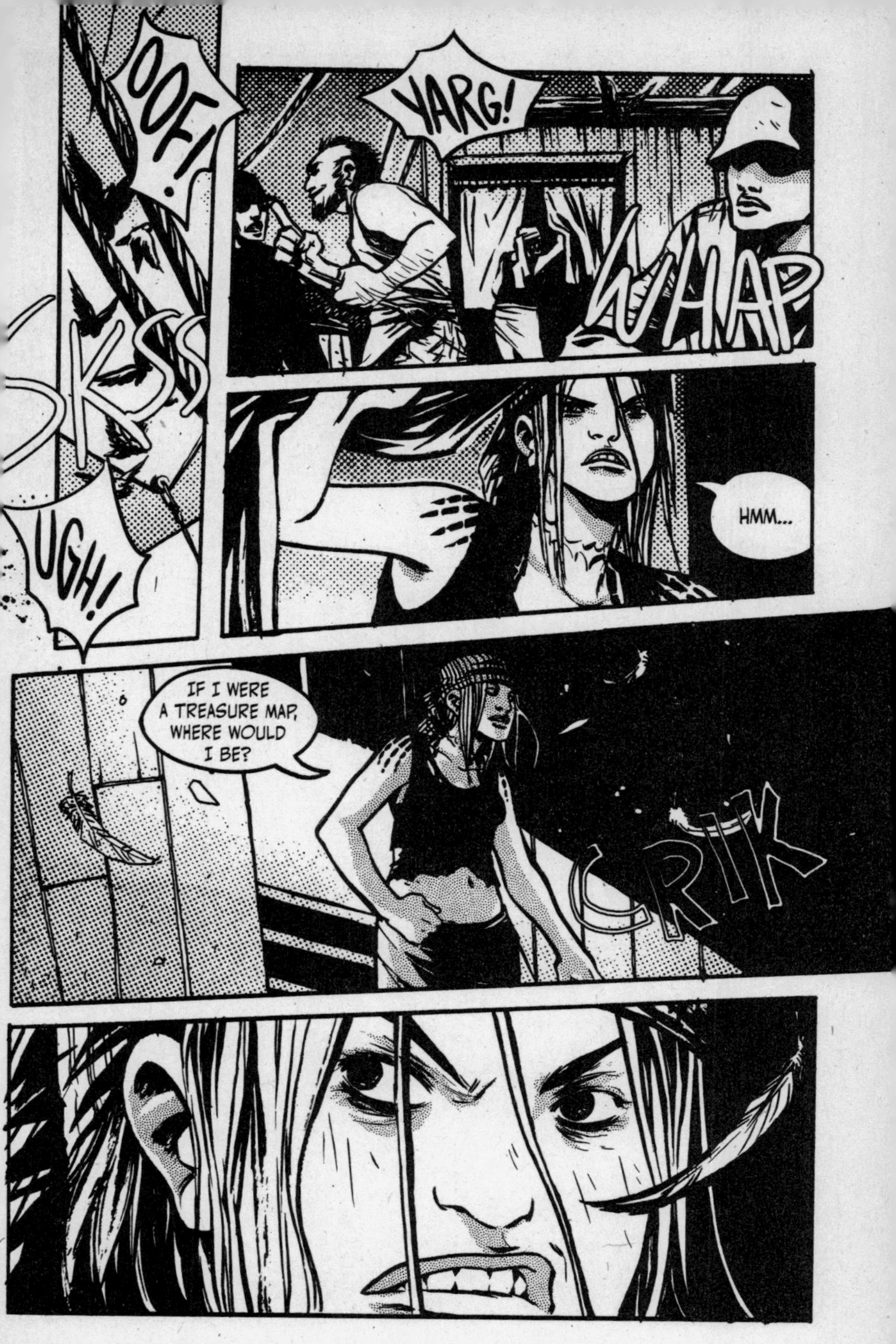
YARG!
WHAP
HMM...
OOF!
SKSS
UGH!
IF I WERE A TREASURE MAP, WHERE WOULD I BE?
CRIK

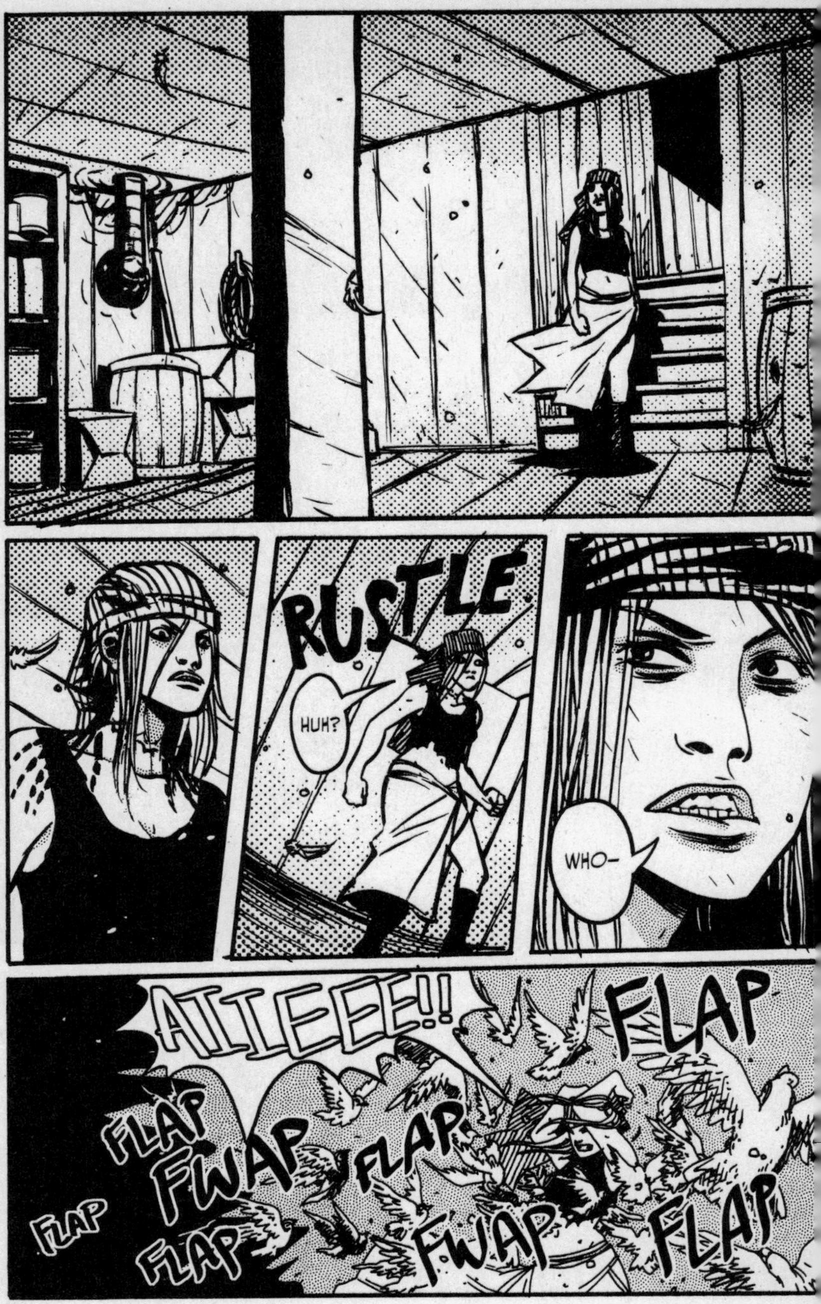
RUSTLE
HUH?
WHO-
AIIEEE!!
FLAP
FLAP
FWAP
FLAP
FLAP
FLAP
FWAP
FLAP

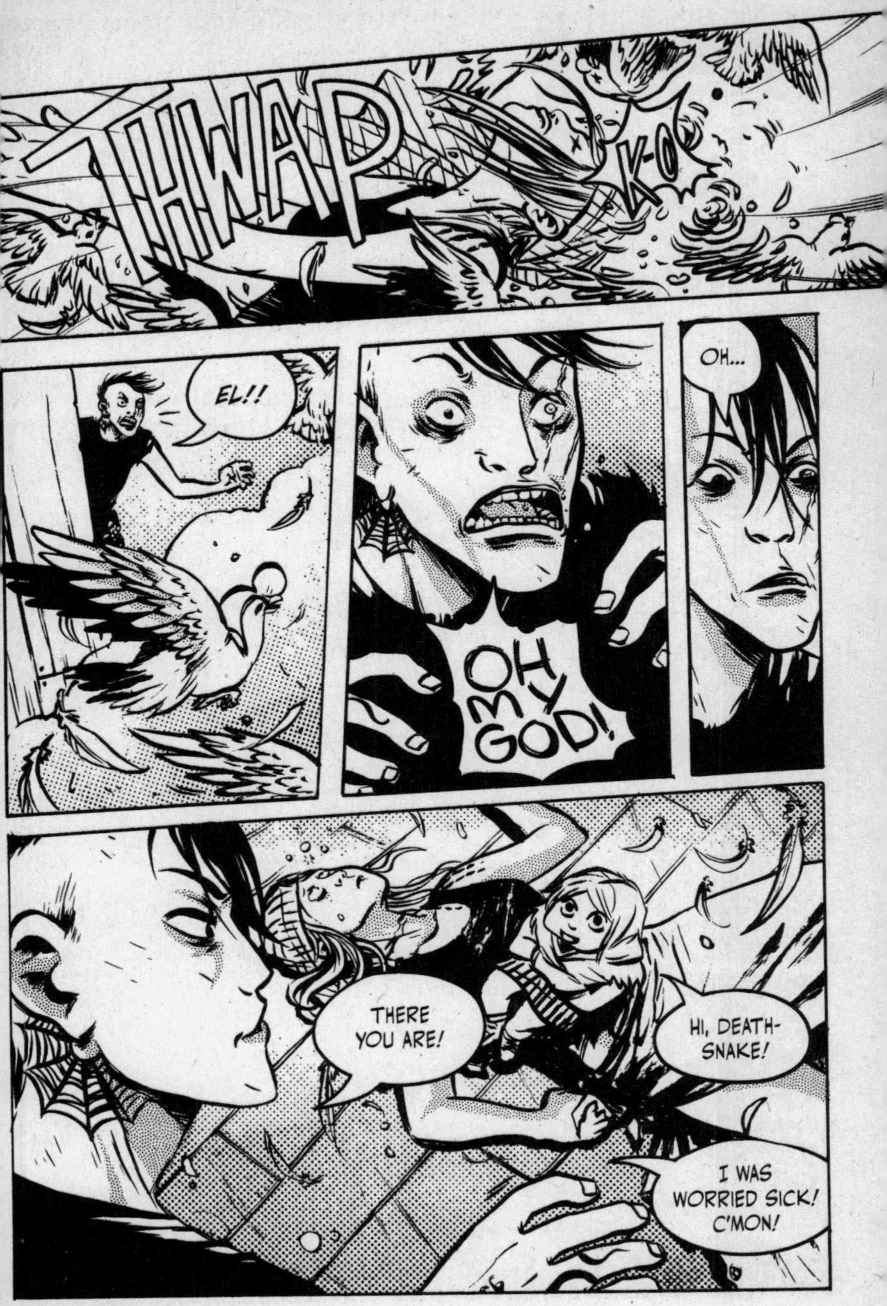
THWAP!
K-O
EL!!
OH MY GOD!
OH...
THERE YOU ARE!
HI, DEATH-SNAKE!
I WAS WORRIED SICK! C'MON!

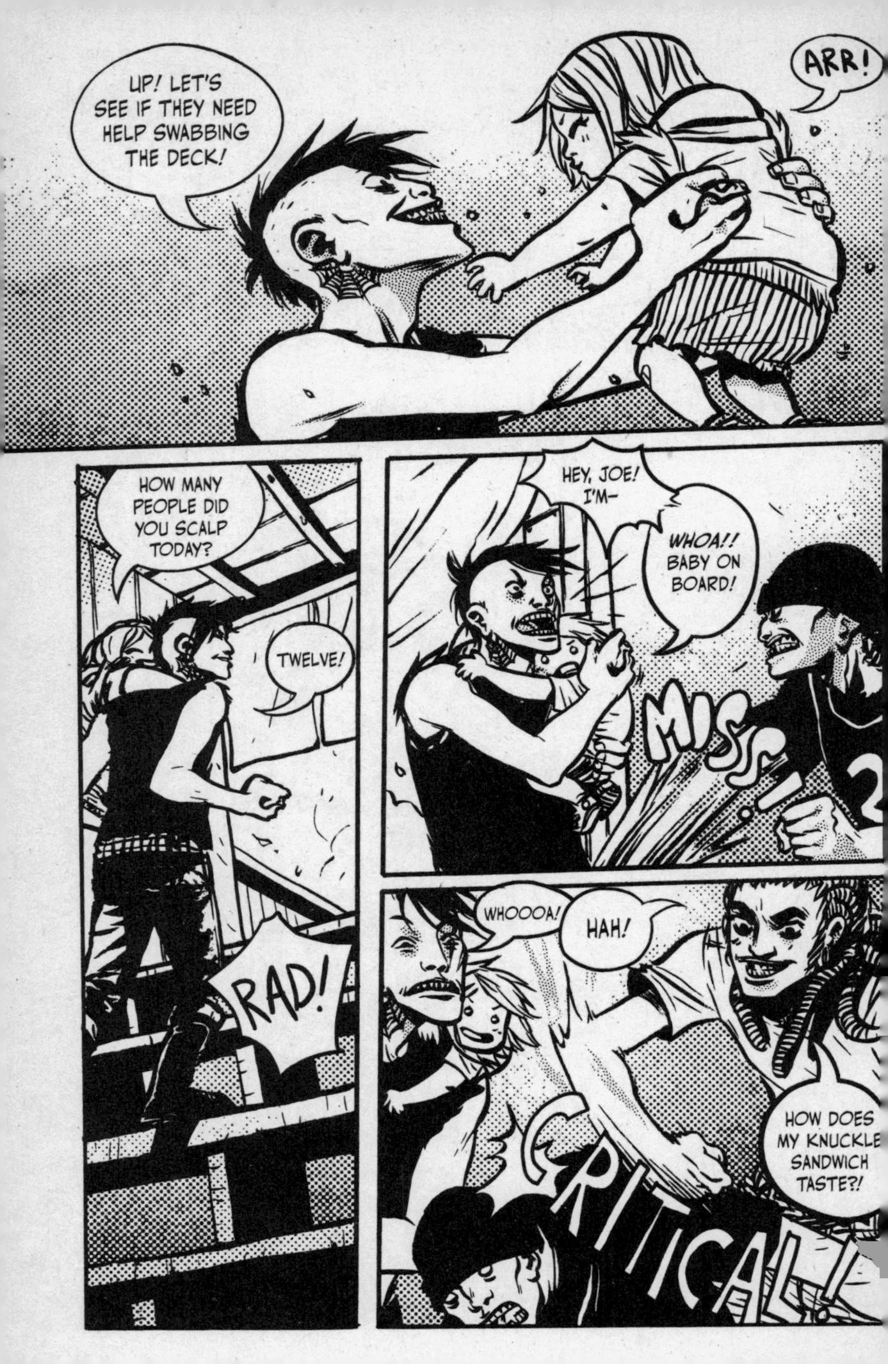
UP! LET'S SEE IF THEY NEED HELP SWABBING THE DECK!
ARR!
HOW MANY PEOPLE DID YOU SCALP TODAY?
TWELVE!
RAD!
HEY, JOE! I'M—
WHOA!! BABY ON BOARD!
MISS!
WHOOOA!
HAH!
HOW DOES MY KNUCKLE SANDWICH TASTE?!
CRITICAL!

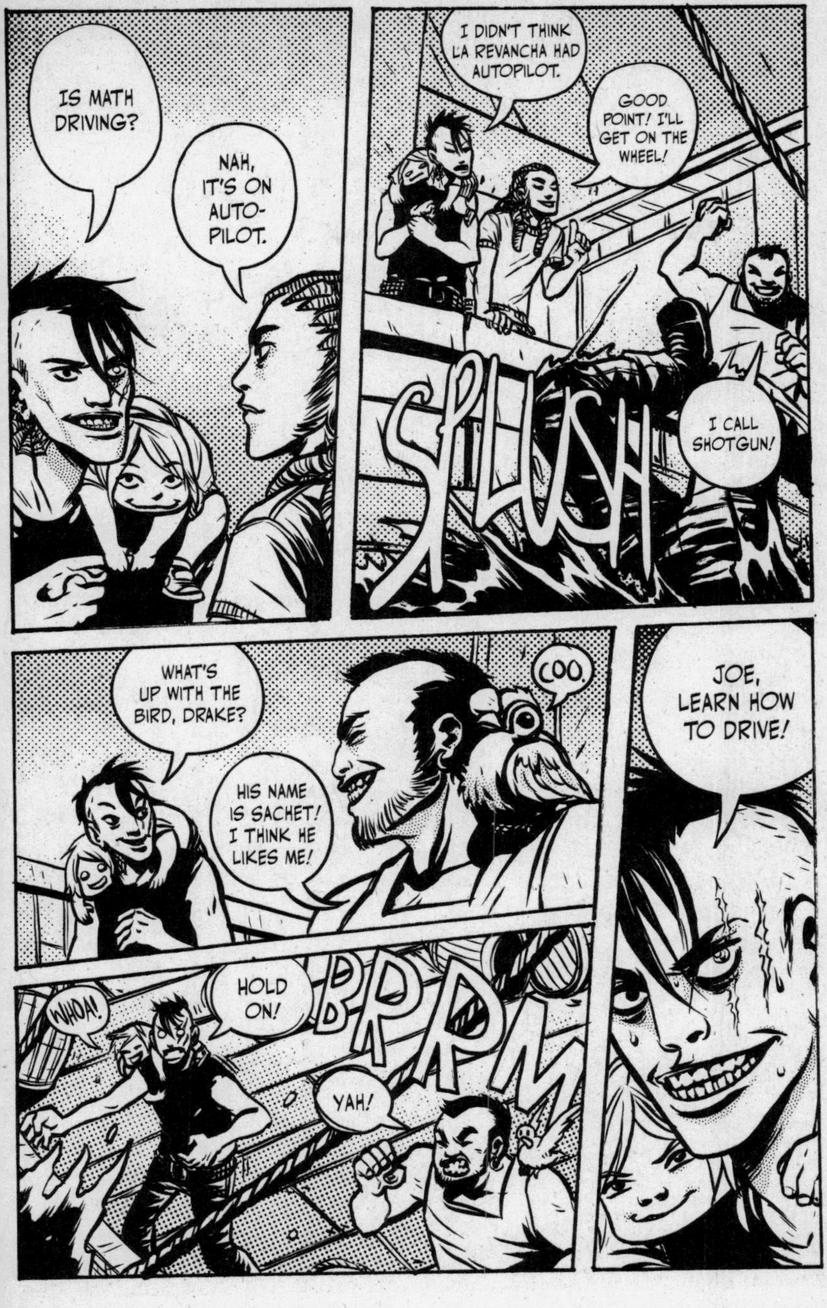
IS MATH DRIVING?
NAH, IT'S ON AUTO-PILOT.
I DIDN'T THINK LA REVANCHA HAD AUTOPILOT.
GOOD POINT! I'LL GET ON THE WHEEL!
I CALL SHOTGUN!
SPLUSH
WHAT'S UP WITH THE BIRD, DRAKE?
COO.
HIS NAME IS SACHET! I THINK HE LIKES ME!
WHOA!
HOLD ON!
BRRM
YAH!
JOE, LEARN HOW TO DRIVE!

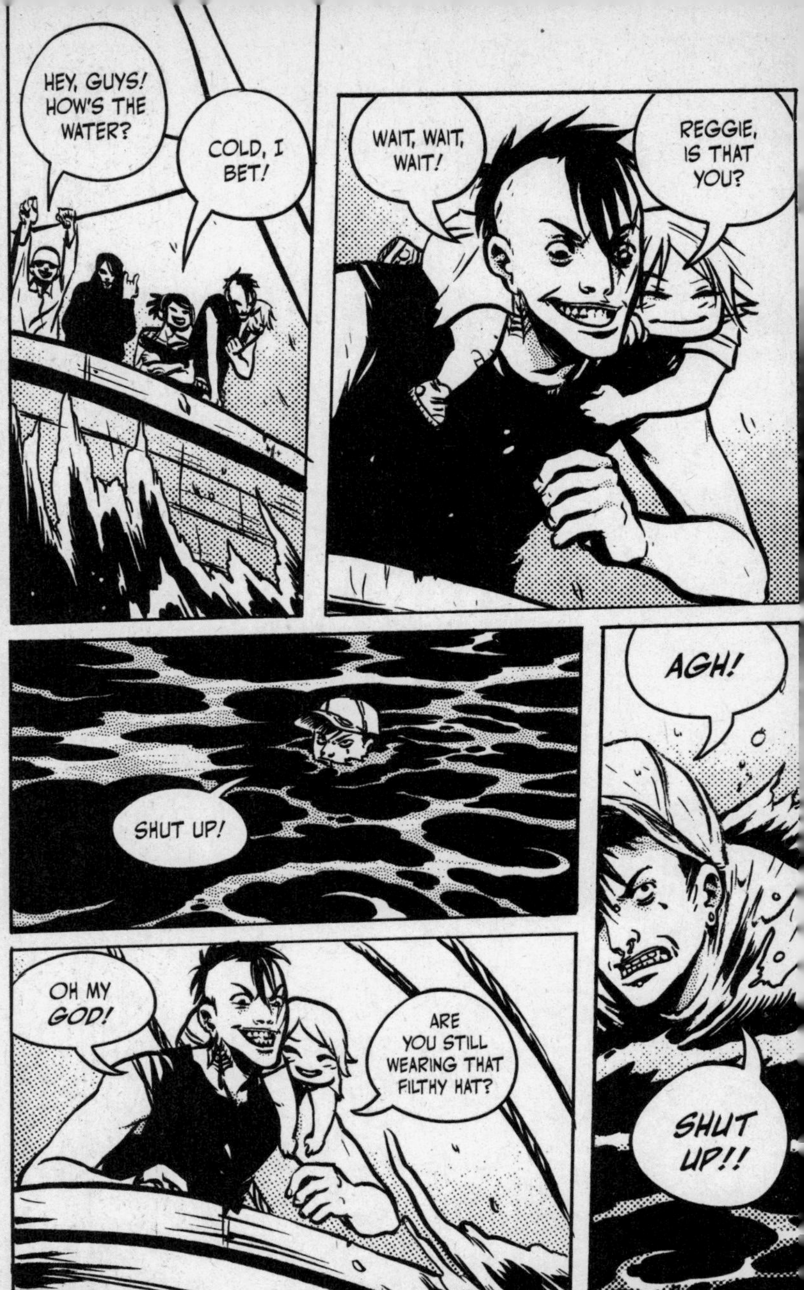
HEY, GUYS! HOW'S THE WATER?
COLD, I BET!
WAIT, WAIT, WAIT!
REGGIE, IS THAT YOU?
SHUT UP!
AGH!
OH MY GOD!
ARE YOU STILL WEARING THAT FILTHY HAT?
SHUT UP!!

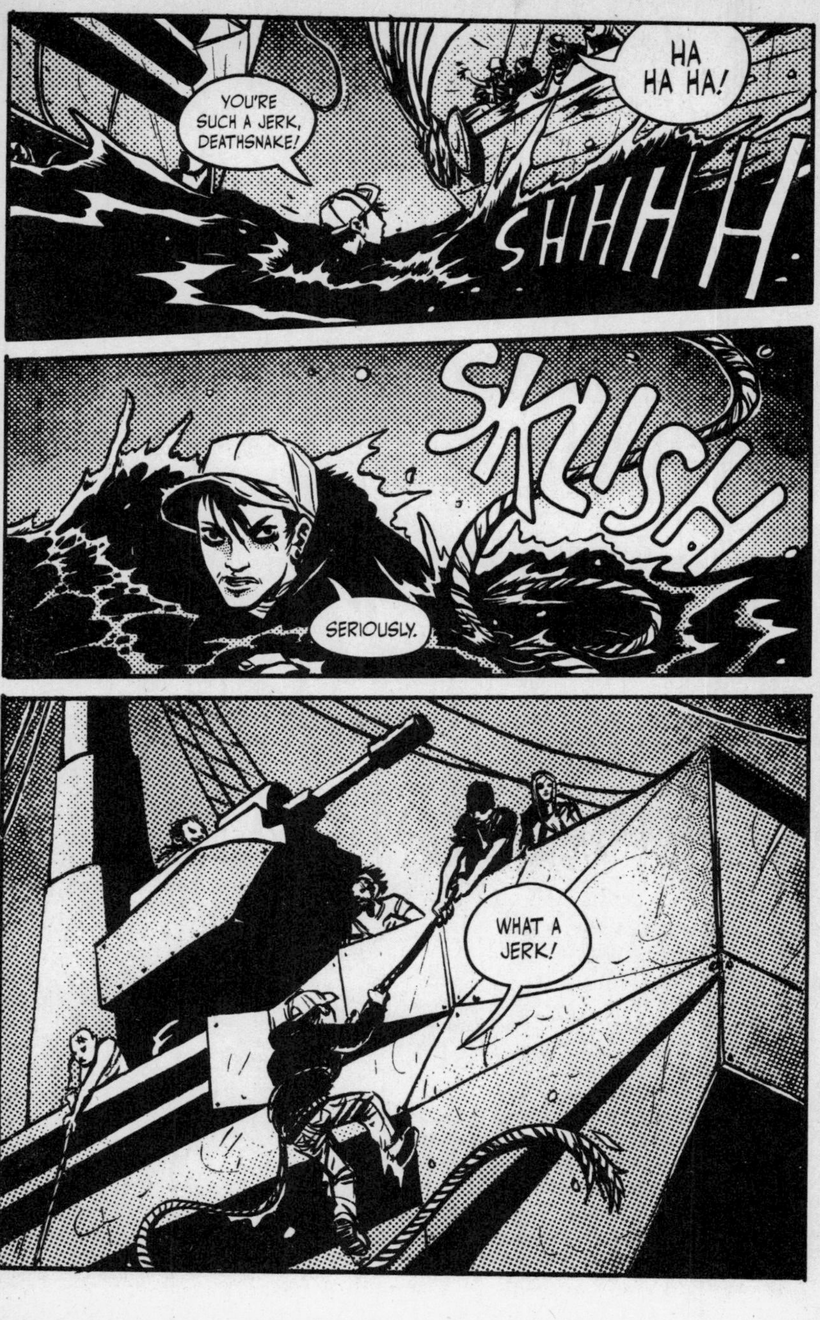
YOU'RE SUCH A JERK, DEATHSNAKE!
HA HA HA!
SHHHHH
SKLISH
SERIOUSLY.
WHAT A JERK!

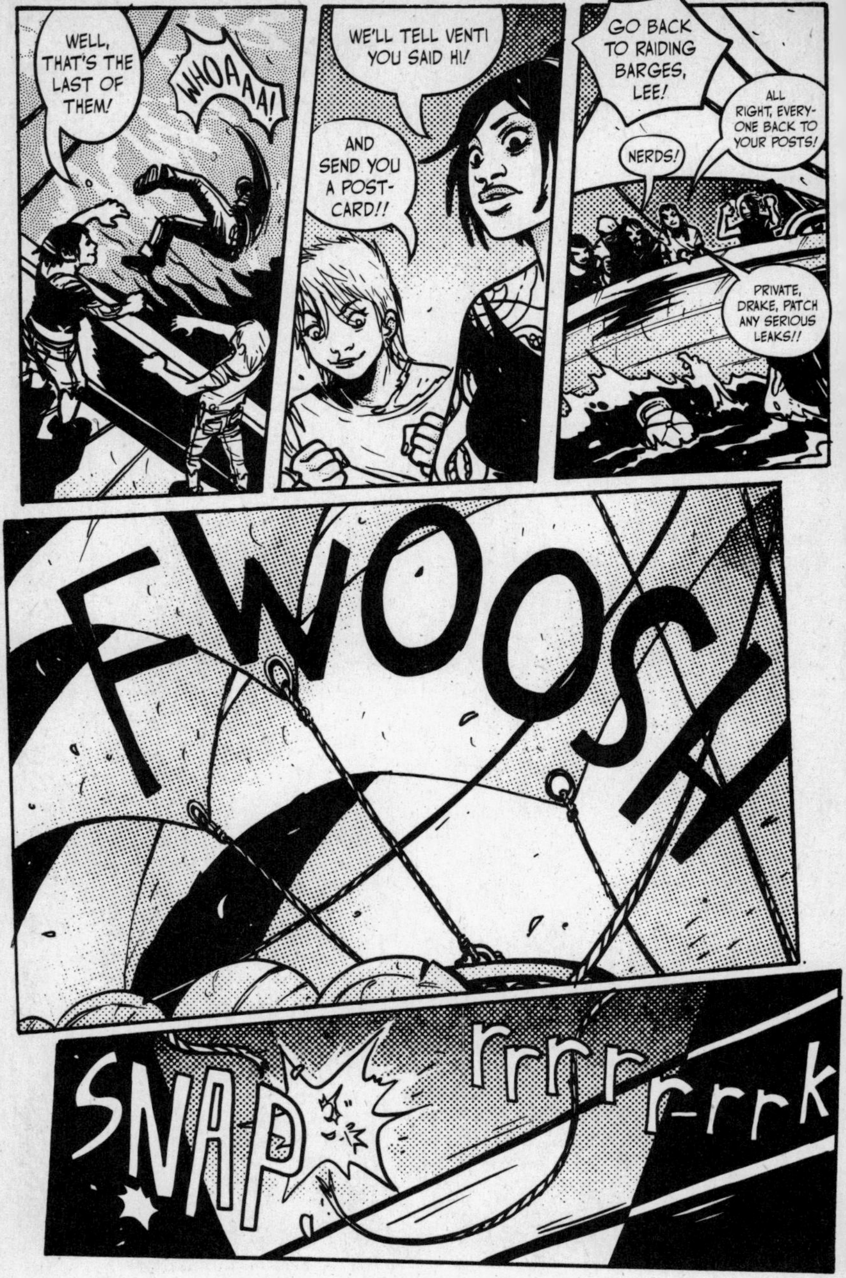
WELL, THAT'S THE LAST OF THEM!
WHOAAAA!
WE'LL TELL VENTI YOU SAID HI!
AND SEND YOU A POST-CARD!!
GO BACK TO RAIDING BARGES, LEE!
NERDS!
ALL RIGHT, EVERY-ONE BACK TO YOUR POSTS!
PRIVATE, DRAKE, PATCH ANY SERIOUS LEAKS!!
FWOOSH
SNAP
rrrrr-rrrk

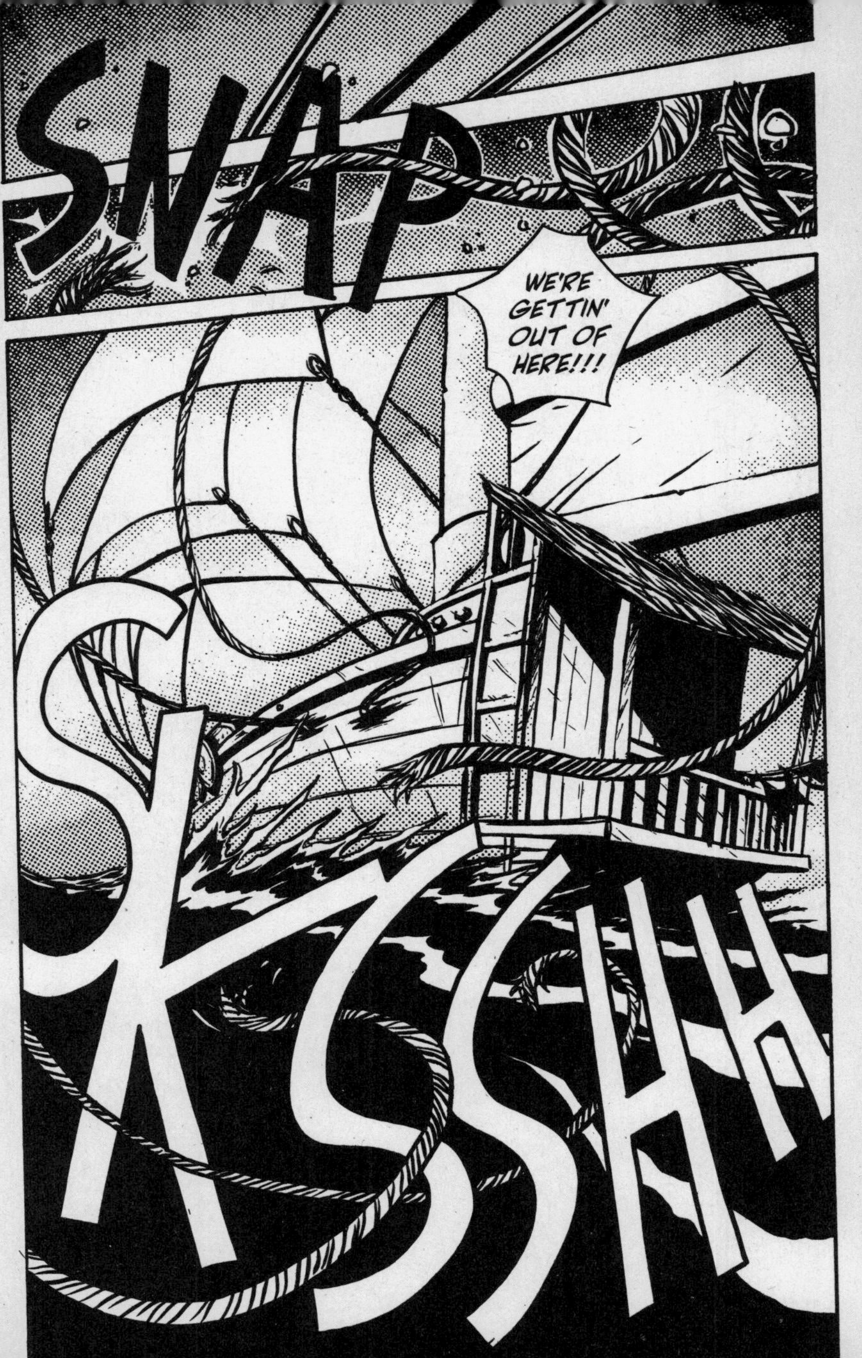
SNAP
WE'RE GETTIN' OUT OF HERE!!!
SKASSHH

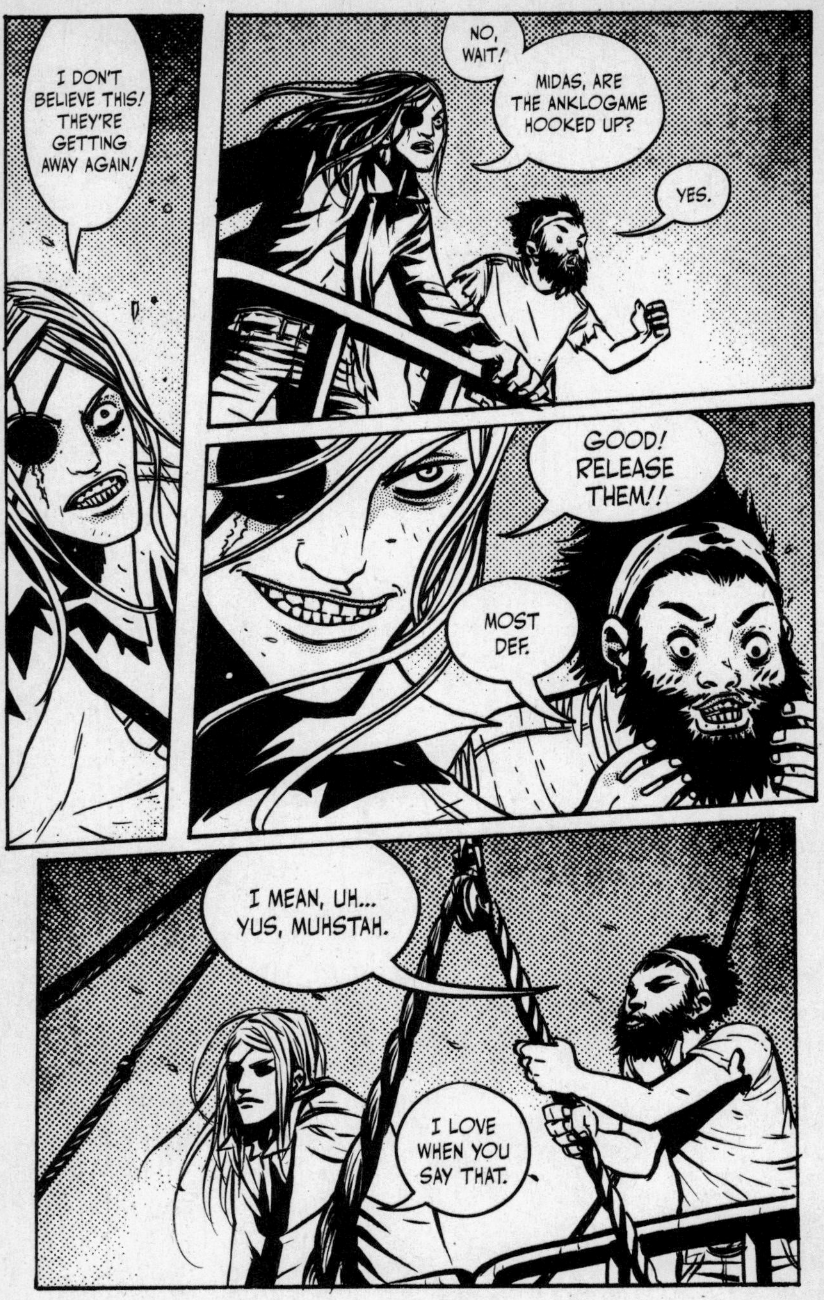
I DON'T BELIEVE THIS! THEY'RE GETTING AWAY AGAIN!
NO, WAIT!
MIDAS, ARE THE ANKLOGAME HOOKED UP?
YES.
GOOD! RELEASE THEM!!
MOST DEF.
I MEAN, UH... YUS, MUHSTAH.
I LOVE WHEN YOU SAY THAT.

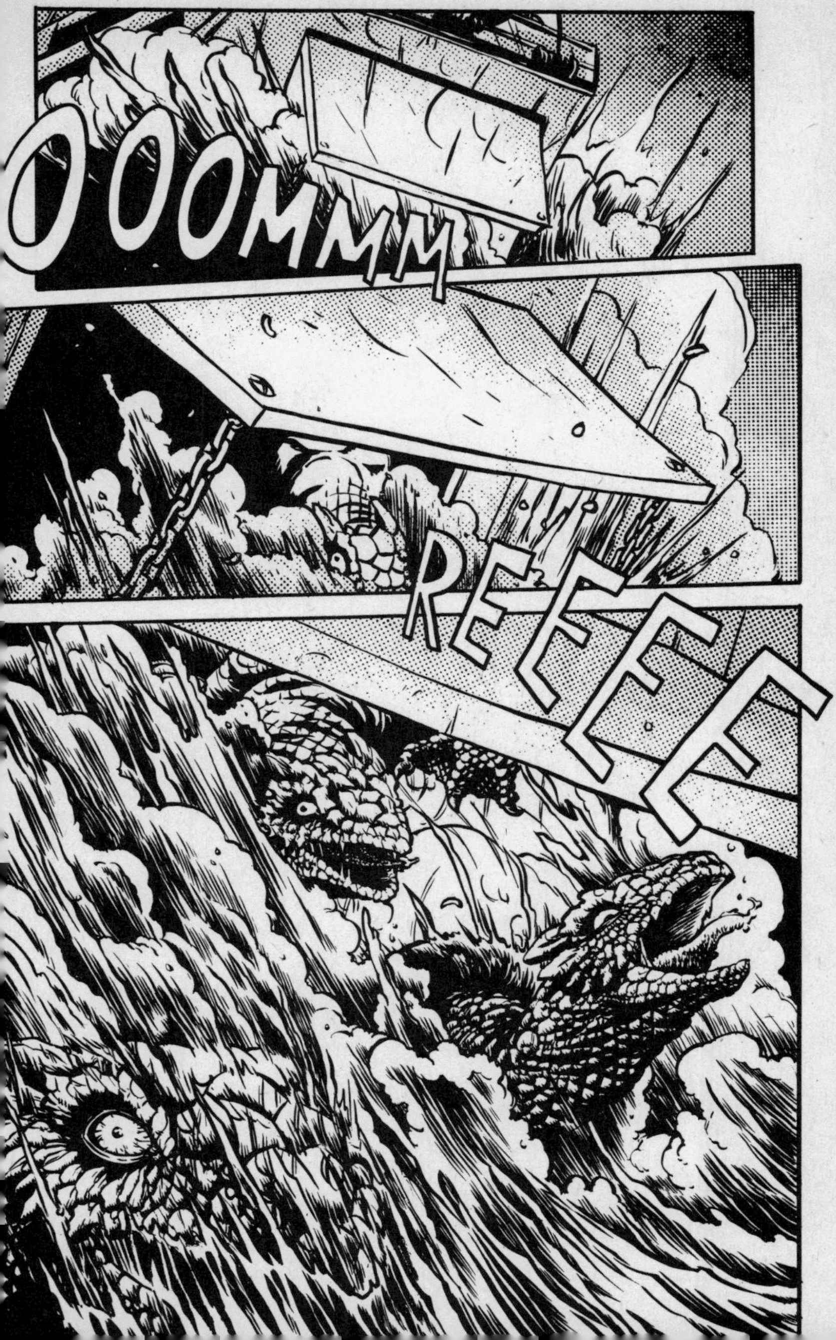
OOOMMMM
REEEE

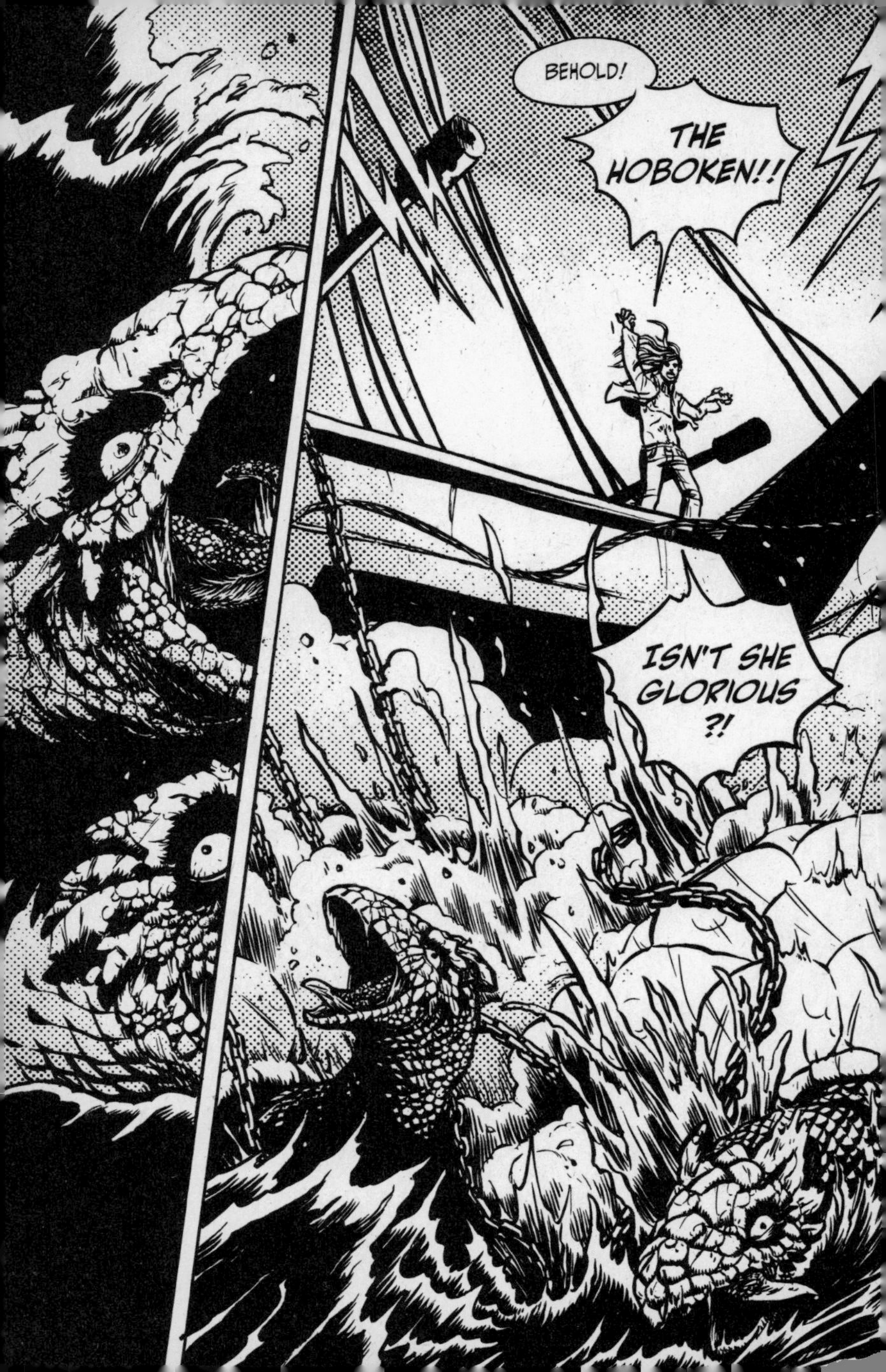
BEHOLD!
THE HOBOKEN!!
ISN'T SHE GLORIOUS ?!

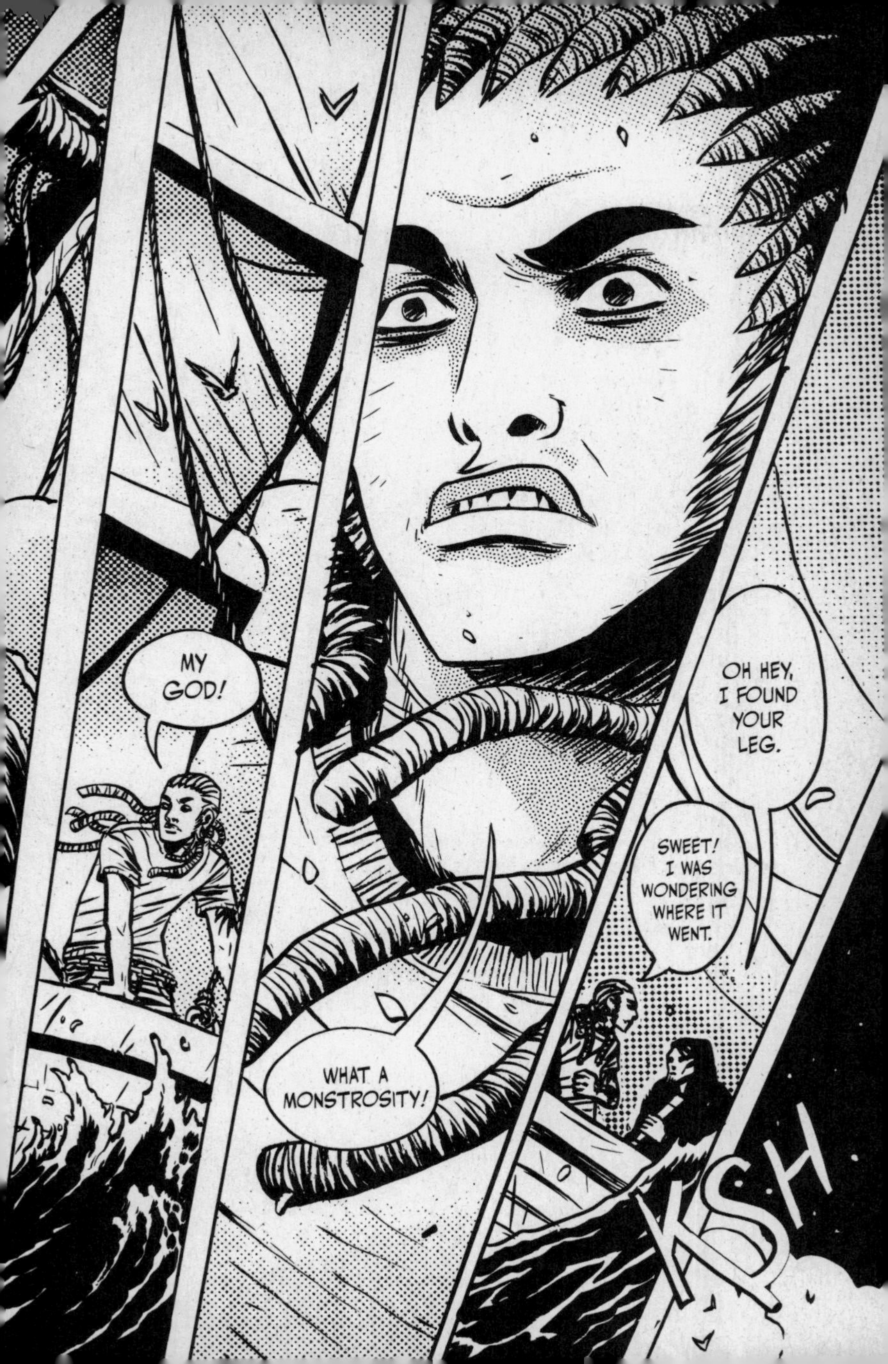
MY GOD!
WHAT A MONSTROSITY!
OH HEY, I FOUND YOUR LEG.
SWEET! I WAS WONDERING WHERE IT WENT.
KSH

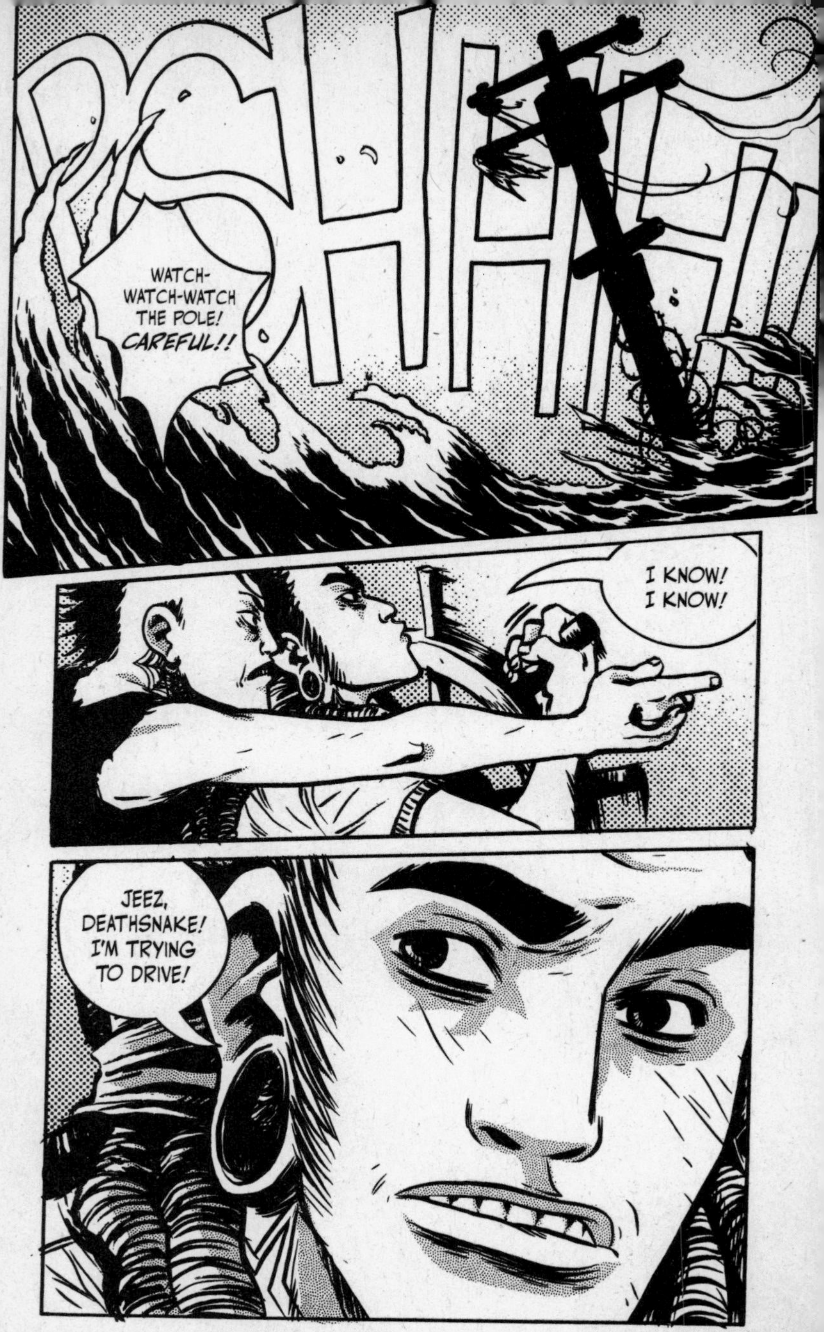
WATCH-WATCH-WATCH THE POLE! *CAREFUL!!*
I KNOW! I KNOW!
JEEZ, DEATHSNAKE! I'M TRYING TO DRIVE!

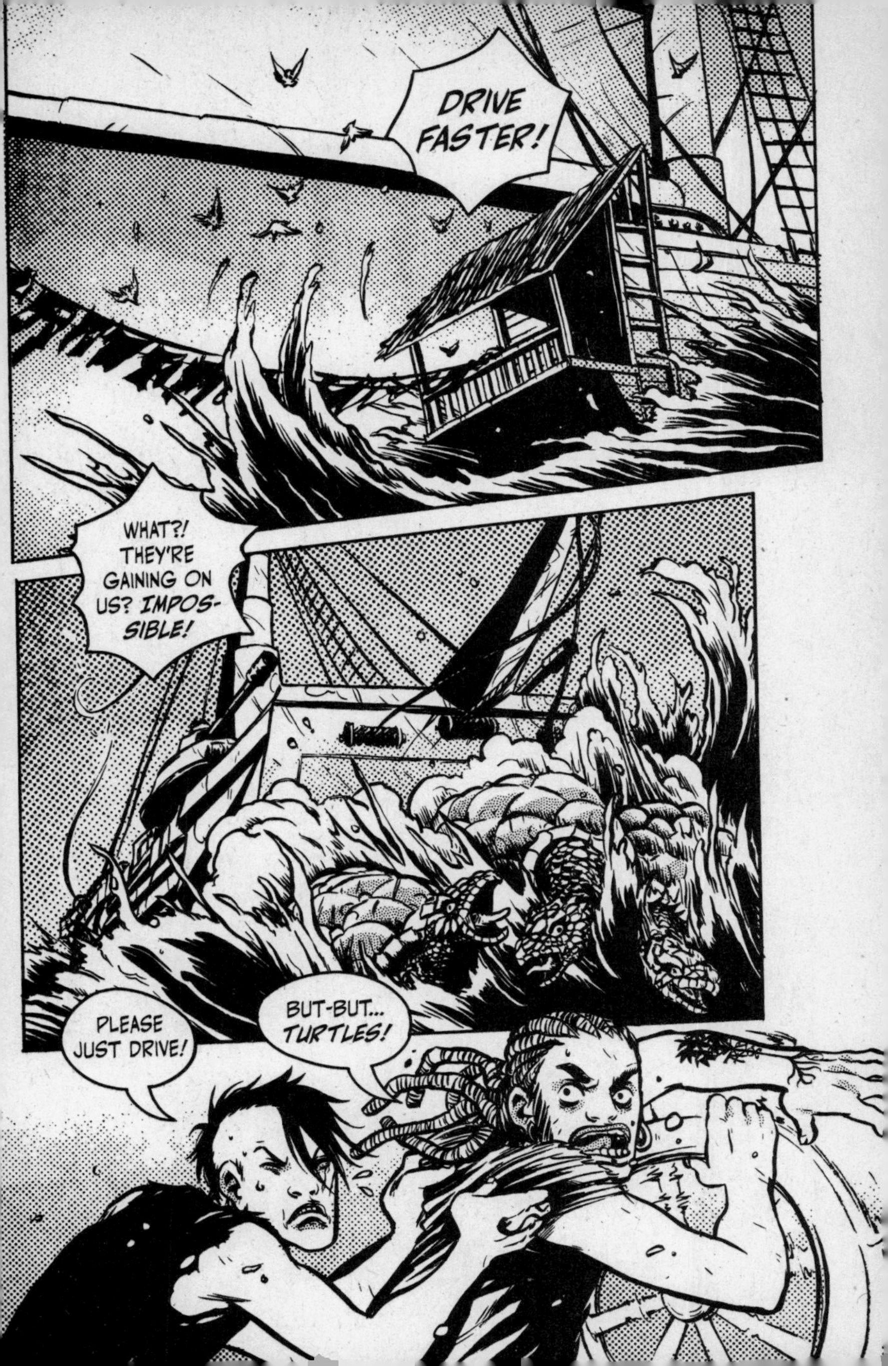
DRIVE FASTER!
WHAT?! THEY'RE GAINING ON US? *IMPOSSIBLE!*
PLEASE JUST DRIVE!
BUT-BUT... *TURTLES!*

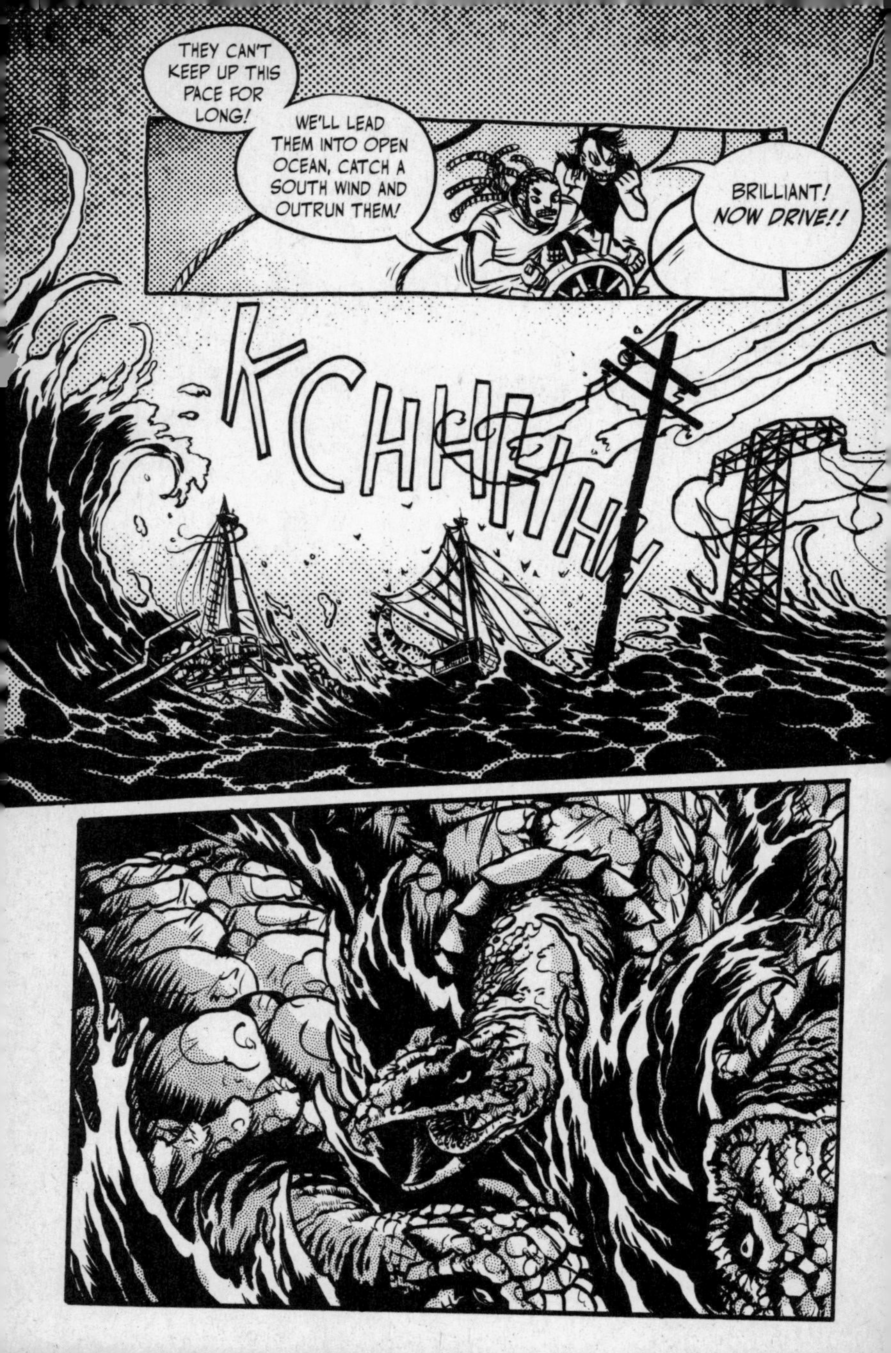
THEY CAN'T KEEP UP THIS PACE FOR LONG!
WE'LL LEAD THEM INTO OPEN OCEAN, CATCH A SOUTH WIND AND OUTRUN THEM!
BRILLIANT! NOW DRIVE!!
KCHHHHHH

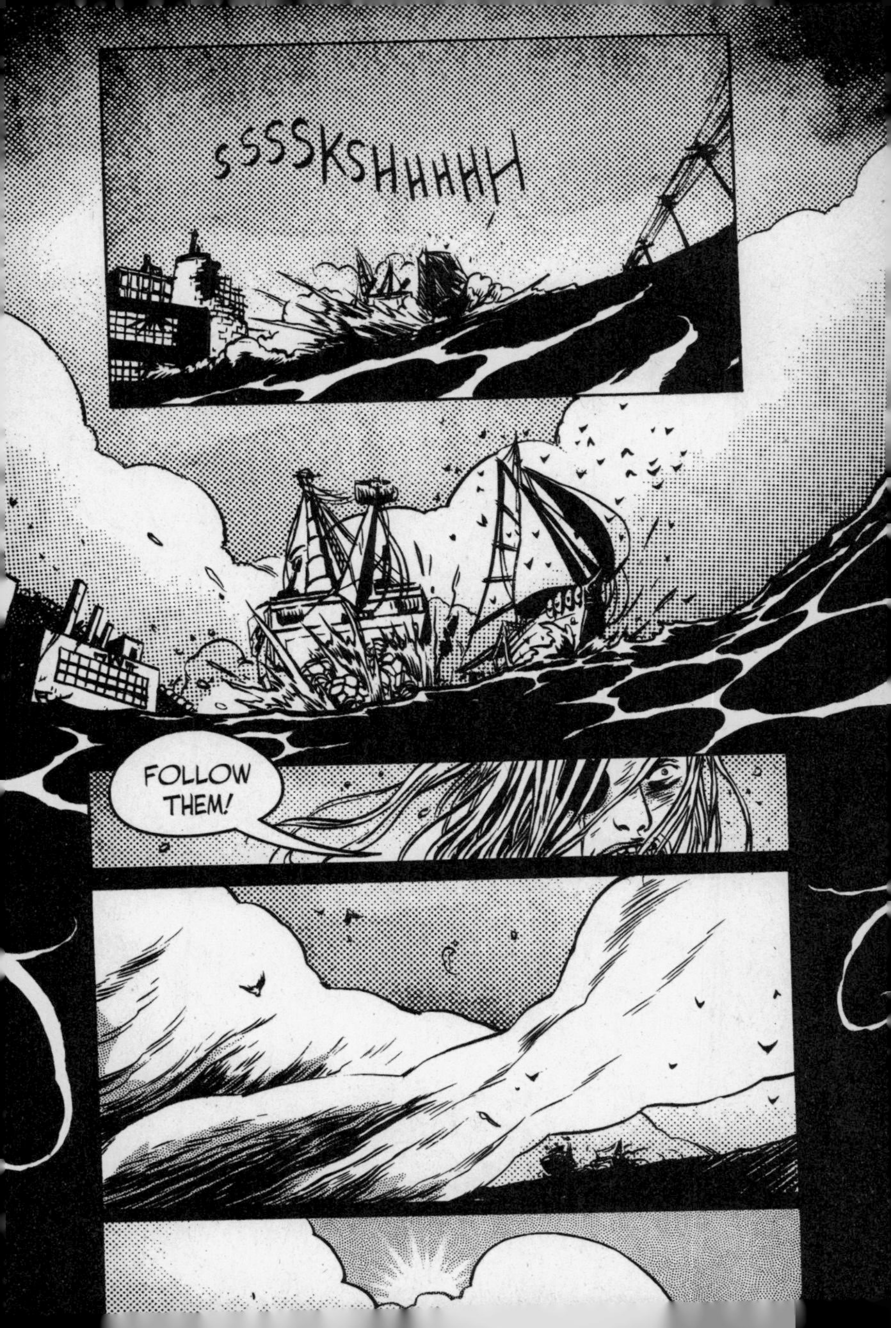
SSSSKSHHHHHH
FOLLOW THEM!

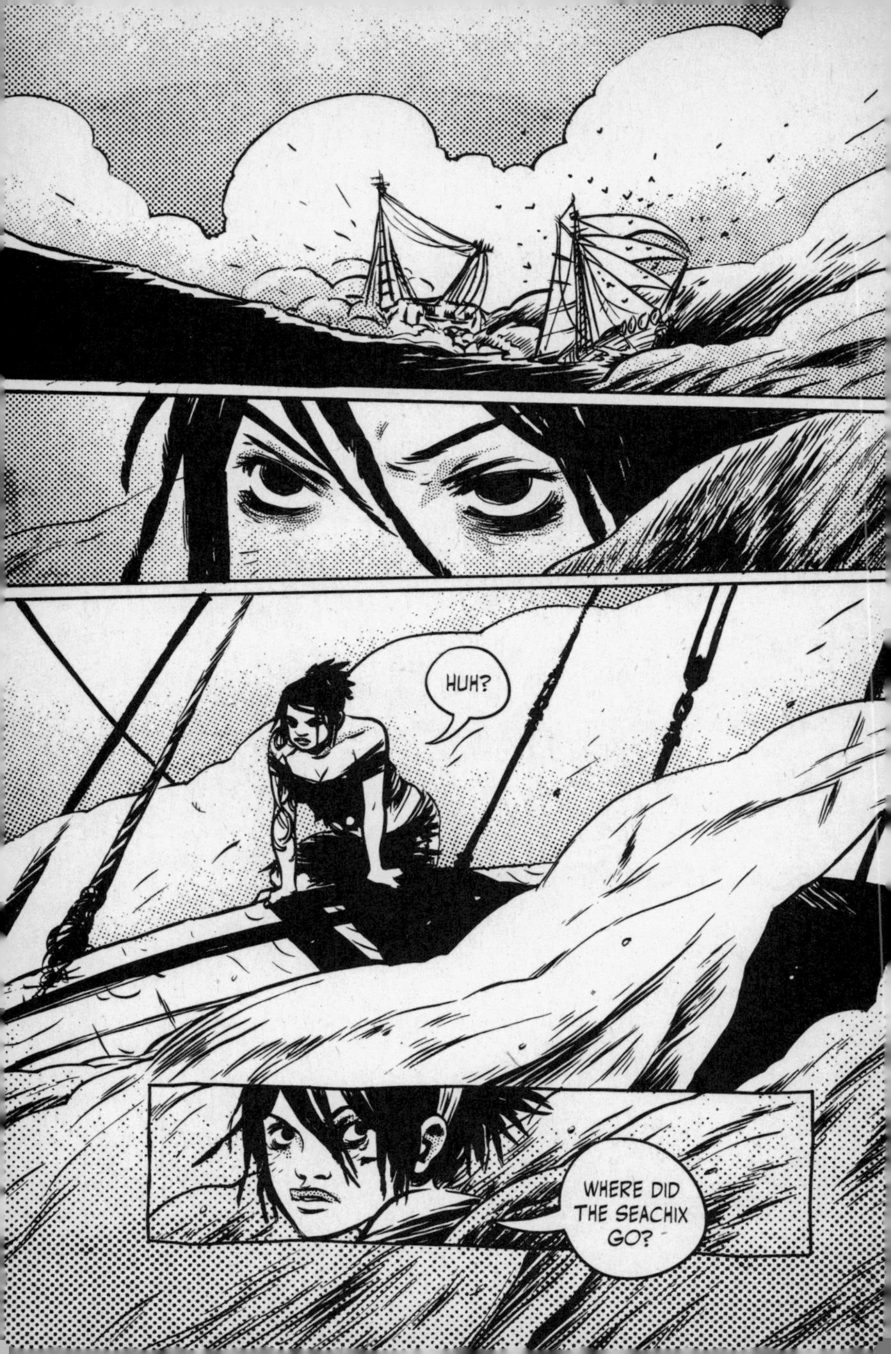
HUH?
WHERE DID THE SEACHIX GO?

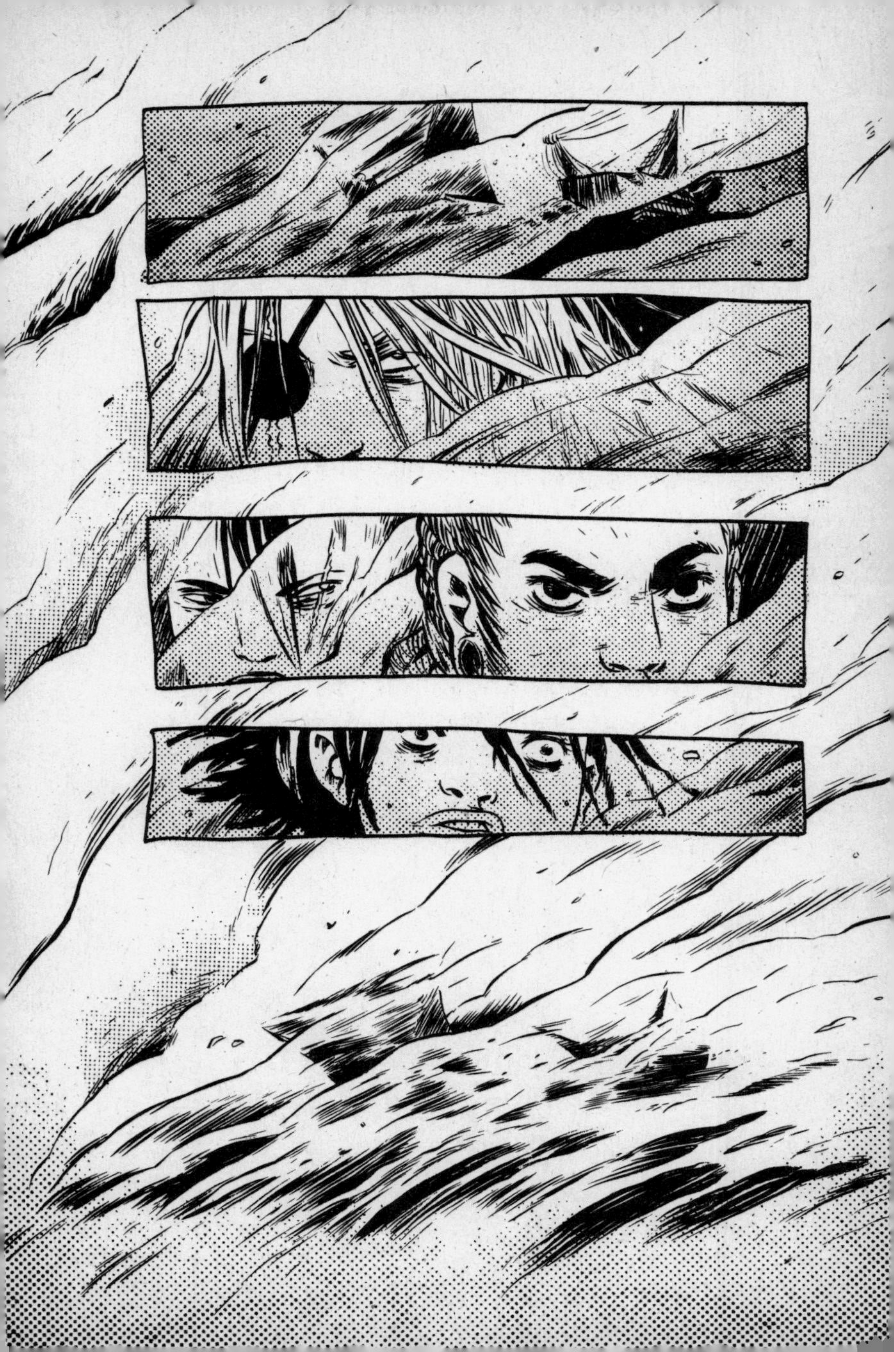

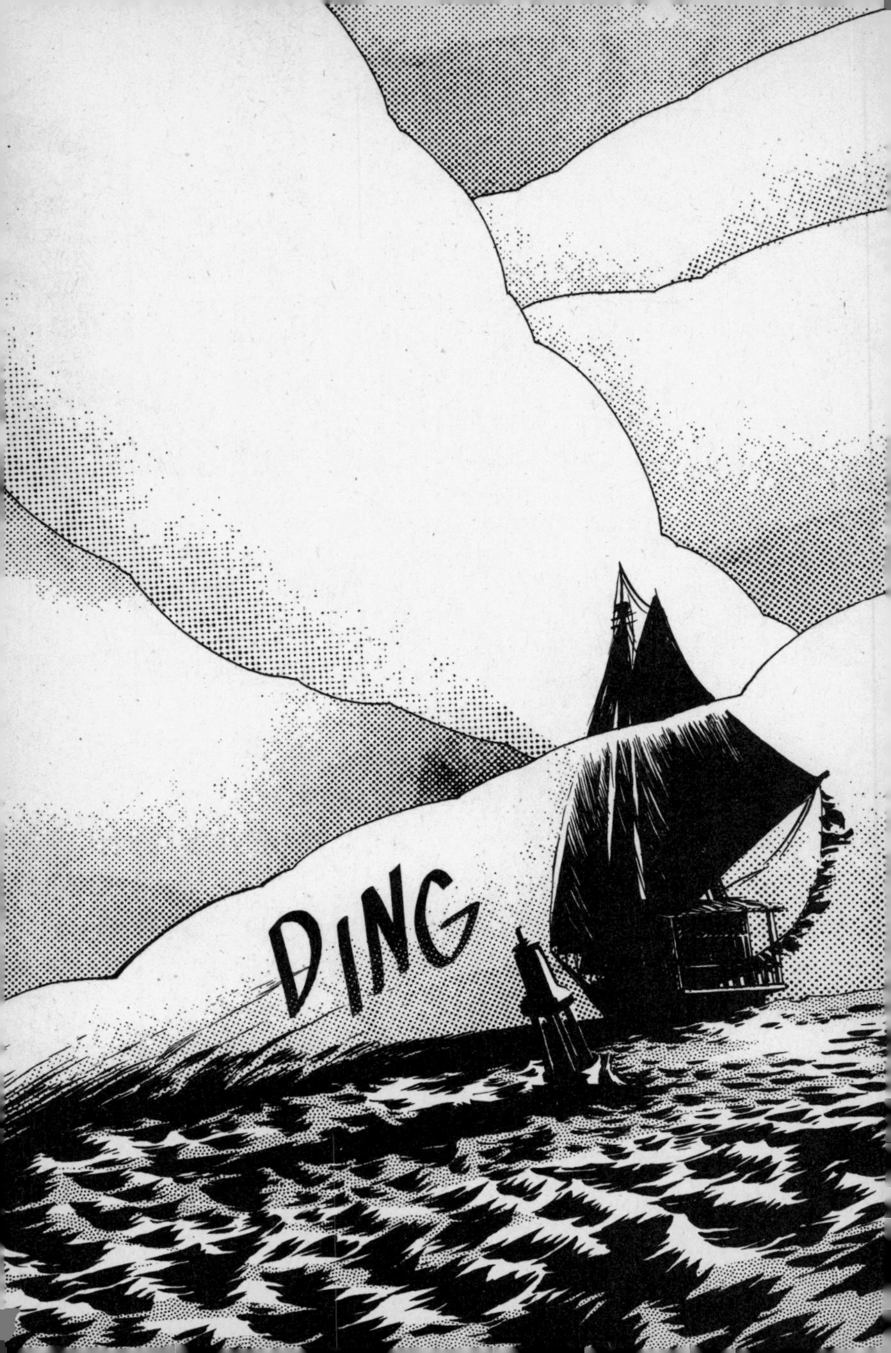
DING

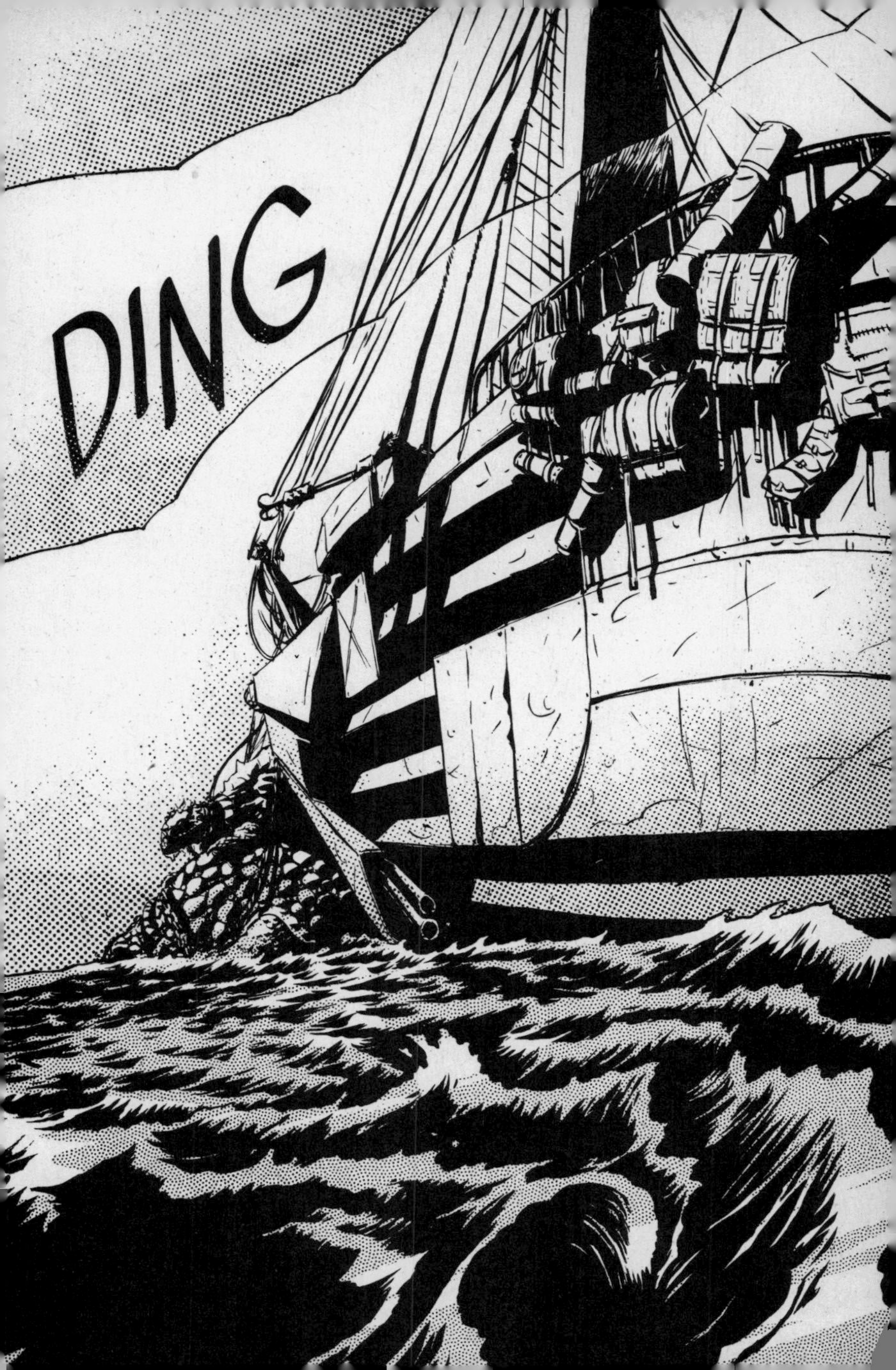
DING

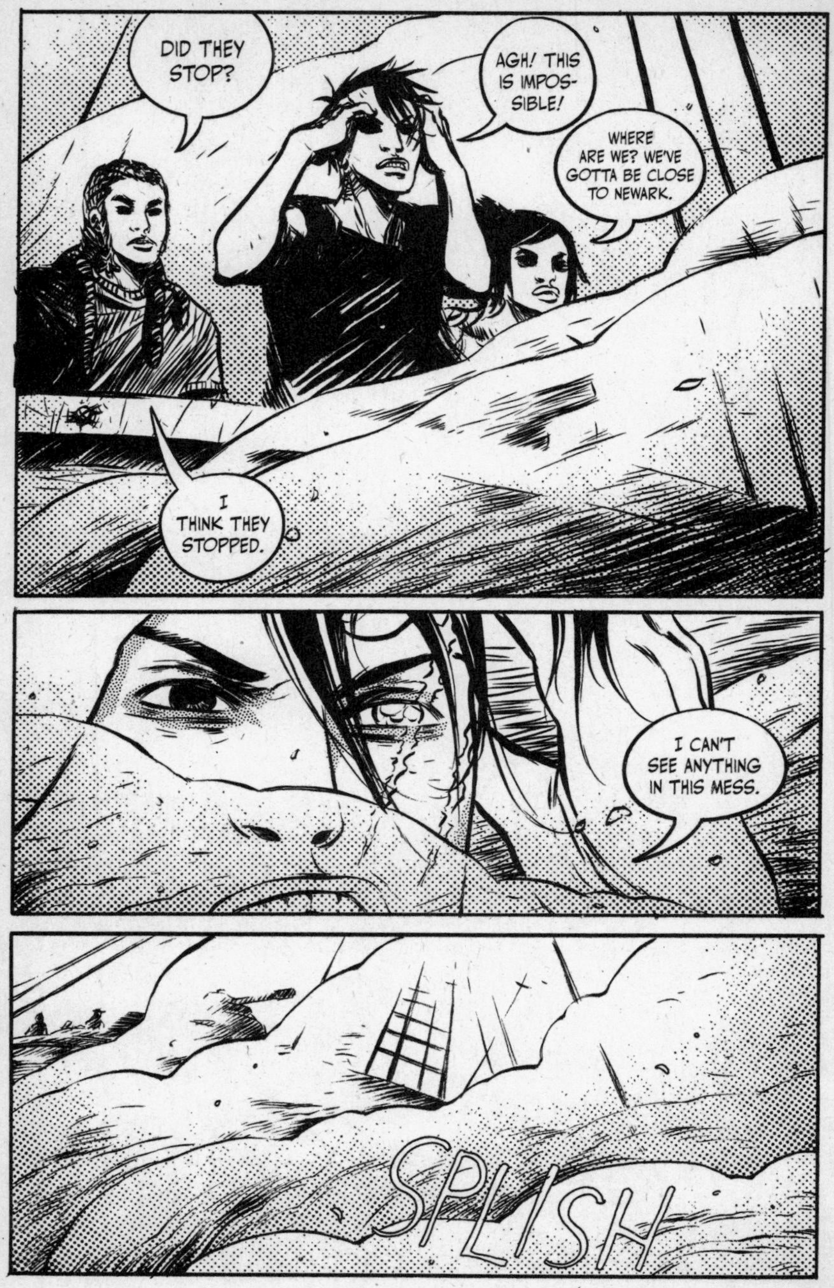
DID THEY STOP?
AGH! THIS IS IMPOS-SIBLE!
WHERE ARE WE? WE'VE GOTTA BE CLOSE TO NEWARK.
I THINK THEY STOPPED.
I CAN'T SEE ANYTHING IN THIS MESS.
SPLISH

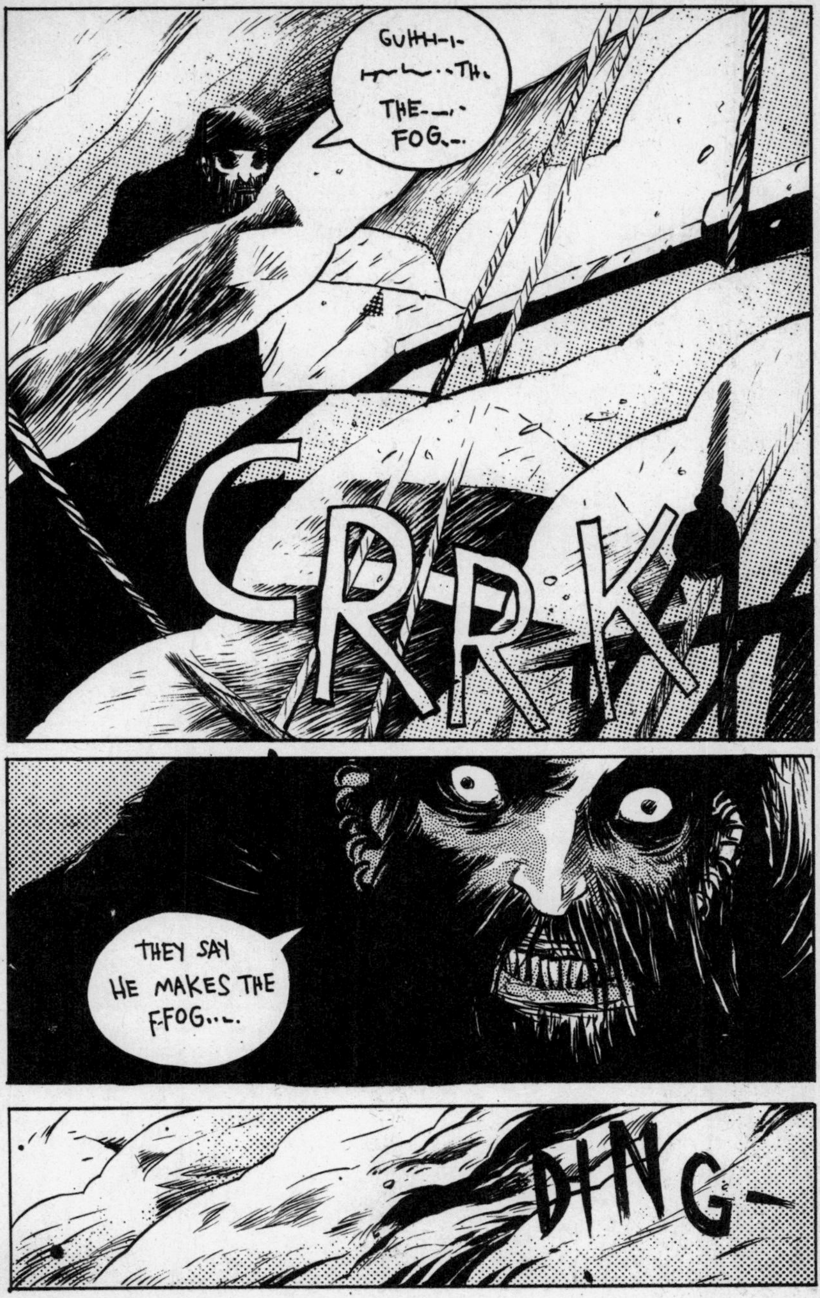
GUHHH-I-
...TH.
THE-...
FOG...
CRRK
THEY SAY HE MAKES THE F-FOG...
DING-

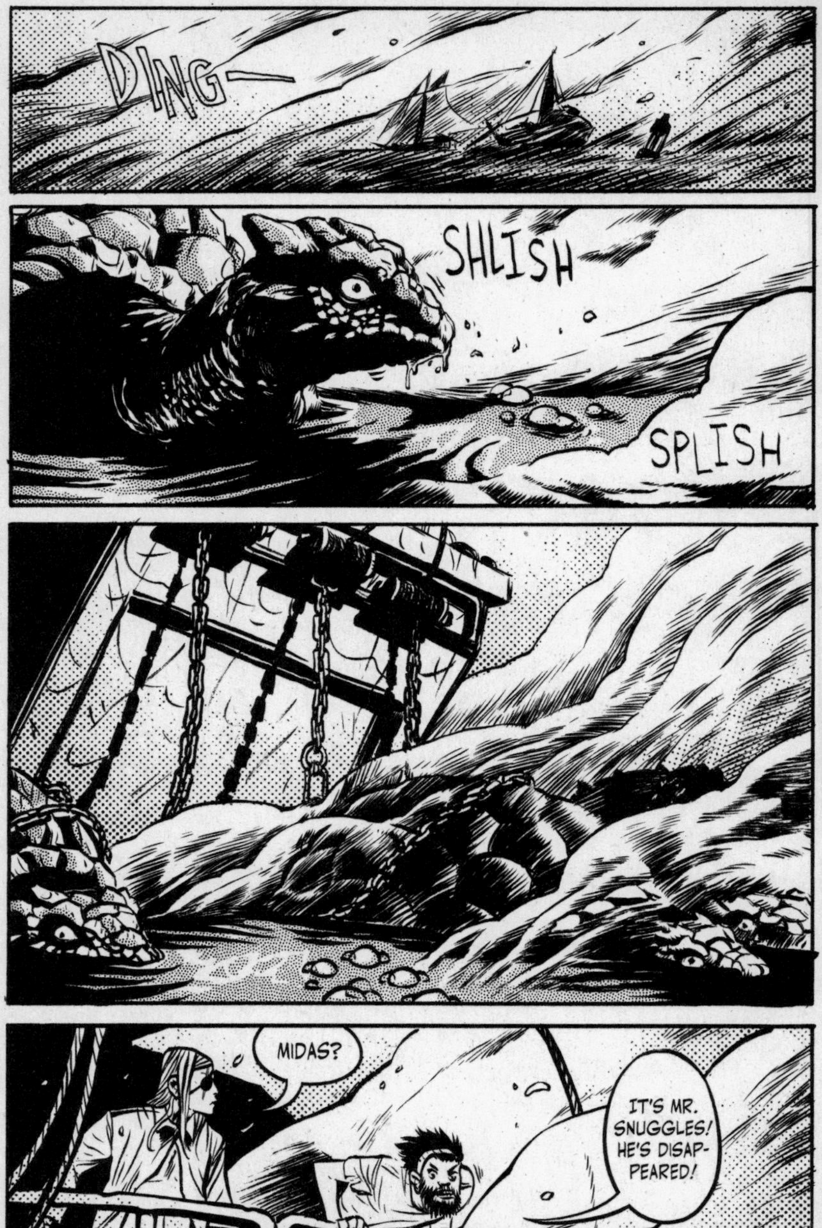
DING—
SHLISH
SPLISH
MIDAS?
IT'S MR. SNUGGLES! HE'S DISAP-PEARED!

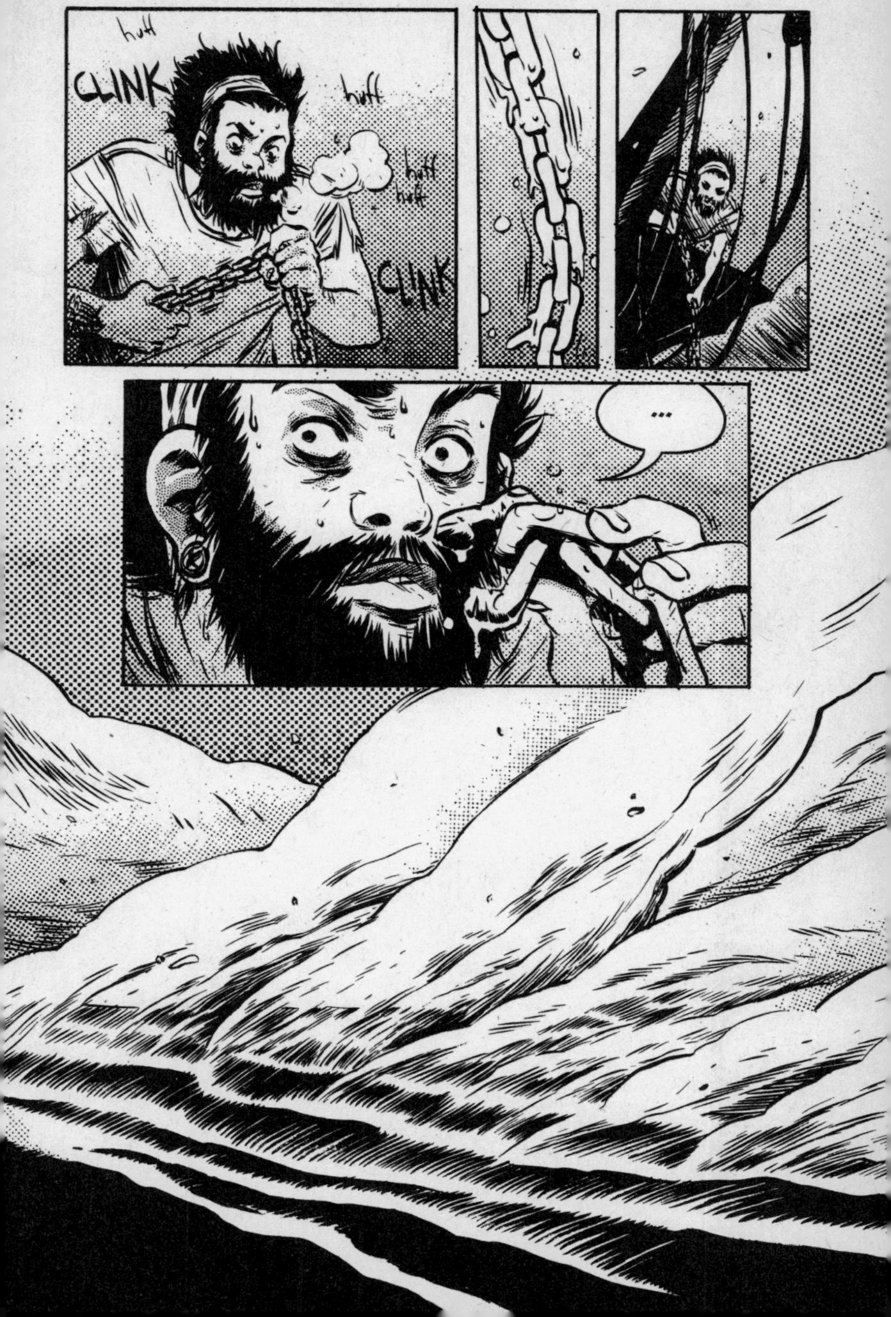
huff
CLINK
huff
huff
huff
CLINK
...

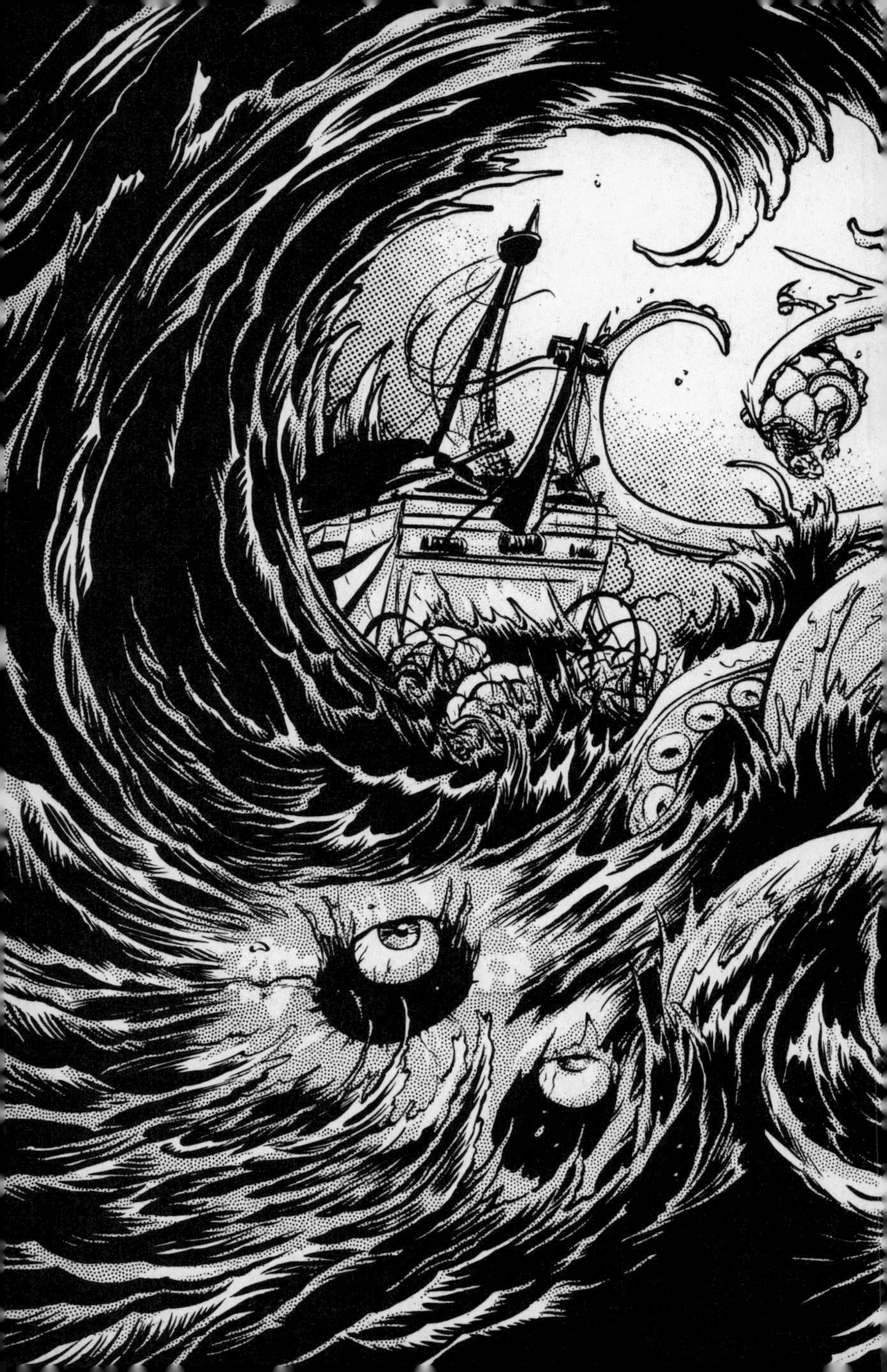

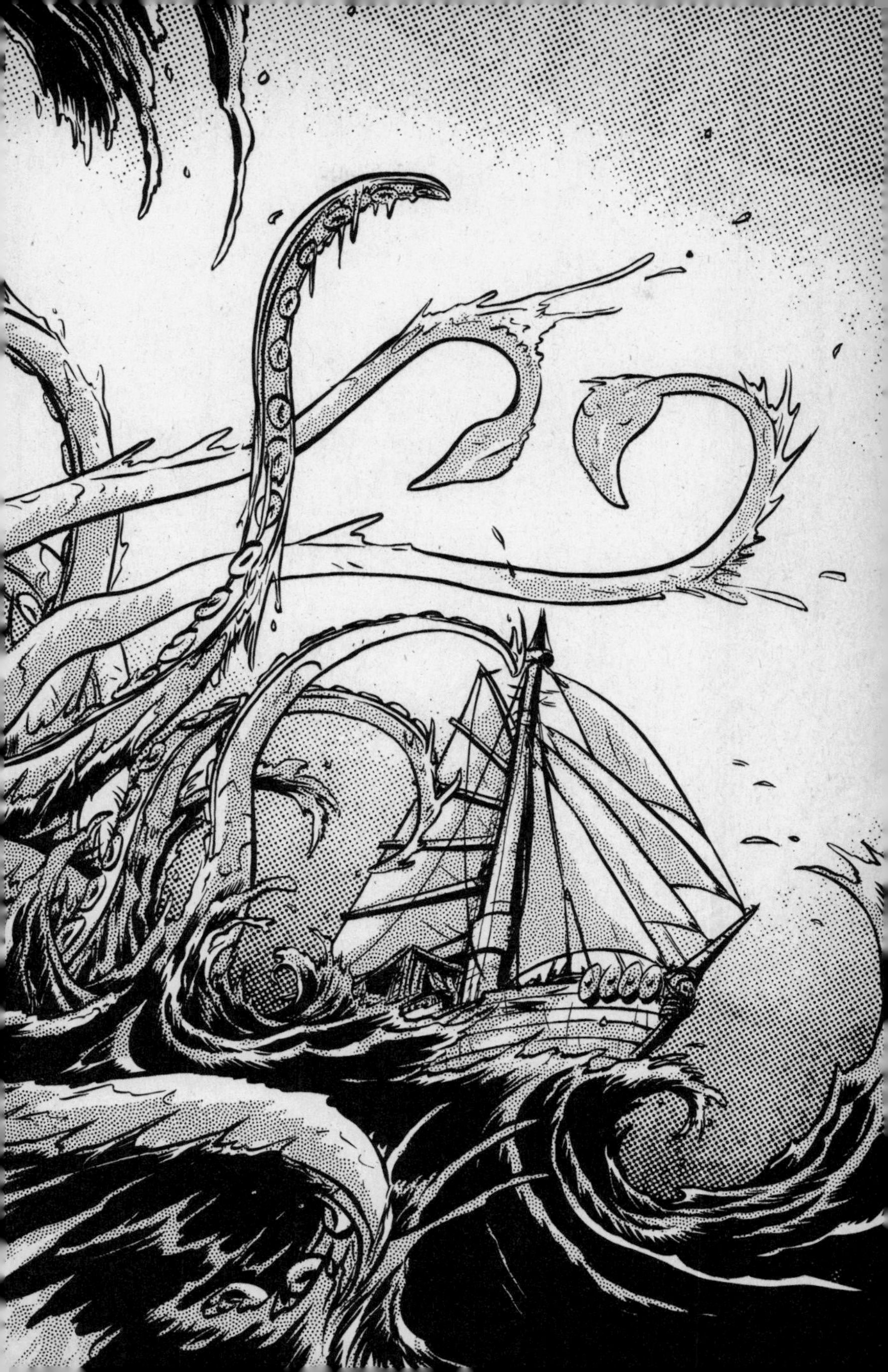

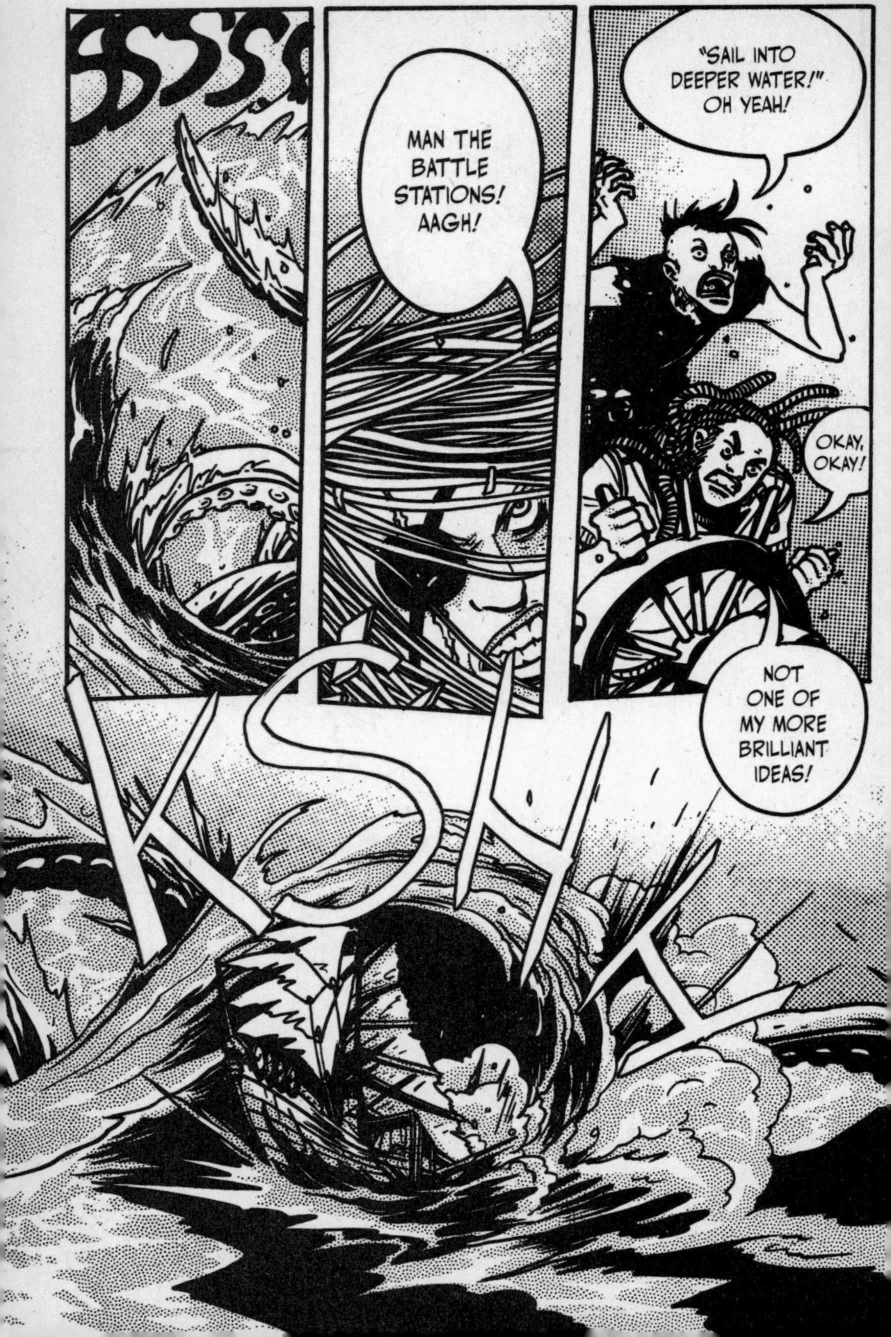
MAN THE BATTLE STATIONS! AAGH!
"SAIL INTO DEEPER WATER!" OH YEAH!
OKAY, OKAY!
NOT ONE OF MY MORE BRILLIANT IDEAS!
KSHH

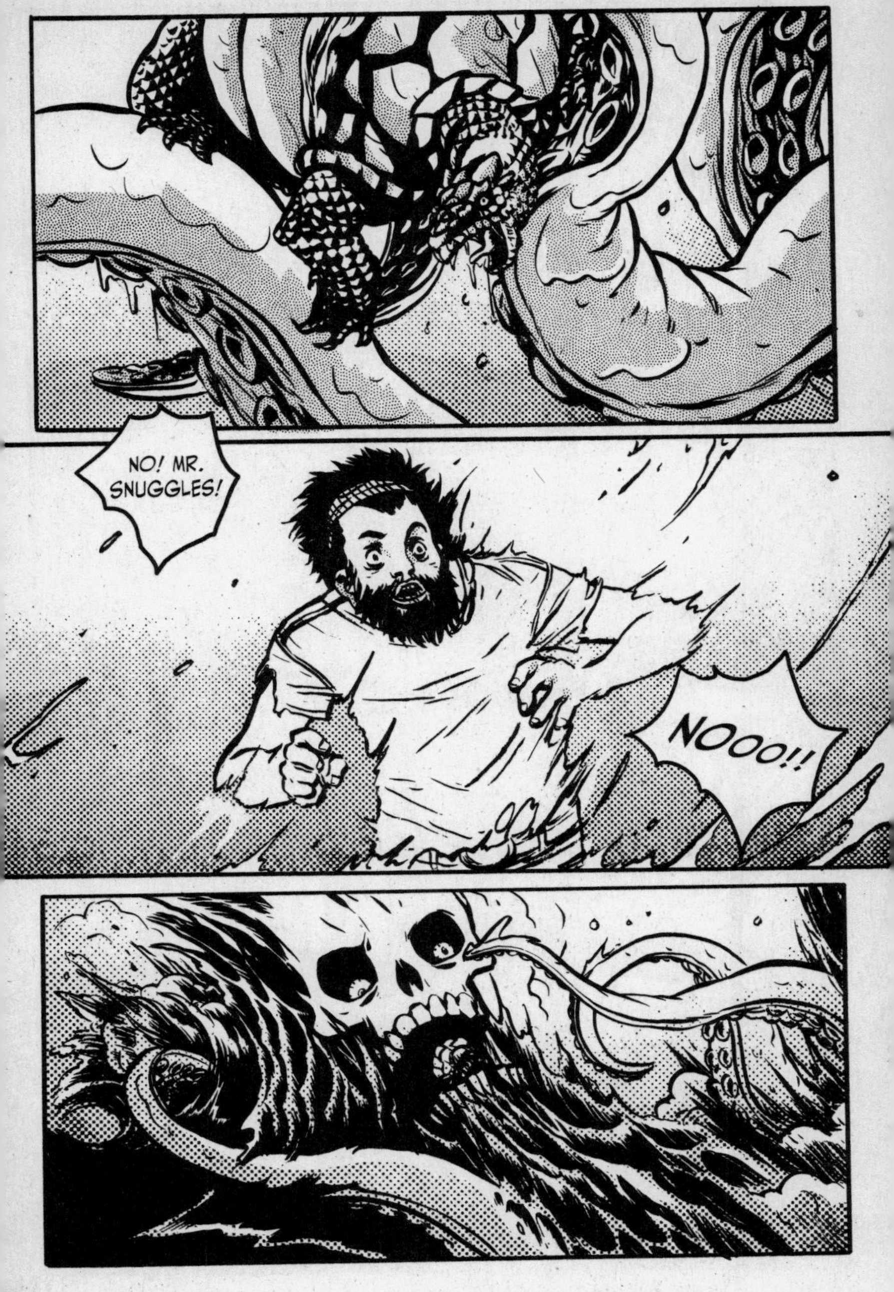
NO! MR. SNUGGLES!
NOOO!!

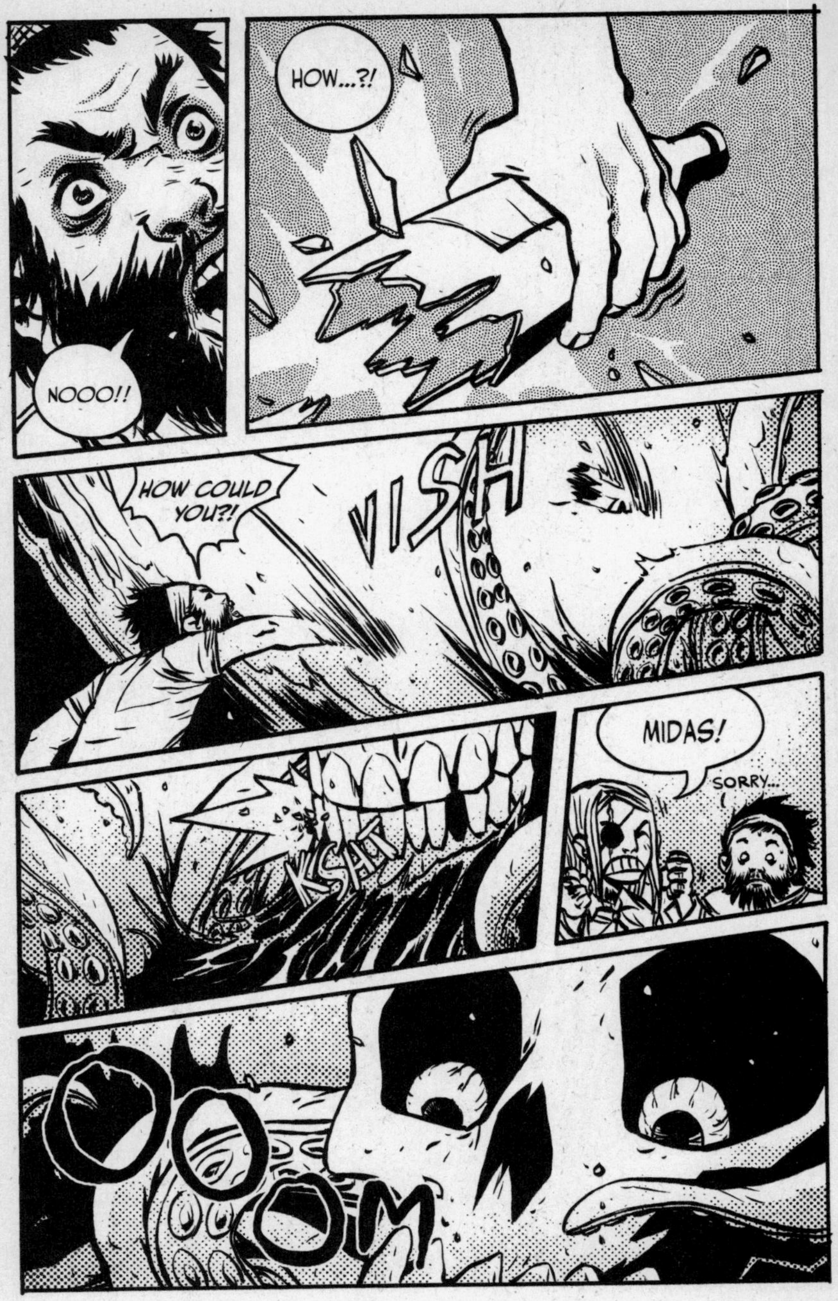
NOOO!!
HOW...?!
HOW COULD YOU?!
VISH
KSHK
MIDAS!
SORRY...
OOOOM

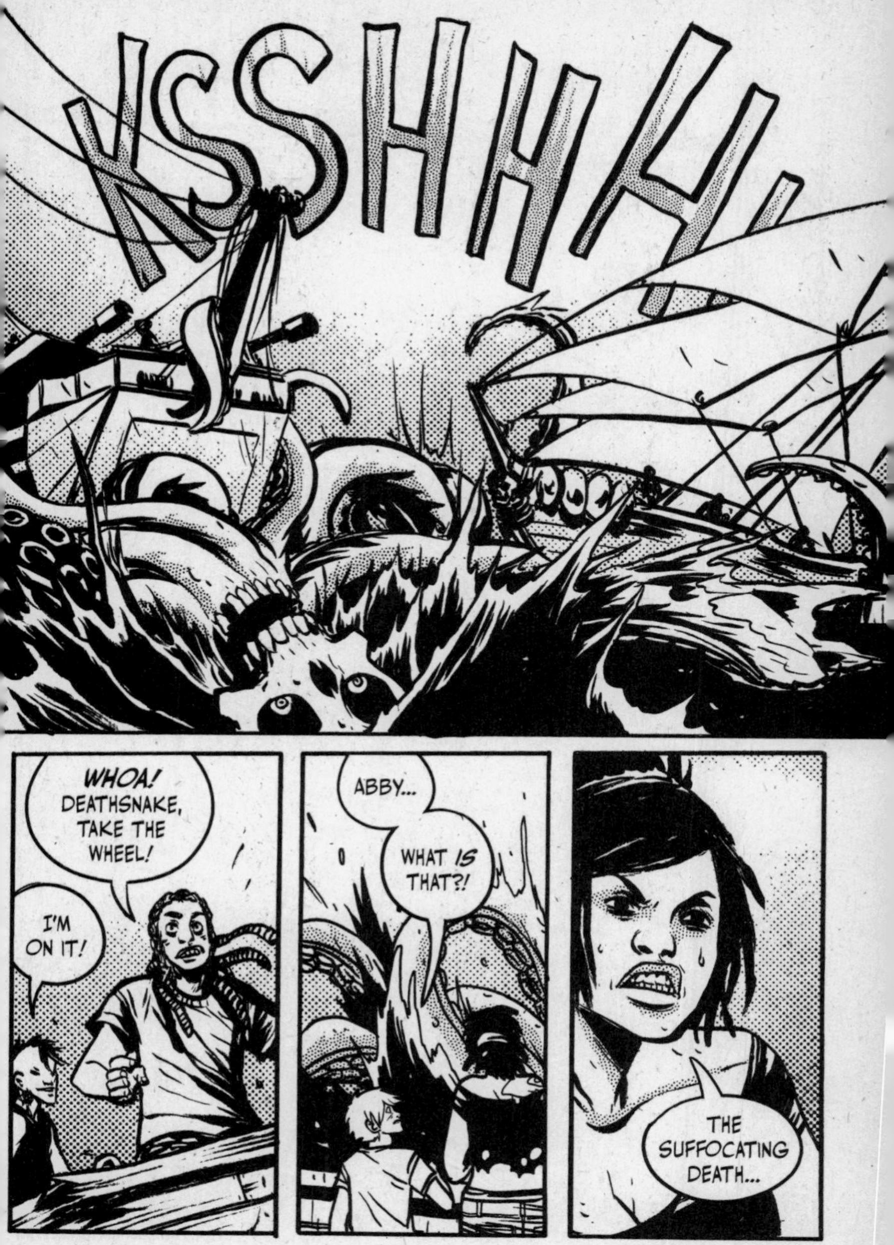
KSSHHHH
WHOA! DEATHSNAKE, TAKE THE WHEEL!
I'M ON IT!
ABBY...
WHAT IS THAT?!
THE SUFFOCATING DEATH...

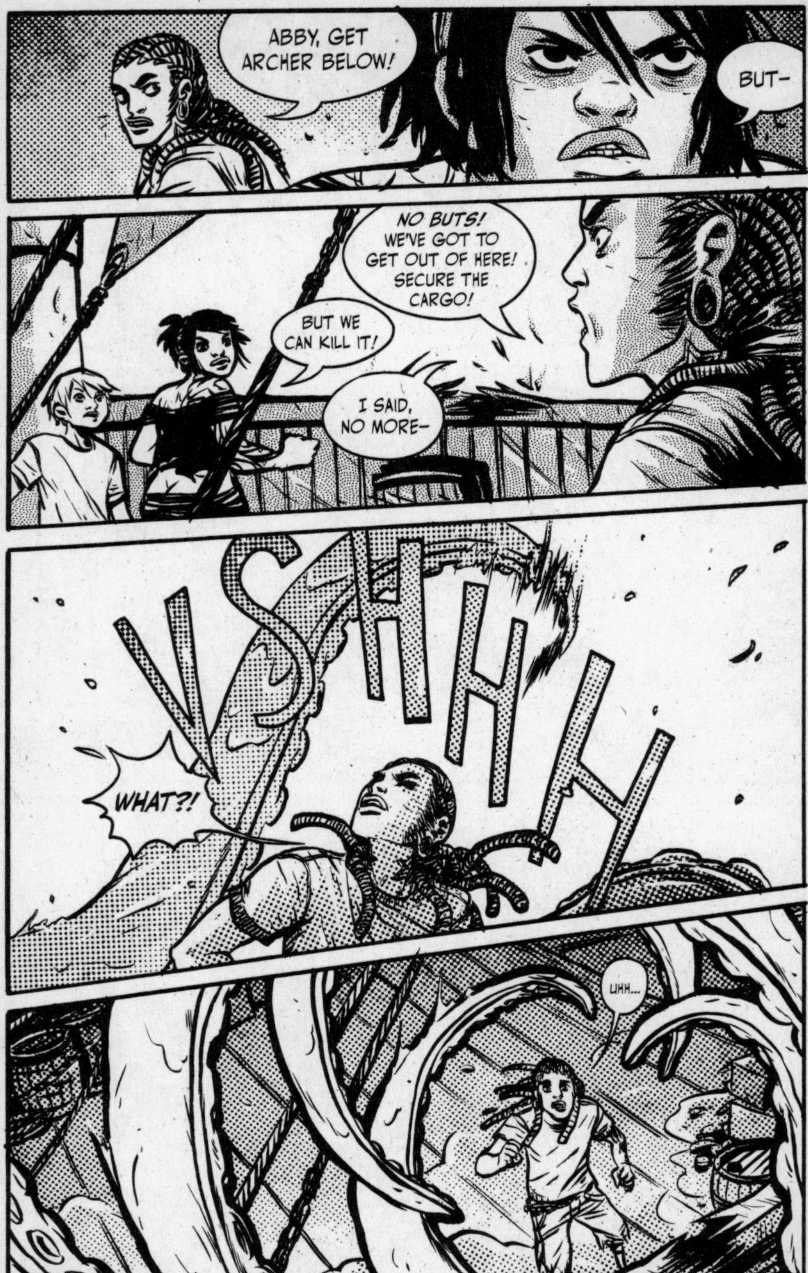
ABBY, GET ARCHER BELOW!
BUT-
NO BUTS! WE'VE GOT TO GET OUT OF HERE! SECURE THE CARGO!
BUT WE CAN KILL IT!
I SAID, NO MORE-
VSHHHH
WHAT?!
UHH...

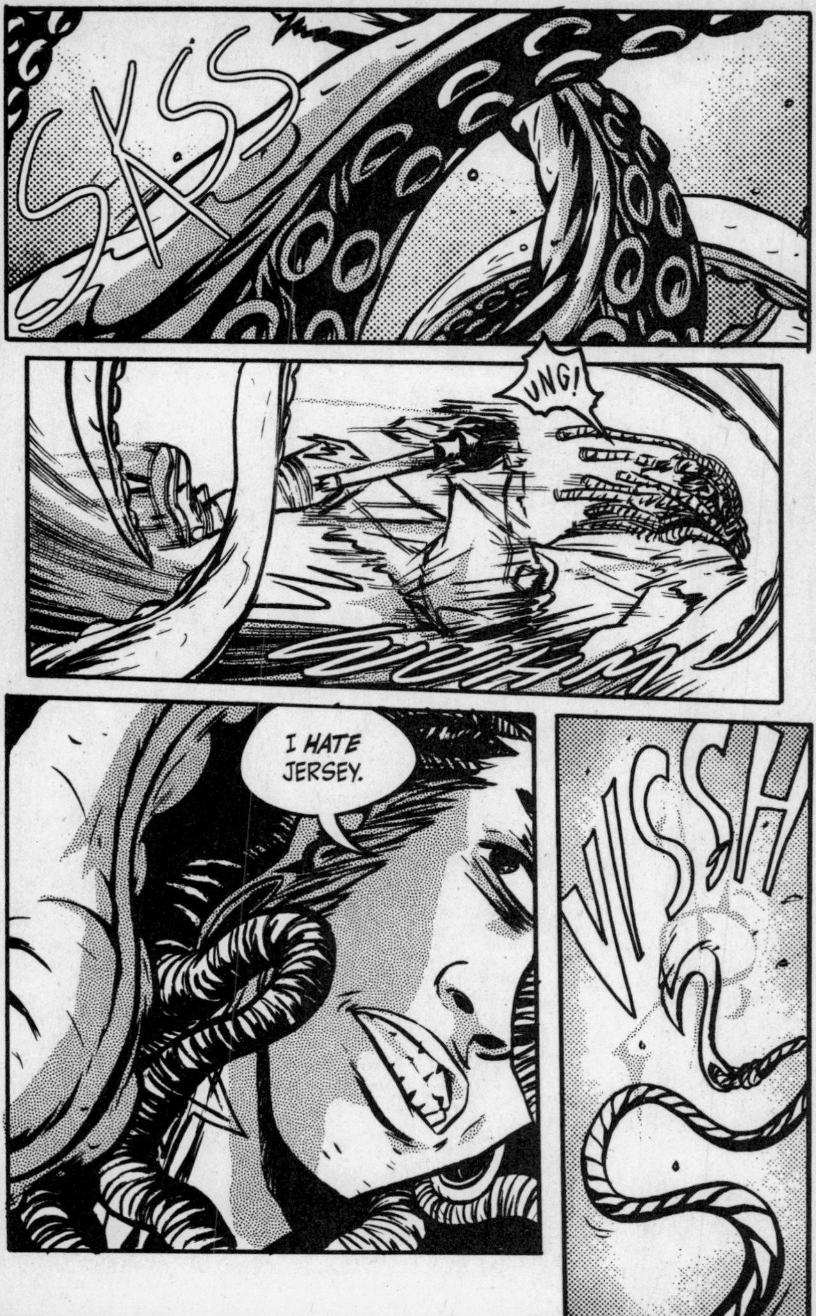
UNG!
I HATE JERSEY.

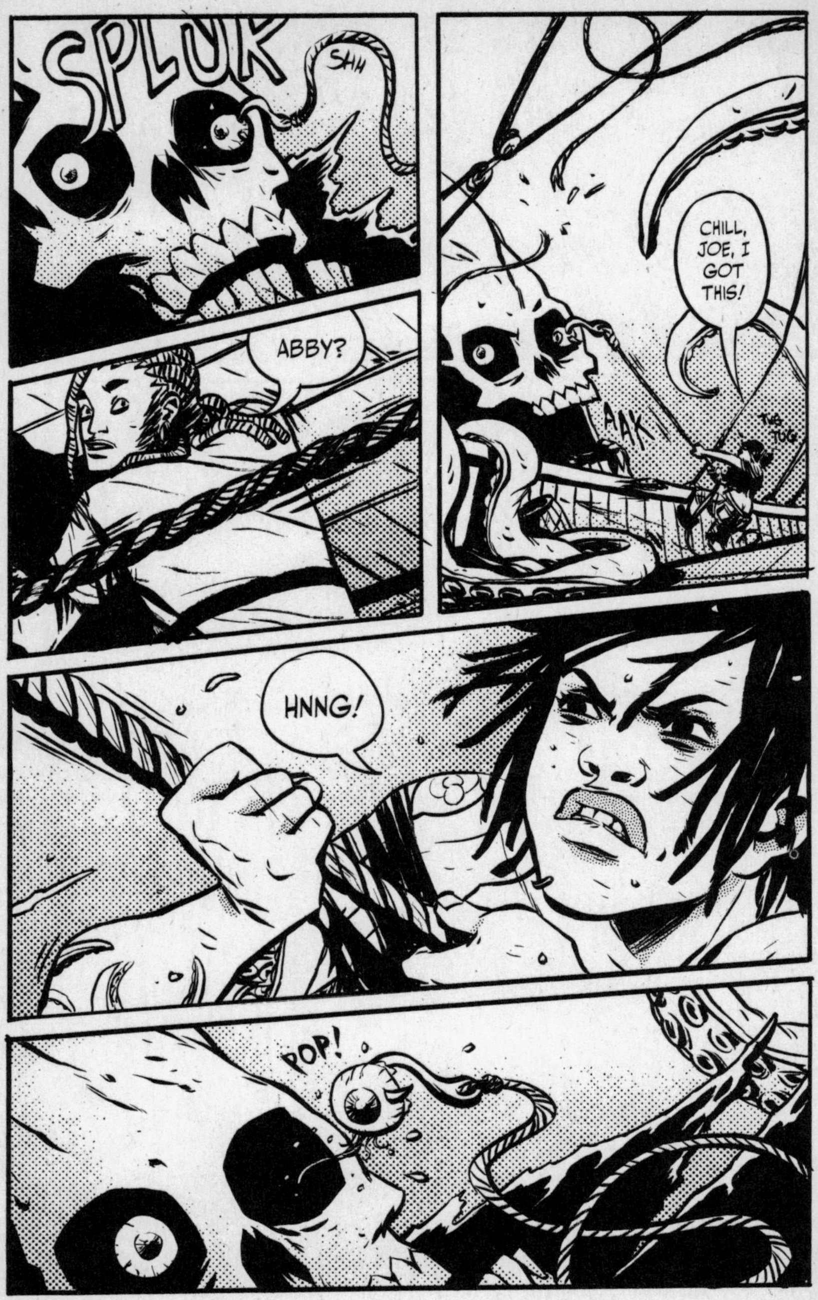
SPLUK
SHH
ABBY?
CHILL, JOE, I GOT THIS!
AAX
TUG TUG
HNNG!
POP!

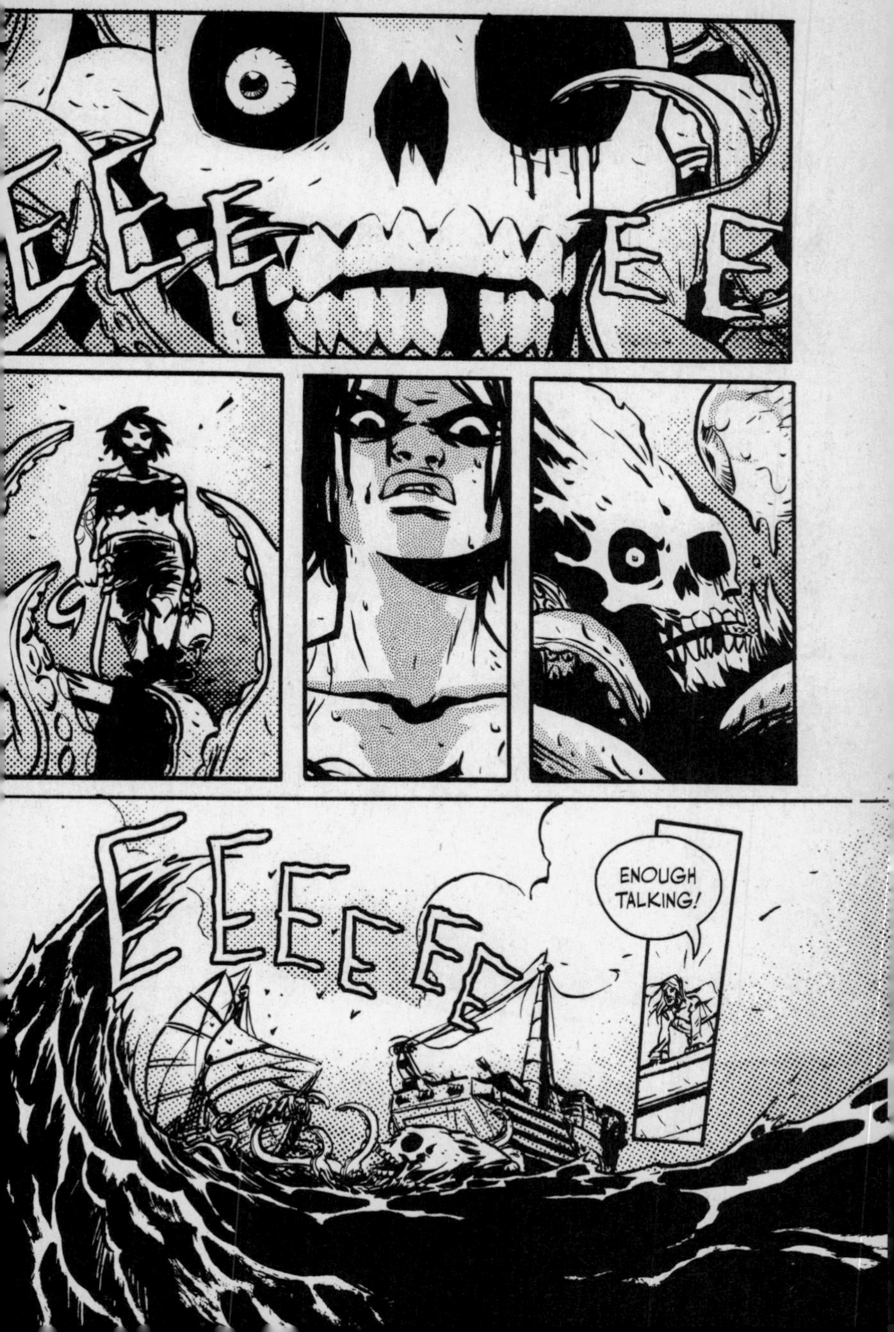
EEEEEE
EEEEEE
ENOUGH TALKING!

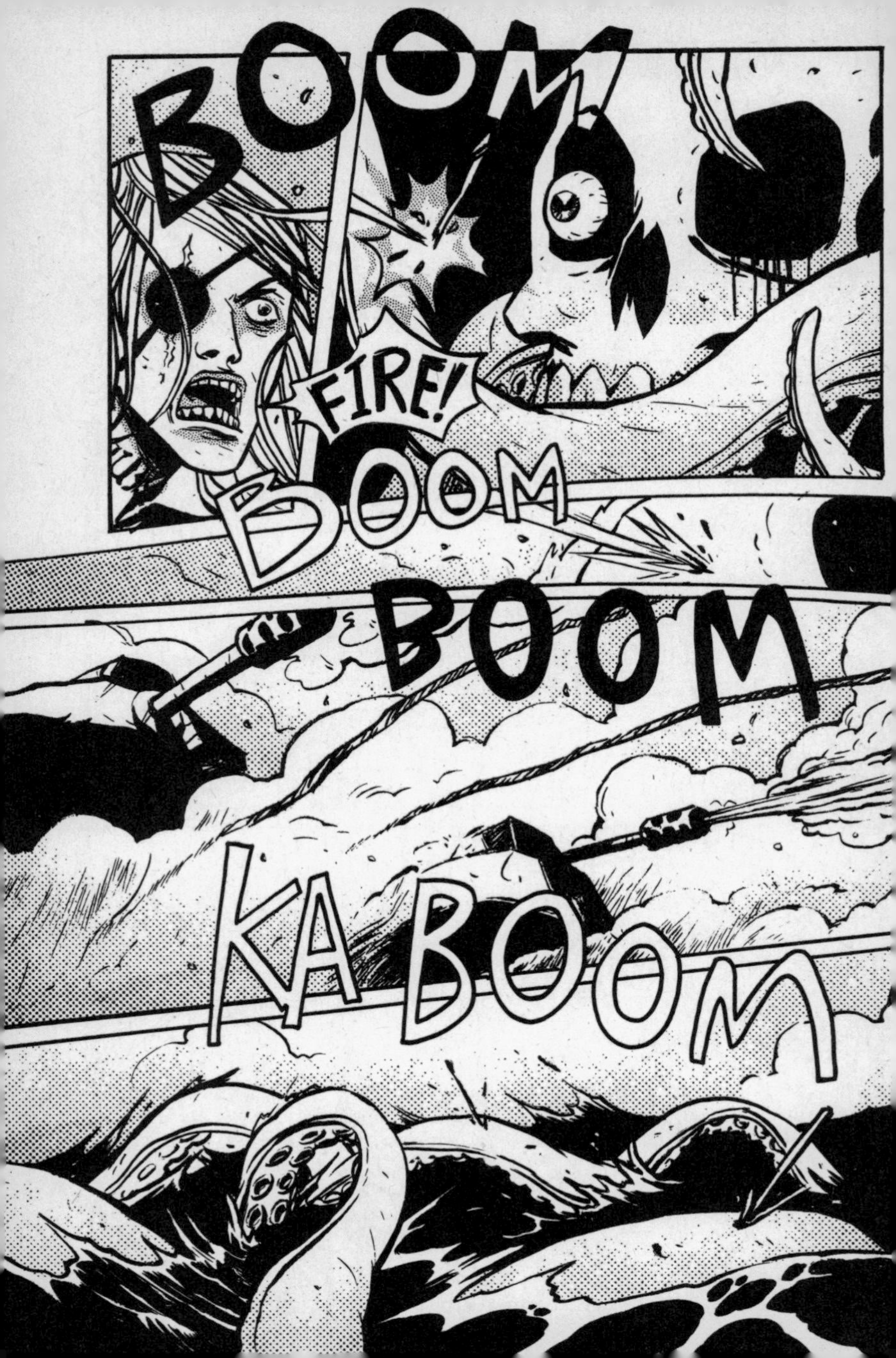
BOOM
FIRE!
BOOM
BOOM
KA BOOM

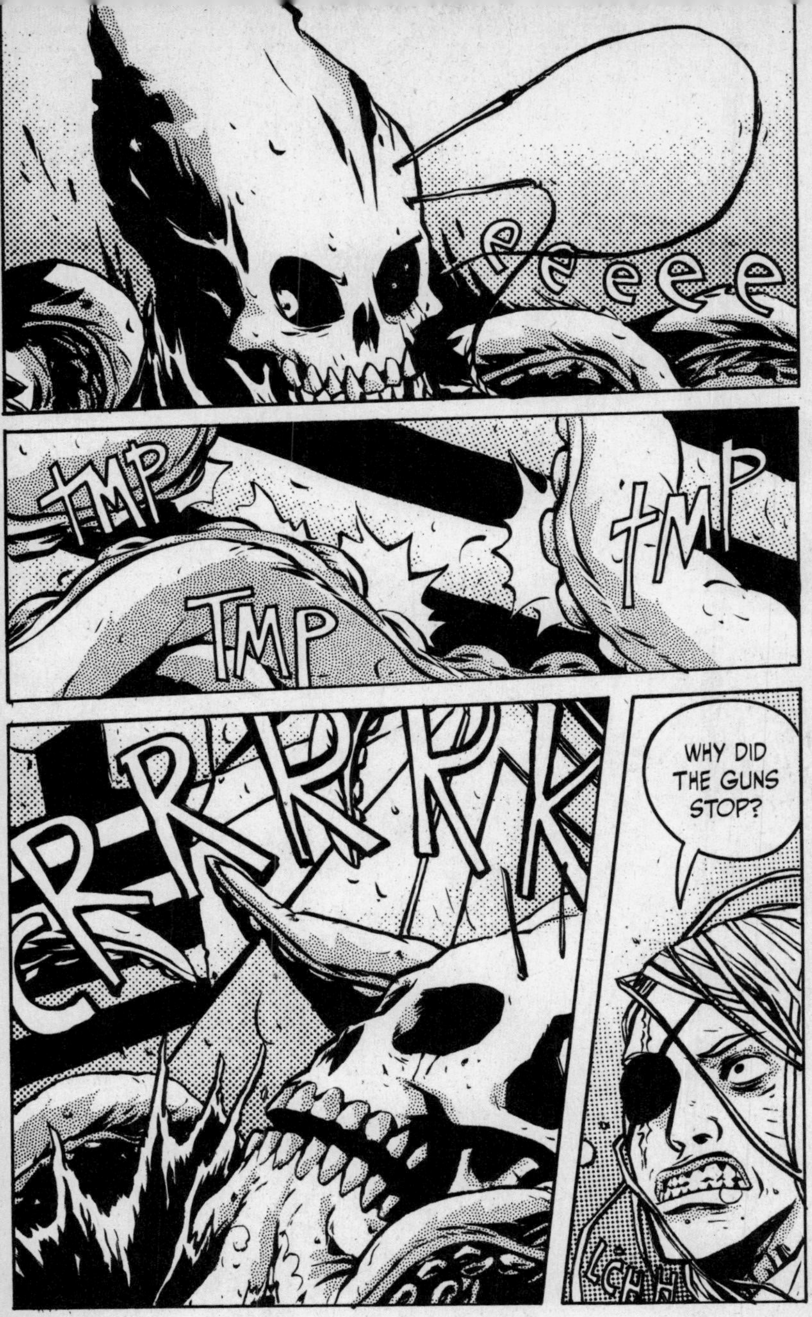
eeeee
TMP
TMP
TMP
CRRRRK
WHY DID THE GUNS STOP?

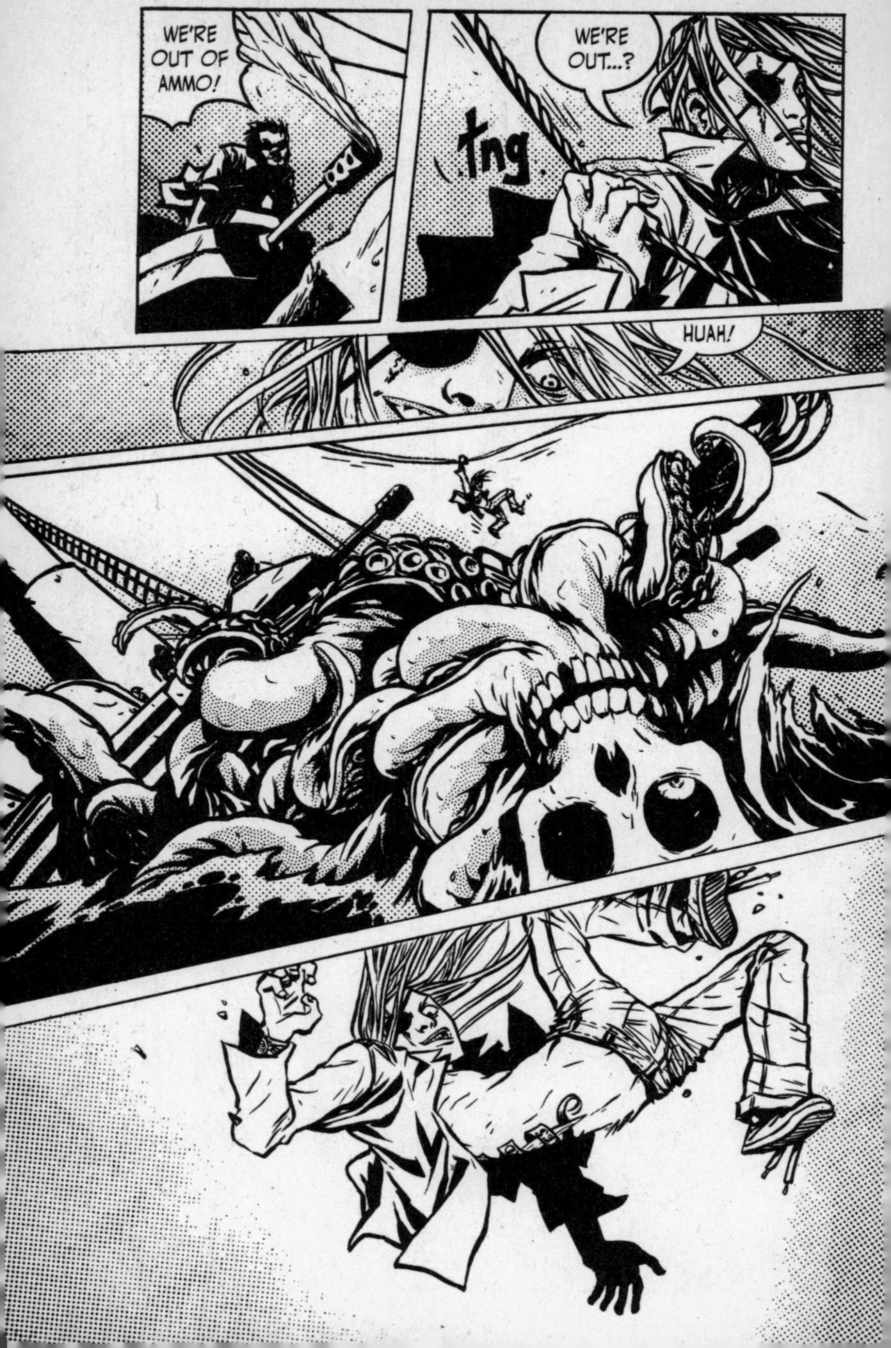
WE'RE OUT OF AMMO!
WE'RE OUT...?
tng
HUAH!

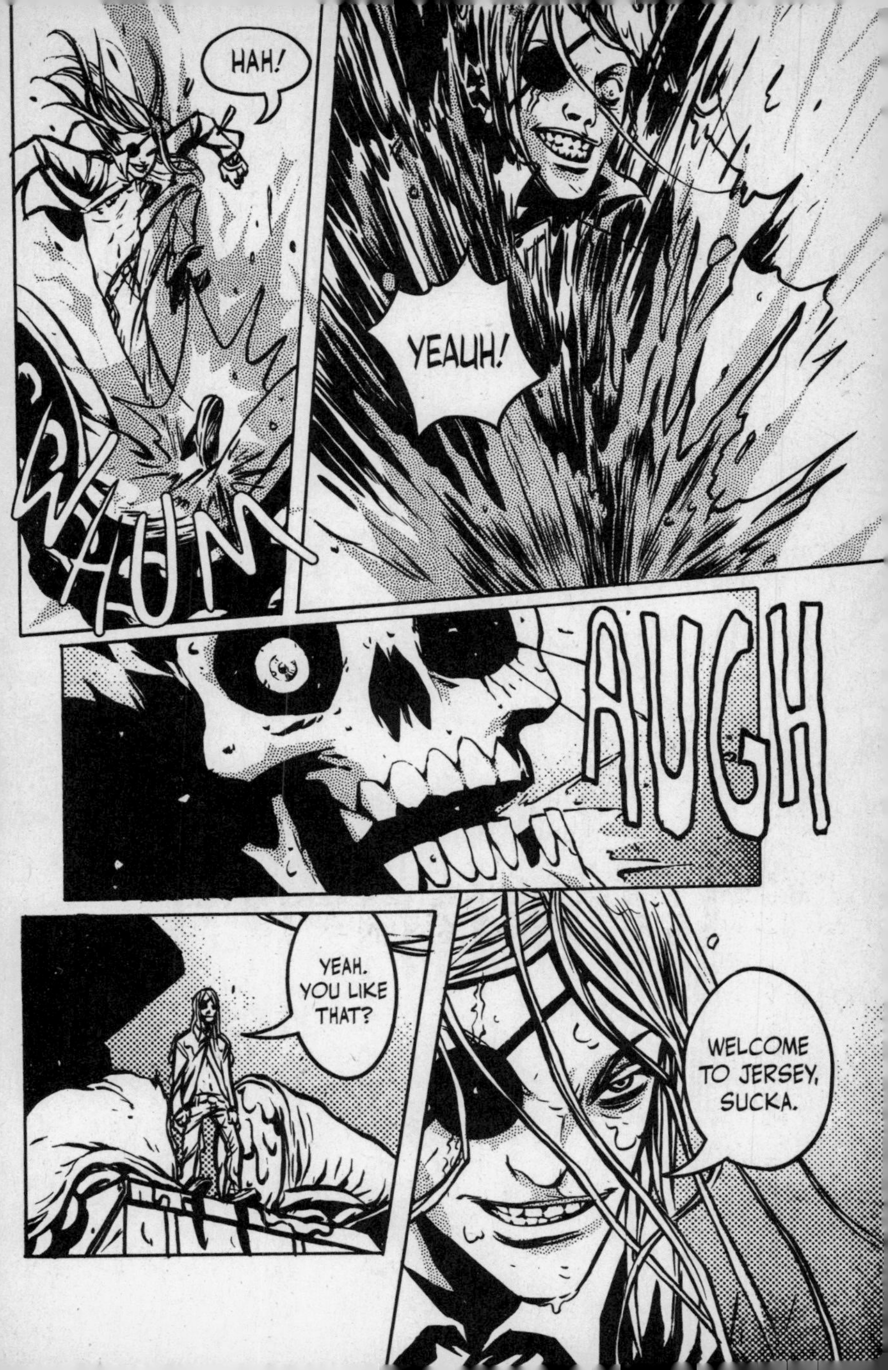
HAH!
WHUM
YEAUH!
AUGH
YEAH. YOU LIKE THAT?
WELCOME TO JERSEY, SUCKA.

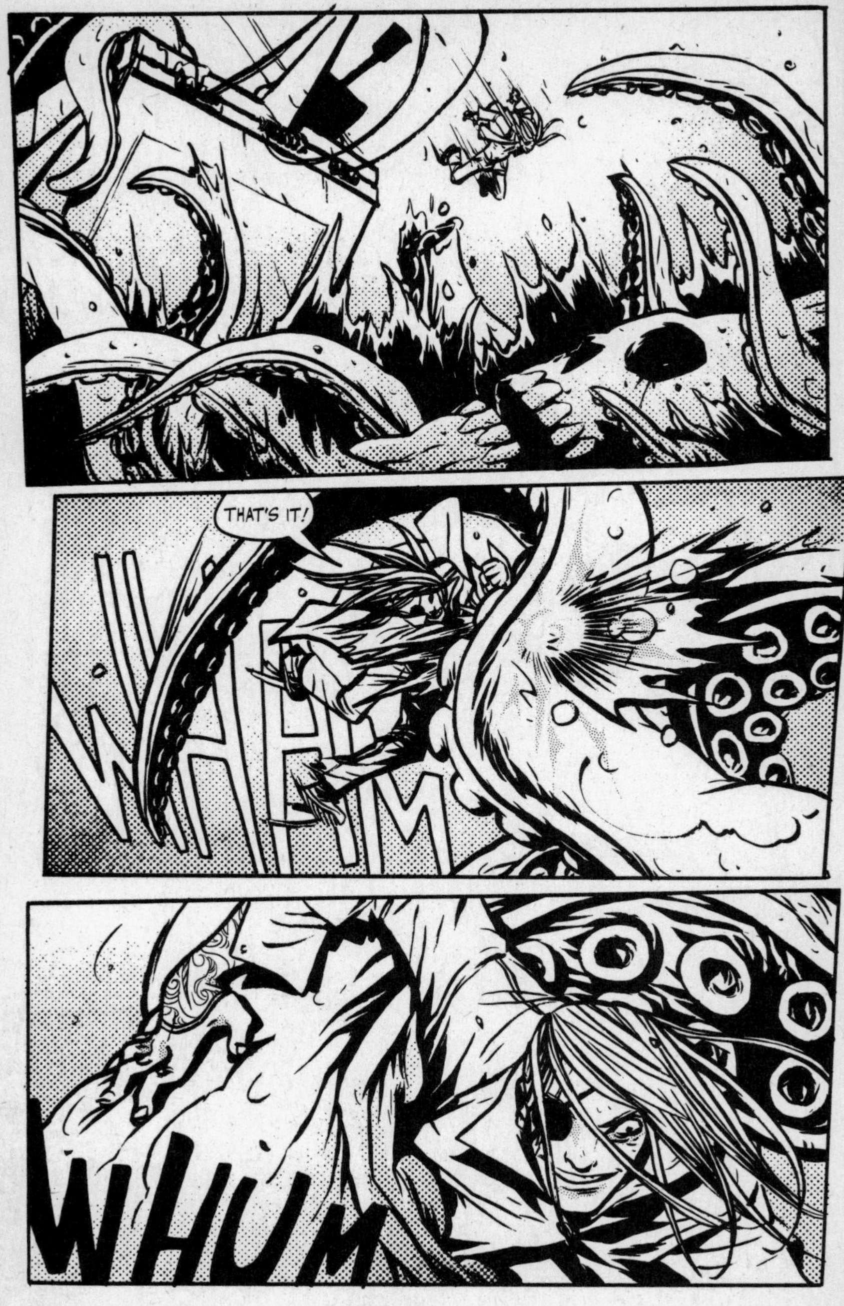
THAT'S IT!
WHUM

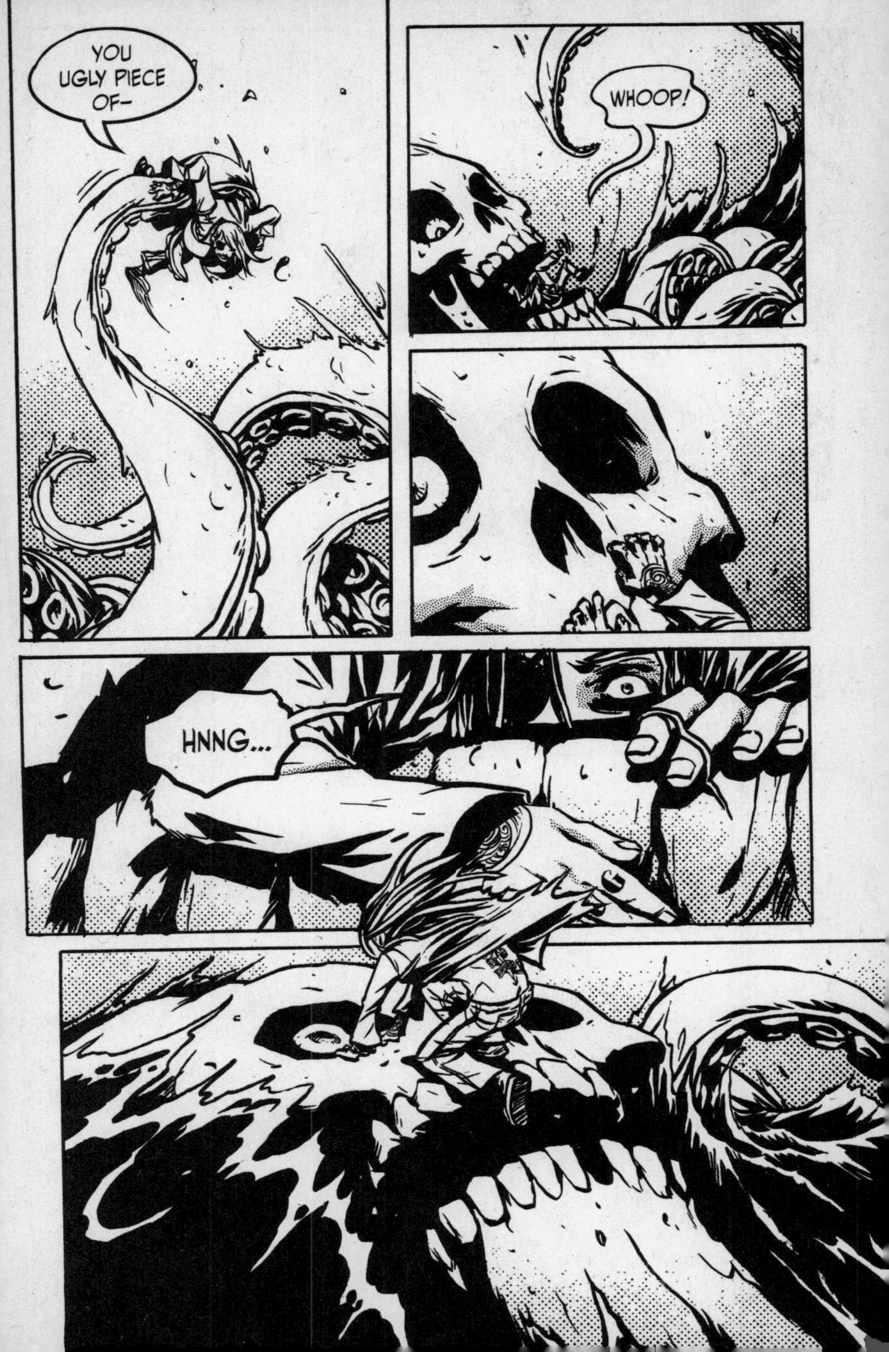
YOU UGLY PIECE OF–
WHOOP!
HNNG...

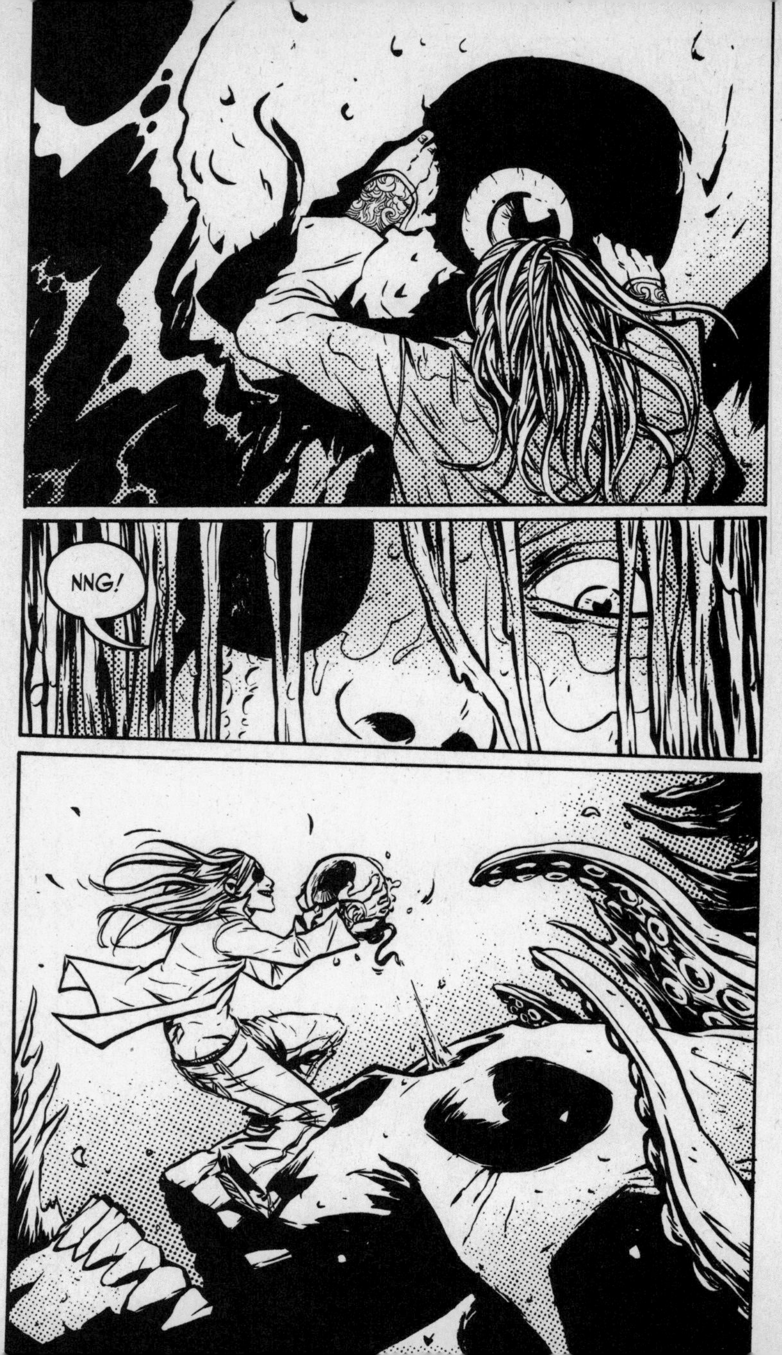
NNG!

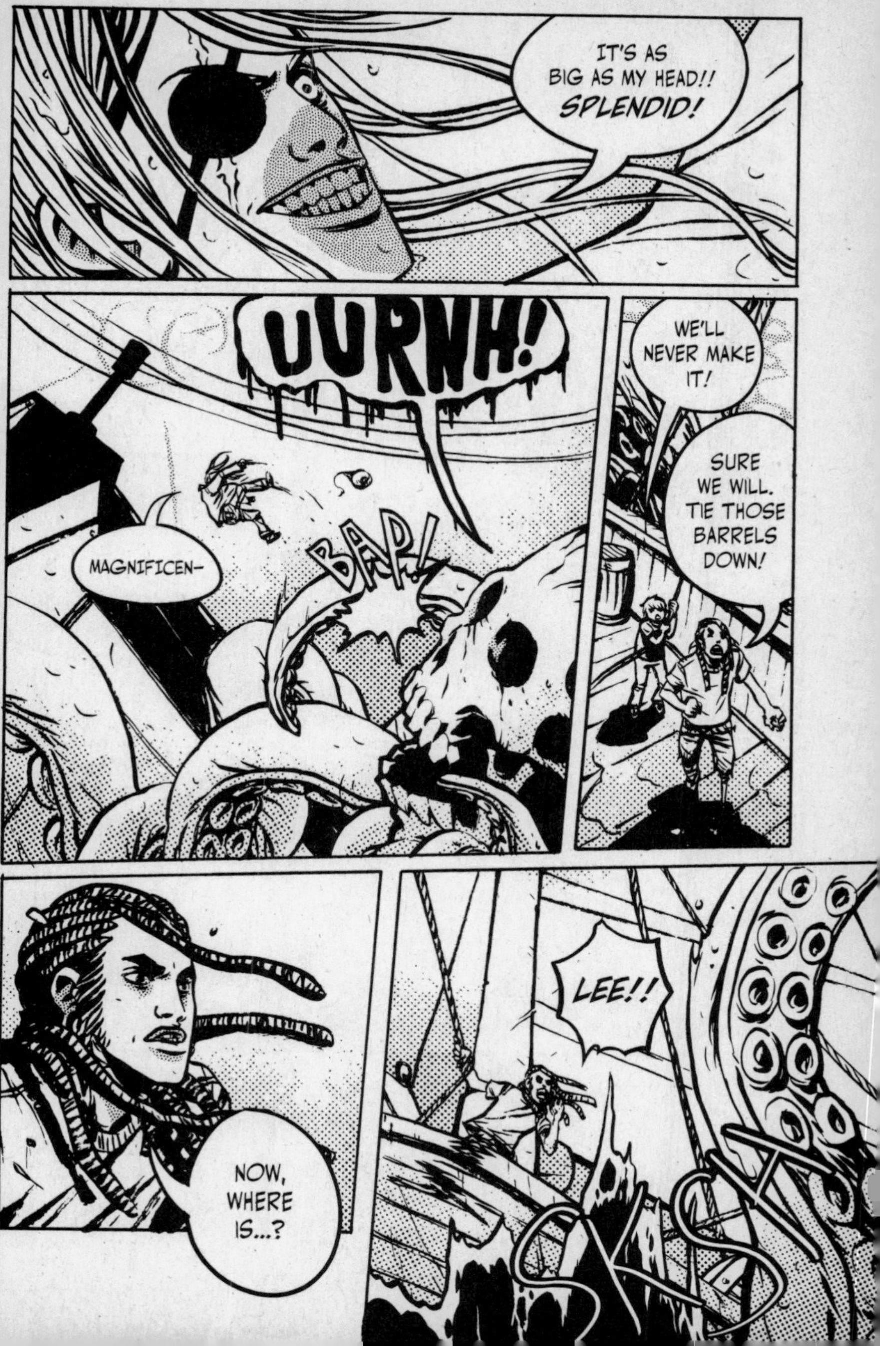
IT'S AS BIG AS MY HEAD!! SPLENDID!
UURNH!
MAGNIFICEN-
BAP!
WE'LL NEVER MAKE IT!
SURE WE WILL. TIE THOSE BARRELS DOWN!
NOW, WHERE IS...?
LEE!!

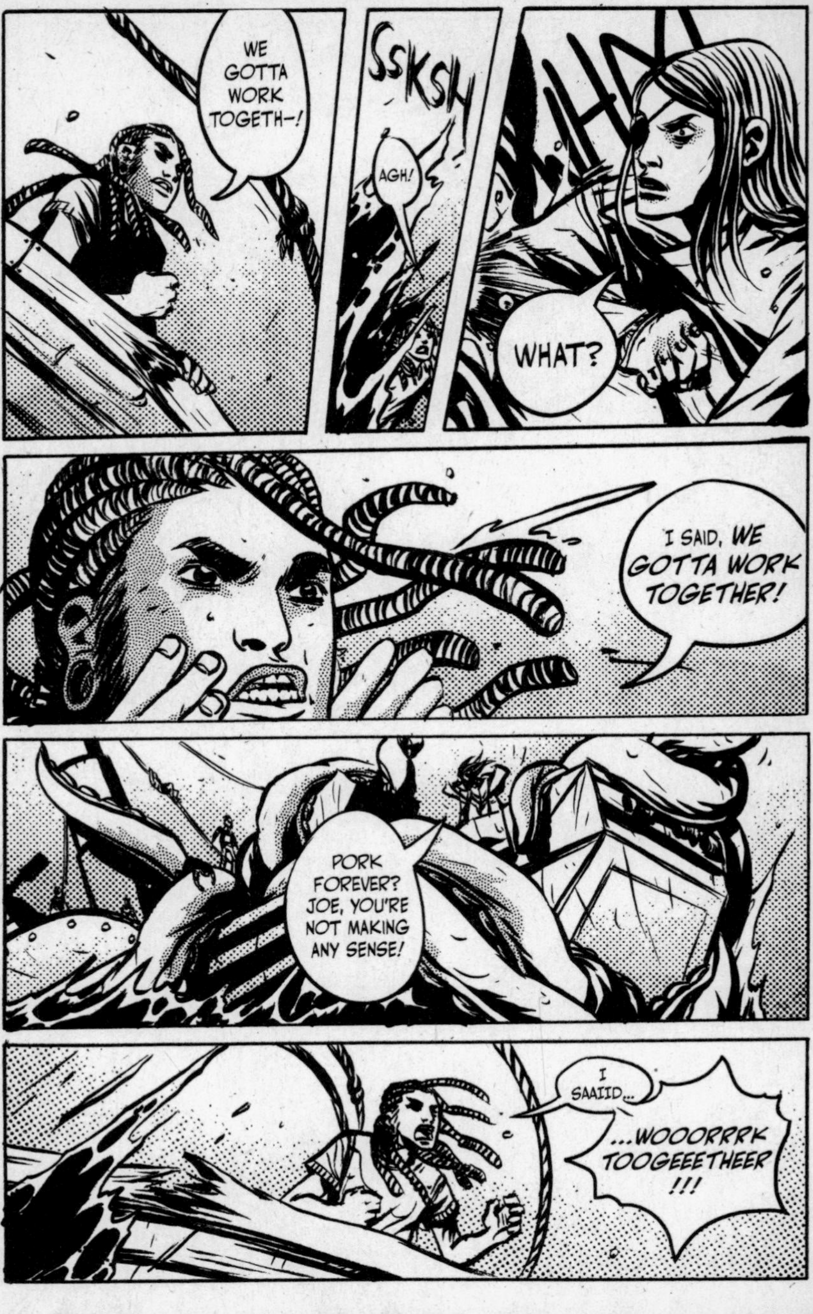
WE GOTTA WORK TOGETH-!
SSKSH!
AGH!
WHAT?
I SAID, WE GOTTA WORK TOGETHER!
PORK FOREVER? JOE, YOU'RE NOT MAKING ANY SENSE!
I SAAIID...
...WOOORRRK TOOGEEETHEER !!!

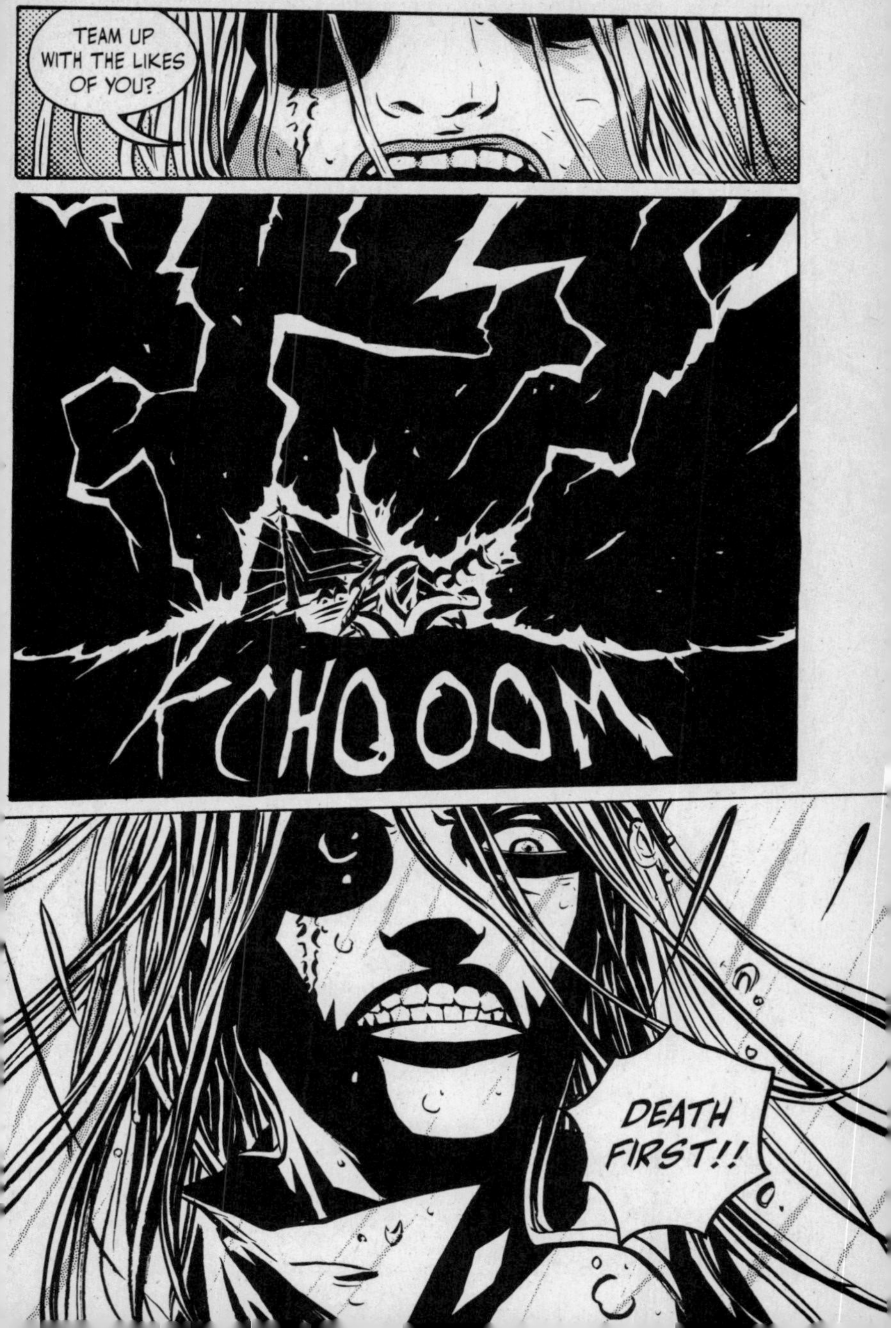
TEAM UP WITH THE LIKES OF YOU?
CHOOOM
DEATH FIRST!!

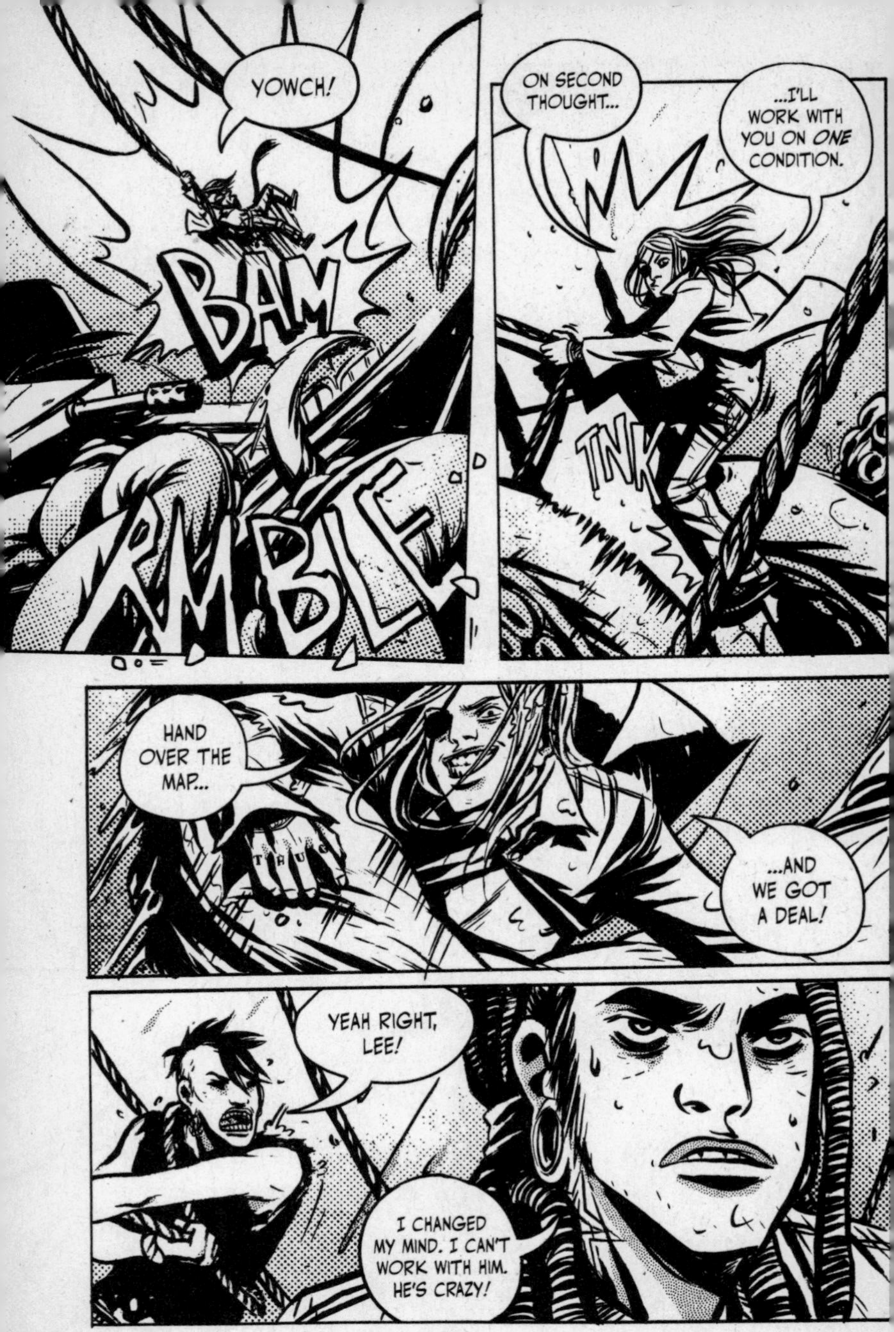
YOWCH!
BAM
RMBLE
ON SECOND THOUGHT...
...I'LL WORK WITH YOU ON ONE CONDITION.
TNK
HAND OVER THE MAP...
THUG
...AND WE GOT A DEAL!
YEAH RIGHT, LEE!
I CHANGED MY MIND. I CAN'T WORK WITH HIM. HE'S CRAZY!

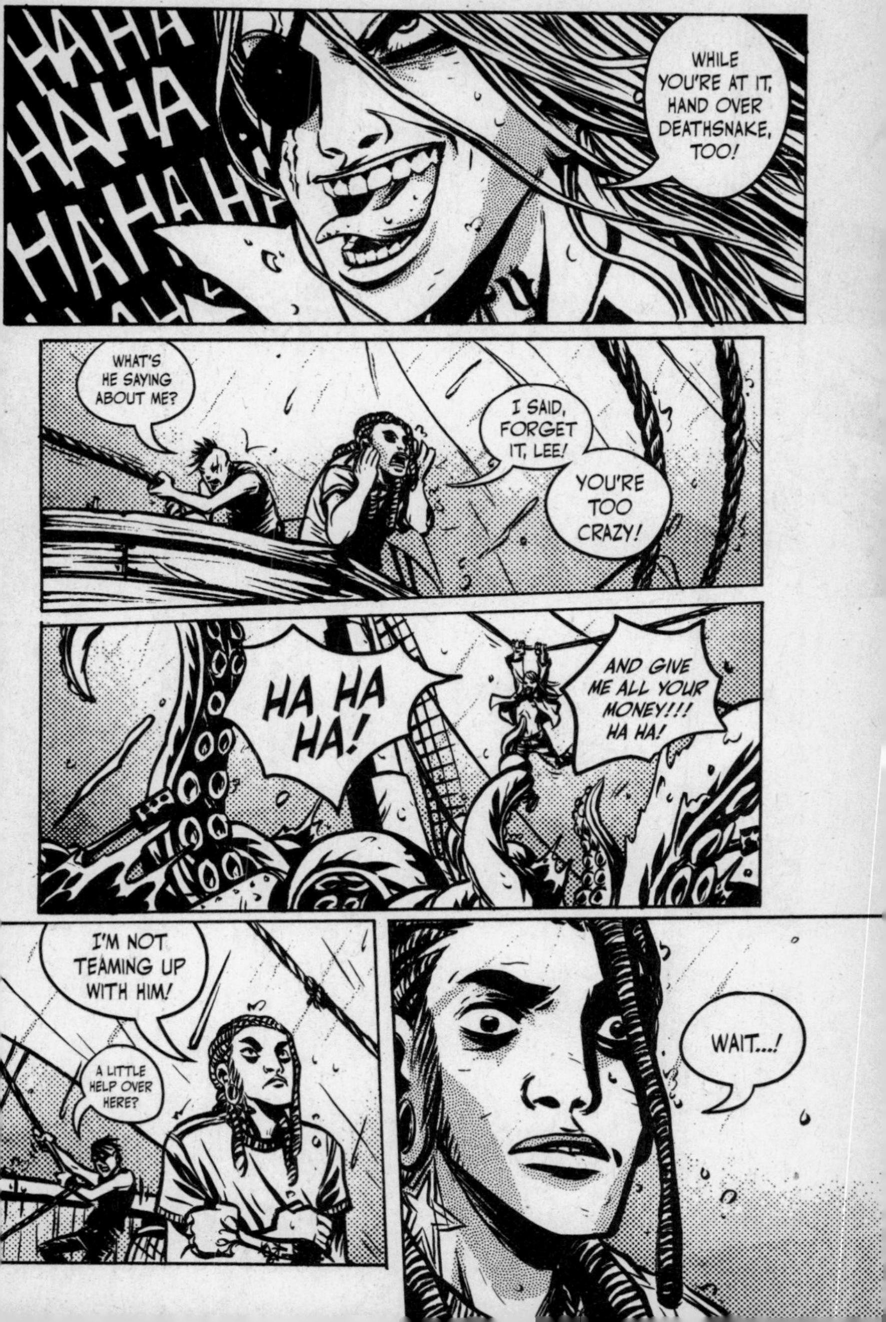
HA HA HAHA HAHAHA HAHAHA
WHILE YOU'RE AT IT, HAND OVER DEATHSNAKE, TOO!
WHAT'S HE SAYING ABOUT ME?
I SAID, FORGET IT, LEE!
YOU'RE TOO CRAZY!
HA HA HA!
AND GIVE ME ALL YOUR MONEY!!! HA HA!
I'M NOT TEAMING UP WITH HIM!
A LITTLE HELP OVER HERE?
WAIT...!

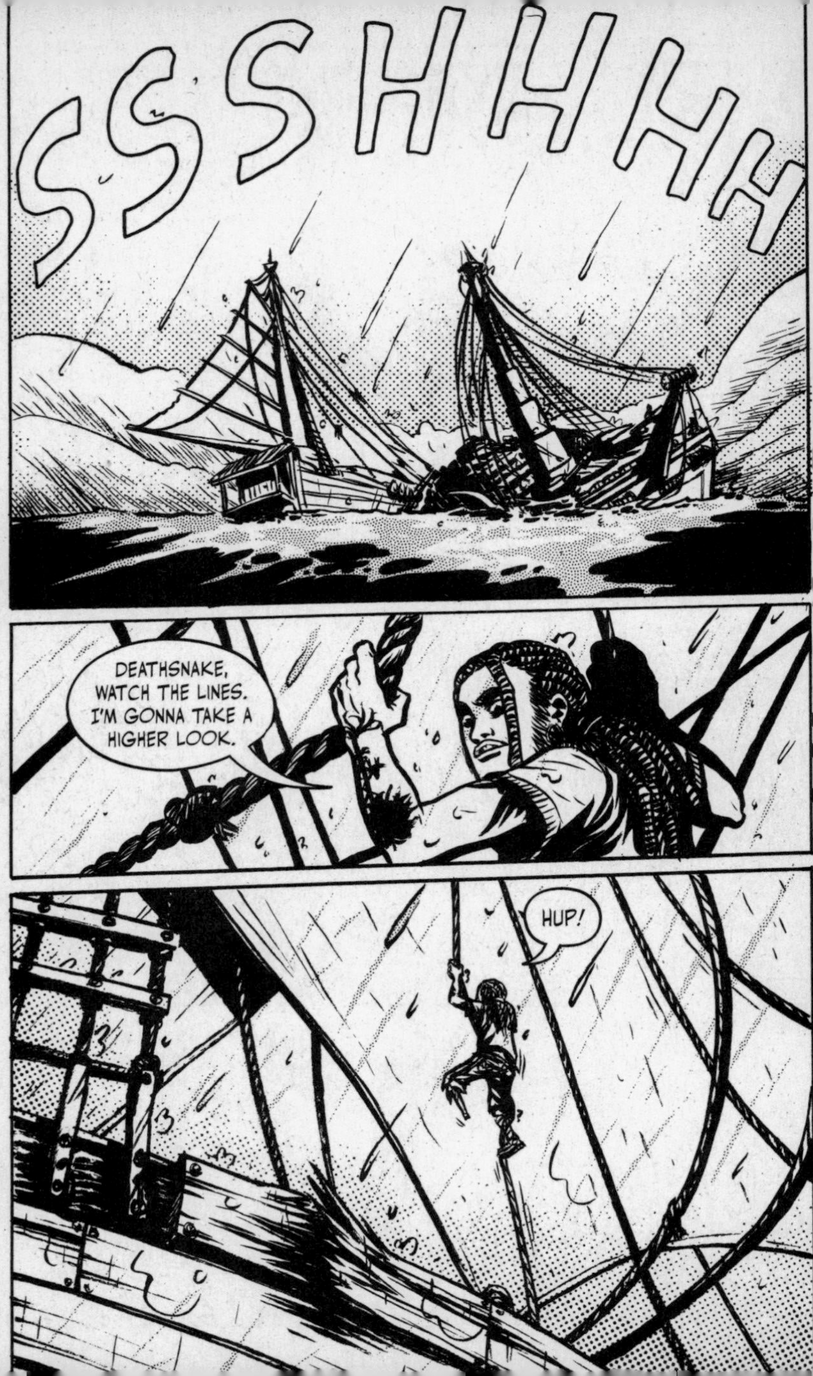
SSSHHHHH
DEATHSNAKE, WATCH THE LINES. I'M GONNA TAKE A HIGHER LOOK.
HUP!

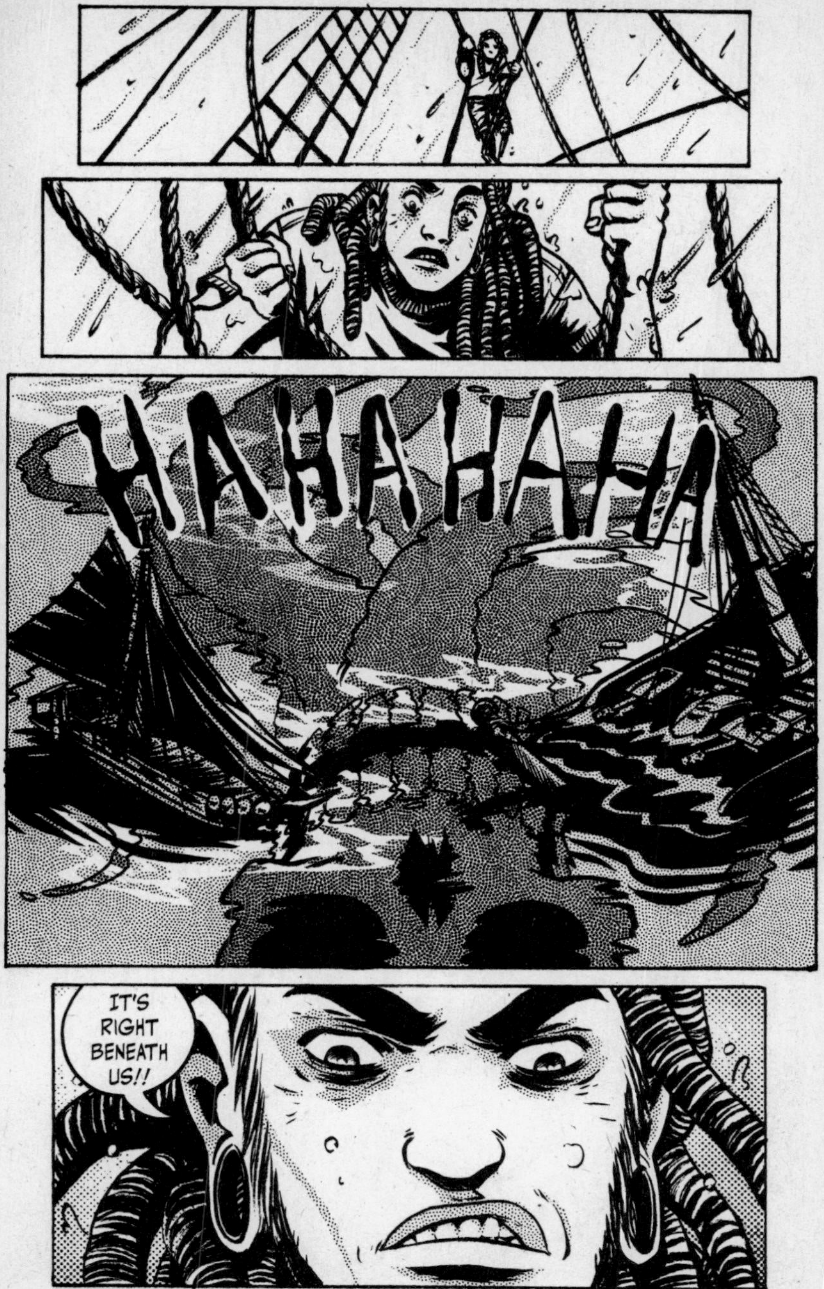
HAHAHAHA
IT'S RIGHT BENEATH US!!

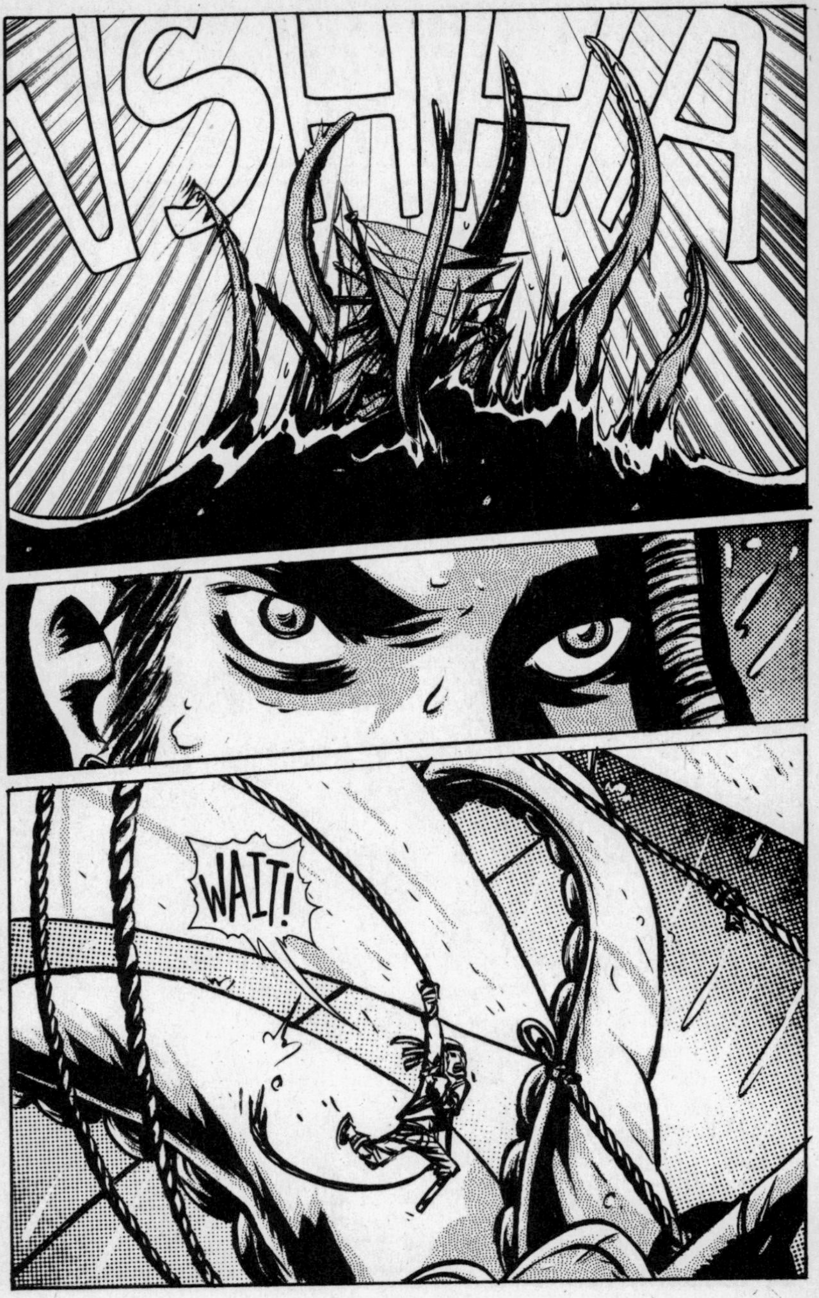
VSHHA
WAIT!

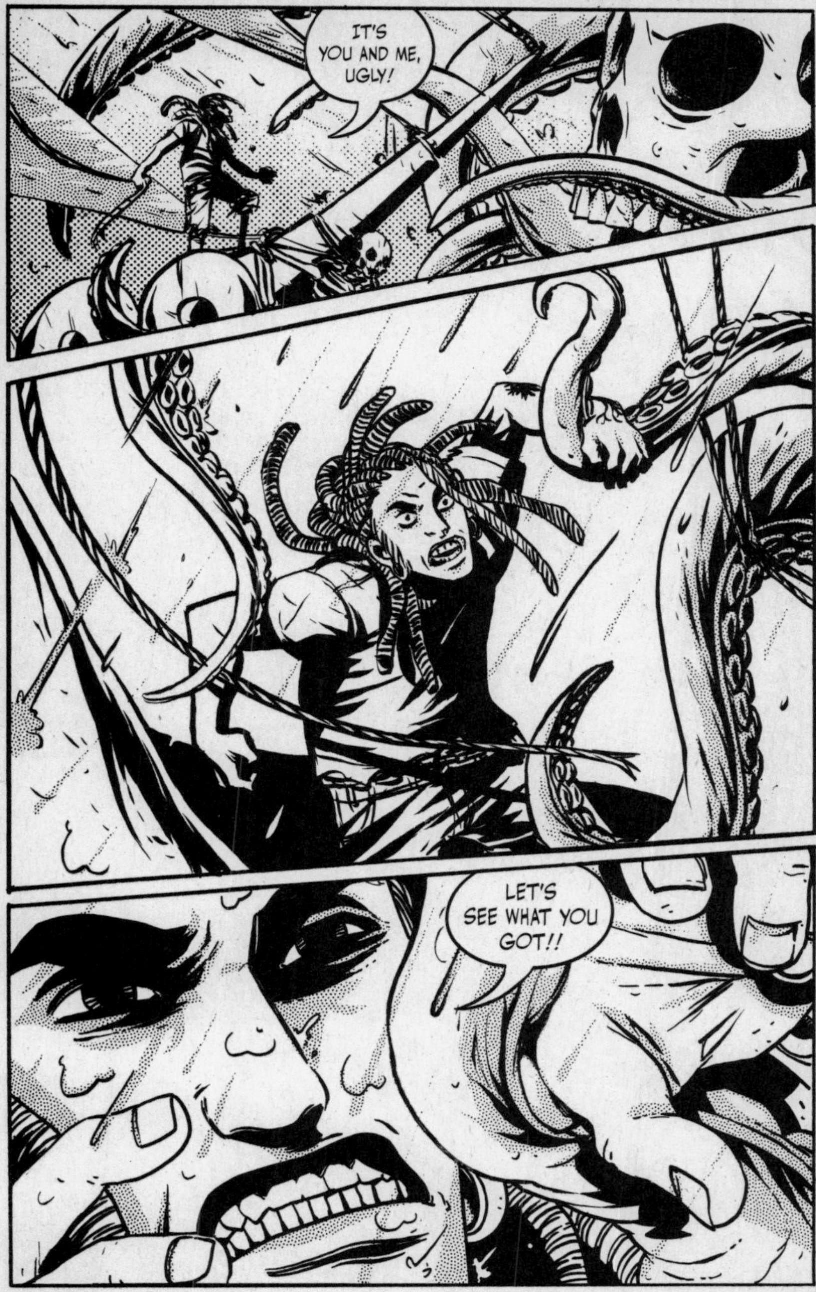
IT'S YOU AND ME, UGLY!
LET'S SEE WHAT YOU GOT!!

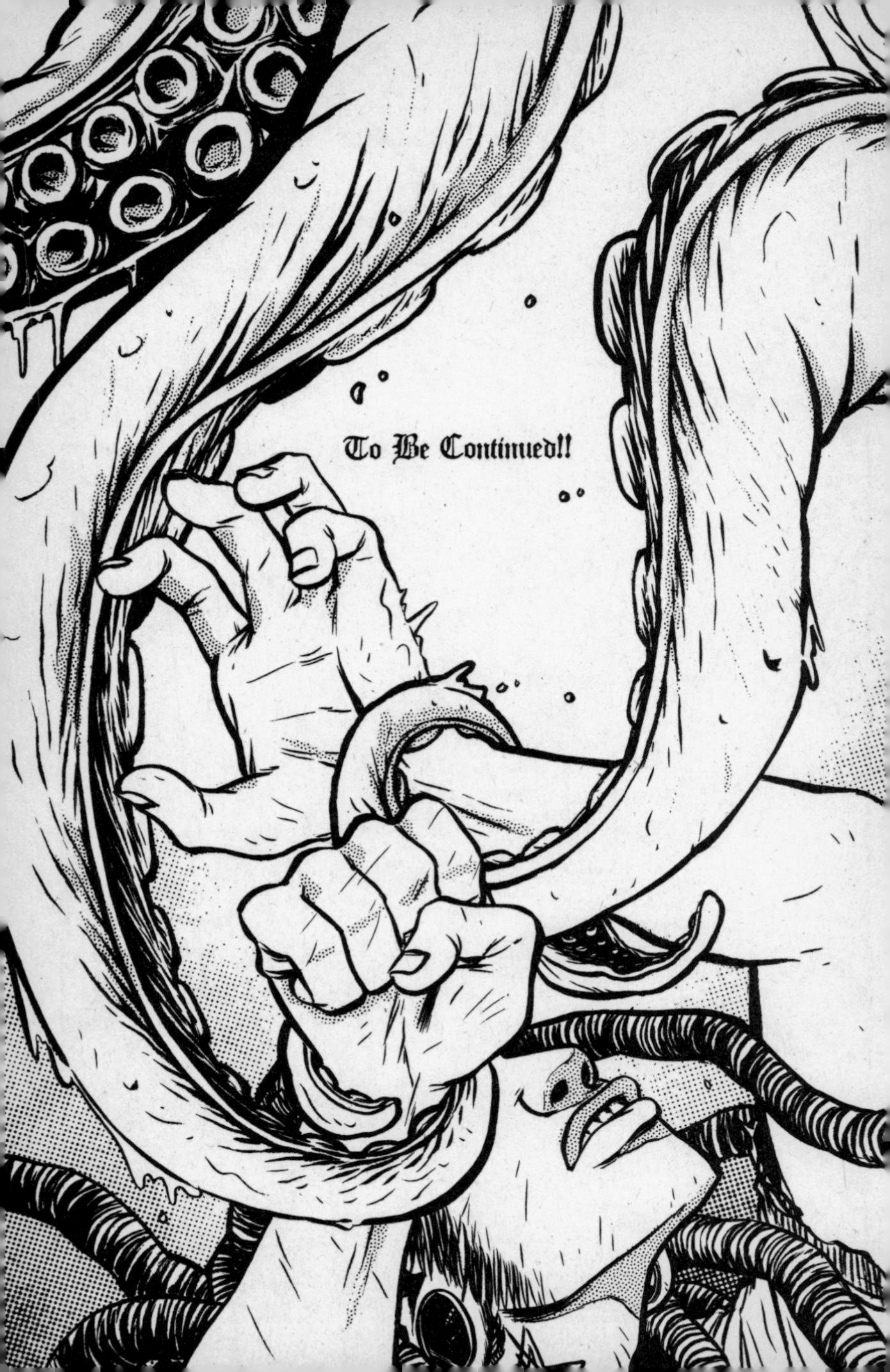
To Be Continued!!

Coming up in Volume Two

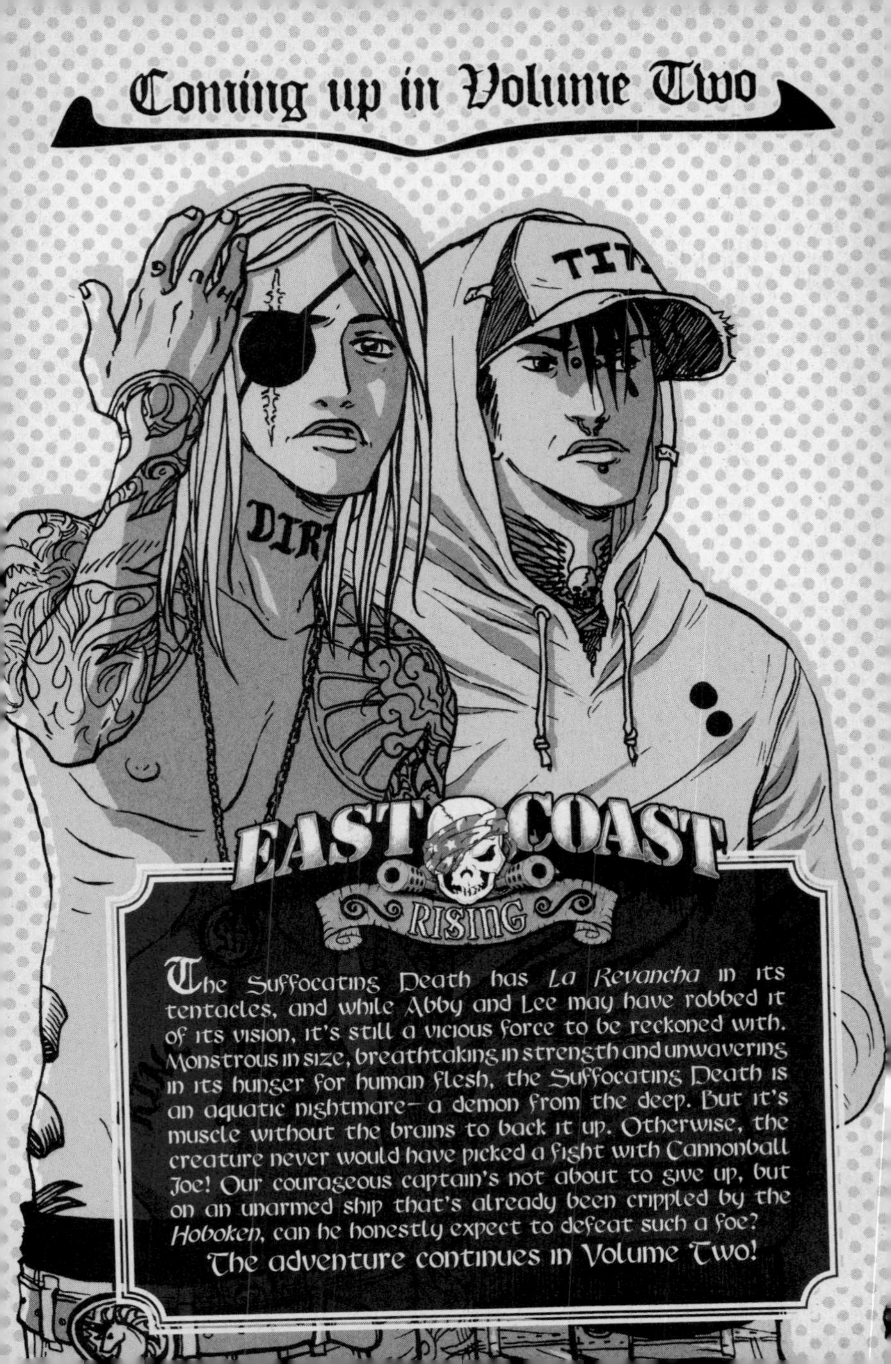

EAST COAST RISING

The Suffocating Death has *La Revancha* in its tentacles, and while Abby and Lee may have robbed it of its vision, it's still a vicious force to be reckoned with. Monstrous in size, breathtaking in strength and unwavering in its hunger for human flesh, the Suffocating Death is an aquatic nightmare—a demon from the deep. But it's muscle without the brains to back it up. Otherwise, the creature never would have picked a fight with Cannonball Joe! Our courageous captain's not about to give up, but on an unarmed ship that's already been crippled by the *Hoboken*, can he honestly expect to defeat such a foe?

The adventure continues in Volume Two!

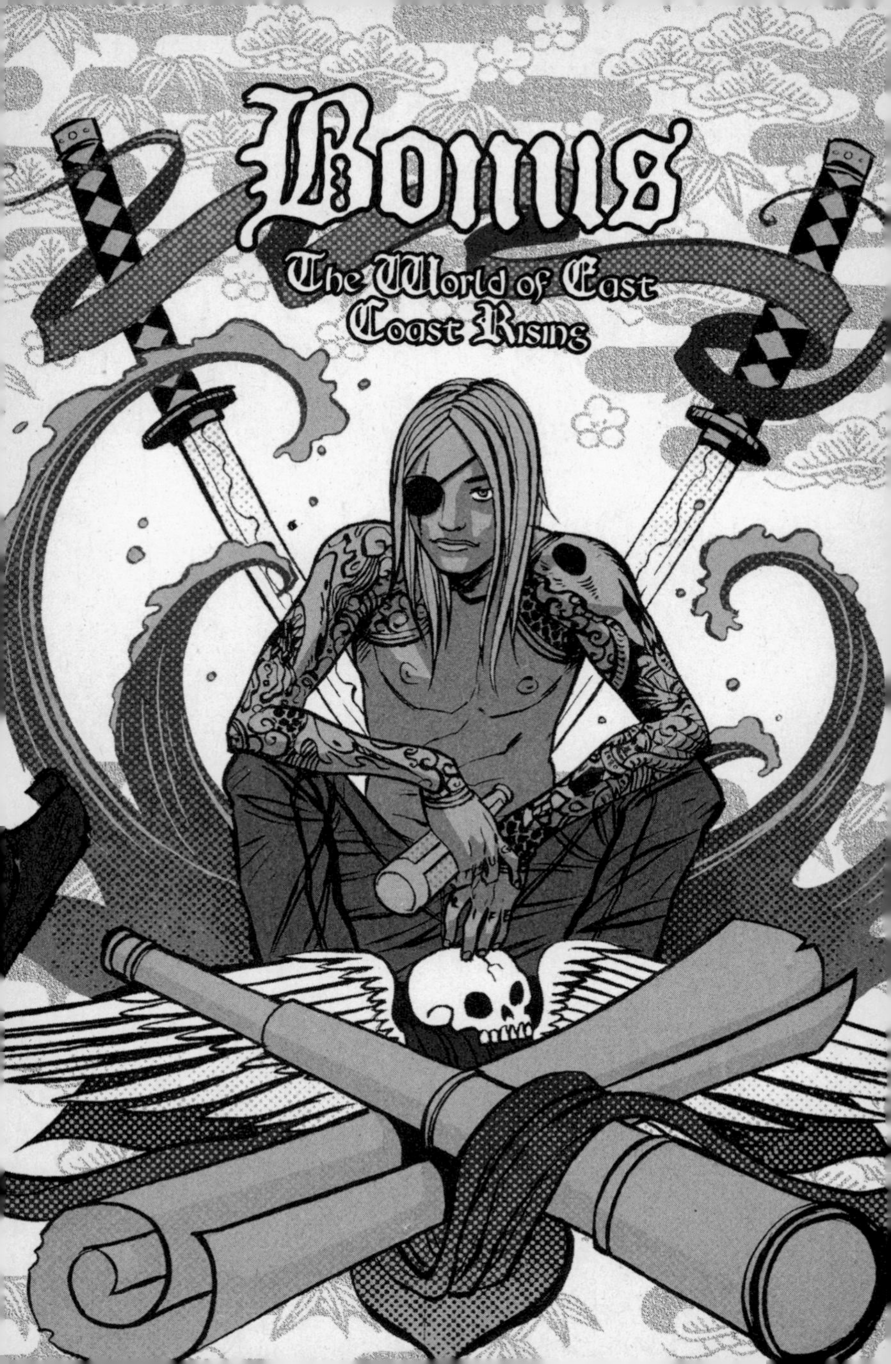
Bonus
The World of East Coast Rising

la revancha

Rumored to be the fastest and most practical ship in the tri-state area. Suitable to house up to ten crew members on long-term voyages. Its speed and agility make up for the lack of weapons on board and also help make the laundry dry very, very quickly.

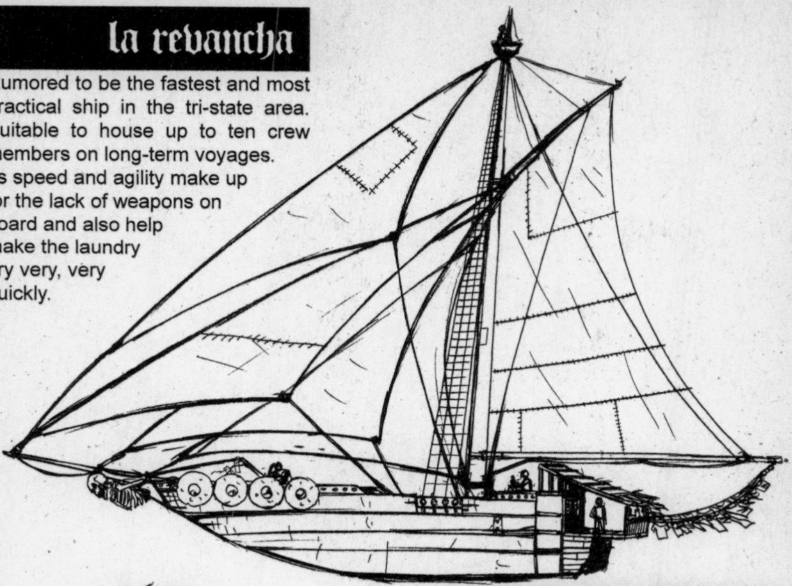

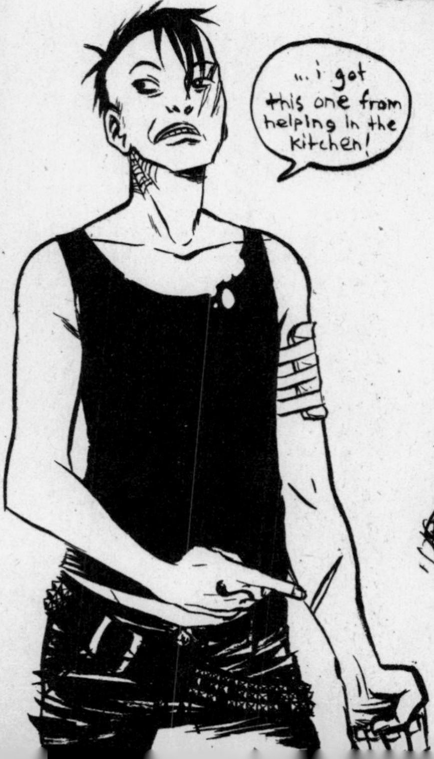
...i got this one from helping in the kitchen!

rat finks

Contrary to popular belief, the crew of *La Revancha* are merchants. They turned to trading after treasure became scarce and treasure-hunting became too difficult to make a living at. They have no interest in pillaging. Plunder, however, is another story...

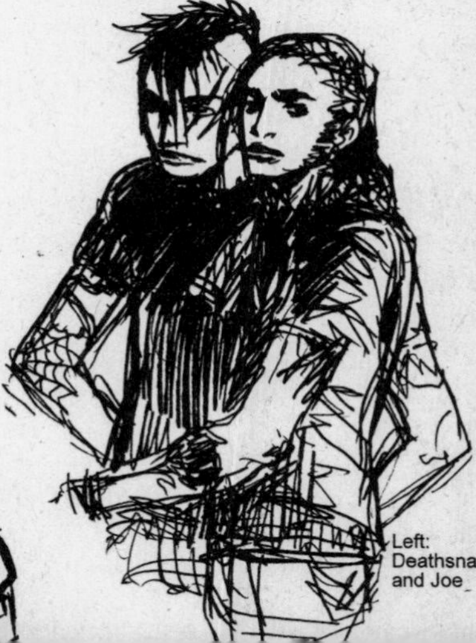

Left: Deathsnake and Joe

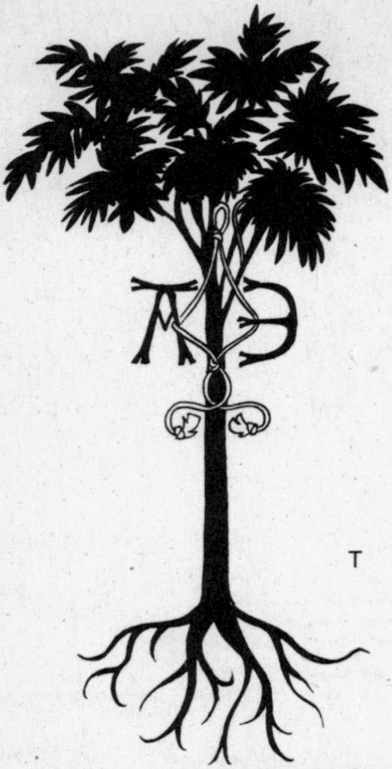

T

venti

Joseph G. Venti was the last mayor of New York before the great floods. After he died, his body was buried inside a family tomb in Queens along with all of the money he had stolen during his time in office. Many have searched in vain for his treasure.

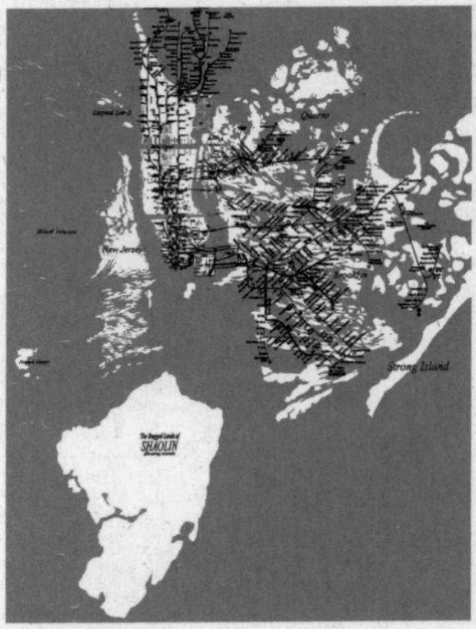
Queens
New Jersey
Brooklyn
Strong Island
The Rugged Lands of
SHAOLIN

Of course, it's never as easy as just following a map.The treasure is said to be guarded by Venti's descendents, who took an oath to protect the tomb from outsiders, and the subways have become an underwater maze infested with slithering demons. It's assumed that whatever they are guarding must be pretty important.

fortune & glory

There is no doubt that Venti had possessed immense wealth, but some also believe that he studied alchemy and the occult to find immortality. If that was the case, then his tomb could contain more than just money.

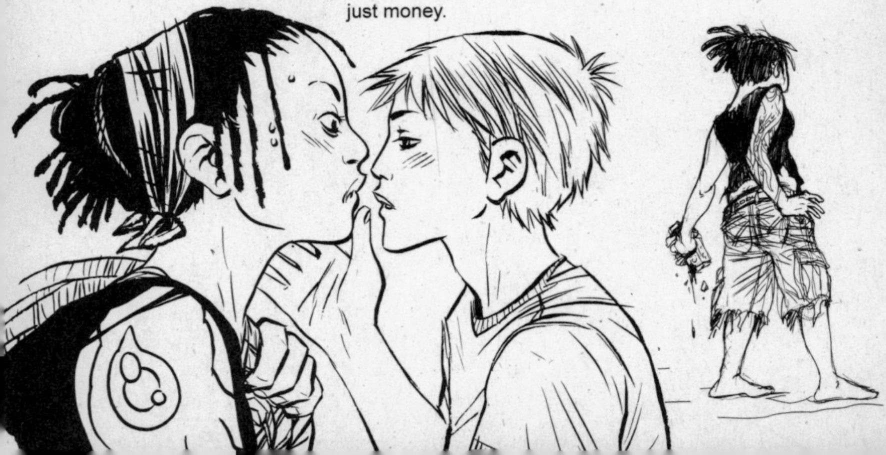

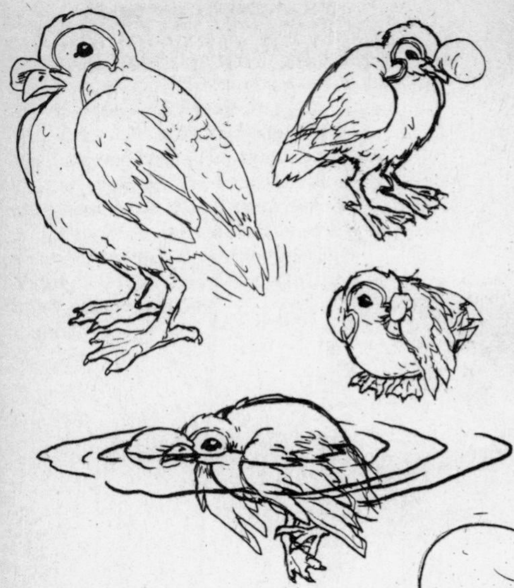

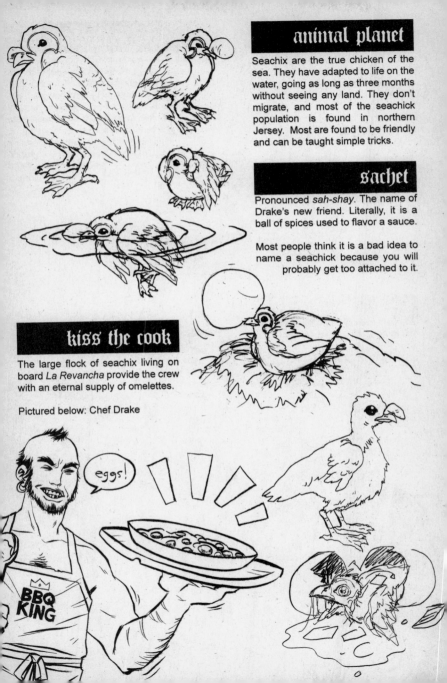

animal planet

Seachix are the true chicken of the sea. They have adapted to life on the water, going as long as three months without seeing any land. They don't migrate, and most of the seachick population is found in northern Jersey. Most are found to be friendly and can be taught simple tricks.

sachet

Pronounced *sah-shay*. The name of Drake's new friend. Literally, it is a ball of spices used to flavor a sauce.

Most people think it is a bad idea to name a seachick because you will probably get too attached to it.

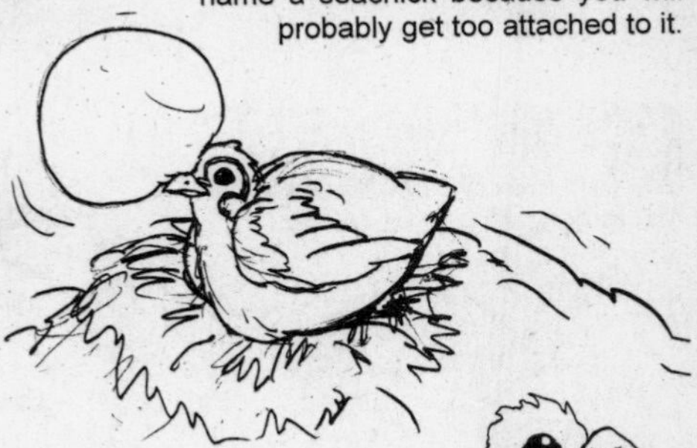

kiss the cook

The large flock of seachix living on board *La Revancha* provide the crew with an eternal supply of omelettes.

Pictured below: Chef Drake

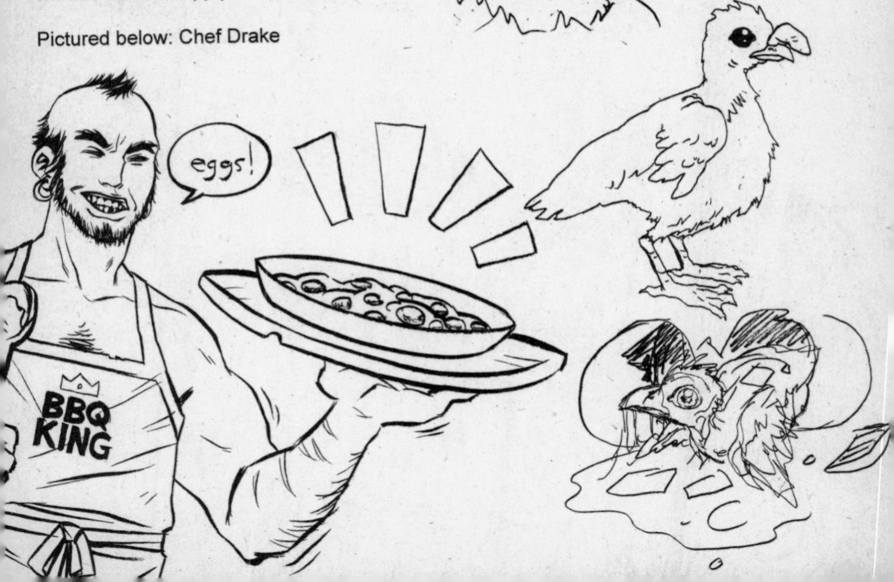
eggs!
BBQ KING

the hoboken

Modified amphibious assault vehicle capable of traveling underwater for short periods of time, the *Hoboken* is perfect for navigating the partially-submerged New Jersey terrain. Well-equipped, with seventeen crew members, three harpoon guns, one drill cannon and four anklogame which, when added together, equal one huge world of hurt.

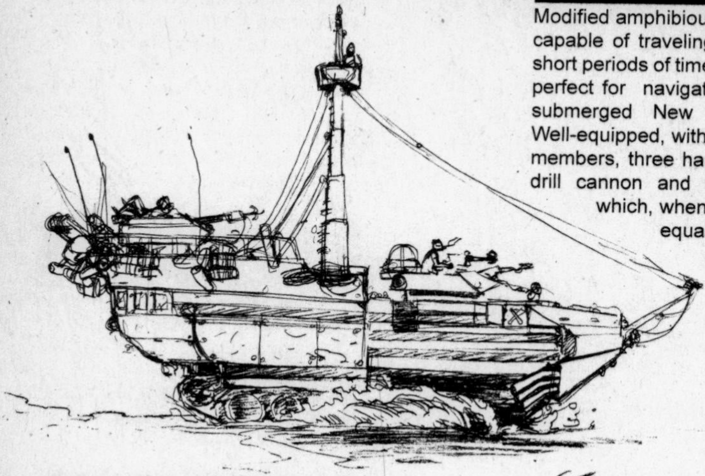

dirty jersey

Left to right: Zeus, Lee, Honey B

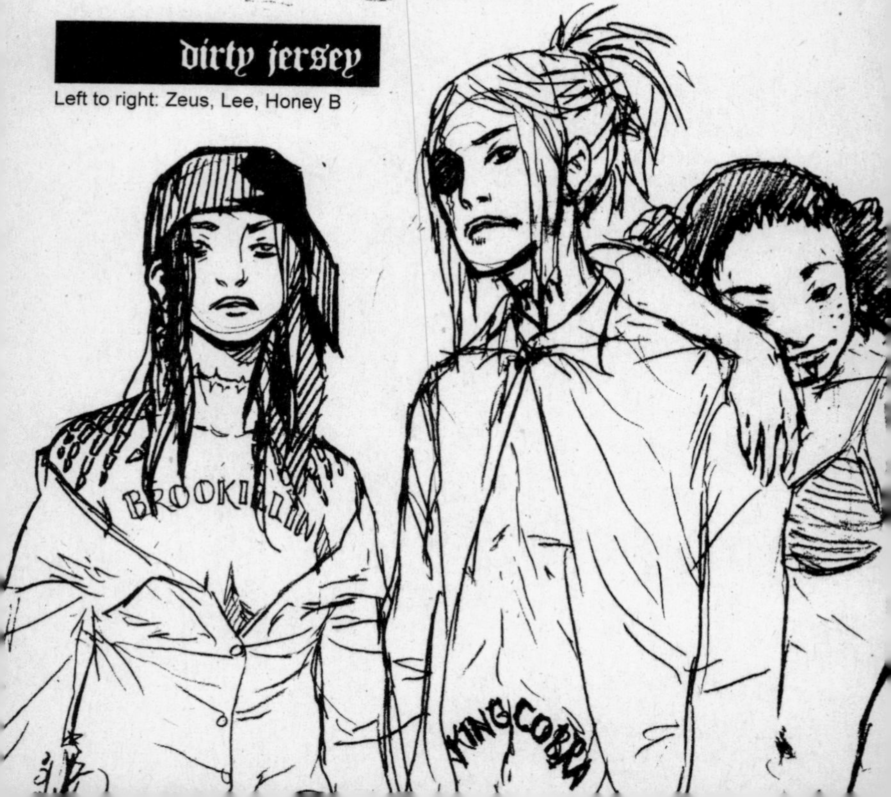
KING COBRA

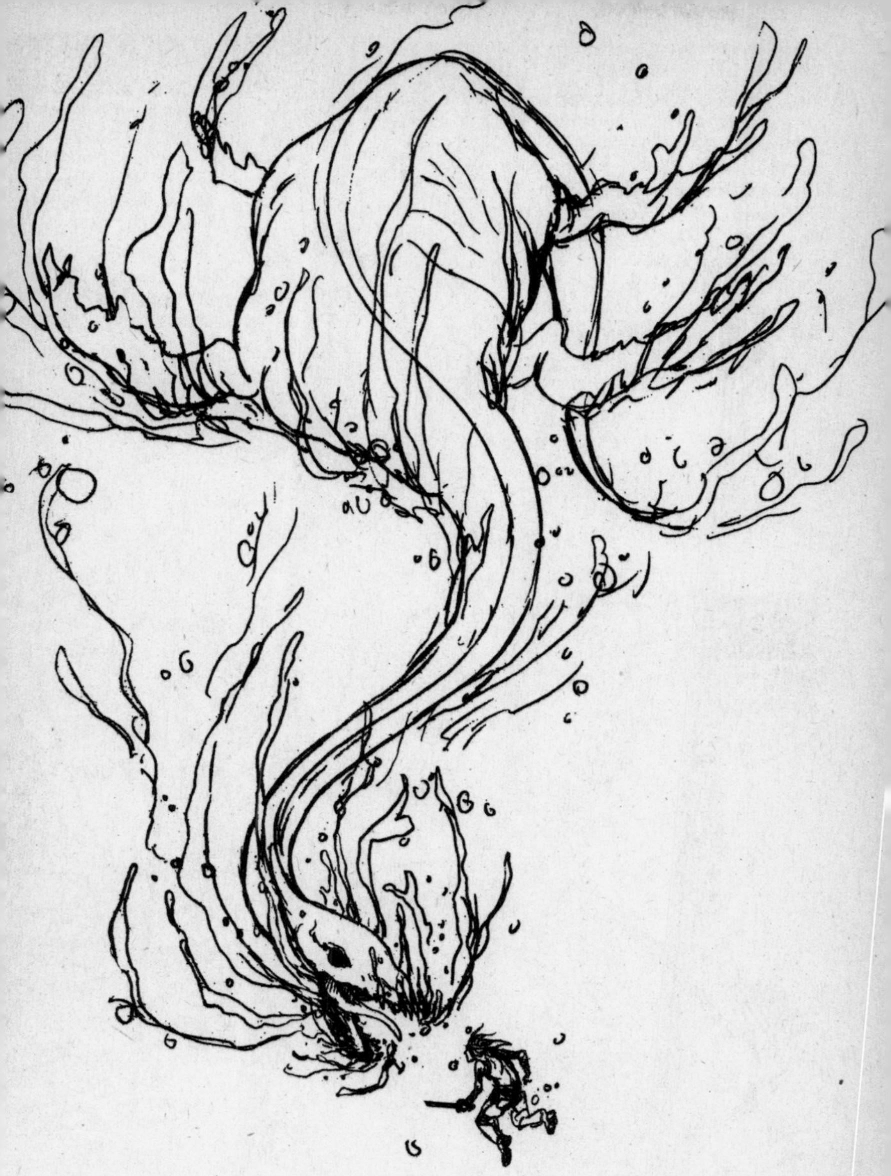

knife fight

Lee killed this monster with a knife.

bunch of jerks

New Jersey is a land almost entirely populated with criminals. This doesn't make them disorganized, however, and their attacks on merchant and trade ships are relentless. Now that the map to Venti's Tomb has surfaced, they will stop at nothing to get it. They also tend to make a lot of weird faces, mostly due to the almost intolerable smell that permeates the state.

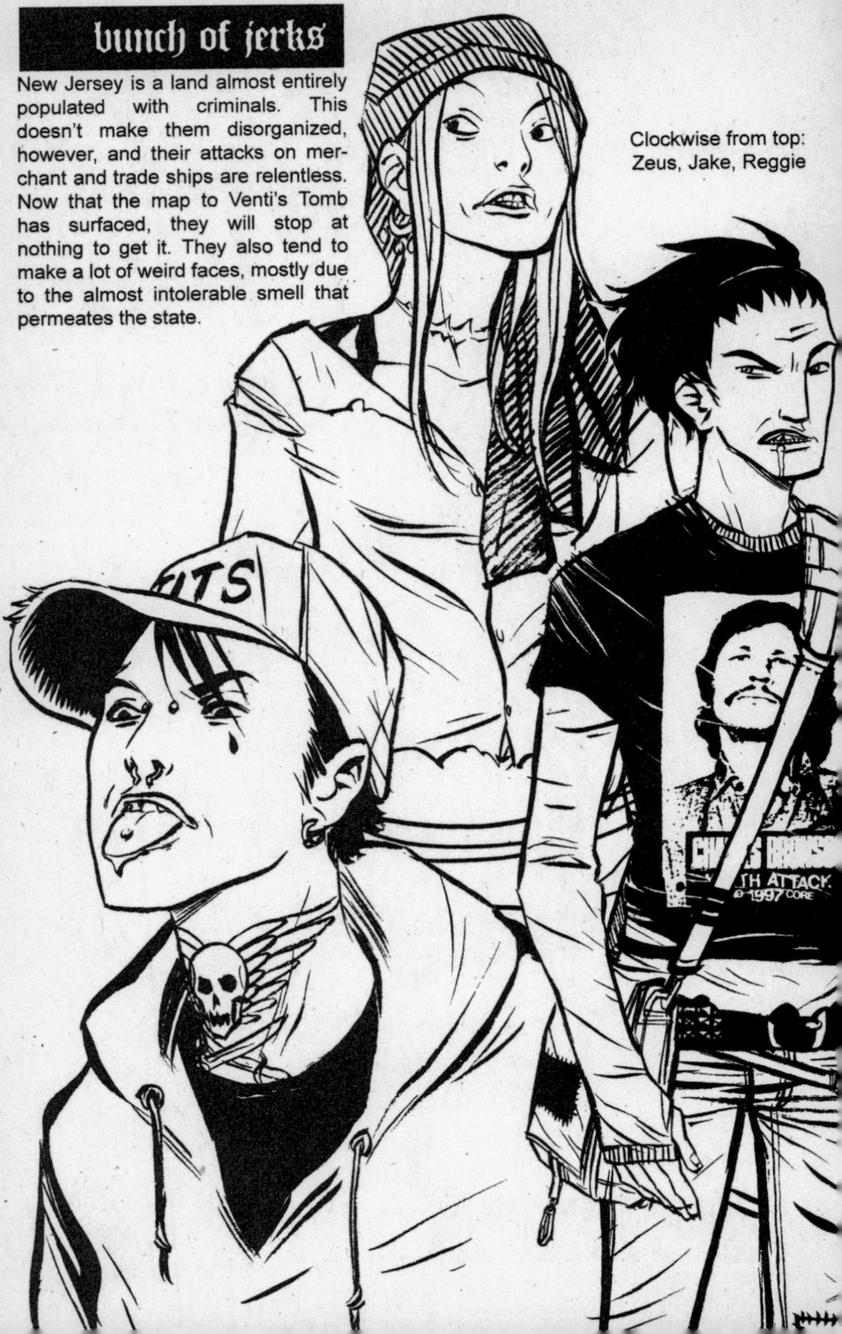
ITS
TH ATTACK
© 1997 CORE

Clockwise from top:
Zeus, Jake, Reggie

tattoos

Each tattoo has a meaning for the character who wears it. Some are for superstition or good luck; others are in remberence of someone. A lot are just old and embarrassing, though.

mr. snuggles

Midas has been raising and training anklogame since he was a wee little boy. He found an abandoned nest of eggs on Shaolin and raised the baby turtles without knowing they would grow to be bigger than an SUV.

The anklogames' favorite food is human flesh, but they also enjoy small sea mammals and crusta-ceans.

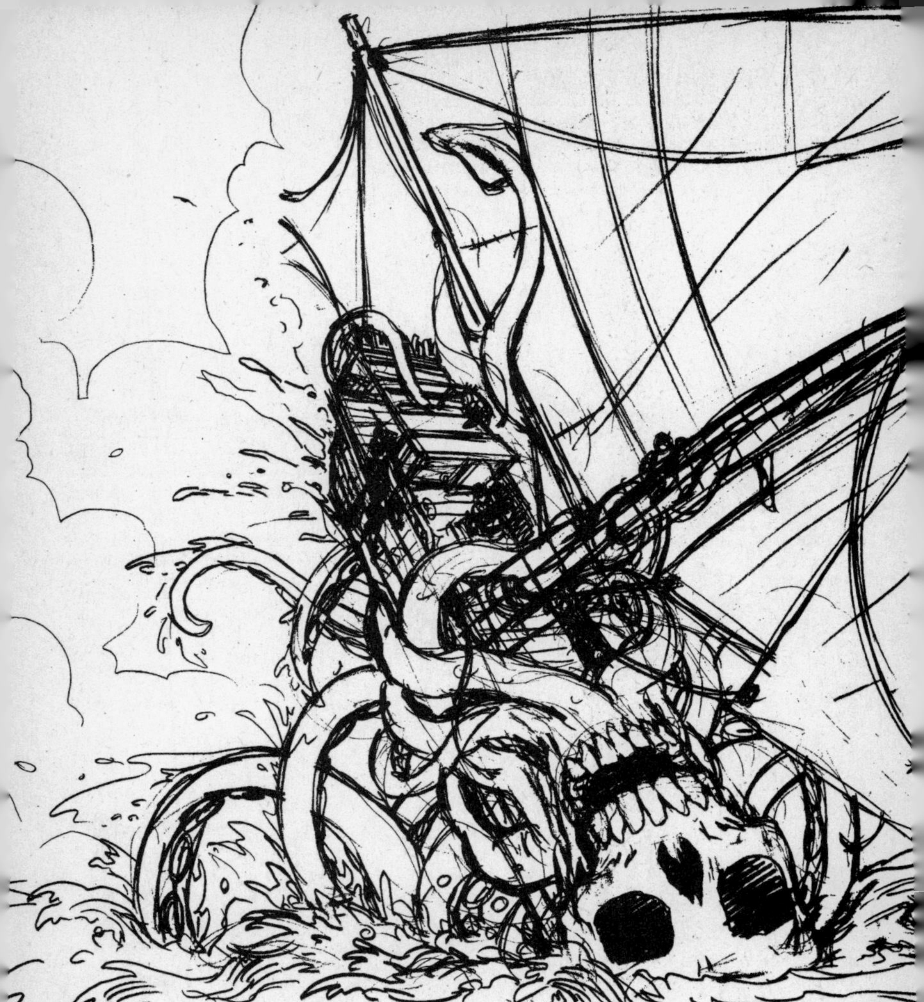

blind death

Few see it and live to tell the tale. Consequently, not much is known about this ancient sea beast, known also as the Caducus or Suffocating Death. The majority of sightings have been close to Newark; however, most have been reported as hoaxes.

Nobody knows for sure, but there is thought to be only one in existence.

The origin of this creature is shrouded in mystery. Legend has it that it is the ghost of a deceased whaler who was beheaded for high treason. His disembodied head was thrown laughing into the ocean, and to this day it still haunts the waves, looking for its body. Most people think of the Suffocating Death as mythological, much like the Loch Ness monster and the Rio Yeti.

Below are a few of the conceptual designs I did over the course of a weekend.

I really enjoy fonts, typography and lettering. I've done a lot of posters and flyers for many different types of shows, so it was fun to take a few days and incorporate that into my comic. It's really quite a challenge.

I think this one might be my favorite of the four, mostly because of the little wavey-type thing at the top. It looks almost like it belongs on a bar of soap. So fresh and so clean!

I was hoping to pull off a kraken-style underwater monster-type feeling with this one. That plus the classic tattoo font, fishing line and bob made this one pretty fun to draw.

The line through the bottom of this logo was going to represent sea level, but instead it turned this logo into the unholy union of Manowar and Husker Du. Am I good or what?

The line through... EAST COAST RISING

When I finished coloring this logo it magically transformed into a lesser Egyptian god.

Less pirates! More Ra!

Most of the art on the following pages was done during the summer of 2003 and remixed recently into this short comic....

legendary treasures

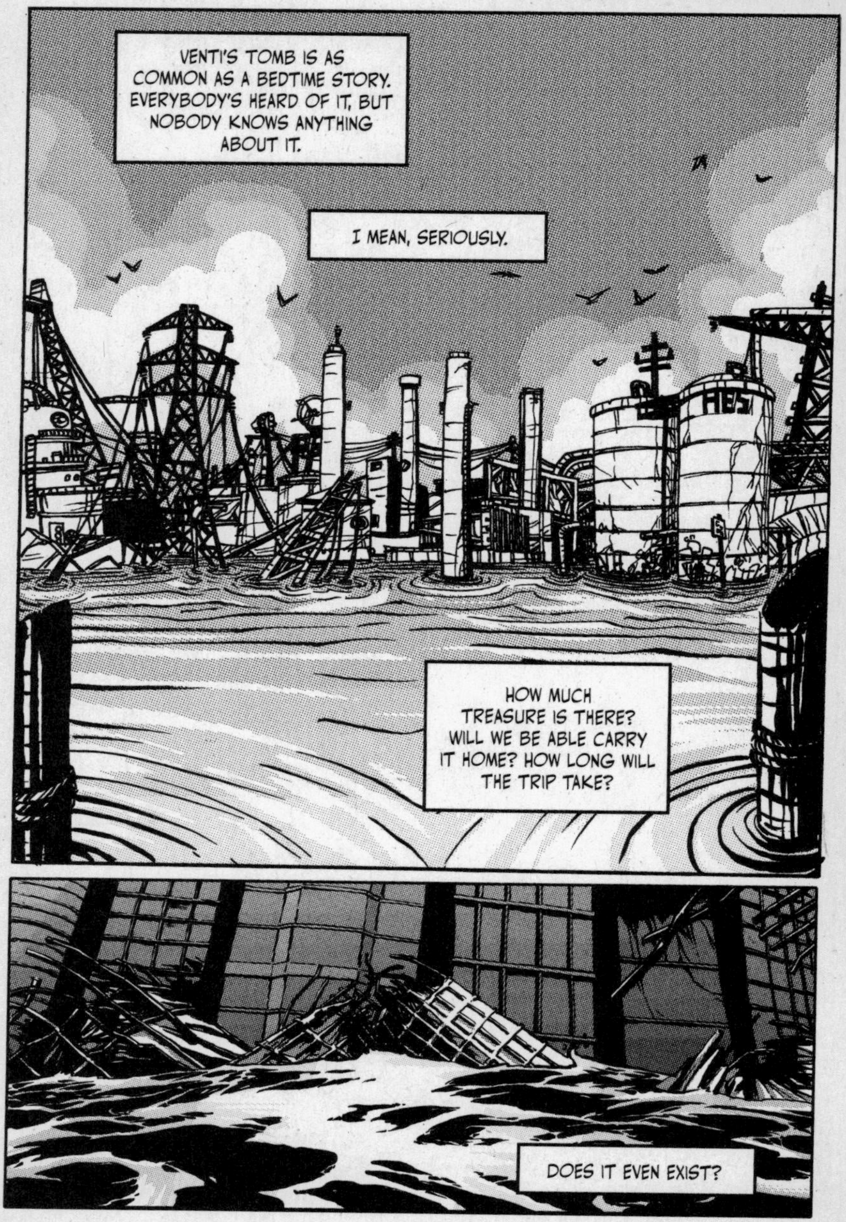
VENTI'S TOMB IS AS COMMON AS A BEDTIME STORY. EVERYBODY'S HEARD OF IT, BUT NOBODY KNOWS ANYTHING ABOUT IT.
I MEAN, SERIOUSLY.
HOW MUCH TREASURE IS THERE? WILL WE BE ABLE CARRY IT HOME? HOW LONG WILL THE TRIP TAKE?
DOES IT EVEN EXIST?

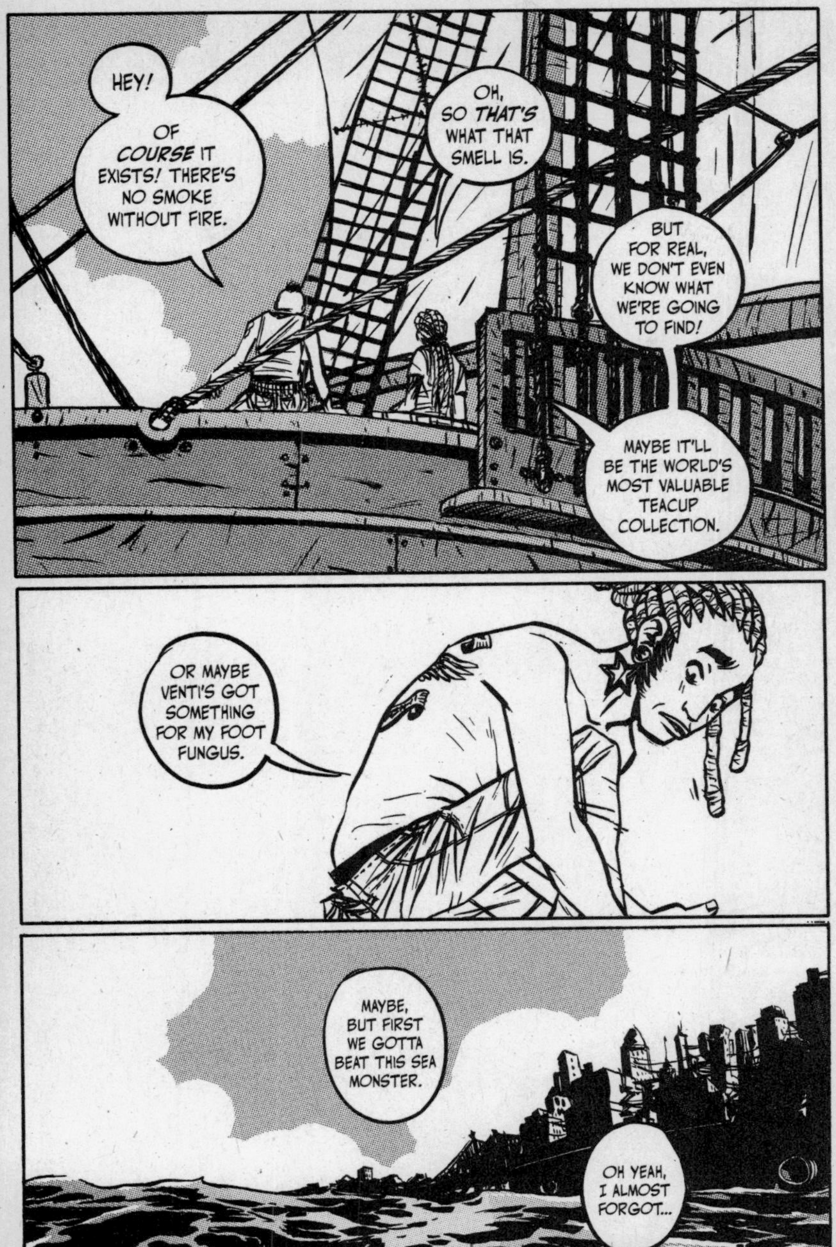
HEY!
OF *COURSE* IT EXISTS! THERE'S NO SMOKE WITHOUT FIRE.
OH, SO *THAT'S* WHAT THAT SMELL IS.
BUT FOR REAL, WE DON'T EVEN KNOW WHAT WE'RE GOING TO FIND!
MAYBE IT'LL BE THE WORLD'S MOST VALUABLE TEACUP COLLECTION.
OR MAYBE VENTI'S GOT SOMETHING FOR MY FOOT FUNGUS.
MAYBE, BUT FIRST WE GOTTA BEAT THIS SEA MONSTER.
OH YEAH, I ALMOST FORGOT...

OFF*BEAT

BY JEN LEE QUICK

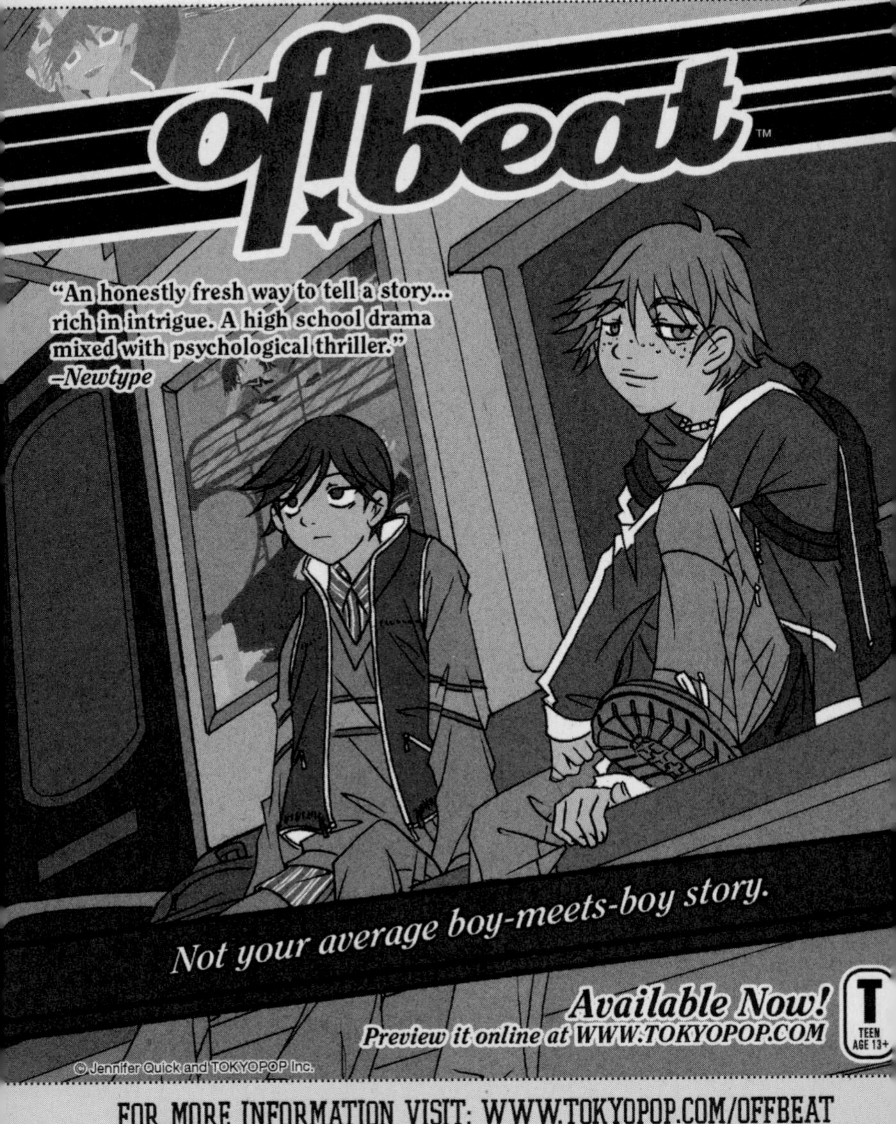
offbeat™
"An honestly fresh way to tell a story... rich in intrigue. A high school drama mixed with psychological thriller."
–Newtype
Not your average boy-meets-boy story.
Available Now!
Preview it online at WWW.TOKYOPOP.COM
T TEEN AGE 13+
© Jennifer Quick and TOKYOPOP Inc.

FOR MORE INFORMATION VISIT: WWW.TOKYOPOP.COM/OFFBEAT

THE DEBUT MANGA FROM HANS STEINBACH

HOT NEW ARTIST!

A MIDNIGHT™ OPERA

Immortality, Redemption, and Bittersweet Love...

For nearly a millennium, undead creatures have blended into a Europe driven by religious dogma...

Ein DeLaLune is an underground Goth metal sensation on the Paris music scene, tragic and beautiful. He has the edge on other Goth music powerhouses—he's undead, a fact he's kept hidden for centuries. But his newfound fame might just bring out the very phantoms of his past from whom he has been hiding for centuries, including his powerful brother, Leroux. And if the two don't reconcile, the entire undead nation could rise up from the depths of modern society to lay waste to mankind.